楚
Ch'u

吴
Wu

Yüeh
越

Sun-tzu

The

Art

of

War

Sun-tzu

The

Translated, with introductions

Art

and commentary by

of

Ralph D. Sawyer

War

With the collaboration of
Mei-chün Lee Sawyer

MetroBooks

In memory of three who forged their own paths:
John, Ralph, and Chad

Contents

Preface

RECENT DECADES have witnessed explosive growth in American and European interest in the Far East. Books and articles about China have enjoyed popularity since the 1970s; those on Japan, especially on Japanese management practices, have proliferated since the early 1980s; and those focusing on business in terms of "corporate warfare" and theories of strategy, including Asian practices and their underlying philosophies, retain currency. The writings of Musashi, the famous Japanese swordsman, and Sun-tzu, the ancient Chinese military theorist, have been repeatedly translated, investigated, and discussed. However, as interesting as they and a few books from the martial arts have proven to be, the vast Chinese military corpus—despite its historical importance and contemporary significance—remains unknown in the West.

Chinese military thought probably originated with neolithic village conflicts four or five thousand years ago, perhaps even as mythologized in the clash of legendary cultural heroes and Sage Emperors. Subsequently, because men were compelled to direct their ingenuity toward combat, weapons were developed, tactics evolved, and power structures arose. Eventually, dominant figures—perhaps clan or lineage chiefs commanding more-warlike peoples—imposed their wills over other groups and widening domains and some groups became significant political powers. At the dawn of the historical age, as preserved in early written materials and revealed by artifacts, frequent, intense clashes were already occurring between these contending forces as they evolved into states and as powerful individuals sought to establish sole rule over the realm and to found dynastic houses. Thereafter the scope of battle expanded; the strength and effectiveness of weapons increased; and military organization, tactics, and technology all developed. Eventually, battlefield lessons and command experience became the focus of conscious study; efforts were made to preserve the insights and avoid the errors of the past; and the science of military tactics and strategy was born.

By the second century B.C. China had already passed through a thousand years of almost unremitting conflict and had been brutally unified into a vast, powerful, imperially directed entity. Along the way, skilled commanders appeared, and major battles were fought. Campaigns became interminable, and the scale of destruction was immense, consuming both men and the thoughts they had committed to writing. However, among the small number of military writings that survived until unification, there were six major ones, including Sun-tzu's famous *Art of War*. They continued to be studied and transmitted down through the centuries until the remnants were collected and edited in the Sung dynasty around twelve hundred years later. Combined with a T'ang dynasty work, they compose the *Seven Military Classics,* a compilation that comprised the orthodox foundations for military thought and the basis for the imperial examinations required for martial appointment.

In the early 1970s, archaeologists excavating the Han dynasty tomb of a high-ranking official discovered a large number of immensely valuable texts written on remarkably well preserved bamboo slips. The military works among them include major portions of several of the *Seven Military Classics,* including the *Art of War* and extensive fragments of Sun Pin's *Military Methods.* Although this last book—by Sun-tzu's descendant—appeared in the bibliographic listings compiled in the Han dynasty, it had apparently vanished in the Han and been lost for over two thousand years. This important find thus increased the total extant military materials from the ancient period to eight classic works in all, supplemented by a few hundred other writings of various, but definitely later, dates.

Even though tactical studies continued to be written throughout Chinese history, much of the vast military corpus has undoubtedly been lost over the centuries through carelessness, natural disasters, deliberate destruction, and warfare. However, ancient epigraphic materials and such early historical records as the *Tso chuan* and *Shih chi* also chronicle the exploits of generals and kings; the *Twenty-five Histories* preserves extensive information about men and actions; and Warring States philosophical works contain discussions of military issues. Thus resources abound, but only a part of the historical writings, including the complete *Tso chuan,* and essentially two of the *Seven Military Classics* (Sun-tzu's *Art of War*—three major versions, several minor ones—and the *Wu-tzu*—which appears as an appendix to Griffith's translation) have been translated and published.

Far from having vanished and being forgotten, these ancient Chinese military works have extensively influenced twentieth-century thought and are experiencing a new vitality in Asia. Not only in the military realm—throughout the century they have been thoroughly studied in Japan and China—do they continue to be discussed, but also in the business and personal spheres their resurgence is particularly evident. In the 1980s a management book that revived Sun-tzu's thought and employed the revitalized figures of several ancient martial heroes to instruct companies in the basics of business and marketing became a bestseller in the draconian Communist environment of the People's Republic of China and eventually in capitalist Hong Kong as well. Japanese companies have regularly held study groups to seek insights from the *Art of War* that may be implemented as corporate strategy. Koreans, enduring intense international pressure to revalue their currency, open their markets, and submit to trade limitations just when prosperity is attainable, are discovering strategies for international business warfare in these books.

In Taiwan, where companies confront a situation similar to Korea's, books applying the thoughts of the ancient strategists to life, business, sports, and the stock market have suddenly surged in popularity, even though modernists have ignored and scorned them for decades. Perhaps more astounding is the penchant of Japanese writers to apply principles and tactics from the *Seven Military Classics* to all the complexities of modern society; they use such tactics, for example, for succesful human relations, romantic liaisons, and company infighting. In addition to at least one scholarly translation, several new paperbacks offering simplified renditions and popularized expansions of selected teachings are published annually in Japan. The ubiquitous *salaryman* may be seen reading them while commuting to work, and there are even comic-book editions of the *Art of War* and novels about Sun-tzu to satisfy those so inclined. Naturally, tactics from the classics also frequently appear in novels, movies, and on television, and their words are quoted in contemporary media throughout Asia. However, in every sphere, Sun-tzu's *Art of War* predominates, eclipsing all the other military writings combined.

. . .

There is a great temptation, given the extensive materials rapidly becoming available from diverse sources, to undertake a truly comprehensive introduction to the entire military enterprise in Ancient China. Many topics critical to understanding strategy, tactics, and the evolution of military thought merit exploration and analysis. However, we have consciously focused upon depicting the historical context and reviewing the essential material aspects, such as armor and weapons, rather than ineffectually sketching comprehensive intellectual issues. Although we have not totally neglected the latter, exploring topics such as the relationships of Taoism and military thought in at least cursory fashion in the introductions and the extensive notes, these areas must largely be consigned to another work and to expert monographs. Similarly, although we have outlined the essentials of Sun-tzu's concepts, such as unorthodox/orthodox, we have not analyzed them in depth, nor have we discussed the details of technology; concrete tactics of deployment; or the implementation of strategy beyond that found in the *Art of War,* supplemented by the historical records of Sun-tzu's era—the *Shih chi, Tso chuan,* and *Wu Yüeh ch'un-ch'iu.* Furthermore, except in an occasional note, we have not explored the relationship of the *Art of War* to the *Kuan-tzu,* the *Book of Lord Shang,* or other Warring States philosophical writings that prominently espouse military policies, administrative measures, and strategic concepts. These and many other topics, including the systematic analysis and integration of ideas and methods and their interrelationship in each of the classics, require extensive studies in themselves. Because their inclusion would be premature and would probably detract from the core teaching of the *Art of War,* we will focus upon them in a future work integrating the interactive development of military technology and tactical thought.

Because this book is intended for the general reader, a rubric we assume encompasses everyone except those few specialists in ancient Chinese studies with expertise in the previously neglected military writings, we have provided somewhat fuller notes on many general aspects than might otherwise be necessary. Overall the notes have been designed for several different audiences; although much of the translation cries out for detailed annotation, in order to minimize the number of notes, we have refrained from exploring deeply every thought, concept, and strategy. Many of the notes simply provide contextual information or identify figures and terms for the convenience of readers unfamiliar with Chinese history and writings. Others are intended for those students of Asia—professional or not—who might benefit from further historical, technical, or military information or from the citation of certain seminal articles. Many notes comment upon the intricacies of translation matters: They provide alternative readings; note emendations we have accepted and commentaries followed; discuss the relevant fragments from the tomb text when differences exist; and sometimes indicate where we have relied upon our own judgment contrary to traditional readings. Finally, some amplify those portions of the introductory material where we sought to avoid dogmatic assertions about the numerous issues, such as textual authenticity, that have only tentatively been resolved or remain the subject of scholarly controversy. Every reader is encouraged to peruse them all, at least briefly, focusing upon those of greatest relevance in the quest to understand these texts.

Full bibliographic information is provided for each work at its first appearance in each chapter, with abbreviated titles thereafter. Consequently, for the bibliography we have departed from the usual format and instead provided a selected listing by subject for those who might wish to investigate the literature on a single topic. Numerous books with only tangential connections with the *Seven Military Classics* and solely of interest to specialists have been excluded. For matters of general knowledge that have not been annotated, the reader should consult the Western-language works listed in the bibliography for further reading.

. . .

A work of this scope, in our case undertaken enthusiastically without fully realizing the many thorny issues it would entail, is necessarily the product of years of reading, study, pondering, sifting, and effort. We have benefited vastly from the commentaries and essays of a hundred generations of Chinese scholars and from the growth of detailed knowledge deriving from the work of Western and Asian scholars in the present century. However, having left the academic community two decades ago, we have enjoyed a rather different, vibrant perspective on these ideas and philosophies—the result of twenty-five years of technical and business consulting at all levels in Japan, China, Taiwan, Korea, Hong Kong, Singapore, and Southeast Asia. For a startling number of our Asian associates, the various military classics—especially the *Art of War*—remain compendiums of effective tactics and strategies, providing approaches and measures that can be profitably adopted in life and employed in business practices. Their discussions and understanding of many of the concrete lessons, although not necessary orthodox or classically based, stimulated our own enlightenment on many issues. In particular, conversations over the decades in Asia with Guy Baer, Cleon Brewer, Ma Shang-jen, Kong Jung-yul, Professor W. K. Seong, Professor Ts'ai Mao-t'ang, and especially C. S. Shim have been both stimulating and illuminating.

Certain early teachers had a lasting influence on my approach to Chinese intellectual history. In particular, as a graduate student at Harvard in the turbulent 1960s I was greatly influenced by Professors Yang Lien-sheng, Yü Ying-shih, Benjamin Schwartz, and especially Dr. Achilles Fang, under whom I was privileged to be thrust into the true study of classical Chinese. Thereafter I was fortunate to read intermittently for more than a decade with Professor Chin Chia-hsi, a *Chuangtzu* specialist and university professor of Chinese at National Taiwan University. However, my greatest intellectual debt is to Professor Nathan Sivin, initially a Sage at M.I.T.; a friend for more than twenty-five years; and ultimately responsible for both illuminating the Way and making the path accessible.

However, these are all general intellectual obligations, not specific, for these scholars have not seen any portion of this work, and the survivors from Harvard would perhaps be astonished to learn that I have been carrying on the Chinese tradition of private scholarship over these many years. Whereas I am responsible for the translations, introductions, and notes, Mei-chün Lee (Sawyer) has not only been an active participant in our discussions and studies over the years but also undertook numerous burdens associated with the detailed research of such historical issues as the evolution of weapons. She also contributed immeasurably through her insightful readings of the translations and the tedious investigation and comparison of various modern commentaries. Her collaborative efforts greatly aided my understanding of many issues and improved the overall work significantly, all while she continued to fulfill her responsibilities in our consulting operations.

Finally we would like to thank Westview Press, in particular, Peter Kracht, senior editor, for his efforts on the original edition of the *Seven Military Classics,* on which this edition of the *Art of War* is based. We benefited greatly from Westview's editorial support and from the intensive, detailed reading of the translation provided through their auspices by Professor Robin D.S. Yates. Many of his numerous emendations and general suggestions substantially improved the work, and all his criticisms stimulated a careful reexamination of the text and many additional materials; nevertheless, final responsibility for their evaluation and integration, where accepted, remains with the translators.

Others who assisted, especially in locating articles and textual materials in the United States and Asia, include Miao Yong-i, Marta Hanson, Yuriko Baer, Anton Stetzko, and Zhao Yong; Lorrie Stetzko provided expertise on horses and the intricacies of riding; Westview Press and Max Gartenberg essentially made the project possible. We express our deep appreciation to all these people and to Lee T'ing-jung, who has honored the work with his calligraphy.

Ralph D. Sawyer

A Note
on the
Translation
and
Pronunciation

THE TRANSLATION IS based upon and rigorously follows the so-called Ming edition of the (Sung dynasty)*Seven Military Classics,* which contains and benefits from Liu Yin's consistent commentary—the *chih-chieh,* or "direct explanations"—throughout all seven books. However, although many of his comments are illuminating and even critical to understanding the actual text, scholarship continued to advance, and over the centuries, a few valuable commentaries and several variant editions that have furthered the process of understanding—particularly of the *Art of War*—have come out. Where the Ming text appears obviously defective, recourse for emendation is made first to the Sung edition and then to other variants. Full information on the individual variants employed is given in the introduction and the notes for each book, and the basic editions are listed in the bibliography.

We have sought to employ contemporary scholarship judiciously, irrespective of its political perspective, and to integrate insights provided by archaeological discoveries. The discovery of early versions, although dramatic and invaluable, precipitates the problem about which text to translate: the "original" versions, which entail numerous problems of their own, or the Sung *Seven Military Classics* edition, which has been historically available and influential for nine centuries. Because the newly recovered tomb text, even when supplemented by additional fragments that may well have been part of the *Art of War* or from Sun-tzu's hand (or school), is only partial, while the book that is read and known throughout Asia remains the traditional text, we have chosen to translate the traditionally received version. Accordingly, we have used the newly recovered textual materials to make emendations only where they resolve highly problematic or completely incomprehensible passages, and to supplement passages where clearly integral to the topic. In addition, we have provided translations of the relevant, important tomb materials in a supplementary section, together with the highly illuminating nine passages on "configurations of terrain" separately preserved in the *T'ung tien.*

In providing a translation for a general readership, rather than a somewhat more literal (and some would claim precise) version for sinologists, we hope to emulate the vibrant translations of Professor Burton Watson and thereby make this amazing text accessible to the widest possible audience. We have thus avoided military jargon because, apart from the thorny question about each term's appropriateness, such terms would render the translation less comprehensible to anyone lacking military experience or unacquainted with military history.

Unfortunately, neither of the two commonly employed orthographies makes the pronunciation of romanized Chinese characters easy. Each system has its stumbling blocks and we remain unconvinced that the Pinyin *qi* is inherently more comprehensible than the Wade-Giles *ch'i*, although it is certainly no less comprehensible than *j* for *r* in Wade-Giles. However, as many of the important terms may already be familiar to Western readers and previous translations have employed Wade-Giles, we have opted to use that system throughout our work. Well-known cities, names, and books—such as Peking—are retained in their common form, and books and articles published with romanized names and titles also appear in their original form.

As a guide to pronunciation, we offer the following notes on the significant exceptions to normally expected sounds:

> *t,* as in *Tao:* without apostrophe, pronounced like *d*
> *p,* as in *ping:* without apostrophe, pronounced like *b*
> *ch,* as in *chuang:* without apostrophe, pronounced like *j*
> *hs,* as in *hsi:* prounounced *sh*
> *j,* as in *jen:* pronounced like *r*

Thus, the name of the famous Chou dynasty is pronounced as if written "jou" and sounds just like the English name "Joe."

Chronology
of
Approximate
Dynastic
Periods

Dynastic Period	Years
Legendary Sage Emperors	2852-2255 B.C.
Hsia	2205-1766
Shang	1766-1045
Chou:	1045-256
Western Chou	1045-770
Eastern Chou	770-256
Spring and Autumn	722-481
Warring States	403-221
Ch'in	221-207
Former Han	206 B.C.-8 A.D.
Later Han	23-220
Six Dynasties	222-589
Sui	589-618
T'ang	618-907
Five Dynasties	907-959
Sung	960-1126
Southern Sung	1127-1279
Yüan (*Mongol*)	1279-1368
Ming	1368-1644
Ch'ing (*Manchu*)	1644-1911

General Introduction and Historical Background

MILITARY THOUGHT, the complex product of both violent war and intellectual analysis, suffered from disparagement and disrepute during almost all the past two millennia in Imperial China. Ignoring the original teachings of Confucius, self-styled Confucians eschewed—whether sincerely or hypocritically—the profession of arms and all aspects of military involvement from the Han dynasty on, growing more vociferous in their condemnation with the passing of centuries.[1] However, regardless of these people's civilized and cultured self-perception, the nation could not be without armies or generals, particularly in the face of constant "barbarian" threats and ongoing conflicts with volatile nomadic peoples. Accordingly, a number of early military treatises continued to be valued and studied and thereby managed to survive, while the turmoil of frequent crises inevitably fostered generations of professional military figures and additional strategic studies. Yet compared to the Confucian classics and various other orthodox writings, the military corpus remained minuscule, numbering at most a few hundred works.

Individual chapters of several writings by influential philosophers of the Warring States period (403–221 B.C.),[2] such as Lord Shang, also focused upon military matters, often with radical impact.[3] Many famous thinkers, including Hsün-tzu and Han Fei-tzu,[4] pondered the major questions of government administration and military organization; motivation and training; the nature of courage; and the establishment of policies to stimulate the state's material prosperity. The *Tso chuan* and other historical writings similarly record the thoughts of many key administrators and preserve the outlines of famous strategies, although their presentation of battlefield tactics is minimal.

A number of the ancient strategic monographs became relatively famous, and scholars in the Sung Period (circa A.D. 1078) collected, edited, and assembled the six important survivors, augmenting them with a T'ang dynasty book; the final product was the *Seven Military Classics*. Thus codified, the seven works thereafter furnished the official textual foundation for government examinations in military affairs and concurrently provided a common ground for tactical and strategic conceptualization.

Despite incessant barbarian incursions and major military threats throughout its history, Imperial China was little inclined to pursue military solutions to aggression—except during the ill-fated expansionistic policies of the Former Han dynasty, or under dynamic young rulers, such as T'ang T'ai-tsung, during the founding years of a dynasty. Rulers and ministers preferred to believe in the myth of cultural attraction whereby their vastly superior Chinese civilization, founded upon Virtue[5] and reinforced by opulent material achievements, would simply overwhelm the hostile tendencies of the uncultured. Frequent gifts of the embellishments of civilized life, coupled with music and women, it was felt, would distract and enervate even the most warlike peoples. If they could not be either overawed into submission or bribed into compliance, other mounted nomadic tribes could be employed against the troublemakers, following the time-honored tradition of "using barbarian against barbarian."[6]

According to Confucian thought, which became the orthodox philosophy and prescribed state view in the Former Han, the ruler need only cultivate his Virtue, accord with the seasons, and implement benevolent policies in order to be successful in attracting universal support and fostering stability. Naturally, there were dissenting views, and even Mencius (371–289 B.C.), the second great Confucian, advocated punitive military expeditions to chastise evil rulers and relieve the people's suffering. However, except under rulers such as Sui Yang-ti (reigned A.D. 605–617), who sought to impose Chinese suzerainty on external regions—and thereby impoverished the nation—military affairs were pressed unwillingly; most of the bureaucracy tended to disdain anything associated with the military and the profession of arms.

Evolution
of Conflict
and Weapons
in China

THE SHANG

Over the centuries Chinese military thought mirrored the evolution in weapons, economic conditions, and political power while creating the framework for strategic conceptualization and stimulating the development of battlefield methods. Tactics appropriate to the dawn of the historical Shang period changed in response to increased manpower, greater speed and mobility, and the invention of more-powerful shock and missile weapons. However, a critical kernel of thought that focused on basic questions, including organization, discipline, evaluation, objectives, and fundamental principles, retained its validity and continued to be applied until the Ch'in eventually conquered and unified the empire, thereby signifying the end of the Warring States period.

The Shang dynasty was a theocratic state whose power arose initially from, and continued to depend upon, the military skills of the nobility, in conjunction with its religious beliefs and institutions.[7] The populace was effectively divided into four classes: ruling families; royal clan members, many of whom were enfeoffed or served as officials, and other members of the nobility; common people, who were essentially serfs; and slaves.[8] The king exercised great power over a central area and enjoyed the allegiance of various lords in the peripheral territory. The nobility, which was educated and cultured, lived in well-organized cities marked by massive complex buildings, such as palaces and temples.[9] The common people, who dwelled in semi-earthen huts, farmed or practiced various specialized crafts during most of the year, although they were also required to provide conscript labor and even to mobilize to assist military campaigns.

Bronze technology advanced rapidly from the official inception of the Shang (traditionally dated as 1766 B.C., when T'ang I mounted his victorious campaign over the Hsia) until its collapse at the hands of the Chou, about 1045 B.C.[10] Intricately detailed ritual vessels, essential to the ancestor worship that underlay the king's power, provide dramatic evidence of the technological achievements and the government's effective management and monopoly of productive resources.[11] Although the weapons for the nobility were fashioned primarily from bronze, the raw materials for agricultural implements and the arms carried by the commoners were largely confined to stone, wood, and animal bones.[12] Millet and, later, wheat, were the staple crops, and they were stored in centralized granaries after harvesting. Rice was known, but it remained an expensive luxury even for the ruler because it was cultivated mainly in the south.[13] The level of material culture had progressed sufficiently to sustain cities with large populations based upon organized farming and systematic exploitation of the hunt. Some animals—such as sheep, oxen, pigs, and dogs—had been domesticated,[14] and both silk and hemp were produced. Vessels for ordinary use were made of pottery, which was marked by intricate designs.

Prior to the Shang dynasty, armed conflict essentially consisted of raids by and engagements between neolithic villages, although certain clan chiefs apparently developed local power bases and some regional strongmen emerged, such as those who founded the Hsia dynasty. However, with the rise of the Shang and the imposition of significant central authority (although not administration), a royal standing army of about a thousand was maintained. The number could be expanded as needed: The subservient lineage chiefs and state rulers would be ordered to furnish supporting armies. Although the king normally commanded in person, a rudimentary military bureaucracy with specialized officials already existed.[15] A royal campaign against border enemies might require three thousand to five thousand men, and a campaign directed toward an insolent state as many as thirteen thousand.[16] Military actions required from a few days to perhaps three months; the actual battles generally were settled in a single confrontation, although engagements lasting several days have also been recorded.[17] The army was divided into three sections—left, right, and middle[18]—formed from two types of units: loosely organized infantry, conscripted from the privileged populace,[19] which acted in a supporting role; and chariots, manned by the nobles fulfilling their martial responsibilities as warriors and sustainers of the state.

Shang warfare objectives included the imposition or reinforcement of royal suzerainty, the mass capture of prisoners, and the seizure of riches.[20] Control over areas outside the central core continued to be imposed through a vassal-like network, rather than through integration under a centrally administered bureaucracy. Plunder increased the wealth of the royal house and also furnished the means to reward loyal service. Some prisoners were enslaved and forced to work in either agricultural or domestic tasks, but large numbers were sacrificed as part of Shang religious ceremonies.[21]

During the several hundred years of Shang rule, bronze weapons formed an integral part of every Shang warrior's arsenal.[22] The preferred weapon was the *ko* (halberd, or dagger-ax),[23] supplemented by spears[24] and the compound bow.[25] Bronze-tipped arrows, propelled by reflex bows whose pull may have reached 160 pounds, provided effective action at a distance. Daggers and hatchets were available for close fighting; leather armor and large shields—the latter used in coordinated fighting tactics—offered considerable protection against shock weapons and projectiles.[26] Bronze helmets were fabricated to deflect missiles and glancing blows, and thin bronze plates were affixed as outer protection on both armor and shields. According to Warring States theory, weapons were usually of mixed type, providing the means for both aggressive and defensive action at close and long ranges. However the sword evolved slowly, apparently from daggers or perhaps the dagger-ax, and true swords did not become common until the middle of the Warring States period.[27]

The chariot functioned as the basic fighting unit during the late Shang, Western Chou, and Spring and Autumn (722–481

B.C.) periods; it remained important until well into the Warring States (403–221), when it was gradually supplanted by large infantry masses and eventually, during the third century B.C., began to be supplemented by the cavalry. Chinese tradition portrays the Shang as having employed seventy chariots during the campaign of rectification to oust the evil Hsia dynasty.[28] However, twentieth-century archaeological discoveries, supplemented by textual research, indicate that the chariot, rather than being an indigenous development, did not reach China from Central Asia until the middle of the Shang dynasty—approximately 1300 to 1200 B.C.[29] Initially, the use of chariot was probably confined to ceremonies and transportation and only gradually was expanded to the hunt and eventually to warfare. Epigraphic materials provide evidence that the Shang relied upon infantry units of nobility to confront their enemies even after the integration of the chariot into their military organization. In fact, throughout the Shang, the chariot may have remained a prestige symbol; its function during military engagements was restricted to providing transport mobility and serving as a command platform rather than constituting a significant military weapon.

The chariots of the late Shang and subsequent Chou periods normally carried three men: the driver in the center, the archer on the left, and a warrior with a dagger-ax on the right. Five chariots constituted a squad, the basic functional unit, and five squads composed a brigade. Each chariot had a complement of 10 to 25 close-supporting infantry, with an additional vanguard of perhaps 125 men in later times.[30] A Shang team consisted of two horses, and the rectangular chariot rode on two sturdy, multispoked wheels. Training for warfare included large-scale royal hunts that utilized chariots, although given the difficulty of developing driving skills and the fighting expertise appropriate to a racing chariot, far more practice must have been necessary.[31] It was an expensive weapon that required craftsmen to build and maintain; thus its use was confined to the nobility, minimally supported by conscripted commoners. Battles accordingly resolved into a number of individual clashes, with personal combat supposedly governed by appropriate ceremonial constraints (probably a later romanticization). A few scholars have seen references to hunting on horseback in certain sentences, but these claims are generally discounted: The horse was employed only in conjunction with the chariot. Lacking stirrups and a saddle and hampered by his long robes, the mounted rider could not become an effective military element until the the third century B.C.

THE CHOU

The Chou came to power by overthrowing the Shang in a decisive battle at Mu-yeh after many years of stealthy preparation and the gradual expansion of their power base through carefully wrought alliances, the submission of some smaller states, and the subjugation of other clans and peoples. Possibly descendants of the Hsia,[32] the Chou originally dwelled to the north but had been forced south into the Wei River valley by more-aggressive peoples.[33] As the Chou were situated on the periphery of Shang culture, they were able to assimilate many of the material and cultural achievements of Shang civilization in relative freedom while successfully developing a strong agricultural base, indigenous technology, and their own cultural identity. External barbarian pressures stimulated their military skills, organizational abilities, and tactical thought simultaneously, and the Shang even entrusted them with the task of subjugating rebellious peoples in the west, which allowed the Chou to increase their military prowess.[34] When they mounted their final campaign against the debauched, enervated Shang, the Chou's weapons and implements were similar to the Shang's. Perhaps the only Chou innovation was the extensive employment of chariots, facilitating more-rapid movement and the conveying of greater quantities of weapons and supplies.[35] The Chou's victory probably stemmed in large part not only from the Shang's disorganization but also from the exhaustion suffered by the Shang in fighting off hostile nomadic peoples to the north and east and from their large-scale commitment to a southern military expedition at the moment of attack.[36]

The Chou's overall campaign and tactics (particularly if the *Book of Documents* and the *Six Secret Teachings* preserve any reliable material) approached the conflict from a new perspective—abandoning ritualistic, formal combat for effective revolutionary activity.[37] Attaining the objective of dynastic revolution required perfecting themselves in the measures and technologies of the time and systematically developing policies, strategies, and even battlefield tactics not previously witnessed in Chinese history. The Chou kings were compelled to ponder employing limited resources and restricted forces to attack a vastly superior, well-entrenched foe whose campaign armies alone probably outnumbered the entire Chou population. In short, they had to create a substantial power base and attract the allegiance of other peoples and states just to create the possibility of militarily confronting the Shang.

The epoch-making clash between the Chou and Shang dynasties, as envisioned by the Chou and idealistically portrayed in later historical writings, set the moral tone and established the parameters for the dynastic cycle concept. The archetypal battle of virtue and evil—the benevolent and righteous acting on behalf of all the people against a tyrant and his coterie of parasitic supporters—had its origin with this conflict. The Shang's earlier conquest of the Hsia, although portrayed as having been similarly conceived, occurred before the advent of written language and was only a legend even in antiquity. However, the Chou's determined effort to free the realm from the yoke of suffering and establish a rule of Virtue and benevolence became the inspirational essence of China's moral self-perception. As dynasties decayed and rulers became morally corrupt and increasingly ineffectual, new champions of righteousness appeared who confronted the oppressive forces of government, rescued the people from imminent doom, and returned the state to benevolent policies. Moreover, in the view of some historians, the Shang-Chou conflict marked the last battle between different peoples because starting with the Chou dynasty, military engagements within China were essentially internal political clashes.[38] However, confrontations between inhabitants of the agrarian central states and the nomadic steppe peoples continued throughout Chinese history, reflecting in part the self-conscious identity emphasized by the people of the central states in contrast with their "barbarian" neighbors.

As portrayed in such historical writings as the *Shih chi*,[39] and in accord with good moral tradition and the plight of the people, the Shang had ascended to power by overthrowing the last evil ruler of the previous dynasty—the Hsia.[40] After generations of rule, the Shang emperors—due perhaps to their splendid isolation and constant indulgence in myriad pleasures—are believed to have become less virtuous and less capable.[41] Their moral decline continued inexorably until the final ruler, who history has depicted as evil incarnate. The many perversities attributed to him included imposing heavy taxes; forcing the people to perform onerous labor services, mainly to provide him with lavish palaces and pleasure centers; interfering with agricultural practices, thereby causing widespread hunger and deprivation; indulging in debauchery, including drunkenness, orgies, and violence; brutally murdering innumerable people, especially famous men of virtue and loyal court officials; and developing and inflicting inhuman punishments. However, as the following brief excerpt from the Shang Annals in the *Shih chi* records, the king was also talented, powerful, and fearsome:

> In natural ability and discrimination Emperor Chou was acute and quick; his hearing and sight were extremely sensitive; and his physical skills and strength surpassed other men. His hands could slay a fierce animal; his knowledge was sufficient to ward off criticism; and his verbal skills [were] sufficient to adorn his errors. He boasted to his ministers about his own ability; he was haughty to all the realm with his reputation; and [he] believed that all were below him. He loved wine, debauched himself in music, and was enamored of his consorts. He loved Ta Chi, and followed her words.[42] Thus he had Shih Chüan create new licentious sounds, the Pei-li dance [of licentious women], and the [lewd] music of "fluttering down." He made the taxes heavier in order to fill the Deer Tower with coins, and stuffed the Chü-ch'iao storehouses with grain. He increased his collections of dogs, horses, and unusual objects, overflowing the pal-

ace buildings. He expanded the Sha-ch'iu garden tower, and had a multitude of wild animals and flying birds brought there. He was disrespectful to ghosts and spirits. He assembled numerous musicians and actors at the Sha-ch'iu garden; [he] made a lake of wine and a forest of hanging meat, and had naked men and women pursue each other in them, conducting a drinking feast throughout the night. The hundred surnames looked toward him with hatred, and some of the feudal lords revolted.[43]

According to traditional sources, the Chou state was dramatically established when Tan Fu, the Chou leader, emigrated over the mountains south into the Wei River valley to avoid endangering his people and subsequently abandoned so-called barbarian customs to embrace the agricultural destiny of his ancestors. These actions immediately characterized him as a paragon of Virtue and endowed the Chou—and subsequently China—with a sedentary, agrarian character. The *Shih chi* records it as follows:

> The Ancient Duke, Tan Fu, again cultivated the [agricultural] occupation of Hou Chi[44] and Duke Liu, accumulated his Virtue and practiced righteousness, and the people of the state all supported him. The Hsün-yü of the Jung and Ti [barbarians] attacked them, wanting to get their wealth and things, so he gave them to them. After that they again attacked, wanting to take the land and people. The people were all angry and wanted to fight. The Ancient Duke said, "When people establish a ruler, it should be to their advantage. Now the barbarians are attacking and waging war because they want my land and people. What difference is there if the people are with them, or with me? The people want to fight because of me, but to slay people's fathers and sons in order to rule them, I cannot bear to do it." Then, with his relatives, he went to Pin, forded the Ch'i River, the Chü River, crossed over Mt. Liang, and stopped below Mt. Ch'i. The people of Pin, supporting their aged and carrying their weak, again all flocked to the Ancient Duke below Mt. Ch'i. When the nearby states heard of the Ancient Duke's benevolence, many also gave their allegiance. Thereupon the Ancient Duke discarded their barbarian customs, constructed

walls and buildings, and established cities to have them dwell separately. He set up officials for the five offices. The people all sang songs and took pleasure in it, praising his Virtue.[45]

General Hsü Pei-ken, a twentieth-century Chinese military historian, believes the Chou easily managed to develop alliances with various peoples—including disenchanted Hsia groups conquered by the Shang—because of their agricultural heritage and specialization. In perpetuating the Hsia's agricultural offices, for many years the Chou had dispatched advisers to instruct other people and states in farming practices and seasonal activities. This not only garnered them respect and goodwill but also gave them an opportunity to gain a thorough knowledge of the inhabitants, customs, and terrain outside the Wei River valley.[46]

However, Chi Li—Tan Fu's third son and heir through the virtuous deference of his two elder brothers—aggressively waged successful campaigns against neighboring peoples and rapidly expanded the Chou's power base. At first the Shang recognized his achievements and sanctioned his actions, granting him the title of earl, but he was eventually imprisoned and died at Shang hands despite having married into their royal house. Although the history of Shang-Chou relations remains somewhat unclear, awaiting further archaeological discoveries, several other members of the Chou royal house—including King Wen—seem to have married Shang princesses. Generations before the Chou had migrated into the Wei River valley, commencing with King Wu Ting, the Shang had conducted several military expeditions to subjugate the Chou. Shang kings had also frequently hunted in the Chou domain but apparently grew apprehensive and abandoned this practice as Chou's might increased.[47]

In his old age, King Wen was also imprisoned by the tyrannical Shang ruler for his loyal remonstrance, but he gained his freedom through lavish bribes gathered by his family and other virtuous men.[48] The gifts presented were so generous and impressive that King Wen, who continued to profess his submission and fealty to the Shang, was even designated the Western Duke, or Lord of the West. When the title was conferred, he was presented with a bow, arrows, and axes—symbols of the attendant military responsibilities that ironically required that he actively protect the empire from external challenges. He immediately returned to his small state on the western fringe of the Shang empire where the remoteness of the Wei River valley proved immensely advantageous. Dwelling in essentially barbarian territory, the people enjoyed the stimulus of vigorous military activity,[49] the harvests of a fertile area, and the secrecy that relative isolation allowed. Because King Wen could implement effective policies to foster the state's material and social strength without attracting undue attention, Chou had the luxury of seventeen years to prepare for the ultimate confrontation.[50]

THE *SIX SECRET TEACHINGS* AND THE CHOU CONQUEST

Three famous individuals have historically been identified with the Chou's ascent and conquest of the Shang: King Wen, King Wu, and the T'ai Kung. King Wen, who ruled for decades, nurtured the state's power, implemented strong economic policies to foster the people's welfare, and fashioned a strong reputation for Virtue. King Wu, who succeeded him just years before the dynastic revolution, completed the Chou's preparations by expanding their alliances, subjugating potential enemies, and forging the armed forces, thereafter undertaking the final military campaign. The T'ai Kung, whose historical authenticity—like Sun-tzu's—is frequently questioned, has been honored throughout Chinese history as the first general and the true progenitor of strategic thought.[51] After meeting King Wen in a "predestined" encounter, he reportedly served as advisor, teacher, confidant, Sage, strategist, and military commander for the twenty years necessary before final victory could be attained.

The *Six Secret Teachings,* one of the *Seven Military Classics,* is said to contain the T'ai Kung's political and tactical instructions to Kings Wen and Wu, preserving his measures for effective state control, attaining national prosperity, and waging psychological warfare. However, much of the work is devoted to analyzing tactical situations and suggesting appropriate concrete measures. These are particularly important to the study of Chinese military strategy, generally being viewed as expanded discourses upon the configurations of terrain first raised by Sun-tzu in the *Art of War* and possibly Wu Ch'i in the *Wu-tzu*. Although the extant text evidently dates from the Warring States period,[52] some scholars believe it reflects the tradition of Ch'i military studies[53] and preserves at least vestiges, if not the core, of the oldest strata of Chinese military thought.[54] After the great conquest over the Shang the T'ai Kung was enfeoffed as king of Ch'i, no doubt as much to stabilize the eastern area as to reward him for his efforts (and simultaneously remove him as a potential military threat). Thereafter the martial tradition and military studies flourished and became identified with Ch'i; Sun-tzu's clan was one of the four powerful ones who later contended for supremacy in the state.

Because of the T'ai Kung's legendary position in China's martial tradition and the importance of historical material from this period for understanding Sun-tzu's era and milieu, his biography in the *Shih chi* is well worth presenting. An elderly, mysterious figure whose early life was shrouded in secrecy even when he first appeared in the Chou, the T'ai Kung had perhaps found the Shang ruler insufferable and feigned madness to escape court life and the monarch's power. He disappeared only to resurface in the Chou countryside at the apocryphal age of seventy-two. Apart from his storied longevity, his initial interview with King Wen was also marked by the mythic aura that frequently characterizes inevitable meetings between great historical figures:

> T'ai Kung Wang, Lü Shang, was a native of the Eastern Sea area.[55] His ancestor once served as a labor director, and in assisting Yü in pacifying the waters, had merit. In the interval between Emperor Shun and the Hsia dynasty he was enfeoffed at Lü, or perhaps at Shen, and surnamed Chiang. During the Hsia

and Shang dynasties some of the sons and grandsons of the collateral lines were enfeoffed at Lü and Shen, some were commoners, and Shang was their descendant. His original surname was Chiang, but he was [subsequently] surnamed from his fief, so was called Lü Shang.

Lü Shang, impoverished and in straits, was already old when, through fishing, he sought out the Lord of the West [King Wen].[56] The Lord of the West was about to go hunting, and divined about [the prospects]. What [the diviner] said was: "What you will obtain will be neither dragon nor serpent, neither tiger nor bear. What you will obtain is an assistant for a hegemon[57] or king." Thereupon the Lord of the West went hunting, and indeed met the T'ai Kung on the sunny side of the Wei River. After speaking with him he was greatly pleased and said, "My former lord, the T'ai Kung, said 'There should be a Sage who will come to Chou, and Chou will thereby flourish.' Are you truly this [one] or not? My T'ai Kung looked out [wang] for you for a long time." Thus he called him T'ai Kung Wang,[58] and returned together with him in the carriage, establishing him as a strategist.[59]

Someone said, "The T'ai Kung has extensive learning, and once served King Chou [of the Shang]. King Chou lacked the Way [Tao], so he left him. He traveled about exercising his persuasion on the various feudal lords,[60] but didn't encounter anyone [suitable], and in the end returned west with the Lord of the West."

Someone else said, "Lü Shang was a retired scholar who had hidden himself on the seacoast.[61] When the Lord of the West was confined at Yu-li, San-i Sheng and Hung Yao, having long known him, summoned Lü Shang. Lü Shang also said, 'I have heard that the Lord of the West is a Worthy, and moreover excels at nurturing the old, so I guess I'll go there.' The three men sought out beautiful women and unusual objects on behalf of the Lord of the West, and presented them to King Chou in order to ransom the Lord of the West. The Lord of the West was thereby able to go out and return to his state."

Although the ways they say Lü Shang came to serve the Lord of the West differ, still the essential point is that he became strategist to Kings Wen and Wu.

After the Lord of the West was extricated from Yu-li and returned [to Chou], he secretly planned with Lü Shang and cultivated his Virtue in order to overturn Shang's government. The T'ai Kung's affairs were mostly concerned with military authority and unorthodox stratagems,[62] so when later generations speak about armies and the Chou's secret balance of power [*ch'üan,*][63] they all honor the T'ai Kung for making the fundamental plans.

The Lord of the West's government was equitable, [even] extending to settling the conflict between the Yü and Jui. The poet [in the *Book of Odes*] refers to the Lord of the West as King Wen after he received the Mandate [of Heaven]. He attacked Ch'ung, Mi-hsü, and Chüan-i[64] and constructed a great city at Feng. If All under Heaven were divided into thirds, two-thirds had [already] given their allegiance to the Chou.[65] The Ta'i Kung's plans and schemes occupied the major part.

When King Wen died, King Wu ascended the throne. In the ninth year, wanting to continue King Wen's task, he mounted an attack in the east to observe whether the feudal lords would assemble or not. When the army set out, the T'ai Kung wielded the yellow battle ax in his left hand, and grasped the white pennon in his right, in order to swear the oath.

> *Ts'ang-ssu! Ts'ang-ssu!*[66]
> *Unite your masses of common people*
> *with your boats and oars.*
> *Those who arrive after will be beheaded.*

Thereafter he went to Meng-chin. The number of feudal lords who assembled of their own accord was eight hundred. The feudal lords all said, "King Chou can be attacked." King Wu said, "They cannot yet." He returned the army and made the Great Oath with the T'ai Kung.[67]

After they had remained in Chou for two years, King Chou killed Prince Pi-kan and imprisoned Chi-tzu. King Wu, wanting to attack King Chou, performed divination with the tortoise shell to observe the signs. They were not auspicious, and violent wind and rain arose. The assembled Dukes were all afraid, but the T'ai Kung stiffened them to support King Wu.[68] King Wu then went forth.

In the eleventh year, the first month, on the day *chia-tzu* he swore the oath at Mu-yeh and attacked King Chou of the Shang. King Chou's army was completely defeated. King Chou turned and ran off, mounting the Deer Tower. They then pursued and beheaded King Chou.[69] On the morrow King Wu was established at the altars: The Dukes presented clear water; K'ang Shu-feng of Wei spread out a variegated mat; the Shih Shang-fu [the T'ai Kung] led the sacrificial animals; and the Scribe I chanted the prayers, in order to announce to the spirits the punishment of King Chou's offenses. They distributed the money from the Deer Tower, and gave out grain from the Chü-ch'iao granary, in order to relieve the impoverished people. They enfeoffed Pi-kan's grave, and released Chi-tzu from imprisonment. They moved the nine cauldrons,[70] rectified the government of Chou, and began anew with All under Heaven. The Shih Shang-fu's [T'ai Kung's] plans occupied the major part.[71]

Thereupon King Wu, having already pacified the Shang and become King of All under Heaven, enfeoffed the T'ai Kung at Ying-ch'iu in Ch'i. The T'ai Kung went east to go to his state, staying overnight on the road and traveling slowly. The inn-keeper said, "I have heard it said that time is hard to get but easy to lose. Our guest sleeps extremely peacefully. Probably he isn't going to return to his state." The T'ai Kung, overhearing it, got dressed that night and set out, reaching his state just before first light. The Marquis of Lai came out to attack, and fought with him for Ying-ch'iu. Ying-ch'iu bordered Lai. The people of Lai were Yi people who, taking advantage of the chaos under King Chou and the new settlement of the Chou dynasty, assumed Chou would not be able to assemble the distant quarters. For this reason they battled with the T'ai Kung for his state.

When the T'ai Kung reached his state he rectified the government in accord with their customs[72], simplified the Chou's forms of propriety [li]; opened up the occupations of the merchants and artisans; and facilitated the realization of profits from fishing and salt. In large numbers the people turned their allegiance to Ch'i, and Ch'i became a great state.[73]

Then when King Ch'eng of the Chou was young,[74] Kuan Shu and Ts'ai Shu revolted, and the Yi people of the Hua River valley turned against the Chou. So [King Ch'eng] had Duke Chao K'ang issue a mandate to the T'ai Kung: "To the east as far as the sea, the west to the Yellow River, south to Mu-ling, and north to Wu-ti, completely rectify and put in order the five marquis and nine earls.[75] From this Ch'i was able to conduct a campaign of rectification and attack [the rebellious], and became a great state. Its capital was Ying-ch'iu.

When the T'ai Kung died he was probably more than a hundred years old. . . .

. . .

The Grand Historian says: "I went to Ch'i—from Lang-yeh which belongs to Mt. T'ai, north to where it fronts the sea, two thousand *li* of fertile land. Its people are expansive,[76] and many conceal their knowledge. It's their Heaven-given nature. Taking the T'ai Kung's Sageness in establishing his state, isn't it appropriate that Duke Huan flourished and cultivated good government, and was thereby able to assemble the feudal lords in a covenant. Vast, vast, truly the style of a great state"[77]

Despite this detailed biography of the T'ai Kung in Ssu-ma Ch'ien's generally reliable *Shih chi,* over the millennia Confucian skeptics even denied his very existence. Others, perturbed by the confusing traditions regarding his origin, consigned him to a minor role. Both groups justified their views by citing the absence of references to the T'ai Kung in the traditionally accepted archaic texts that supposedly provide an authentic record of these epoch-making events—the *Shang shu*[78] and *Ch'un ch'iu* [*Spring and Autumn Annals.*] Thus, skeptics generally appear to follow the thinking of the second great Confucian, the pedantic Mencius, in refusing to accept the brutal nature of military campaigns and the inevitable bloodshed.[79] King Wu's herculean efforts over the many years prior to the conquest, and his achievements in imposing rudimentary Chou control over the vast Shang domain also tend to be slighted. Consequently, the two figures historically associated with sagacity, virtue, and the civil—King Wen and the Duke of Chou—are revered while the strategist and final commander, the representatives of the martial, are ignored and dismissed. However, after examining numerous stories and references in disparate texts and winnowing away the legendary and mythic material, other scholars and historians have concluded that the T'ai Kung not only existed but also played a prominent role in Chou history—much as described in the *Shih chi* biography.[80] Although the details of his initial encounter with King Wen seem likely to remain unknown, the T'ai Kung was probably a representative of the Chiang clan with whom the Chou were militarily allied and had intermarried for generations.[81] No doubt, as with the Hsia dynasty, whose formerly mythic existence assumes concrete dimensions with the ongoing discovery of ancient artifacts, the T'ai Kung will eventually be vindicated by historical evidence.[82]

Consolidation and the Western Chou

The Chou kings were confronted with the immediate problem of ruling an empire of disparate peoples and far-flung territories with only a small Chou population. Although the Chou had apparently enjoyed the allegiance of roughly eight hundred states in the final campaign against the Shang, many had also opposed them. These enemy peoples, the tens of thousands of Shang nobility, and even the populace of their own allies all had to be effectively controlled, and smoldering rebellions quenched. Immediately after the famous battle at Mu-yeh, King Wu had the T'ai Kung secure the Chou hold over the surrounding area. Next, when returning to the capital, the Chou vanquished a number of recalcitrant states lying along the corridor of their march.[83] Finally, the Western Chou consolidated their rule through several political and military measures, the most important of which was the enfeoffment of powerful clan members among both allied and dissident states. Each person so enfeoffed would establish a collateral family line and would emigrate with his family members, retainers, and military forces. They would constitute a Chou enclave among the local people and would immediately construct a walled town, which would function as the Chou military, political, economic, administrative, and cultural center.[84]

The Chou also forced thousands of Shang noble families to emigrate to the eastern capital region, where they could be adequately supervised and controlled, although they were allowed to retain most of their own officials, customs, and laws.[85] Thereafter, the early Chou kings imposed their rule and consolidated their power through close connections with all the vassals thus established. The obedience of these feudal lords was ensured by their participation in clan activities and power, was reinforced by their military and political inferiority, and was emphasized by their relative isolation—all of which necessitated mutual cooperation under the king's directives. The Shang's theocratic character was displaced by a more worldly approach, although the Chou king preserved and emphasized his right to sacrifice to the ancestors, whose intimate involvement in state affairs remained necessary, and to Heaven, which had sanctified Chou's revolutionary activity.

In addition to maintaining six royal armies[86] and posting garrison units throughout the realm, the Chou also incorporated eight armies from the vanquished Shang and could summon the forces of their own vassals as necessary. These units were still composed essentially of nobility, although they were assisted by commoners, personal retainers, and servants in a secondary role. No doubt the *shih*—minor descendants of the ruling house, younger sons of earls and dukes, and other members of the lesser nobility—also furnished many of the combatants and foot support. Throughout the Western Chou period, the actual fighting was conducted by men of rank and was marked increasingly by mutual deference and respect, with the chariot dominating as the focus of power and mobility.

Following the final conquest of the peripheral areas and their integration under central authority through the imposition of a feudal system, the first few hundred years of the Western Chou period witnessed no dramatic changes in military technology or strategy. Armor more suited to the increasingly active role played by infantrymen appeared and evolved, thanks to improvements in tanning and leather-working capabilities. Coincident with the consistent advances in metallurgical skills, the shape of weapons continued to evolve slowly, becoming longer, stronger, and more complex, eventually resulting in the development of the true sword, which appeared in limited quantities by the end of the Western Chou in 771 B.C. However, long weapons persisted—for fighting either from chariots or dismounted—with the halberd (dagger-ax) predominating. After only four generations, the central power of the Western Chou began to erode, dissipated partly by fatal expansionist campaigns into the south. Early on, the Western Chou became preoccupied with barbarian threats from the north and west, and they were impoverished as the kings continued to grant fiefs and rewards to the loyal vassals who sustained the government. Consequently, the feudal lords gradually rose in power, and although still reluctantly obedient to the king's demands, they became increasingly self-conscious about their regional identities, particularly as they interacted with local peoples and cultures. The ruling house was also plagued by weak and incompetent rulers, some of whom had obviously forgotten that King Chou's debauchery was among the justifications cited when King Wu presumptuously claimed the sanction of the Mandate of Heaven. Eventually, in 771 B.C., a Chou king, restored to the throne through the efforts of vassal states, was compelled to move the capital ignominiously to the east to avoid barbarian pressures and prolong the myth of dynasty. Ironically, one of his defensive actions was to enfeoff the ancestors of the state of Ch'in as a reward for their horsebreeding efforts, in the expectations that they (who were semibarbarians themselves) would form a bulwark against the nomadic tide.

THE SPRING AND AUTUMN

The Spring and Autumn period (722–481 B.C.), named after the famous Confucian classic chronicling the era, witnessed the rise of state power, development of internecine strife, and destruction of numerous political entities. At its inception, descendants of the various Chou feudal lords still ruled in most states, generally in conjunction with other members of their immediate families and the local nobility.

members of their immediate families and the local nobility. Although they appeared to exercise supreme power, their positions depended largely upon the kinship system and the state as extensions of the greater clan. With the Chou's continued decline, the states were effectively freed of their subservient status and therefore were able to exercise increasing independence in their activities. Their new assertiveness reflected not only the shift in the balance of power from a central authority to peripheral actors but also the distinct weakening of the original ties of kinship upon which enfeoffment had been based. The passing of generations, combined with the inherent difficulties of traveling to the capital to participate actively in the Chou court, had contributed to this estrangement. Although the feudal lords continued to seek Chou sanctification and strongmen later appeared to wield power as hegemons in the dynasty's name, their acquiescence in major political and military affairs had to be sought—rather than being mandated—by the king. Freed of old constraints, the feudal lords focused on internal strife and interstate conflict instead of devoting themselves to performing the duties of vassals.

The locus of state power also tended to shift from the enfeoffed ruling house to the contending parties. From the beginning to the middle of the era, the ministerial families—mostly collateral descendants of the first feudal lord—grew more powerful. In many states they even wrested control of the government from the legitimate line, only to exterminate each other in the next century. By the end of the period the surviving states all had effective despots—either members of the founding family who had managed to reseize power or survivors from one of the great families that had usurped the throne. Because more than a hundred states were annexed or extinguished during the Spring and Autumn period—with their ruling clans and great families reduced to commoners, enslaved, or killed—much of the original feudal nobility ceased to exist.[87]

As a result of the predatory campaigns of the stronger states, the scope of warfare in the Spring and Autumn period in-of peasants as integral elements because it could not depend solely upon the nobility. Sustained combat, at least on open terrain, apparently remained centered on the chariot supported by infantry forces, which grew more and more numerous. Concepts of chivalry initially prevailed, and the ethics of battle dictated adherence to the *li* (forms of propriety), although conscripted infantry were little bound by them. Within a century, however, only the foolish and soon-to-be-defeated were burdened by the old code of ethics, and the ancient style of individual combat—despite personal challenges still offered to instigate battles—was outmoded.[88]

Early in the period, campaign armies consisted of roughly several hundred to a thousand chariots, accompanied by perhaps ten thousand men. However, by the end of the Spring and Autumn period in 481 B.C., the strong states of Ch'in and Ch'i fielded approximately four thousand chariots each, supported by forty thousand infantrymen. Cavalry remained unknown, and in 541 B.C. the Chin commander even compelled his reluctant chariot forces to dismount and—as infantrymen—engage barbarian foot soldiers.[89]

Combat weapons throughout the period were similar to those of the Western Chou, with the infantrymen depending more upon spears and short swords than the dagger-ax (halberd), which was the weapon par excellence of charioteers.[90] Metalworking skills continued to advance, resulting in stronger, sharper, larger, and more-deadly combat tools. Yet bronze technology remained the norm, with the newly discovered processes of iron and steel technology (in the late Spring and Autumn period) confined largely to the production of agricultural implements.[91]

Wars occurred frequently, and even the most powerful state, should it fail to prepare its defenses and train its soldiers, could be vanquished. Consequently, the recognition and retention of individuals proficient in the military arts became essential, and rewards—including position, honors, and rank—for valor, strength, and military achievements were initiated. Basic physical qualifications for members of the standing army and for those selected to more elite units were maintained.[92]

As talent grew in importance, resulting in social mobility, bureaucracies staffed by capable individuals began to expand, supplementing and then displacing government by members of the ruler's clan and the entrenched nobility. More-direct forms of administration, through the establishment of districts rather than through enfeoffment, apparently emerged, permitting the central government to wield greater power over the entire state. Peasants slowly began to gain land tenancy instead of being serfs; they prospered economically as property gradually became a transferable commodity rather than the sole possession of the king.

THE WARRING STATES PERIOD

At the beginning of the Warring States period in 403 B.C., the pace of events accelerated. The conflicts of the Spring and Autumn period had segmented China into seven powerful survivor-states,[93] each contending for control of the realm, and fifteen weaker states for them to prey upon. The feudal lords had by then evolved into despotic monarchs who were compelled to nurture the development of extensive economic and political bureaucracies just to survive. In order to suppress external threats effectively, virtually every ruler had to expand his state's agricultural base. The immigration of disaffected people from other states was encouraged by policies providing them with land, and tenancy and landownership continued their swift development. After 500 B.C. iron implements came into general use, and drainage and irrigation projects vastly increased the food reserves—and therefore strength—of some areas. Trade and commerce flourished, and as a result, a class of influential merchants arose, although they continued to be officially despised.

During the Warring States period, the scale of conflict surged phenomenally, sustained by the increasing agricultural productivity and expanding material prosperity. In the Shang a few thousand men had once constituted an army, whereas now the weaker states easily fielded 100,000 and the strongest, in the third century B.C., reportedly maintaining a standing army of nearly a million, is said to have even mobilized 600,000 for a single campaign. In the battle between Ch'in and Ch'u the total number of combatants apparently exceeded a million, an astounding figure even after discounting for inaccuracy and exaggeration. Numerical strength had become critical, for in the previous campaign Ch'in, with 200,000 soldiers, had suffered a severe defeat. Naturally, casualties also escalated rapidly, with 100,000 from Wei dying at the battle of Ma-ling in 341B.C.; 240,000 in the combined forces of Wei and Han perishing at I-ch'üeh in 295 B.C.; and 450,000 men of Ch'u being slaughtered at Ch'ang-p'ing in 260 B.C. Campaigns of such magnitude required lengthy periods for logistical preparation, mobilization, and engagement. Instead of a few days or weeks on the march, with perhaps a couple of days in battle, as in the Shang, months and even years were necessary, with the battles raging for tens of days, or stalemates persisting for a year or more.

Managing the employment of such vast resources and manpower demanded great expertise, and the profession of arms quickly developed. Whereas the newly free masses were generally registered and subjected to military training on a seasonal basis and were conscripted for combat when needed, the army's core had to be composed of practiced, disciplined officers and soldiers. Drill manuals and deployment methods, as well as the tactics they would be designed to execute, suddenly became indispensable. An extensive body of military theory appeared, stimulated not only by battlefield and training requirements but also by new political theories and individual philosophies. Numerous military books—remnants of which survive—were no doubt composed during the early part of the Warring States, and their theories found rigorous employment thereafter.

The commander's qualifications and responsibilities also changed during the period, with strategy becoming so complex that the replacement of a general could, and frequently did, result in an army's defeat and the endangerment of an entire nation. Although rulers continued to meddle in army matters—with catastrophic results—often at the instigation of jealous ministers or corrupt officials acting on behalf of foreign powers, in general, professional officers who specialized solely in military affairs appeared. Early in the Warring States period the ideal commander was normally an effective, even exemplary, civilian administrator, such as Wu Ch'i, but toward the end, the civilian realm became increasingly estranged from the realities of warfare.[94]

During the Shang and early Chou periods, battles were fought on agricultural and otherwise open, undefended terrain, with mobilized armies encountering only scattered cities during their advances. Some fortifications seem always to have existed—such as the famous thick neolithic and Shang dynasty stamped-earth walls that are still being discovered—but forces could essentially roam through the countryside unhampered until encountering them. In the Warring States period the feudal lords undertook the expanded defense of borders, constructing "great walls," ramparts, forts, and guard towers throughout the countryside to defend the entire territory against incursion.[95] States protected their land more than their people, and the objective of warfare changed as each state sought not to capture prisoners and plunder for riches but to vanquish its enemies by seizing their lands, exterminating their armies, gaining political control of their populace, and administratively annexing their territory.

Fortified cities, previously military and administrative centers, grew enormously in significance as industry, trade, and population all flourished, and they became focal points in the road network. Accordingly, whereas in the Western Chou and Spring and Autumn periods it was advisable to circumvent these isolated cities rather than to waste men and resources besieging and assaulting them, their capture or destruction now assumed critical importance. Techniques for assault and defense advanced simultaneously, with siege engines, mobile shields, battering rams, catapults, mobile towers, and similar mobile devices appearing in substantial numbers. Specialists in the technologies of assault and defense were needed: The Mohists, who created and mastered defensive techniques and measures, became famous for their dedication to assisting the targets of aggression. Therefore, Sun-tzu's condemnation of besieging and assaulting cities had become outdated by the time of Sun Pin's analysis of vulnerable and impregnable targets in his *Military Methods.*[96]

The growth of mass infantry armies was also accompanied by the perfection and widespread use of the crossbow during the fourth century B.C.;[97] by further developments in articulation, deployment, and maneuvering capabilities; and by the reluctant adoption of barbarian practices to create the cavalry.[98] Under constant pressure from mounted steppe horsemen, various perceptive commanders and rulers realized the need to develop their own cavalry. Although the history of the horse in China is still emerging, it appears that in 307 B.C. King Wu-ling of North Chao, over vehement objections, deliberately—to facilitate adoption of the cavalry—forced on his troops the "barbarian style of dress" (short jacket and trousers) instead of the indigenous and much-revered long coat of the Chinese. Since the fifth century mounted horsemen had apparently been challenging the Chinese states. The skill of riding probably evolved from Iran and the steppe region, and foreign horses had long been famous in China for their speed and endurance. Wu-ling created the first known cavalry, immediately providing the state with a vastly increased offensive potential.

The saddle, when there was one, was extremely primitive—only a rolled blanket, and stirrups did not appear until the end of the Han. Consequently, the rider was burdened with the task of simultaneously controlling his horse and either shooting his bow or striking with his shock weapon. The effectiveness of the horsemen, acting from such an unstable platform, was inevitably limited and stemmed more from their great speed and mobility than inherent fighting power. However, the development of the cavalry—mentioned only briefly in the military books prior to T'ang T'ai-tsung—freed armies from being confined to open, chariot-accessible terrain and allowed their diffuse deployment in ravines, valleys, forests, hilly fields, and mountains, fully exploiting the terrain.[99] Supported by vast hordes of armored infantrymen wielding spears, cross-bows, and swords (possibly of iron),[100] warfare on an unprec-edented scale suddenly became both possible and inevitable. In the final century of conflict—the third century B.C., which witnessed the growth and decisive triumph of Ch'in—massive campaigns requiring hundreds of thousands of men executing both "explosive" and "persisting" strategies decimated the populace and the countryside. In those days the strategies and methods of the famous tacticians were repeatedly tested and applied and were proven to have a timeless validity.

The State of Wei

The history of Wei, an important participant in the politics of the era, reflects the evolution of military affairs during the Warring States period. Wu Ch'i[101] became a famous general and military administrator in Wei, whereas both Mencius, the early Confucian standard-bearer, and Wei Liao-tzu, reputed progenitor of the military classic bearing his name, squan-dered their persuasive skills on King Hui. One of the seven powers in the Warring States period, Wei had become an inde-pendent political entity in 434 B.C. when three powerful fam-ilies carved the large, formerly mighty state of Chin into Wei, Chao, and Han. In 403 B.C. the Chou king recognized the de facto rulers as feudal lords, and in 376 B.C. they completely ex-terminated the remnants of the Chin ruling house. Situated in the central part of China between the contending powers of Ch'in to the west and Ch'i to the east, Wei was the strongest of the so-called three Chin. Initially, the capital was at An-i, but the fertile plains area in which it was located lacked such nat-ural defenses as mountains and ravines, and the government suffered from constant pressure from hostile neighbors in all directions. When the government was strong and prosperous, it could retain control over the West Ho region and thus fend off any threat from the belligerent Ch'in; when weak—through the ruler's ineptitude or some disaster—it suffered repeated defeats in the incessant warfare. Furthermore, whereas Ch'in had been successfully stymied by the strength of the great Chin, once the latter was segmented, the successor states—indifferent to mutual cooperation—lacked the power necessary for independent survival.

King Wen, who reigned from the inception of Wei until 387 B.C., realized the need for talented advisers and welcomed worthy men irrespective of their regional origin. Li K'o, one of the outsiders who responded to this policy, was appointed to high office and had great impact. He rewrote the laws, promulgated measures to increase agricultural production, established private property, and fostered a stable commodity-price policy. Hsi-men Pao focused his efforts upon irrigation, thereby greatly increasing the nation's wealth. Wu Ch'i, appointed commanding general, conducted numerous successful campaigns against the Ch'in and secured the defense of the West Ho region. King Wen's son King Wu continued Wu Ch'i's basic policy, thereby compelling the other Chin states of Han and Chao to respect Wei's might and prosperity, although Wu Ch'i was ignominiously forced by court intrigues to flee for his life.

Unfortunately, King Hui—who assumed power in 370 B.C.—was more successful in antagonizing people than in employing them, and he forfeited the services of many talented individuals, such as Lord Shang (who subsequently was instrumental in strengthening Ch'in). Instead of nurturing harmonious relations with his neighbors, he appears to have annoyed them constantly, greatly exacerbating the pressures and conflicts on all sides. Furthermore, he eventually lost the West Ho region, thereby opening the state to incursions by Ch'in, and was forced to move the capital to Ta-liang, thereafter calling the state Liang.

Two famous battles illustrate the nature of warfare in this period. The first, at Kui-ling, stemmed from King Hui's desire to recoup losses suffered at the hands of Ch'in in the west. Wei's army, under the command of P'ang Chüan, attacked Chao in the north. Finding itself hard-pressed, Chao requested aid from Ch'i, in the east, on the premise that as Chao presented a natural barrier and defense against Wei, it would be strategically advantageous for Ch'i to support Chao's efforts. Although the Ch'i ruler assented, Sun Pin—the famous strategist whose book has recently been rediscovered—advised waiting for the two antagonists to exhaust themselves, thereby ensuring maximum gain with minimum risk and effort. In 352 B.C., under the command of T'ien Chi, Ch'i mobilized an army to effect an indirect strike at the Wei homeland, the critical city of Ta-liang, in accord with the principles of "first seize what they love," "attack vacuity," and "strike where undefended." P'ang Chüan, flushed with his victories in Chao, reacted as predicted, racing back to mount a counterattack. Ch'i then feigned concern and withdrew to its chosen battlefield to await the Wei army, thereby following a number of basic tactical principles from Sun-tzu and Sun Pin, such as "with ease await the tired." From its fortified positions and high terrain Ch'i was able to quickly defeat the exhausted Wei army, inflicting severe casualties at minimal cost.

Some years later, Wei found itself being increasingly squeezed by a newly vigorous Han, to the south; Ch'in, to the west; Ch'i, to the east; and Chao, to the north. King Hui embarked on a campaign against Han, which had become formidable through the administrative efforts of the famous theorist Shen Pu-hai and by forming an alliance with and returning to Chao the cities previously lost. P'ang Chüan, again entrusted with command, struck directly at the Han capital. Han, as Chao had before, sought aid from Ch'i, citing the benefits of mutual defense. Again Sun Pin advised waiting for the forces to decimate each other, further weakening Wei. Han mounted a total defensive effort but lost five major battles in succession and was forced to submit to Ch'in in a desperate effort to survive. Ch'i then sallied forth, following the previous strategy, with Sun Pin as strategist and T'ien Chi in command. P'ang Chüan immediately abandoned his campaign in Han, turning back toward his home state. Meanwhile, King Hui mobilized all his resources, placing his son in command of the home-defense troops, with the sole aim of seeking a decisive confrontation with Ch'i.

Under Sun Pin's direction the Ch'i armies, which were advancing into Wei, followed the dictum "Be deceptive." P'ang Chüan arrogantly believed the men of Ch'i to be cowards who would flee rather than engage mighty Wei in battle. Therefore, Sun Pin daily reduced the number of cooking fires in the encampment to create a facade of ever-increasing desertion. He also effected a tactical withdrawal to further entice P'ang Chüan into the favorable terrain at Ma-ling where the Ch'i commander concealed ten thousand crossbowmen among the hills. P'ang Chüan, apparently afraid that he would miss an opportunity to inflict a severe blow on the retreating Ch'i army, abandoned his heavy forces and supply train and rushed forth with only light units. Arriving at night, the combined Wei forces were ambushed as soon as they penetrated the killing zone. In addition to being decisively defeated by Ch'i's withering crossbow fire, 100,000 Wei soldiers needlessly perished because of their commander's character flaws and hasty judgment.[102]

Thereafter, Wei not only never regained its former power but also suffered numerous incursions by the now-unchecked mighty Ch'in, which would eventually subjugate all China. In 340 B.C. Wei was forced to cede 700 *li* to Ch'in after sustained defeats, and felt compelled to move its capital to Ta-liang to avoid the incessant danger. Although a strong figure occasionally emerged to effect a temporary resurgence in Wei's strength, its territory continued to shrink until the state, together with the royal house, was finally extinguished in 225 B.C.

The Military Writings

In order to appreciate the great value and inherent importance of the Chinese military classics, one should note several brief historical and political points. First, military works were not normally permitted in private hands, and their possession could be construed as evidence of a conspiracy. (Possession of the T'ai Kung's *Six Secret Teachings*—a book advocating and instructing revolution—would be particularly fatal.) Second, almost all these teachings were at first transmitted through the generations, often orally and always secretly. Eventually they were recorded—committed to written form on bamboo slips—and sometimes became public knowledge. Government scribes and designated officials gathered the slips for state use, depositing them in imperial libraries, where they were so highly valued that they were exempted from the infamous book burnings of the Ch'in dynasty. Once stored away, they were accessible to a few professors of the classics, a restricted number of high officials, and the emperor himself. Even these privileged individuals might still be denied access to the critical writings, especially if they were related to the imperial family.

Even after the teachings were recorded in manuscript form on bamboo, silk, or eventually paper (after the Han dynasty), patriots sometimes felt compelled to remove them from public domain. General Chang Liang, who played a fundamental role in the overthrow of the tyrannical Ch'in dynasty and in the establishment of the Han, for example, supposedly had the sole copy of the *Three Strategies of Huang Shih-kung*, from which he had personally profited, buried with him in his casket. According to one tradition, however, the text resurfaced when his tomb was vandalized in the fourth century A.D. Another example is the well-known (although perhaps apocryphal) refusal of Li Wei-kung, a famous strategist and effective general, to provide the T'ang emperor with more than defensive knowledge and tactics. In the view of Li Wei-kung, strategies for aggressive action should not be disseminated because, with the empire already at peace, they could only aid and interest those who wanted to precipitate war and incite revolution.

The seven military books, as they have been traditionally arranged in the *Seven Military Classics* since the Sung dynasty, are:

Sun-tzu's Art of War
Wu-tzu
The Methods of the Ssu-ma (Ssu-ma Fa)
Questions and Replies Between
   T'ang T'ai-tsung and Li Wei-kung
Wei Liao-tzu
Three Strategies of Huang Shih-kung
T'ai Kung's Six Secret Teachings.

Although uncertainty abounds regarding the authorship and dates of several of the classics, as well as to what extent they are composite books drawing upon common ground and lost writings, the traditional order unquestionably is not chronological. Sun-tzu's *Art of War* has generally been considered the oldest and greatest extant Chinese military work, even though the purported author of the *Six Secret Teachings*—the T'ai Kung—was active hundreds of years earlier than the (possibly) historical Sun-tzu. Materials preserved in the *Ssu-ma Fa* reputedly extend back into the early Chou; the *Wu-tzu* may have been recorded by Wu Ch'i's disciples, although suffering from later accretions; and the *Three Strategies* probably follows the *Wei Liao-tzu,* yet traditionalists still associate it with the T'ai Kung. Accordingly, one possible order (with many caveats and unstated qualifications) might well be:

INITIAL PERIOD	*Ssu-ma Fa*
	Art of War
SECOND PERIOD	*Wu-tzu*
THIRD PERIOD	*Wei Liao-tzu*
	Six Secret Teachings
	Three Strategies
T'ANG-SUNG	*Questions and Replies*

Much of the evidence for ascribing dates of composition to particular periods is tenuous and often circular, and the systematic study of the evolution of strategic thought and military concepts remains to be undertaken. However, the preceding sequence—although possibly infuriating Sun-tzu advocates—seems sustainable in the light of both traditional textual scholarship and recent tomb discoveries. The relative order of books in the third period (which probably coincides with the latter half of the third century B.C.) remains to be defined.[103] A summary discussion of the various viewpoints on the *Art of War* and their purported justifications, as well as a consideration of whether Sun-tzu even existed and what historical role he might have played, will be found at the end of the introduction to the translation.

Ancient
Warfare
and its
Equipment

In recent decades the histories of the horse, chariot, cavalry, and weapons in the first millennium B.C. have become fairly clear due to China's innumerable archaeological discoveries and their systematic publication. Although a detailed reconstruction of their evolution and impact would require more than a few monographs, for the convenience of readers interested in the tools of warfare available to the ancient tacticians in Sun-tzu's era, brief overviews are presented here.

THE CHARIOT

The role and importance of chariots as well as the date of their introduction have been the subject of several articles in recent decades. Unquestionably, the chariot was introduced from the West through central Asia around the fourteenth century B.C., and then the transmission route was probably severed because major Western developments were never reflected in China. (Hayashi Minao confidently asserts that the Shang had chariots by 1300 B.C. and that they were used in hunting.[104] Edward L. Shaughnessy holds that the chariot's introduction should be dated to 1200 B.C.[105]) Support for the theory of diffusion rather than indigenous origin is seen in the absence of any precursor, such as oxen-pulled wagons or four-wheeled carts, although horses were domesticated prior to this period.[106]

Although the construction of the Chinese chariot was substantially the same as its Western prototype, the earliest chariots unearthed thus far have several distinctive characteristics:

Each wheel has many more spokes—sometimes as many as forty-eight; wheel shape is conical; and the chariot box is rectangular and larger than is the case in the West and can accommodate three men standing in triangular formation.[107] (Some of these developments are also seen in an intermediate stage in the Trans-Caucasus versions discovered in this century.[108]) No major alterations occur after its introduction, although there was a historical tendency toward stronger, heavier, swifter vehicles. Significant minor innovations and refinements naturally continued over the centuries, such as in the method of mounting the chariot box on the axle and in the yoking, with a continuing differentiation into types by use. (Even the Shang apparently had specialized chariots or carriages for ordinary transport, chariots designed for combat and the hunt— perhaps in limited numbers—and something similar to wagons for conveying goods.[109])

In the Shang the chariot was a highly visible symbol of rank and power and was elaborately decorated, often being covered with imperial gifts of insignia. However, perhaps because of their greater numbers, chariots in the Chou were more pragmatic and functional, although they still conspicuously displayed marks of royal favor.[110] Finally, in the Spring and Autumn and Warring States periods, highly specialized chariots and other wheeled vehicles were created to suit the requirements of siege warfare and other specialized assault tasks; they were equipped with large shields, towers, battering rams, movable ladders, and multiple arrow crossbows.[111]

Tradition holds that Hsi Chung—either as a minister under the Yellow Emperor or in the Hsia dynasty—created the chariot. The Shang reputedly employed either seventy or three hundred chariots to overthrow the Hsia, but this is improbable. The actual degree to which the Shang employed chariots remains somewhat controversial; some scholars find no evidence that the Shang employed chariots as a battle element,[112] whereas others—especially traditionally oriented experts such as Ku Chieh-kang—maintain qualified opposing views.[113] However, certain facts are known. For example, even in the later years of the dynasty, Shang knights were apparently fighting on foot as infantrymen rather than from chariots. Some of their enemies, however, seem to have employed them in substantial numbers compared with their overall forces.[114]

The Chou are traditionally noted for increasing the horsepower of their assault chariots, using four rather than two horses.[115] (Shang tombs also have chariots with four horses, but these may have been for funerary display rather than for actual use.) One explanation for the Chou's startling victory—apart from their superior Virtue and the support of the people—is the swiftness of their movement and the unexpected crossing of the Yellow River to the south, thereby avoiding Shang defenses to the west. (According to the *Shih chi*, the Shang ruler significantly furthered the Chou's efforts by consciously ignoring their approach until they were suddenly upon him.) In the actual battle three hundred chariots were probably employed, which matches the reported three thousand members of the Tiger Guard, assuming the ten-to-one ratio that is frequently suggested.[116] The swiftness and ferocity of the assault surprised the Shang and might be attributed to the Chou's superior and perhaps first effective use of chariot power.

Significant clashes between the Chou and their steppe neighbors in which considerable numbers of chariots were employed apparently commenced in the first centuries of Chou rule; in one such encounter 130 enemy vehicles were reportedly captured.[117] Massed chariot battles were occurring by the ninth century B.C. and continued throughout the Western Chou era and into the Spring and Autumn period. However, the effectiveness of the chariot under actual combat conditions has been questioned in recent decades by Creel[118] and others. Although the chariot promised power, speed, and mobility—at least in contrast to foot movement—it may have been more symbolic and have served largely as a command platform rather than an overwhelming assault weapon. This is not to deny that chariot combat—often involving great numbers—took place. However, as Yang Hung has discussed, the chariot demanded a large area, and the warriors positioned on either side in the back (especially the one on the right who wielded the halberd) could only engage the enemy when the chariots passed each other perfectly—neither too far apart nor too head on.[119] In addition, their stability and maneuvering ability—which were restricted by a fixed axle that rendered turning extremely difficult, especially at speed—were minimal, even on the flatest plain. (Imagine racing across a corn field without shock absorbers and attempting to fire a bow or strike a moving, equally unpredictable opponent with a shock weapon at the last instant.)

The failure of Wu and Yüeh to adopt the chariot, despite explicit efforts to inculcate them in their use around 541 B.C., further indicates a realization of terrain-imposed limitations; both states were mountainous regions crisscrossed by rivers and streams and marked by lakes, ponds, and marshes.[120] In response to these insurmountable constraints, Wu and Yüeh stressed infantry and naval forces and developed weapons for close combat—such as the sword—to such a high degree that they were famous throughout the realm; when unearthed today, they still retain their surface and edge qualities.[121]

Despite their inherent faults, chariots did permit the comparatively rapid conveyance of men, and under the direction of a skilled driver and reasonable conditions of terrain, they could undoubtedly be formidable. The romantic image of courageous knights challenging each other from their glistening, leather armored chariots rings as true for China as the West, and the chariot was particularly suited to individuals valiantly racing out and provoking the enemy into hasty action. (However, Creel has observed that the Age of Chivalry did not begin until the Spring and Autumn period.[122])

The difficulty of maintaining close formations required advancing at a measured pace (as edicted by King Wu in his prebattle instructions preserved in the *Shih chi* and *Ssu-ma Fa*) in order to coordinate not only chariots with chariots but also chariots with supporting infantry. The necessary imposition and observance of such constraints must have severely tempered an assault thrust's maximum speed and, insofar as the book reflects antique practices, no doubt underlies the *Ssu-ma Fa's* repeated stress on adhering to proper measures. It was possible for coordinated infantry to take advantage of the chariot's difficulties and surround, overturn, or otherwise obstruct it; according to the *Tso chuan,* they also constantly failed of their own accord—suffering broken axles, becoming mired, getting tangled in branches, and falling into unseen gullies. Perhaps because of these limitations, coupled with their cost and extensive training requirements, the only effective way for armies to expand was with infantrymen. However, the growth of infantry divisions obviously reflected changing social and political conditions as well as a number of other factors, and experts such as Yang Hung explicitly deny that the problems of chariot employment caused them to be replaced.[123]

THE HORSE AND CAVALRY

The horse was domesticated in China in neolithic times but was not ridden. The indigenous breed, which had a distribution through the steppe region, was apparently rather small—especially compared with the mounts of the nomadic peoples who appeared on China's western borders around the fifth century B.C. (Creel dogmatically asserts that no evidence exists for mounted riders in China prior to about 300 B.C.,[124], but Shaughnessy suggests the Chinese were encountering mounted riders by the end of the Spring and Autumn period in 484 B.C.[125] Some traditional scholars, on the basis of scant archaeological evidence, have argued for a long indigenous development period and for the existence of riding and hunting as early as the Shang, but this view is largely discredited.[126] Others claim that a *Tso chuan* entry indicates that barbarians were waging mounted warfare by 664 B.C.[127] Pulleyblank[128] and Yetts[129] basically concur with Creel. However, there are historical references to the famous general Wu Ch'i (440?–361 B.C.) riding on horseback; a similar passage is found in the *Wu-tzu* (which is conveniently employed to discredit the work's authenticity). Passages in the *Six Secret Teachings* that discuss the tactical employment of cavalry are also consigned to a late Warring States date on the basis of King Wu-ling's innovation in 307 B.C.[130])

Prior to the fifth century B.C. the nomads were still on foot and fought as infantry or employed chariots. In the fourth century the Hu peoples initiated the first mounted incursions against the northern border states of Chao and Yen. Their horses offered them the obvious advantages of speed, mobility, and freedom in targeting, immediately spreading the requirements of static defense over much larger areas. Consequently, King Wu-ling of Chao resolved to force his warriors to imitate the barbarian mode of dress (trousers and short jackets) because he believed such attire was critical in unleashing the cavalry's power. Apparently, his intent was to increase the army's aggressive potential rather than simply to cope with the Hu, who were not particularly formidable, because he subsequently attempted to flank and invade Ch'in from the north.[131] Thereafter, the horse and cavalry grew in importance but until the Han dynasty, they remained a minor element in the army despite the tactics proposed by strategists such as Sun Pin and the T'ai Kung (of the *Six Secret Teachings* rather than the historical figure). According to their works, the cavalry provides mobility; frees the army from having its main assault weapon (hitherto the chariot) confined to level terrain, and permits the development of unorthodox maneuvers. Throughout the Warring States period, chariots remained more important than the cavalry (although in terms of power and numbers, the infantry came to play a greater role). Even the conquering Ch'in army, however, only included about ten percent cavalry. Liu Pang, founder of the Han, created an elite cavalry unit to turn the tide in his final battles with Hsiang Yü, but this still only amounted to twenty percent of his total forces.[132]

Subsequently, Han Wu-ti, the great expansionist emperor of the Former Han—determined to secure the famous, superior horses from the distant nomads—dispatched major campaign armies into central Asia to subjugate recalcitrant peoples and seize the horses by force.[133] One hundred thousand cavalry, accompanied by as many supply wagons, embarked on the campaign of 128 to 119 B.C. From this time on the chariot ceased to have any tactical fighting role (although there was an abortive attempt by Fang Kuan in the T'ang era to reconstruct and follow the antique ways). From perhaps the middle of the Former Han era, the cavalry became an independent battle element that provided focal power for orthodox tactics and flexibility for executing unorthodox tactics.[134] With the invention of stirrups and the development of an effective saddle, heavy cavalry became possible, although it was displaced again by light cavalry with the approach of the T'ang. T'ang Tai-tsung made particularly effective use of the cavalry in wresting control of the empire and was famous for his horsemanship. He was perhaps of nomadic ancestry and well understood the effectiveness of cavalry (as is seen in the military work bearing his name and the accompanying translator's introduction).

ARMOR AND SHIELDS[135]

The primitive armor of the predynastic neolithic period and the Hsia probably consisted of animal skins, including those of the fearsome tiger, with little alteration. From the Shang through the end of the Warring States, leather—generally fashioned from cowhide, although sometimes from rhino or buffalo—comprised the basic material. When employed in conjunction with large shields, leather armor apparently provided adequate protection against the bronze weapons of the period. Based on evidence from the Chou (and assuming essential continuity between the Shang and Chou), the mighty Shang warriors wore two-piece leather armor that covered the front and back, as well as bronze helmets. As the scope and intensity of conflict increased in the early Chou, construction techniques changed dramatically—shifting from two large pieces to multiple small rectangles strung into rows with leather thongs, the rows then being overlaid to create a lamellar tunic. The individual pieces were cut from leather that had been tanned, lacquered, and finally colored (frequently with red or black pigmented lacquer or perhaps decorated with fierce motifs). Due to the perishable nature of such materials, the exact course of their evolution remains indistinct, but such armor probably displaced two-piece models by the Spring and Autumn period.

Armor was apparently specialized, suited to the warrior's

function and his mode of fighting. For example, that for charioteers—who remained basically stationary once ensconced in
their vehicle—was generally long and cumbersome, protecting the entire body while leaving primarily the arms free.
However, the infantry—which was heavily dependent on agil-
ity and foot speed for both its survival and aggressiveness—
obviously fought with shorter leather tunics, fewer restrictive
leg protectors, and far less overall weight. When the cavalry
developed, although they could easily sustain more weight
than infantrymen, their legs had to be unrestricted (but protected against outside attacks), which accounts for the adoption of barbarian-style trousers and short tunics. Furthermore,
until the invention of the stirrups, excess weight would also
contribute to the rider's instability. Thus heavy cavalry did not
develop until the post-Han, only to be again displaced by
swifter, lighter elements within a few centuries.

Even after the development of iron and its application for
agricultural implements and weapons, iron armor—which
was necessary to withstand the greater firepower of the crossbow as well as perhaps stronger iron swords—did not displace
leather until well into the Han (coincident with the replacement of the bronze sword). Bronze armor may have have
existed in the early Chou, and the use of some combination of
leather with perhaps a reinforcing bronze outer piece (particularly for the shield) is evident. However, until the advent of
iron plates imitating the leather lamellar construction—thus
ensuring flexibility and endurable weight—metal appears to
have been extremely rare. Even in the Han and thereafter,
leather never entirely disappeared, being employed in a supplementary fashion.

Shields—an essential adjunct to every warrior's defensive
equipment—were generally constructed on a wooden frame
over which lacquered leather or various lacquered cloth materials were stretched. All-wood shields as well as those made
from reeds and rushes obviously existed in some regions and
in different eras, although their history has yet to be reconstructed. But as with body armor, leather was the material of
choice, sometimes with additional protective layers of bronze.

With the rise of iron weapons and the crossbow, iron shields also appeared but apparently not in great numbers until late in the Warring States or the Han dynasty. Helmets were fashioned from bronze throughout the period, although iron helmets had appeared by the beginning of the Warring States. However, as with the iron sword and armor, they did not dominate until at least the Han. Chariots, which evolved little over the period, also used lacquered leather for reinforcement, as is noted in Wu Chi's initial interview with the king in the *Wu-tzu*. Protection for the horse—the prime target—was also considered important and may have originated late in the Warring States period. However, again it was not until the Han that equine armor became both massive and extensive, reflecting the newly dominant role of the cavalry and the need to protect the valuable steeds. Outside stimuli from the mounted, highly mobile steppe peoples may have also contributed to the development of armor (and perhaps some weapons), but most developments were indigenous rather than imitative.

THE SWORD

Although there are a few dissenting voices and much controversy about the origin, evolution, and numbers of swords, it appears that the true sword—one with the blade more than double the length of the haft—did not really develop in China until late in the Spring and Autumn period.[136] Prior to this time warriors carried daggers, spear heads, and sometimes a short sword—all of which were fashioned from bronze.[137] (However, based on recent archaeological evidence, some traditionally oriented scholars have deduced that Western Chou warriors carried bronze swords.[138] An occasional artifact from the Shang is also classified as a "sword" in the literature, but when its dimensions are considered, the blade rarely exceeds the length of the haft by much—consigning it instead to the category of short swords or long daggers.)

Swords in the Western Chou and Spring and Autumn periods were designed for piercing and thrusting, not for slashing and cutting attacks.[139] With the advent of the infantry, weapons for close combat necessarily supplemented and then began to displace the halberd and other chariot-oriented war implements. In addition to the sword, the short or hand *chi* (spear-tipped halberd capable of thrusting attacks much like a spear[140]) became very common among Warring States infantrymen—particularly in states where chariots were tactically unsuitable, such as Wu and Yüeh.[141]

Some scholars have coupled the final evolution and proliferation of the sword to the development of the cavalry in the late Warring States period and subsequently the Han dynasty.[142] Extremely long swords, especially double-edged ones, would be both dangerous and unwieldy for cavalrymen;[143] therefore, the excessively long swords that developed in the late Warring States and early Han were probably exclusively for infantrymen or were simply ceremonial.

Theories of origin range from imitation of steppe weapons to totally indigenous development without any nonmetallic precursors.[144] One theory holds that warriors in the Shang and Early Chou carried spearheads as a sort of short dagger and that from these—especially as the spearheads became longer and stronger—the short dagger with a handle and then the elongated sword evolved.[145] As the technology of metalworking progressed, improvements in shape, durability, sharpness, and appearance rapidly followed. However, whatever their origin, swords with slashing power and considerable length in comparison with the handle really only flourished in the late Warring States, Ch'in, and Han.[146]

As the cavalry became the dominant battle element in the armed forces, the sword evolved to match its requirements. Thus from the Han onward, a single-edged sword with a ring handle—actually termed a "knife"—gradually displaced the long swords of the Warring States. Thereafter, metalworking continually improved, especially layering and surface treatment; and two distinctive trends emerged—one toward high-quality, shorter, functional-edged weapons; the other toward purely ceremonial and elaborately decorated symbolic swords. Steel "knives" became the sword of choice for both infantrymen and cavalrymen as the T'ang—the era of the last of the *Seven Military Classics*— approached.

Although this brief sketch is inadequate for any true understanding of the sword and its history, a more extensive consideration requires a separate book. Readers with a command of Asian languages should consult Hayashi Minao's detailed but somewhat dated work[147] and similar writings in Chinese.[148]

MILITARY ORGANIZATION

Military organization in all its aspects—such as the development of administrative districts, population registration, and universal military service obligations—requires a separate study. Opinions on many aspects—including fundamentals, questions of origin, and early history—are far from unanimous. However, because knowledge of the basic organizational methods and principles is helpful to understanding much of the *Seven Military Classics,* a brief overview is undertaken here.

The critical problem in characterizing organization in the Shang dynasty is the uncertain role the chariot played because some scholars believe the chariot comprised the core element around which the company—the basic military unit—was formed. If chariots were insignificant or only played a transport role, this would obviously not be possible. Consequently, two theories must be considered: chariot-centered and clan-centered. In the former, the chariot—manned by three members of the nobility—would be accompanied by conscripted commoners, probably ten men per chariot.[149] Their function was strictly supportive; because they would be drawn from the state's farming and artisan populations as well as from each noble's personal retainers—in an age when bronze weapons were expensive and limited in numbers—they were only minimally armed.[150] Based on burial patterns, this line of thought holds that the chariots were organized into squads of five, with either three or five squads to a company. Each squad would be supported by a one-hundred-man infantry company with (in some views) a complement of twenty-five officers. A battalion composed of three or five squads with associated infantry would constitute an operational unit. (Conclusive evidence for these reconstructions is lacking.[151])

Another view—based on excavated tombs—suggests the total number per *tsu,* or company, was one hundred: three officers for the chariot and seventy-two infantry organized into three platoons, supported by a supply vehicle staffed by twenty-five. However, this conceptualization seems to derive from the later idealization found in the *Chou li* and more likely describes the state of affairs late in the Spring and Autumn.[152]

Considerable textual evidence suggests that the clan composed the basic organizational unit, with the *tsu* (a different character than that above) again numbering one hundred men.[153] The members would all be from the nobility, under the command of the clan chief—who would normally also be the king, an important vassal, or a local feudal lord. Thus organized, they probably fought as infantry units, although chariots could also have been integrated for transport and command purposes. (According to Hsü Cho-yün, clan units [*tsu*] still actively participated in the pitched battles of the Spring and Autumn.[154]) Ten such companies probably comprised a *shih,* which was basically an army of one thousand men; in fact, the term *shih* should be considered synonymous with "army" in this period.[155] The word normally translated as "army"—*chün*—does not appear until the Spring and Autumn.[156]

Early Western Chou military organization would have been essentially the same, but with the units definitely chariot-centered. As already noted, the three thousand famous Tiger Warriors at the epoch-making battle of Mu-yeh would appropriately work out to a ratio of ten men per chariot. Thereafter, the infantry expanded as the number associated with each chariot gradually increased, until by the early Spring and Autumn the ratio was perhaps twenty, twenty-two, or even thirty foot soldiers per vehicle.[157] In the Spring and Autumn period—the classic age of chariot warfare depicted in the *Tso chuan*—the systematic grouping of men into squads of five, with a vertical hierarchy mapped out on multiples of five, seems to have developed and become prevalent.[158] This is the period described by passages in several of the *Military Classics* and the *Chou li,* during which seventy-two infantrymen accompanied each chariot, deployed in three platoons characterized as left, center, and right. (These designations were nominal; actual positioning depended on their function. For example, on easy terrain the center platoon would follow the chariot, whereas on difficult terrain it would precede it—both as a defensive measure and to clear obstacles.[159]) Whether the officers were included among the one hundred also seems to be a matter of debate.[160]

From the *Chou li* and some of the military writings, the following chart can be constructed, with rough Western equivalents as indicated:

UNIT	STRENGTH	POSSIBLE WESTERN EQUIVALENTS	
wu	5	squad	
liang	25	platoon	
tsu	100	company	
lü	500	battalion	(regiment)
shih	2,500	regiment	(brigade)
chün	12,500	army	(corps)

The Western equivalents are relative; their definition depends on the era and country of organization.[161] The columns represent a set of alternatives, so that if regiment is used for *lü,* then brigade (or perhaps division) should be used for *shih.* The term *lü* is an ancient one; it was originally used by the Shang to designate a military unit that reportedly expanded to ten thousand for one campaign, but it also may have referred to the standing army.[162] Subsequently, in the Spring and Autumn and Warring States periods, it was combined with the character for army—*chün*—as *chün-lü* to indicate the army or military units in general. In its original meaning, it apparently referred to "men serving under a flag."

As already noted, the term for army—*chün*—appeared only in the Spring and Autumn and then only in the central states because the peripheral states, such as Ch'u, had their own distinct forms of organization.[163] The term "Three Armies" (*san chün*) encountered throughout the military texts normally refers to the army in general, not just to three units of army strength according to the above chart.[164] Early Chou theory asserted that the king alone had the right to maintain six armies (*shih*); a great feudal lord, three armies; lesser lords, two armies; and the least of them, one army. All of the vassal armies could and would be called on to supplement the royal forces and support the dynasty in the military campaigns that were generally mounted to suppress either rebellious states or nomadic peoples. With the rise of the hegemons in the Spring and Autumn period, states such as Chin simply disregarded both the Chou house and its prerogatives, eventually fielding as many as six armies.[165]

In the earliest stage of the Shang and Chou, force size was apparently irregular; it was enumerated, constituted, and organized to meet the situation and the demand. However, with the vastly augmented scope of conflict in the Warring States and the imposition of universal service obligations, military hierarchy and discipline became essential, as is evident from the emphasis on them in the *Seven Military Classics*. Actual service demands made on the newly registered populace also increased from the Spring and Autumn into the Warring States; at first, only a single male in each family was required to serve, then all males were so required. This mirrored early Chou trends when all the people who dwelled within the state (*kuo*) trained and were obligated to fight but were universally mobilized in only the most dire circumstances.[166] With the creation and imposition of hierarchical administrative systems for the populace (both variants—the village and district—began late in the Spring and Autumn in Chin and Ch'u, perhaps originating with Kuan Chung), the male population could be quickly summoned for active duty. The village and district groups of five and twenty-five were immediately translated into squads and platoons. Local officials at all levels would immediately become officers at the respective unit level, although there were professional military personnel for the higher ranks and a standing army to form the army's core.[167] This meant that the total qualified populace could be mobilized for military campaigns, and that virtually an entire country could go to war.[168]

Introduction

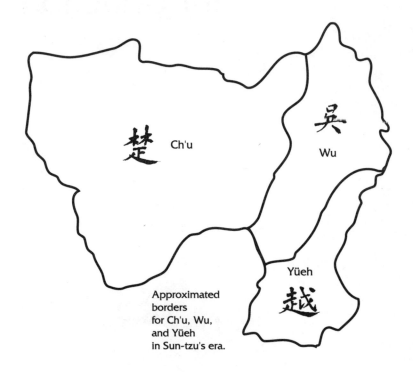

楚 Ch'u

吴 Wu

Yüeh 越

Approximated
borders
for Ch'u, Wu,
and Yüeh
in Sun-tzu's era.

OF THE *Seven Military Classics* only Sun-tzu's *Military Strategy*, traditionally known as the *Art of War*, has received much exposure in the West. First translated by a French missionary roughly two hundred years ago, it was reportedly studied and effectively employed by Napoleon and possibly by certain members of the Nazi High Command. For two thousand years it remained the most important military treatise in Asia, known at least by name even to the common people. Chinese, Japanese, and Korean military theorists and professional soldiers have all studied it, and many of the strategies played a significant role in Japan's storied military history, commencing about the eighth century A.D.[1] Over the millennia the book's concepts have stimulated intense debate and vehement philosophical discussion, commanding the attention of significant figures in all realms. Although rendered into English numerous times, with the translations of Giles[2] and Griffith[3] still being widely available, further translations continue to appear. Some of these are merely versions of Giles, acknowledged or otherwise, under a different cover, while others represent entirely new works.[4]

The *Art of War* has long been recognized as China's oldest and most profound military treatise, all other works being relegated to secondary status at best. Traditionalists attribute the book to the historical Sun Wu, who is portrayed in the *Shih chi* and *Spring and Autumn Annals of Wu and Yüeh* as active in the last years of the sixth century, beginning about 512 B.C. In their view the book preserves his strategic and tactical concepts and principles and should therefore be dated to this period. Over the ages, however, more skeptical scholars have questioned the work's authenticity, citing certain historical discrepancies and anachronisms to justify their positions. Although all the arguments have varying degrees of merit and credibility, and will be separately considered at the end of the introduction, the most extreme not only deny Sun Wu's military role, but even his very existence. The critical element in their argument is the absence of any material in the *Tso chuan*, the classic record of the period's political events, which would confirm Sun Wu's existence and corroborate his strategic role in the wars between Wu and Yüeh as preserved in the *Shih chi* biography.[5]

The *Shih chi*, famous throughout Asia as China's first true history and a literary masterpiece, includes several biographies devoted to distinguished military strategists and generals, including Sun-tzu.[6] However, the *Spring and Autumn Annals of Wu and Yüeh* recount a very similar but somewhat more interesting version of Sun Wu's career and experiences:

> In the third year of King Ho-lü's reign Wu's generals wanted to attack Ch'u, but no action was taken. Wu Tzu-hsü[7] and Po P'i[8] spoke with each other: "We nurture officers and make plans on behalf of the king. These strategies will be advantageous to the state, and for this reason the king should attack Ch'u. But he has put off issuing the orders, and does not have any intention to mobilize the army. What should we do?"
>
> After a while the King of Wu queried Wu Tzu-hsü and Po P'i: "I want to send forth the army. What do you think?" Wu-tzu Hsü and Po P'i replied: "We would like to receive the order." The King of Wu secretly thought the two of them harbored great enmity for Ch'u. He was deeply afraid that they would take the army out only to be exterminated. He mounted his tower, faced into the southern wind and groaned. After a while he sighed. None of his ministers understood the king's thoughts. Wu Tzu-hsü secretly realized the king would not decide, so he recommended Sun-tzu to him.
>
> Sun-tzu, whose name was Wu, was a native of Wu.[9] He excelled at military strategy, but dwelled in secrecy far away from civilization, so ordinary people did not know of his ability. Wu Tzu-hsü, himself enlightened, wise, and skilled in discrimination, knew Sun-tzu could penetrate and destroy the enemy. One morning when he was discussing military affairs he recommended Sun-tzu seven times. The king of Wu said: "Since you have found an excuse to advance this *shih*, I want to have him brought in." He questioned Sun-tzu about military strategy, and each time that he laid out a section of his book the king couldn't praise him enough.
>
> Greatly pleased, he inquired: "If possible, I would like a minor test of your military strategy." Sun-tzu said: "It's possible. We can conduct a minor test with women from the inner

palace." The king said, "I agree." Sun-tzu said: "I would like to have two of your Majesty's beloved concubines act as company commanders, each to direct a company." He ordered all three hundred women to wear helmets and armor, to carry swords and shields, and stand. He instructed them in military methods, that in accord with the drum they should advance, withdraw, go left or right, or turn around. He had them know the prohibitions and then ordered, "At the first beating of the drum you should all assemble, at the second drumming you should advance with your weapons, and at the third deploy into military formation." At this the palace women all covered their mouths and laughed.

Sun-tzu then personally took up the sticks and beat the drums, giving the orders three times, and explaining them five times. They laughed as before. Sun-tzu saw that the women laughed continuously, and wouldn't stop.

Sun-tzu was enraged, his eyes suddenly opened wide, his sound was like a terrifying tiger, his hair stood on end under his cap, and his neck broke the tassels at the side. He said to the Master of Laws, "Get the executioner's axes."

Sun-tzu [then] said: "If the instructions are not clear, if the explanations and orders are not trusted, it is the general's offense. When they have already been instructed three times, and the orders explained five times, if the troops still do not perform, it is the fault of the officers. According to the rescripts for military discipline, what is the procedure?" The Master of Laws said: "Decapitation!" Sun-tzu then ordered the beheading of the two company commanders, the king's favorite concubines.[10]

The King of Wu ascended his platform to observe just when they were about to behead his beloved concubines. He had an official hasten down to them with orders to say, "I already know the general is able to command forces. Without these two concubines my food will not be sweet. It would be appropriate not to behead them."

Sun-tzu said: "I have already received my commission as commanding general. According to the rules for generals, when I, as a general, am in command of the army even though you issue orders to me, I do not [have to] accept them." [He then had them beheaded.]

He again beat the drum, and they went left and right,

advanced and withdrew, and turned around in accord with the prescribed standards without daring to blink an eye. The two companies were silent, not daring to look around. Thereupon Sun-tzu reported to the King of Wu: "The army is already well ordered. I would like your Majesty to observe them. However you might want to employ them, even sending them forth into fire and water, will not present any difficulty. They can be used to settle All under Heaven."

The King of Wu was suddenly displeased. He said: "I know that you excel at employing the army. Even though I can thereby become a hegemon, there is no place to exercise them. General, please dismiss the army and return to your dwelling. I am unwilling to act further."

Sun-tzu said: "Your Majesty only likes the words, he isn't able to realize their substance." Wu Tzu-hsü remonstrated: "I have heard that the army is an inauspicious affair[11] and can not be wantonly tested. Thus if one forms an army but does not go forth to launch a punitive attack, then the military Tao will be unclear. Now if Your Majesty sincerely seeks talented *shih* and wants to mobilize the army to execute the brutal state of Ch'u, become hegemon of All under Heaven, and overawe the feudal lords, if you do not employ Sun-tzu as your general, who can ford the Huai, cross the Ssu, and traverse a thousand *li* to engage in battle?" Thereupon the King of Wu was elated. He had the drum beaten to convene the army's staff, assembled the troops, and attacked Ch'u. Sun-tzu took Shu, killing the two renegade Wu generals, Princes Kai-yu and Chu-yung.[12]

➤ The *Shih chi* biography differs from the above version in two fundamental respects: first, it identifies Sun-tzu as a native of Ch'i rather than Wu.[13] This would place his background in the state that enjoyed the heritage of the T'ai Kung's military thought. Accordingly, many traditional scholars have asserted that he was well versed in the *Six Secret Teachings* and similar writings, although it should be noted that the *Six Secret Teachings* was probably composed well after Sun-tzu's *Art of War*. Moreover, the state of Ch'i, originally on the periphery of the ancient Chou political world, was well known for nurturing a diversity of views and imaginative theories. Since the *Art of War* clearly reflects many

Taoist conceptions[14] and is philosophically sophisticated, he may well have been a man of Ch'i.

Second, the *Shi chi* biography adds a brief description of Sun-tzu's achievements: "To the West [the king] defeated the powerful state of Ch'u, and advanced into Ying. To the north he overawed Ch'i and Chin, and manifested his name among the feudal lords. This was due to Sun-tzu imparting power to him."[15] Some military historians have identified Sun Wu with the campaigns against Ch'u that commenced in 511 B.C., the year after his initial interview with King Ho-lü. Although he is never mentioned in any recorded source as having sole command of the troops, following Wu's conquest of Ying, the capital of Ch'u, his name completely disappears. Perhaps he realized the difficulty of surviving under the unstable political conditions of his time, or possibly feared he would be executed by the new king, Fu-ch'ai, after becoming entangled in Po P'i's machinations, and set an example for later ages by retiring to obscurity, leaving his work behind.[16]

The view that Sun-tzu simply vanished of his own volition was commonly held in later centuries, possibly reflecting the famous example of Fan Li, the great Yüeh strategist and commander who, eschewing further service despite the impassioned entreaties of King Kou-chien once Yüeh had completed its lengthy conquest of Wu, willingly set off and disappeared at sea. The *Tung-chou lieh-kuo-chih,* a highly popular Ming dynasty novel closely based upon historical materials from the Eastern Chou period, romanticizes a similar departure for Sun-tzu:

> When Ho-lü discussed comparative achievement in Ch'u's destruction, he ranked Sun Wu first. Sun Wu was unwilling to occupy an official position, so he steadfastly requested permission to return to the mountains. The king had Wu Tzu-hsü detain him. Sun Wu personally addressed Wu Tzu-hsü "Do you know the Tao of Heaven? When summer goes winter comes; after spring returns autumn will arrive. The king now relies upon his strength flourishing; the four borders are free of worries; arrogance and pleasure will inevitably be born. Now

when achievements are complete, failing to retire will invariably result in later misfortune. I am not trying to preserve myself alone, but I also want to preserve you." Wu Tzu-hsü said he didn't find it to be so. Sun Wu subsequently drifted away. Having been presented with several carriages of gold and silks, he scattered them all among the impoverished common people along his route. Later no one knew how he ended up.[17]

Sun Wu remains an enigma not only because of the absence of historical data in the so-called authentic texts of the period, but also because his life never generated the anecdotes and illustrative stories frequently found about famous figures in the works of succeeding periods. In contrast, Wu Ch'i, the extraordinary general and likely progenitor of the *Wu-tzu*, became the focus of many incidents in such widely read compilations as the *Shuo yüan, Han-shih wai-chuan,* and *Lü-shih ch'un-ch'iu,* as well as staid philosophical works like the *Han Fei-tzu.* Many theories have been vociferously advanced to explain Sun Wu's invisibility, chief among them that most of the credit that was rightly his was attributed to his mentor, Wu Tzu-hsü, because the latter was more prominent and his life, a living melodrama writ large, provided a natural focal point for tales of intrigue and portraits of achievement. Remarkably, among those who deny Sun-tzu's very existence, some have advanced the theory that he and Wu Tzu-hsü were identical, one and the same individual. These and other inseparable issues will be discussed in a subsequent section on the text and its dating.

Historical
Background
of Ch'u, Wu,
and Yüeh

Whether or not Sun-tzu existed, in order to gain a better understanding of his era—including the nature of warfare, the complexities and astounding effects of political intrigue, and the significant historical figures with whom he would have interacted—it is worthwhile to reconstruct many facets of Spring and Autumn political and economic life and analyze the battles in which he purportedly served as strategist or commander. The period overflows with strong personalities, intrigue, murder, and machination on an extreme scale, creating human drama in which entire states perished at the whim of a single man. Since Wu Tzu-hsü was a pivotal figure in the clashes between Ch'u and Wu, and later a forlorn voice in the destructive wars between Wu and Yüeh, his biography provides an informative focal point for exploring Sun Wu's world and era.

As discussed in the general historical introduction, from its inception the Chou had an avowed policy of dispatching royal clan groups to both enemy and unsettled domains. Within a few generations it also began experiencing pressure from nomadic "barbarian" peoples to the north and west; therefore, any further activity in the quest for allies, resources, and political strength tended to be directed toward the south and southeast. Several Early Chou kings enthusiastically undertook military campaigns to the south (with mixed results), and King Chao, the fifth to reign, even perished mysteriously, leading to the frequently repeated charge that Ch'u had murdered him.[18] While members of the Chi and Chiang clans emigrated to these areas for defensive purposes, the southern offensive became essentially a cultural one, gradually sinicizing the peoples around initial Chou enclaves, particularly as they acquired a need for Chou products and associated technology. Numerous small states proudly claimed descent from one or another Chou royal family member, and most at least nominally allied themselves with the Chou, and later with the stronger northern states that emerged when Chou power visibly declined.

The Spring and Autumn period witnessed the rise of the great families and their inevitable, often brutal conflict with the older ruling nobility in the various domains, as well as the destructive emergence of seven great states, each reputedly capable of fielding ten thousand chariots. In the early sixth century the state of Chin had already formed six armies, visibly usurping a Chou royal prerogative, and was probably capable of mobilizing seventy-five thousand men if necessary. (These same six armies, under the direction of individual factions, would later split the state apart as the six ministerial families contended for ultimate authority.) Awesome Chin, originally also founded by the Chi clan—the royal house of Chou—claimed the role of hegemon in officially sustaining the Chou, coercing the other states into formally recognizing and even sanctifying its prestigious role.

Although the central states vigorously contended among themselves for relative supremacy, they retained a joint sense of identity, consciously distinguishing themselves from the uncivilized "barbarian" areas and peoples. Consequently, with both disdain and trepidation they observed the rapid development of the wild southern areas where the states of Ch'u, Wu, and Yüeh were forming, and also feared the ever less-submissive state of Ch'in in the old Chou heartland. The south was not only distinctly different, it also enjoyed numerous advantages. First, the climate was warmer, resulting in a greater variety of plants, crops, and products. Second, the longer growing season, coupled with plentiful water resources, provided the populace with bountiful harvests, including rice. Third, the area was crisscrossed by rivers, filled with lakes, and dense with mountains and forests; the latter provided abundant wild life, the former seafood, to supplement the agricultural diet. A natural bastion that made chariot-centered land warfare—which was feasible only on the relatively flat, open land of the northern plains—frequently useless, the terrain compelled the development of extensive naval forces. These early, essentially inland navies capitalized upon the indigenous skills that had evolved to exploit the Yangtze, Han, and Huai rivers, the numerous lakes, and expansive marshes.[19] Even though there was a natural tension between the original culture of the central plains area and that of the "wild, uncivilized, and forbidding south," the south also enjoyed a virtual monopoly on many resources, ensuring that the "northern states" could not ignore trade possibilities. For example, copper mainly derived from the south, and when iron technology evolved late in the Spring and Autumn period, the main production centers arose in the southern states. In fact, claims have been advanced that Wu and Yüeh became prosperous not only through trade, but also because they were the first states to employ iron tools in agriculture, significantly increasing the yields. Furthermore, their bronze weapon technology was spectacularly advanced, with the most famous swords of the era coming from Wu and Yüeh in the fifth century B.C.[20]

THE THREE STATES AND THEIR CONFLICTS

The three significant southern states, in the order of their emergence, were Ch'u, Wu, and Yüeh. Ch'u lay to the south of the northern plains area, generally in modern day Hupei, Hunan, Honan, and Anhui. While there were a number of smaller states between it and the "Chinese" entities, Ch'u's northern border was basically contiguous with the latter.

Wu lay to the east of Ch'u, and therefore to the southeast of the northern states, reaching to the sea. Its capital was in the Suchou area, and it occupied essentially present Chiangsu province. Yüeh lay to the south of Wu, largely falling in northern Chechiang, and was the last state to develop.

The state of Ch'u—Wu's nemesis and the object of Wu Tzu-hsü's and Sun Wu's strategy and efforts—was originally a barbarian state, but by the middle of the Spring and Autumn period it had become largely sinicized. The government had adopted many of the forms and practices of "civilization," including government organization and the *li* (the rites or forms of etiquette), although the populace remained a mixture of indigenous peoples, descendants of original Chou settlers, and later migrants. Its stronghold was the area between the Yangtze and Han rivers, with the capital located at Ying. In the seventh century B.C. it had already become militarily active, subjugating and obliterating various small Chou states, such as Ts'ai, Shen, and Cheng, with the total annexed or destroyed eventually rising to more than forty.[21] A state marked by an aggressive, energetic populace, stimulated by terrain and sometimes harsh climatic conditions, and under often belligerent leadership, its expansionist policies threatened the northern states, especially Chin, its closest significant neighbor. By 632 B.C. its immense territory already covered a thousand *li*.

In that year—632 B.C.—at the famous great battle of Ch'eng-p'u, the allied states of Chin, Ch'i, Ch'in, and Sung defeated Ch'u's army.[22] This forced Ch'u, at least temporarily, to redirect their campaigns of expansion toward the south and southeast, whereupon they subjugated many smaller states along the Han River. The direction of this new thrust inevitably brought them into conflict with the state of Wu, particularly after they suffered another defeat at the hands of Chin in 575 B.C.

Even though Chin had been reasonably successful in its ongoing efforts to contain Ch'u, when confronted by additional threats from Ch'in's growing strength in the West, its own internal dissension, and its rapidly declining prestige, it sought to develop an external counterbalance to Ch'u's might. In 584 B.C. Chin therefore dispatched Wu-ch'en, duke of Shen—a former high-ranking Ch'u official who had fled his native state for ostensibly political reasons—with 125 Chin warriors and officers and 9 chariots to Wu for the express purpose of introducing the chariot and instructing them in the land warfare techniques of the northern states.[23] Although his visit is generally seen as marking not only a military turning point, but also, at least symbolically, bringing Wu culturally into the sphere of the civilized states, in reality Wu's growing strength no doubt suggested the constructive possibilities of such a mission.[24] The true impact and overall effectiveness of Wu-ch'en's instructions are also debatable, for naval and infantry forces continued to predominate, with chariots only being sporadically mentioned in the *Tso chuan's* accounts of Wu's various battles.[25] Since Wu's important attacks against Ch'u required launching along water routes, or at least fording extensive rivers, boats were inevitably required for transport; therefore the number of cumbersome chariots that could be conveyed would be limited, and infantry units invariably played the focal role.

The state of Wu claimed an antiquity even greater than the Chou itself, having supposedly been founded by the eldest son of King T'ai, who, being disinclined to inherit the throne, had fled to the south.[26] The indigenous peoples in the Wu and Yüeh region were known for having short hair and tatooing their bodies, perhaps because their lifestyle was closely connected with water activities.[27] Since much of Wu occupied an alluvial plain formed by the Yang-tze River, it lacked more than small hills, but approximately 15 percent of its land area was wet, consisting of marshes, rivers, lakes, and ponds. In 585 B.C. Shou-meng became the first ruler to assume the title of king, styling himself as the "king of Wu." This marked another step toward the more formal administrative style found in the north, and also constituted a blatant effort to increase his prestige. (The northern states, while also witnessing the birth of additional "kings," still had many states governed only by "dukes" and lesser royalty. The Chou king alone theoretically merited and inherited the right to such a grand title.)

The duke of Shen's diplomatic mission marked two important developments: he was the first "guest advisor" to be honored in Wu, commencing a practice that would later see Wu Tzu-hsü and Sun Wu gain employment, and his visit entangled it in an alliance with Chin, thereby confirming its future enmity with Ch'u. Although Wu did not receive formal Chou recognition until 576 B.C., clashes between Ch'u and Wu immediately began in 584 B.C. as the former sought to expand into the region between them, while the latter mounted its initial preemptive strike against Ch'u's subordinate state of Hsü. Thereafter, clashes continued at least every few years for the next six decades as the two states strove to dominate the region.

During this initial period Wu emerged victorious from every significant encounter, greatly blunting Ch'u's power and curtailing its influence. These repeated defeats forced Ch'u to constantly reassess its military organization and methods, bringing about pauses in the hostilities for up to five years while Ch'u sought to rebuild and retrain its forces. Most of the attacks were launched by water routes and featured naval engagements followed by limited land assaults. In virtually every case Wu was better prepared and therefore managed either to stop and eventually rout the Ch'u forces, or to employ subterfuge and stratagems to turn the tide. Whenever a ruler died or another destabilizing opportunity presented itself in one state, the other state would quickly launch an attack, although Wu again proved more successful in exploiting such transitory possibilities.

As the decades passed, Wu commenced increasingly aggressive actions against Ch'u's cities, forcing Ch'u (from 538 B.C. on) to undertake massive defensive preparations, including the construction of walled cities and other fortifications.[28] Wu also constantly benefited from Ch'u brutally suppressing the various minority peoples and smaller states in the region, easily finding numerous allies and local support among them. By exploiting the sense of common identity fostered by confronting a mutual enemy, Wu was able to draw upon them for material support, local guides, and field intelligence. For example in 537 B.C. Ch'u mounted a large-scale attack in conjunction with several of its subordinate states and assistance from Yüeh (marking the latter's first conflict with Wu), only to suffer a defeat. Later in the same year Ch'u again attempted an advance, but withdrew after finding Wu fully prepared for their invasion. Consequently, Ch'u grew increasingly weaker, having dissipated its people and resources in futile efforts to dominate Wu, and was spared even further distress only because Wu engaged the great northern state of Ch'i in battle in 521 B.C. and suffered the temporarily crippling loss of two full armies.[29]

Chinese military historians examining this initial period tend to draw several conclusions about the nature of the two states and their conflict.[30] First of all, before Ch'u directed its attention toward Wu—primarily because it wanted to expand and thereby encircle the northern states, but also because it was constrained by the north—engagements were between the single state of Ch'u and members of the Chou alliance. However, once it redirected its focus toward the Huai River basin area, the nature of warfare changed to engagements between two single states contending over territory populated by various, unintegrated peoples. Ch'u's previous military experience had been limited to chariot-centered land warfare; although it possessed naval forces, its members were not well practiced in the requisite underlying skills or their employment in combat. It appears that assimilating land warfare methods proved easier and more successful for Wu than Ch'u's attempts to adopt naval measures. Despite Ch'u's theoretical inherent advantage in moving downstream to engage Wu forces, they amassed an abysmal battle record.[31]

The respective populaces, styles of government, and general policies of the two states also displayed distinctive characteristics. For example, even allowing for archetypal distortion, Ch'u's leadership seems to have been remarkably brutal, suppressing not only external peoples, but also exhausting and exploiting the energies of its own inhabitants. The demands of incessant military activity imposed heavy burdens on the populace both in terms of material resources (various taxes and impositions) and the (often unwilling) supply of manpower. Their government seems to have suffered more than other states from frequent intrigues while the rulers distinguished themselves by emulating the last Shang dynasty king, constructing extravagant pleasure facilities that further debilitated the people and interfered with the agricultural seasons. (These and other themes merit note not only because of their inherent veracity and impact, but also because they became pivotal doctrines in the military and philosophical writings of the time.[32]) The leadership also seems to have been muddled, lacking direction as well as a clear recognition of their goals when engaging Wu in battle.

Conversely, Wu was a younger state marked by a growing self-consciousness, one generally governed by dynamic leaders who largely avoided the pitfalls of extravagance and debauchery. Instead of exploiting and exhausting the people, its kings generally fostered policies to nurture them, increase the population, and stimulate productivity. Throughout their numerous military campaigns Wu's warriors seem to have been more courageous, more spirited and energetic, able to endure great difficulties and turn defeat into victory. Its leadership also seems to have been more unified, no doubt largely accounting for their ability to respond quickly. Realizing that they would be outnumbered in virtually every clash with Ch'u armies, they had to create imaginative tactics and consistently avoid any frontal, brute-force confrontation that could decimate their numbers. Consequently their attacks stressed speed and mobility, frequently employed deceit and clever stratagems, and focused upon frustrating the enemy's plans and movements—all cardinal principles found in the *Art of War*. In many cases Wu mounted such formidable defenses that when the Ch'u armies arrived they couldn't detect any weakness to attack. Clearly Wu's pre-Sun-tzu efforts exemplified and perhaps furnished the historical basis for several pivotal teachings from the *Art of War*, such as

> Subjugating the enemy's army without fighting is the true pinnacle of excellence.[33]

> The strategy for employing the army is not to rely on their not coming, but to depend upon us having the means to await them. Do not rely on them not attacking, but depend upon us having an unassailable position.[34]

> When someone excels at defense the enemy does not know where to attack . . . . If I do not want to engage in combat, even though I merely draw a line upon the ground and defend it, they will not be able to engage me in battle because we thwart his movements.[35]

Roughly a century later the great general Wu Ch'i analyzed Ch'u's character for Marquis Wu of Wei. His remarks are apparently preserved in the chapter entitled "Evaluating the Enemy" in the *Wu-tzu:*

> Ch'u's character is weak, its lands broad, its government troubling [to the people], and its people weary. Thus while they are well-ordered, they do not long maintain their positions. The way to attack them is to suddenly strike and cause chaos in the encampments. First snatch away their *ch'i*—lightly advancing and then quickly retreating, tiring and laboring them, never actually joining battle with them. Then their army can be defeated.

THE BATTLE OF CHI-FU

The last major battle between Ch'u and Wu before Sun Wu assumed his advisory role in Wu occurred in 519 B.C. around Chi-fu, well within Ch'u territory on the northeastern side of the mountain range falling between Ch'u in the west and Wu in the east. Ch'u's defeat resulted in significant consequences: the peoples dwelling in the disputed region between the two states, as well as those that had already been annexed by Ch'u in the north and east, realized that while Ch'u continued to repress and hold them in bondage, it could not defend them against Wu's strength. Feeling vulnerable to Wu's incursions and generally filled with hatred for Ch'u's ruler, they increasingly turned their hopes and even allegiance to Wu.

Second, this clash is an example of the "few defeating the many, the weak overcoming the strong," as advocated in Sun-tzu's writings. Although Wu apparently ferried some chariots upriver with their naval and infantry forces, they were vastly outnumbered by Ch'u's land-based armies. Therefore they were compelled to (deceitfully) rouse the enemy into movement and take advantage of the ensuing confusion and disorder, as well as the terrain, to startle, terrorize, and strike them. In these efforts they proved enormously successful, no doubt due to the quality of their military intelligence.

Convinced that Ch'u was becoming a much greater threat, King Liao of Wu, together with the future King Ho-lü (who proved a brilliant commander throughout), decided to launch a preemptive strike rather than passively await Ch'u's next aggressive act. For roughly five years each side had been nurturing its forces, so their strength levels were at maximum. When Ch'u learned of Wu's final preparations they hurriedly coerced six smaller allied states into joining with them in a coordinated campaign under Chu's general command. The armies assembled at Chi-fu in preparation for moving against the Wu forces laying siege to Chou-lai. Wu's armies, under Ho-lü's command, anticipating that Ch'u's overwhelming forces would effect the town's rescue, discontinued the siege and withdrew somewhat to occupy more favorable terrain and await the onslaught (probably on the principle "with the rested await the tired"). However, en route Ch'u's commander-in-chief fell ill and died, immediately throwing their central command into turmoil. Since his replacement was decidedly less capable and the officers and soldiers generally felt his death to be an ill omen, they were disorganized and clearly dis- spirited. Once Wu learned of these developments and the state of their morale, they naturally decided to exploit these weaknesses.[36]

Wu's tactics proved to be both brilliant and inventive. First, they targeted the armies of the coerced states as their primary objective on the premise that they would be little inclined to fight for a hated overlord and the recognition that their com- manders had little respect for the new commander-in-chief. Second, they decided to attack on the last day of the lunar cal- endar, traditionally a time when armies remained docilely encamped because they feared undertaking military activities when the balance of yin and yang became so clearly inauspi- cious.[37] Third, they deliberately disrupted Ch'u's defensive posture by employing an advance attack force of three thou- sand ill-trained convicts, knowing that even under conditions of total surprise they would probably be repulsed, panic, and flee, drawing out the defenders in a wildly disorganized pursuit.

The battle proceeded as envisioned, as forces from three of the six state armies (which had been entrusted with defending the center of the forward perimeter behind which Ch'u's main army was encamped) rushed forward into Wu's well-prepared ambush. The Wu armies deployed on the left and right then fervently attacked, while their main force, concealed directly ahead of the onrushing Ch'u troops, launched the main thrust, completely enveloping the enemy. Incredible chaos ensued, with the majority of the alliances's soldiers being killed or captured, and the rulers of the three states being summarily executed. Their executions, very deliberately performed and visibly staged, further increased the panic of the surviving soldiers, many of whom were then allowed to flee, as if by accident, in order to sow the seeds of chaos among the three remaining perimeter armies.

Coincident with the returning onslaught of allied troops, Wu launched a coordinated attack against the three still emplaced state armies. As anticipated, they quickly buckled under the combined pressures of external assault and internal turbulence, panicking as they became engulfed in the turmoil. They naturally fled in an uncontrolled rout, only to directly collide with the main Ch'u army, which, although not yet deployed into fighting formation, had begun to advance. The unimaginable chaos combined with the sheer weight of numbers no doubt prevented them from ever assuming any attack posture, and the rout quickly became a total defeat. Wu's victory marked the first incursion and occupation of Ch'u territory by any state. It also exposed Ch'u to the threat of future invasion, for only three routes existed for penetrating the interior of Ch'u because of the numerous mountains and dense forests protecting it to the east and north.

THE BIOGRAPHY OF WU TZU-HSÜ

Shortly after this great battle, Wu Tzu-hsü was forced to emigrate from Ch'u to Wu by the machinations of a corrupt and evil official, Fei Wu-chi. Remarkably, King Liao of Wu deemed him a worthy individual and despite his origins and

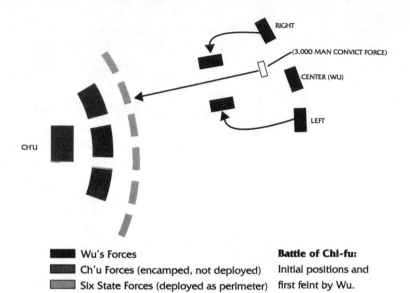

Wu's Forces
Ch'u Forces (encamped, not deployed)
Six State Forces (deployed as perimeter)

Battle of Chi-fu:
Initial positions and
first feint by Wu.

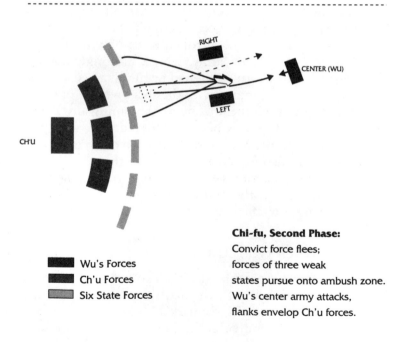

Wu's Forces
Ch'u Forces
Six State Forces

Chi-fu, Second Phase:
Convict force flees;
forces of three weak
states pursue onto ambush zone.
Wu's center army attacks,
flanks envelop Ch'u forces.

96   SUN-TZU

background in Ch'u, appointed him to a central position. Thereafter he became an influential advisor to King Ho-lü, successor to King Liao, and was instrumental in creating Wu's great power and fashioning the strategy for the final great invasion of Ch'u. However, before reconstructing the battle for Ying and analyzing the various tactical principles employed, it is appropriate to present Wu Tzu-hsü's dramatic biography from the *Shih chi* as it provides a portrait of the principal characters and the politics of the era:[38]

> Wu Tzu-hsü, a native of Ch'u, was named Yün. Yün's father was called Wu She; Yün's older brother was called Wu Shang. Their ancestor, called Wu Chü, had served King Chuang of Ch'u with his direct remonstrances and thereby become illustrious. Thus his descendants were famous in Ch'u.
>
> The Heir apparent to King P'ing of Ch'u was his son Chien. He employed Wu She as Grand Mentor, and Fei Wu-chi as Junior Mentor. Wu-chi was not loyal to Heir Apparent Chien. King P'ing dispatched Wu-chi to Ch'in to obtain a wife for the Heir Apparent.[39] The woman of Ch'in was beautiful, so Wu-chi raced back to report to King P'ing: "The Ch'in woman is absolutely beautiful. Your majesty can take her for himself, and then

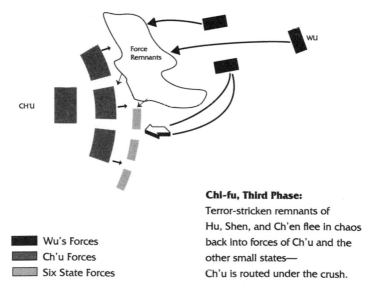

Chi-fu, Third Phase:
Terror-stricken remnants of Hu, Shen, and Ch'en flee in chaos back into forces of Ch'u and the other small states—
Ch'u is routed under the crush.

select another woman for the Heir Apparent." King P'ing subsequently took the Ch'in woman for himself and exceedingly loved and favored her. She gave birth to a son, Chen. Then he obtained another woman for the Heir Apparent.

Because he had already pleased King P'ing with the woman of Ch'in, Wu-chi abandoned the Heir Apparent and served the king. Fearing that one day King P'ing would die and the Heir Apparent, once established, would kill him, he slandered Heir Apparent Chien. Chien's mother, a woman of Ts'ai,[40] did not enjoy King P'ing's favor. King P'ing gradually distanced himself from Chien, and had Chien undertake the defense of Ch'eng-fu, preparing the border troops [against incursions].

A little later Wu-chi again began to speak day and night about the Heir Apparent's shortcomings to the king: "Because of the woman of Ch'in the Heir Apparent can not be without animosity. I would like your majesty to prepare himself somewhat. The Heir Apparent dwells in Ch'eng-fu and commands the troops while externally establishing relationships with the feudal lords; surely he wants to enter [the state] and mount a rebellion." King P'ing thereupon summoned Grand Mentor Wu She and interrogated him. Wu She knew that Wu-chi had slandered the Heir Apparent to King P'ing, so he said: "How is it that your majesty, on account of a slanderous and villainous minor official, estranges himself from his relatives of bone and flesh?" Wu-chi said: "If your majesty does not now take control of the situation the [rebellious] affair will be accomplished! Moreover, your majesty will be captured." Thereupon King P'ing, being angered, imprisoned Wu She and had Fen Yang, the *Ssu-ma* (Commander) for Ch'eng-fu, go out to kill the Heir Apparent. Before his forces arrived Fen Yang had a man first announce to the Heir Apparent: "You must urgently depart; otherwise we will execute you." Heir Apparent Chien escaped by fleeing to the state of Sung.

Wu-chi spoke to King P'ing: "Wu She has two sons, both worthies. If you do not execute them they will cause trouble for Ch'u. You can summon them by using their father as a hostage; otherwise they will cause disaster for Ch'u." The king had an emissary address Wu She: "If you can bring in your two sons you will live; if you are unable to do so then you will die." Wu She said: [My son] Shang's character is benevolent. If I call he will certainly come. Yün's character is hard and stubborn, and able to endure disgrace. He is capable of accomplishing great affairs.[41] When he sees that if he comes in he will also be captured, under such circumstances he certainly will not come." The king didn't listen, but had men summon the two sons, saying: "If you come, I will let your father live; if you don't come, today I will kill Wu She."

Wu Shang wanted to go. Wu Tzu-hsü said: "The king hasn't summoned us two brothers because he wants to keep our father alive, but because he fears that those who escape will later cause disaster. Thus he uses our father as a hostage to deceitfully summon his two sons. When the two of us arrive, we will die together with our father. Of what advantage will this be to our father's death? Our going would make it impossible to avenge our grievance. It would be better to flee to some other state and borrow their strength to wipe away our father's shame. If we are all exterminated there will be no one to act."

Wu Shang said: "I know that even if we go, in the end we will be unable to preserve our father's life. Yet I hate it that, in seeking to live, our father summons us but we do not go. Later, if we are unable to wipe away the shame, in the end all the world will laugh at us." Addressing Wu Tzu-hsü he said: "You can run away! You will be able to avenge the grievances of father and son; I will return to die."

Shang then submitted to custody. The emissary [tried to] detain Wu Tzu-sü. Wu Tzu-hsü fully drew his bow and pointed the arrow toward the emissary. The emissary did not dare advance; Wu Tzu-hsü then fled. He heard that Chien, the Heir Apparent, was in Sung, so he went to follow him. When Wu She heard about Tzu-hsü's escape he said: "The ruler and ministers of Ch'u will soon suffer the bitterness of warfare!" After Wu Shang arrived in Ch'u, the king killed both She and Shang.

After Wu Tzu-hsü arrived in Sung the state experienced the turbulence of the Hua clan [revolt], so with Heir Apparent Chien he fled to Cheng. The people of Cheng treated them exceptionally well. Heir Apparent Chien also went on to Chin where Duke Ch'ing of Chin said: "You are already well treated in Cheng, and the people of Cheng trust you. If you can mount a response from within on our behalf when we attack from without, Cheng's destruction will be certain! If we extinguish

Cheng I will enfeoff you." The Heir Apparent then returned to Cheng. The affair had not yet been accomplished when it happened that for some personal reason he wanted to kill [one of] his followers. This follower knew of his plans so he informed Cheng of them. Duke Ting of Cheng, together with Tzu-ch'an, executed Heir Apparent Chien.

Chien had a son called Sheng. Wu Tzu-hsü was afraid, so he fled with Sheng to Wu. When they reached Chao Pass, [the guards] wanted to detain him. Wu Tzu-hsü and Sheng each escaped alone on foot, almost not getting away.[42] Wu Tzu-hsü's pursuers were right behind him. When he reached the Yangtze river there was a fisherman in a boat who realized Wu Tzu-hsü's extremity and ferried him across. When they had already crossed he unfastened his sword and said: "This sword is worth a hundred pieces of gold. I present it to you." The fisherman said: "According to the laws of Ch'u anyone who catches you will be granted fifty thousand piculs of grain and the rank of Jade Baton Holder, not just a sword worth a hundred pieces of gold!" He did not accept it.[43] When Wu Tzu-hsü had not yet reached Wu he fell ill and halted along the way to beg for food.[44] When he reached Wu, King Liao had just gained power and Prince Kuang was the commanding general. Wu Tzu-hsü then sought an audience with the King of Wu through Prince Kuang.

Some time thereafter King P'ing of Ch'u became enraged because two women from the border towns of Chung-li in Ch'u and the Pei-liang clan in Wu, both silkworm producers, had attacked each other over a mulberry tree. It reached the point where the two states mobilized troops to attack each other. Wu had Prince Kuang attack Ch'u; he returned after seizing their towns of Chung-li and Chü-ch'ao.

Wu Tzu-hsü exercised his persuasion on King Liao of Wu, saying: "Ch'u can be destroyed. I request that you again dispatch Prince Kuang." Prince Kuang addressed the king of Wu: "This Wu Tzu-hsü's father and elder brother were murdered by Ch'u. Thus he encourages your majesty to attack Ch'u because he wants to gain revenge for their grievances. An attack on Ch'u would not yet destroy them." Wu Hsü knew that Prince Kuang harbored a hidden ambition to kill the king and establish himself [on the throne]. Since he could not yet persuade him to undertake external affairs, he introduced [the future assassin] Chuan Chu to Prince Kuang, retiring to plow the fields with Sheng, the Heir Apparent's son.

Five years later King P'ing of Ch'u died. In the beginning the woman of Ch'in who the king had taken from Heir Apparent Chien gave birth to a son, Chen. When King P'ing died Chen was finally established as his successor, becoming King Chao. King Liao of Wu, taking advantage of Ch'u's mourning, dispatched two princes in command of the army to go forth and strike Ch'u. Ch'u mobilized its troops and cut off the rear of Wu's forces, so they were unable to return. Wu's interior was empty, so after Prince Kuang had Chuan Chu suddenly stab King Liao, he ascended the throne himself as King Ho-lü of Wu.[45] Once enthroned as Ho-lü, now that he had attained his ambition, he summoned Wu Tzu-hsü to serve as a protocol officer for foreign envoys and plan state affairs with him.

Ch'u executed its chief ministers Hsi Yüan and Po Chou-li. Po Chou-li's grandson, Po P'i[46] fled to Wu, and Wu also established him as a high official. Earlier the troops King Liao had dispatched under the command of the two princes to attack Ch'u had had their route cut off and couldn't return home. Later, when they heard that Ho-lü had assassinated King Liao and established himself as king they surrendered with their troops to Ch'u. Ch'u then enfeoffed them at Shu.

When Ho-lü had ruled for three years he mobilized the army and with Wu Tzu-hsü and Po P'i attacked Ch'u, taking Shu and going on to capture the two turncoat Wu generals. Then he wanted to proceed to Ying [the capital], but general Sun Wu said: "The people are weary. It's not yet possible; still wait a while." Then they returned.

In his fourth year Wu attacked Ch'u seizing Liu and Ch'ien. In the fifth year he attacked Yüeh and defeated it. In the sixth year King Chao of Ch'u had Prince Nang Wa command the troops in an attack on Wu. Wu had Wu Tzu-hsü respond with a counterstrike; he extensively destroyed Ch'u's army at Yü-chang and seized Ch'u's city of Chü-ch'ao.

In his ninth year King Ho-lü of Wu addressed Wu Tzu-hsü and Sun Wu: "In the beginning you said that Ying could not yet be invaded. Now, after all, what about it?" The two of them replied: "Ch'u's general Nang Wa is greedy while [the small states of] T'ang and Ts'ai both bear animosity toward him.[47] If you really want to mount a major attack against Ch'u, you must first gain [the support of] T'ang and Ts'ai before it will be possible." Ho-lü listened [to their advice] and together with T'ang and Ts'ai fully mobilized the army to attack Ch'u. Their combined forces and Ch'u's army both deployed close upon either side of the Han River. The king of Wu's younger brother, Fu-kai, in command of his troops, requested permission to accompany him, but the king would not listen.[48] Thereupon with his five thousand men he struck Ch'u's general Tzu-ch'ang (Nang Wa). Tzu-ch'ang was defeated and fled, running off to Cheng. Wu then took advantage of the victory to advance, and after five battles reached Ying. On the day *chi-mao* King Chao of Ch'u fled. On *keng-ch'en* [one day later] the king of Wu entered Ying.

When King Chao was fleeing he entered [the marshes of] Yün-meng. Brigands suddenly attacked the king, so he raced off to Yün. The duke of Yün's younger brother Huai said: "King P'ing killed our father. If we kill his son, wouldn't it be appropriate!" The duke of Yün was afraid his younger brother would kill the king, so he fled with him to Sui. Troops from Wu besieged Sui, and then addressed the populace: "The sons and grandsons of the Chou along the Han River have all been exterminated by Ch'u."[49] The people of Sui wanted to kill the king, but Prince Ch'i hid him and disguised himself like the king in order to substitute for him. The people of Sui divined about whether to hand the king over to Wu, but it was not auspicious to do so. They therefore declined Wu's demand and did not turn over the king.

In the beginning Wu Tzu-hsü had known Shen Pao-hsü. When Wu Tzu-hsü fled he said to Shen Pao-hsü "I must overturn Ch'u." Pao-hsü said: "I must preserve it." When Wu's troops entered Ying, Wu Tzu-hsü sought out King Chao. Since he could not get him he dug up King P'ing's funeral mound, disinterred the corpse, and whipped it three hundred blows before stopping. Shen Pao-hsü, having fled to the mountains, had a man say to Tzu-hsü: "Your revenge is far too excessive! I have heard that if masses of men overcome Heaven, Heaven certainly can also destroy men. Now you are King P'ing's former subject. You yourself faced north to serve him, but today you treat a dead man contemptuously. Isn't this the extremity of lacking the Tao of Heaven?" Wu Tzu-hsü said: "Please apologize to Shen Pao-hsü on my behalf, saying 'For me the day was late and the road far, so I contravened normal actions and employed contrary measures.'"

Thereupon Shen Pao-hsü fled to Ch'in to announce [Ch'u's] extremity and seek aid from Ch'in. When Ch'in did not grant it, Pao-hsü stood in the Ch'in court, crying aloud day and night, his sound unbroken for seven days. Duke Ai of Ch'in took pity on him, saying: "Even though Ch'u behaved immorally, since it has a minister such as this, how can we not preserve it?" Then he dispatched five hundred chariots to rescue Ch'u and strike Wu. In the sixth month they defeated Wu's troops at Chi.

It happened that the king of Wu had long remained in Ch'u seeking King Chao while his younger brother Fu-kai had fled and returned [to Wu], and established himself as king. When Ho-lü heard about it he released Ch'u and returned, mounting a sudden strike against his younger brother Fu-kai. Fu-kai fled in defeat, and subsequently raced into Ch'u. When King Chao of Ch'u saw that Wu suffered from internal turbulence, he again entered [his capital of] Ying. He enfeoffed Fu-kai at T'ang-ch'i where he assumed the clan name of T'ang-ch'i. Ch'u again engaged Wu in battle and defeated them. The king of Wu returned home.

Two years later Ho-lü had Fu-ch'ai, the Heir Apparent, command the troops in an attack on Ch'u, seizing P'an. Ch'u feared that Wu would again come in great strength so they abandoned Ying and moved [the capital] to Jo. At this time the state of Wu, employing the strategies of Wu Tzu-hsü and Sun Wu, had destroyed the strong state of Ch'u to the west, overawed Ch'i and Chin to the north, and forced the people of Yüeh in the south to submit.

Four years later Confucius was made minister in Lu.[50] Four years thereafter they attacked Yüeh. King Kou-chien of Yüeh mounted a counterattack and defeated Wu at Ku-su, injuring Ho-lü's toe.[51] Wu's army withdrew. King Ho-lü, who had fallen ill from his wound and was about to die, addressed Heir Apparent Fu-ch'ai: "Will you forget that Kou-chien killed your father?" Fu-ch'ai replied: "I would not dare forget it." That evening Ho-lü died. Fu-ch'ai was then enthroned as king; appointed Po P'i as Grand Steward; and practiced warfare and archery.

Two years later he attacked Yüeh, defeating Yüeh at Fu-chiao. Kou-chien, king of Yüeh, with his remaining five thousand troops ensconced himself on the heights of K'uai-chi, and had the *ta-fu* [high official] Chung dispatched with generous gifts to seek peace through Wu's Grand Steward P'i, offering to subordinate his state, like a subject or wife, to Wu. The king of Wu was about to give his assent when Wu Tzu-hsü remonstrated with him: "The king of Yüeh's character is such that he is capable of enduring hardship. If your majesty does not exterminate him you will certainly regret it later." The king of Wu did not listen, but instead employed the Grand Steward's plans, making peace with Yüeh.

Five years later the king of Wu heard that Duke Ching of Ch'i had died and that the great ministers were contending for favor [under the new king]. Since the new ruler was weak, he mobilized the army to go north and attack Ch'i. Wu Tzu-hsü remonstrated: "Kou-chien does not have two flavors in is food. He consoles the [families of] the dead and inquires about the ill, for he wants to employ them. If this man doesn't die, he will inevitably cause disaster for Wu. Today Wu's having Yüeh is like a man having an acute illness in his abdomen. But if your majesty does not make Yüeh his priority but focuses upon Ch'i, won't this truly be an error?" The king of Wu did not listen, but instead attacked Ch'i, greatly defeating Ch'i's army at Ai-ling, going on to overawe the rulers of Tsou and Lu and then return. He increasingly distanced himself from Wu Tzu-hsü's plans.

Four years later, when the king of Wu was about to go north to attack Ch'i, Kou-chien, king of Yüeh, employing Tzu-kung's strategy, led his masses to assist Wu while greatly augmenting the treasures that he had presented to the Grand Steward P'i. Having already received bribes from Yüeh on several occasions, Grand Steward P'i's love and trust for Yüeh became vastly greater, and day and night he spoke on their behalf to the king of Wu. The king of Wu trusted and employed P'i's plans. Wu Tzu-hsü remonstrated: "Now Yüeh is an abdominal illness. Today you trust their specious phrases and false behavior while coveting Ch'i. If you destroy Ch'i it will be like [having] a rocky field, of no utility. Moreover the Announcement of P'an Keng said: "If there are those who overturn, overstep, or are disrespectful [to my orders], then cut off their noses, utterly exterminate them. Ensure that they will not leave behind any posterity, do not allow their seed to be moved to this city."[52] This is the way by which the Shang arose. I would like your majesty to abandon Ch'i and give priority to Yüeh. If you don't, later you will experience immeasurable regret." But the king of Wu did not listen, and sent Wu Tzu-hsü to Ch'i. When Tzu-hsü was about to depart [to return to Wu] he addressed his son: "I have remonstrated with the king several times, but the king has not employed [my plans]. I can now perceive that Wu is lost. For you to perish together with Wu would be of no advantage." Then he entrusted his son to Pao Mu of Ch'i, and returned to report to Wu.

Wu's Grand Steward Po P'i had already had disagreements with Tzu-hsü, so he slandered him: "Tzu-hsü's character is hard and brutal, of little charity, suspicious and malevolent. I fear his enmity will cause great disaster. Previously your majesty wanted to attack Ch'i, but Tzu-hsü felt it was not possible. In the end your majesty attacked it with great success. Tzu-hsü was ashamed that his plans and strategies were not employed, so he reacted with rancor toward you. And now that you are again about to attack Ch'i, Tzu-hsü alone opposes it and strongly remonstrates against it. He obstructs and slanders those in authority, and would rejoice if Wu should be defeated since his own plans would prevail. Now your majesty is himself going forth, assembling the entire military force of the state in order to attack Ch'i. Because Tzu-hsü's remonstrances have not been heeded, he declines to participate, and feigns illness and inability to travel. Your majesty must be prepared—for this to turn into a disaster would not be difficult.

Moreover, I dispatched men to observe him secretly. When he was an emissary to Ch'i he entrusted his son to the Pao clan of Ch'i. Now he is a minister who within has failed to attain his ambition, and without relies on the feudal lords; who personally acted as the former king's minister for planning but now is not used. He is constantly discontented and resentful. I would like your majesty to plan for it early on."

The king of Wu said: "Not only do you speak about it, I also have doubted him." Then he had an emissary present Wu Tzu-hsü with the Shu-lü sword, saying: "You should use this to die."

Wu Tzu-hsü looked toward Heaven and sighed: "Alas! The slanderous minister P'i causes chaos, but the king turns around and executes me! I caused your father to become hegemon. When you had not yet been established [as Heir Apparent] and the various princes were contending for the designation, I engaged in a death struggle on your behalf with the former king.[53] You almost were not established. When you gained the throne, you wanted to divide the state of Wu with me, but I wouldn't dare hope for it. Yet now you listen to the speeches of sycophants and thereby kill your elders." Then he instructed his retainers: "You must plant my grave with catalpa trees in order that they may be used for vessels [coffins]. And gouge out my eyes and suspend them above Wu's East gate so that I may see Yüeh's invaders enter and destroy Wu." Then he cut his throat and died. When the king of Wu heard about it he was enraged and seized Tzu-hsü's corpse, stuffed it into a leather sack, and floated it out onto the Yangtze River. The people of Wu pitied him so they erected a shrine above the river. Thereafter it was called "Mount Hsü."

When the king of Wu had executed Wu Tzu-hsü he proceeded to attack Ch'i. The Pao clan of Ch'i assassinated their ruler Duke Tao and set up Yang Sheng. The king of Wu wanted to mount a punitive expedition against the brigands, but was not victorious and abandoned it. Two years later the king of Wu summoned the rulers of Lu and Wei to a meeting at T'ao-kao. The year after, he convened a great meeting of the feudal lords in the north at Yellow Pool, forcing the Chou to come. Kou-chien, king of Yüeh, suddenly attacked, killing Wu's Heir Apparent and destroying his forces. When the king of Wu heard about it, he returned and had envoys arrange a truce with Yüeh with generous presents. Nine years thereafter, Kou-chien, king of Yüeh, went on to exterminate Wu, killing King Fu-ch'ai. He also executed the Grand Steward P'i because he had been disloyal to his ruler, accepted heavy bribes from external sources, and colluded with him.

The Grand Historian comments:
How extreme is the poison of vengeance among men!

Wu Tzu-hsü's dramatic biography immediately suggests certain observations. First, the ease with which men shifted allegiances and were willingly embraced by other factions or even states is astounding. A general who suddenly lost favor, whether through battlefield defeat or political machination, might flee to the enemy and—contrary to expectation—not only avoid execution but actually be enfeoffed, his troops and followers being equally welcomed. A political figure who became entangled in court intrigues might also find hospitable refuge in either friendly or enemy states, and be granted significant power as a minister, advisor, or even a strategist for military campaigns against his former state. Clearly, although loyalty was a much espoused virtue in Sun Wu's era—Confucius, identified throughout Chinese history with promoting it, is even mentioned in Wu Tzu-hsü's biography—it was frequently slighted in favor of personal ambition.

Second, the intensity and extensiveness of the court intrigues—even allowing that exaggeration and romantic embellishment may have affected the historical materials available to the Grand Historian four centuries later—is startling.[54] Many officials fled or perished because greed and lust propelled them into conflict with others, including the previously mentioned duke of Shen.[55] Although the ancient rulers portrayed in the *Tso chuan* and *Shih chi* tend to have an archetypal cast, the contrast between frugal, dedicated, and intensely committed young kings such as Ho-lü and Kou-chien and their enemies—such as the licentious Ch'u kings—remains striking. Worthy, conscientious rulers seem to have been a minority despite the much-proclaimed watchwords that flourished from the Chou's victory onward: "nourish the people," "provide for the people's welfare."[56] Obviously Mencius, more than a century later, had many contemporary examples to rail against.

Third, the role of spirit, or *ch'i,* much emphasized in the *Art of War,* can be seen as a significant factor throughout ancient history from biographies such as these. On the whole, states that were well governed by reasonably compassionate, dynamic rulers enjoyed much greater support and even enthusiastic commitment from both the populace and officials. Their people went forth into battle ungrudgingly, with determination and intensity, unified and disciplined in defense of their interests. In contrast, under corrupt and extravagant rulers the people began military campaigns already weary and exhausted, and could only grow more disspirited and filled with rancour, even if initially motivated by "national antagonisms" to fight the enemy. The habits and behavior of such rulers brought about, of themselves, many of the objectives of T'ai Kung's so-called "civil offensive"—spreading dissension, demoralizing the populace, and incapacitating the government.[57] King Kou-chien's bribing of Po P'i provides an extreme example of the effects attainable through successfully implementing such policies. By acting submissively, feigning loyalty, and playing upon King Fu-ch'ai's desires for victory and power over the northern Chou states through Po P'i's persuasions, Yüeh insidiously deflected attention away from itself and ensured that Wu would dissipate its military strength and energy.

Sun-tzu is only mentioned twice in Wu Tzu-hsü's biography: first as a general in the campaign of 512 B.C. that took Shu, and later just prior to launching the campaign that penetrated Ch'u's interior to sieze its capital of Ying and doubtlessly sowed the seeds for its own eventual demise. The absence of any further mention thereafter lends support to the possibility that, having witnessed King Ho-lü's sudden transformation from a worthy, self-controlled ruler to a man enamored of the pleasures found in the Ch'u capital (where he lingered long after he should have simply annexed the city and returned to Wu), Sun-tzu realized the moment had passed, and the time to depart had arrived. Presumably he would have at least been granted generous rewards if he had not already acquired his share of the plunder.[58] Therefore, if he didn't disperse them among the people—contrary to the fictionalized account—Sun-tzu could easily have survived for many years in secret retirement, developing the sophisticated doctrines expressed in the *Art of War.*

THE CONQUEST OF CH'U

In the first year of King Ho-lü's reign, after some years of preparation, Wu moved its capital to Ku-su (approximately modern Su-chou). The new city, constructed on the Chou model with inner and outer fortified walls, provides clear evidence of the effectiveness of Wu's bureaucratic administration, as well as their material resources and planning capabilities. The city was immense, with the inner wall's perimeter reportedly being thirty *li,* and the outer wall's fifty *li.* Constructed at the edge of T'ai Hu (Vast Lake), it was also sited along the first section of an eventual network of extensive canals that were to prove of great significance in Chinese history. Ostensibly developed to transport grain and facilitate trade, this first canal section was of course primarily strategic in importance, facilitating the movement of troops toward the north.

Commencing with Ho-lü's third year, Wu launched a series of nearly annual attacks against Ch'u, always emerging victorious. With each attack it subjugated additional Ch'u client states, sometimes permanently absorbing them, at other times merely freeing them from the yoke of Ch'u dominance. At the same time Wu sought to ensure that any of the smaller, powerful states that might mount a surprise attack on its homeland—should it mobilize extensively to undertake a far-reaching campaign—had their military potential negated through preemptive aggressive action. The battles listed in Wu Tzu-hsü's biography as commencing with Ho-lü's reign, while not complete, include the major ones. Of particular importance was the victorious attack in 511 B.C. on Shu, a Ch'u state in the region where the former Wu generals were emplaced. Because of the two royal brothers' detailed knowledge of Wu (and potential factional support within it), they had constituted a formidable threat until thereby eliminated. Wu also directed its first strike against Yüeh in 510 B.C.; thereafter, apparently fearing Yüeh's great military potential,

King Ho-lü had Wu's already extensive fortifications expanded and strengthened in order to encompass all the populace.[59] In 509 B.C. Ch'u finally decided to attempt an attack against Wu only to be repelled and suffer the loss of additional towns.

Unmentioned in the biography but reported in other sources is that Wu, under King Ho-lü, had deliberately adopted a temporizing strategy for this period in order to enervate Ch'u and dissipate its resources. According to the *Tso chuan*, this policy of temporizing and harassment was advanced by Wu Tzu-hsü rather than Sun-tzu, although it initially may have been formulated by Sun Wu for his mentor's presentation. The record runs:

The King of Wu inquired of Wu Yün: "When you first spoke about attacking Ch'u I knew it would be possible, but I feared [King Liao] would dispatch me. Moreover, I detested the fact that other men would therefore gain [the benefit of] my achievements. Now I will have it myself. What about an attack on Ch'u?"

[Wu Tzu-hsü] replied: "In Ch'u those who hold the reins of government are numerous and at odds with each other. None of them is willing to undertake the responsibility for [resolving] Chu's misfortunes. If we create three armies to harass them, when one of them arrives [at Ch'u's border] all [their troops] will certainly come forth. When they come forth then [our army] should withdraw; when the enemy retires, we should then go forth. Ch'u will certainly be fatigued from [moving back and forth over] the roads. Do this several times to exhaust them; employ many methods to bring about misjudgment. If, after they are exhausted, we follow up with our three armies, we will certainly realize a major conquest." Ho-lü followed his advice, and thenceforth Ch'u began to be debilitated.[60]

Wu accordingly divided its forces into three field armies, each dispatched to engage the enemy in turn, but always directed to never become involved in protracted battles or decisive confrontations. Mobility was emphasized in effecting a long-term campaign of harassment that not only had physical objectives, but also focused on disrupting their command, sowing doubt and dissension, and making Ch'u's leadership both feel and be incapable of coping with Wu's threats. The strategy of mounting a marauding campaign was ostensibly chosen to allow Wu's forces time to rest and rebuild, as well as to undermine and weaken the enemy. However, Ch'u's overwhelming might and the largely impenetrable nature of its state also dictated the need to avoid headlong confrontations in which Wu would inevitably be outnumbered. Wu was therefore forced to contemplate employing the confining characteristics of the terrain and rivers to its tactical advantage, spreading the enemy out, choosing its objectives carefully, and suddenly concentrating its forces where unexpected—all principles found in Sun-tzu's *Art of War,* which itself emphasizes segmenting and combining, changing and transforming as necessary:

> The army is established by deceit, moves for advantage, and changes through segmenting and reuniting. Thus its speed is like the wind, its slowness like the forest; its invasion and plundering like a fire; unmoving, it is like the mountains. It is as difficult to know as the darkness; in movement it is like thunder.[61]

If Sun-Tzu's biography is at all credible, it would seem reasonable, as claimed by traditionalist scholars, that Sun-tzu was entrusted with overall command of Wu's military forces for the purpose of effecting their reorganization and training. From the *Art of War* and other military classics it is clear that even at this early date, approximately 509 B.C., small unit organization, segmentation, articulation, and maneuver were all primary objectives of military preparation, furnishing the basis for implementing complex battlefield tactics.

Unlike in the north and in the "system of five" later advocated by Lord Shang and most of the *Seven Military Classics,* Wu apparently organized its military on a decade system.[62] The squad consisted of eleven men, comprised of ten men and an officer. A company, being ten squads, numbered 110 men; a battalion (or regiment) 1,100 men and officers; and an army 11,200 men—10 regiments plus an additional 100 command personnel. These would all be combat troops, primarily infantry, and would be supplemented by chariots for open terrain engagements against states such as Ch'i. In contrast, the armies found in the north were centered upon the chariot, with infantry forces supplementing them, although the latter become the central tactical element as time progressed and tactics evolved during the Spring and Autumn period. In the campaign against Ch'u that eventually reached Ying, Wu's three armies thus totalled 33,600 highly disciplined, well-organized combat soldiers capable of following orders and executing tactics.[63]

Space does not permit recounting or analyzing the battles prior to the campaign of 506 B.C. against Ch'u, although in virtually all of them Wu seized the initiative, manipulated Ch'u's armies, and employed deceit and unorthodox tactics extensively. Wu's experience turned talented generals into effective commanders, and unified the soldiers behind a king who willingly shared every hardship with them.[64] Conversely, Ch'u increasingly antagonized the allied and subordinate states upon whom it might draw; debilitated the people; and oriented itself toward self-destruction.

Ch'u's monumental defeat at Ying was in part made possible because of the greed of a single man, Nang Wa, who held virtual power as prime minister in Ch'u over the youthful ruler. Foolishly yielding to his own avarice, he imprisoned the rulers of Ts'ai and T'ang, two northern client states (whose domains had been incorporated within Ch'u territory) when they individually refused to yield gifts he desired.[65] After being imprisoned for three years they were finally released in 506 B.C., ostensibly as the result of diplomatic pressure exerted by Chin and the other states in the northern alliance.[66] While en route back to his native place the marquis of Ts'ai, ruler of a state long known for its military prowess and unyielding spirit, attacked the minor but ancient state of Shen, slaying its ruler for abandoning him during his imprisonment.[67] Naturally this stimulated Ch'u into undertaking reprisals, and they prepared to send forth a punitive military force.

Ts'ai, although protected by walls that Ch'u had in fact erected earlier, realized it would certainly be vanquished, possibly even exterminated, and therefore appealed to Wu for assistance. As the result of one man's foolish acts Wu thus acquired an ally deep within Ch'u territory, far along one of the few possible invasion routes. This ensured that they would have local guides and additional military forces, and that they could be reprovisioned well onto enemy terrain. Consequently, Wu's fixed number of vessels could be employed to transport more troops or a small number of chariots up the Huai river. Furthermore, Ts'ai's forces not only increased the overall number of troops challenging Ch'u, but also immediately constrained Ch'u's tactical possibilities, forcing them to consign a significant army to a fixed location.

Because Ch'u was well protected by mountains and dense forests, its leaders no doubt felt reasonably secure. Any land approach would have to negotiate one of three narrow passes, none of which were characterized by wide roads or improved routes of passage. While the Ch'u capital of Ying was theoretically accessible by boat to any force undertaking the arduous task of working up the Yangtze river, the disadvantages of such a choice were obvious: the great expenditure of energy en route would make the sailors too weary to supplement the infantry forces. A limited marine infantry force would therefore have to effect a landing and then launch an assault against a fortified city manned by a vastly superior number of entrenched enemy troops. However, the density of the forests and narrowness of the roads also guaranteed that they would be relatively undefended and an army moving through them would in fact be following Sun-tzu's dictums: "To travel a thousand *li* without becoming fatigued, traverse unoccupied terrain. . . . To effect an unhampered advance, strike their vacuities."[68]

The campaign itself, reconstructed from the *Tso chuan*, can be outlined as follows.[69] Wu, perhaps with Sun Wu in command and Wu Tzu-hsü and Po P'i assisting, divided its troops into two operational field units. The larger force, which could proceed by land, was dispatched to invade Ch'u from the south, while a smaller force worked up the Huai river to the north and had as its initial objective breaking the siege around Ts'ai in order to attain all the advantages enumerated above. Both forces chose largely unpopulated and undefended areas through which to advance, thereby minimizing the difficulties—apart from natural obstacles of terrain—they would encounter.

Ch'u's intelligence was apparently faulty, for it learned only of Wu's northern invasion force, and reacted by abandoning the siege at Ts'ai to confront the enemy at a forward position. Nang Wa, bellicosely exercising general command despite his previous defeat at Wu's hands, divided his armies: A holding force was deployed in a defensive posture to await Wu's infantry forces, which were moving inland after having disembarked from their boats at the Huai river. A second, smaller force was deputed to destroy their vessels and thereby prevent an escape once the frontal attack managed to rout them, as well as to launch a crushing ambush from Wu's rear. The main strength, under Nang Wa's personal command, was to advance and strike the trapped invaders after crossing the Han river and moving up.

While his plan was admirably conceived and potentially effective, it was rendered useless by the threatening incursion of Wu's southern armies. Once Nang Wa learned of this additional thrust he was persuaded to disregard the northern advance (which was then continuing along three routes, Wu having effectively segmented its forces to traverse the narrow terrain successfully), cross the Han River, and attack the southern invaders. According to the *Tso chuan,* Nang Wa feared losing the fame and glory of victory to another general, and therefore determined to engage the enemy himself.[70] Unfortunately, his move proved precipitous, and Wu's forces, having penetrated deeply into enemy territory, were united and determined, just as Sun-tzu observes in the *Art of War:*

> In general the Tao of an invader is that when one has penetrated deeply [into enemy territory] the army will be unified, and the defenders will not be able to conquer you. . . . When the soldiers and officers have penetrated deeply they will not

be afraid. Where there is nowhere to go they will be solid. When they have advanced deeply they will cling together. When there is no alternative they will fight. . . . If there is no escape from death, the officers and soldiers will fully exhaust their strength.[71]

Nang Wa's hasty advance achieved the confrontation he so urgently desired, but Ch'u's army was defeated in three successive battles, forcing him ever backward into the interior. Suddenly displaying the cowardice of the belligerent, he wanted to flee for his life, but was dissuaded when upbraided for his cowardice. Therefore he timorously withdrew to reform his forces on the west bank of the Han river, directly opposite Wu's army, which soon deployed on the east bank.

Events then proceeded as summarized in Wu Tzu-hsü's biography: Fu-kai, a decisive commander accompanied by spirited troops, seized the moment to attack a perceived weakness in the enemy, and emerged victorious. Initially he had counseled King Ho-lü to allow him to launch the first attack:

> Nang Wa of Ch'u is not benevolent, while none of his ministers have the will to fight to the death. If I first launch a fierce attack against him, his troops will certainly run off. And if you then sustain the attack with the main army, we will certainly conquer them.[72]

When permission was denied he boldly proceeded on his own, reportedly exclaiming: "What is referred to as a subject acting righteously without awaiting [his ruler's] edicts is just this! If I die today Ch'u can be invaded."[73] The *Art of War*, addressing commanders on the necessity for acting independently of the ruler's constraints once empowered (as exemplified by Sun-tzu's own actions in his biography), states:

> If the Tao of Warfare [indicates] certain victory, even though the ruler has instructed that combat should be avoided, if you must engage in battle it is permissible. If the Tao of Warfare

[indicates] you will not be victorious, even though the ruler instructs you to engage in battle, not fighting is permissible.[74]

Sun-tzu also said, "One whose general is capable and not interfered with by the ruler will be victorious."[75] (However, it should be remembered that Ho-lü was still acting as his own field commander, just as kings in the Early Chou and beginning of the Spring and Autumn period normally had.)

The attack proved successful, routing Nang Wa's troops in what came to be known as the battle of Po-chü. Fu-kai then led his aroused warriors on a well-disciplined pursuit of the vanquished Ch'u army, engaging them again at the Ch'ing fa River. After repelling a counterattack by a second, newly arrived Ch'u army, Wu's forces pressed on until reaching the capital./The remaining portion of the invasion, apparently requiring five distinct battles, must have constituted essentially a running engagement from the decisive clash at Po-chü until the fall of Ying. Furthermore, the overall campaign has been characterized as the first lengthy encounter of the Spring and Autumn period, and a harbinger of developments in the Warring States period.[76] Surprisingly, once King Ho-lü entered Ying, discipline among the high command immediately broke down, and they tangled over the splendors and spoils of Ch'u's vast wealth. This unfortunately provided an opportunity for Yüeh and Ch'in to profit aggressively, as will be discussed below.

Fu-kai, who shortly thereafter was defeated by the Ch'in army dispatched as a result of Shen Pao-hsü's entreaties and then made his way back to Wu to usurp the throne in Ho-lü's absence, was otherwise a brilliant and decisive commander. His tactics in pursuing and engaging Ch'u's army at the Ch'ing-fa River also provide evidence of the general currency of several concepts found in the *Art of War,* especially the importance of maneuver in order to manipulate and exploit the enemy's *ch'i* (morale). This excerpt from the *Tso-chuan* proves illuminating, although the accuracy of his words is open to suspicion:

Wu followed Ch'u's [army] up to the Ch'ing-fa River and was about to strike it. King[77] Fu-kai said: "Since a distressed animal will still fight, how much the more so will men! If they know they will not be spared and commit themselves to die, they will certainly defeat us. We should cause those who ford the river first to think that they have escaped; those behind them will long to join them, and no one will have the heart to do battle. When half have forded the river they can be attacked." They followed his plan and again defeated them.

[Ch'u's soldiers] were preparing food when the men of Wu reached them. They ate [Ch'u's] food and then followed them, defeating the various forces at Yung-shih River. In five engagements they reached Ying.[78]

According to the *Art of War,* "If there is no place to go it is fatal terrain."[79] Common military wisdom advised against deploying an army between the enemy and a river because it could easily become deadly or fatal ground. Furthermore, it was generally recognized that pursuing a retreating foe was a dangerous undertaking, fraught with possibilities of deception and ambush. Sun-tzu noted:

Do not pursue feigned retreats. Do not attack animated troops. Do not swallow an army acting as bait. Do not obstruct an army retreating homeward. If you besiege an army you must leave an outlet. Do not press an exhausted invader.[80]

Similarly, he discussed some of the problems related to maneuvering an army near rivers:

After crossing rivers you must distance yourself from them. If the enemy is fording a river to advance, do not confront them in the water. When half their forces have crossed, it will be advantageous to strike them.

If you want to engage the enemy in battle, do not array your forces near the river to confront the invader, but look for tenable ground and occupy the heights. Do not confront the current's flow. This is the Way to deploy the army where there are rivers.[81]

While Ch'u's retreat was so hasty and disordered that there was no possibility of it being a ruse to draw them forth into an ambush, exactly this was almost accomplished when Wu's forces paused and a second, fresh Ch'u army suddenly struck. However, Nang Wa clearly had not acted in accord with Sun-tzu's principles, for he deployed his troops on the side of the Han River to confront an invading enemy. Fu-kai, on the other hand, allowed the enemy an opening to encourage their hope that they would escape. He thus deflated their will to fight, avoided "casting them onto fatal terrain," and ensured his next strike would evoke fright and terror. Again the *Art of War,* speaking about the necessity for manipulating the *ch'i* of one's own troops, advises:

> Cast them into hopeless situations and they will be preserved; have them penetrate fatal terrain and they will live. Only after the masses have penetrated dangerous terrain will they be able to craft victory out of defeat.[82]

Fu-kai's own troops, having penetrated deeply into enemy territory, had already been thrust into this exact situation, whereas his controlled advance defused any possibility of the enemy suddenly experiencing a surge of determination from finding themselves on fatal terrain. Thus he was able to realize Sun-tzu's principle for striking the enemy when their *ch'i* had abated:

> The *ch'i* of the Three Armies can be snatched away, the commanding general's mind can be seized. For this reason in the morning their *ch'i* is ardent; during the day their *ch'i* becomes indolent; at dusk their *ch'i* is exhausted. Thus one who excels at employing the army avoids their ardent *ch'i,* and strikes when it is indolent or exhausted. This is the way to manipulate *ch'i.*[883]

(Sun-tzu's discussion of *ch'i* varying with specific times of the day is of course merely an observationally based analogy cited for illustrative purposes rather than a time-based tactic.) Through his restraint at Ch'ing-fa, Fu-kai opportunely managed to feed his own army and thereby realize two more of Sun-tzu's dictums:

> The wise general will concentrate upon securing provisions from the enemy. One bushel of the enemy's foodstuffs is worth twenty of ours; one picul of fodder is worth twenty of ours.[84] With the sated await the hungry.[85]

Surprisingly, after victoriously occupying Ying, Wu then suffered two quick defeats, Fu-kai himself exercising command in one of them before returning to Wu to usurp the throne. The five hundred chariots dispatched by Ch'in as a rescue force were in themselves formidable, especially on Ch'u's more favorable terrain. Despite the problematic aspects of chariot employment, when supplemented by thirty-six thousand infantrymen, they probably proved decisive in successfully engaging an infantry force only minimally supported by chariots.

Wu's campaign strategy had been designed for long-term implementation rather than achieving an immediate, suicidal, direct confrontation. The state, which to some degree lagged behind Ch'u both materially and culturally, employed its fewer numbers more effectively, stressed mobility, and deliberately selected advantageous sites for its battles. In addition, Wu benefited extensively from the willing support of indigenous peoples and enjoyed the strong allegiance of its own populace. The value of the former in supplying information and guidance, as well as material support, should not be underestimated. As Sun-tzu advised:

> One who doesn't know the plans of the feudal lords can not forge preparatory alliances. One who doesn't know the topography of mountains and forests, ravines and defiles, wetlands and marshes, can not maneuver the army. One who does not employ local guides will not secure advantages of terrain. One who does not know these four or five cannot [command] the army of a hegemon or true king.[86]

Furthermore, Wu not only nurtured its own people but also embraced foreign advisors, whereas Ch'u debilitated its people and repeatedly drove away talented and capable officials, frequently into Wu. Wu therefore succeeded first in blunting Ch'u's incursions and then in totally defeating it, achieving an objective hitherto unattainable by the northern states.

THE WAR BETWEEN WU AND YÜEH

Wu's precipitous rise to power preceded its even swifter collapse, self-destruction, and eventual decimation at the hands of Yüeh. The record of their conflict has been famous throughout Chinese history, giving rise to many stories and paradigms current even today. Since Yüeh is mentioned in the *Art of War,* the succeeding decades are relevant to any study of Sun-tzu's thought and era. However, whether Sun Wu personally lingered to participate in the government of King Ho-lü's son and successor, Fu-ch'ai, is doubtful, particularly as the latter was headstrong, extravagant, and licentious, vividly in contrast with his father. The overall developments, however, merit a few paragraphs of summary and analysis because they provide evidence of the strategic concepts and practices of the time, and may have either derived from Sun-tzu's own studies or influenced their formulation.[87]

In 496 B.C., nearly a decade after the conquest of Ch'u, the king of Yüeh died and was succeeded by his talented son Kouchien. King Ho-lü, having already been attacked by Yüeh while tarrying in Ying and thus ever conscious of their military potential, was determined to take advantage of the opportunity provided by Yüeh's internal discord and national mourning to effect a strike. However, contrary to expectation, Wu was in fact defeated by the youthful king, and Ho-lü, as noted in Wu Tzuhsü's biography, died from the fatal infection that developed from a foot wound sustained in battle. Thereafter his son, Fu-ch'ai, who immediately dedicated himself to avenging Ho-lü's death, embarked upon an extensive two-year program of military preparation. Although the task of retraining and drilling the entire army should naturally have fallen to Sun Wu, his name is not mentioned in the records at this time.

King Kou-chien was cast in the mold of the late Ho-lü—

frugal, solicitous of the people's welfare, courageous, and aggressive—and he was aided by two advisors from Ch'u, the military strategist Fan Li and the administrator Wen Chung. (Both had an opportunity to flee to Wu but preferred not to aid an enemy of their native state, whatever their own personal difficulties in Ch'u.) With Ch'u's collapse, Wu and Yüeh soon found themselves colliding over military supremacy and hegemony, even though no one yet regarded Yüeh as a serious contender.

In 494 B.C., after reorganizing, training, and drilling the troops for two years, King Fu-ch'ai felt prepared to attack Yüeh. King Kou-chien, having acquired intelligence about the impending campaign, decided to mount a preemptive naval strike despite Fan Li's opposition, only to suffer a total defeat and be forced to flee for refuge accompanied by five thousand picked troops. As Wu Tzu-hsü's biography indicates, Fu-ch'ai was dissuaded from capitalizing upon the hard-won opportunity to exterminate Yüeh's ruling house and annex its territory, instead acceding to their specious entreaties (accompanied of course by generous bribes and profferings of fealty and submission) to be permitted to survive.[88] An anguished Wu Tzu-hsü, observing the king's character and behavior, accurately prophesized that Yüeh would be revived and go on to extinguish Wu in two decades. As the *Art of War* asserts, "If someone is victorious in battle and succeeds in attack, but does not exploit the achievement, it is disastrous and his fate should be termed 'wasteful and tarrying.'"[89]

In the years prior to Yüeh's sudden attack on Wu, King Kou-chien skillfully played the role of a submissive vassal, first dwelling in Wu's capital for three years (coincidentally providing him with an excellent opportunity to study the state and acquire vital military intelligence), and thereafter in Yüeh (from where he made semiannual pilgrimages to Wu). In sum, Kou-chien fervently embarked upon a campaign devoted to fostering strength and prosperity while conducting a "civil offensive" against Fu-ch'ai.[90] Whenever possible he increased Fu-ch'ai's arrogance, played upon his desires, and encouraged him in his deluded campaigns against Ch'i in the north.[91]

In 482 B.C. the dramatic moment finally arrived. King Fu-ch'ai coerced several states (including an enervated Chin) into convening a meeting at Yellow Springs in the north, traveling up the new canal with his elite forces and the bulk of his army. This vain and wasteful display of power was mounted for the sole purpose of overawing the recalcitrant states into acknowledging Wu's preeminent position among the alliance and according him the status of hegemon. Consequently the interior of Wu was devoid of stalwart troops; only the old and incapacitated remained to man the fortifications against potential invaders.

Yüeh sent forth an army of approximately 49,000 men, including 6,000 elite royal troops, and through a combination of timing and the implementation of unorthodox tactics, including feigned withdrawals, managed to destroy much of Wu's navy, strike its capital, and wrest several easy victories.[92] However, when Wu' main force raced back to engage them and Fu-ch'ai requested a truce, Fan Li advised granting it to avoid a potentially dangerous confrontation with superior forces.

In 478 B.C. Wu suffered from a famine, possibly brought about by Yüeh having supplied them with nongerminating rice that Fu-ch'ai may have foolishly ordered distributed to the people as an improved stock. Kou-chien, while basically acting on Fan Li's new estimation that Wu's situation could be exploited, also relied upon Fu-ch'ai's willingness to fight. Yüeh first employed certain subordinate states to initiate the conflict, then moved forward itself. Wu, with sixty thousand troops, clearly outnumbered them and possessed the advantage of holding a fortified position on the east bank of the river. Yüeh therefore resorted to creating the unexpected by developing a plan that would stir confusion in Wu's entrenched, well-organized forces, manipulating them to advantage by compelling them into movement. As Sun-tzu observed, "One who excels at warfare compels men and is not compelled by others."[93]

As indicated in the simplified accompanying diagram, Yüeh split its troops into four forces, and secretly dispatched one each north and south about two *li* along the river bank. The main army, with strength equal or greater to the detached units, remained arrayed directly opposite Wu's encampment. Then, in the middle of the night, Yüeh had its two flank forces cross the river, deliberately raising a clamor rather than stressing silence and stealth. This startled Fu-ch'ai's command into assuming they were coming under a sudden, two-pronged flanking attack designed to envelop them; therefore they hastily sped their troops to the northern and southern perimeters to counter both of them.

Once Wu's forces had been coerced into precipitous movement, Yüeh's main army, spearheaded by six thousand elite royal warriors, silently crossed the river, reformed, and then suddenly drummed the attack with a horrendous din. Panic-stricken, the Wu forces already en route to defend the flanks chaotically turned about to contend with a frontal attack, only to be subjected to the flanking assault they had just turned away from. As the *Art of War* remarks, "When someone excels in attacking, the enemy does not know where to mount his defense."[94] More concretely:

> The location where we will engage the enemy must not become known to them. If it is not known, then positions that they must prepare to defend will be numerous. If the positions the enemy prepares to defend are numerous, then the forces we will engage will be few. Thus if they prepare to defend the front, to the rear there will be few men. If they defend the rear, in the front there will be few. If they prepare to defend the left flank, then on the right there will be few men. If they prepare to defend the right flank, then on the left there will be few men. If there isn't any position left undefended, then there won't be any place with more than a few. The few [are the ones] who prepare against others; the many [are the ones] who make others prepare against them.[95]

By manipulating Wu's defensive forces Kou-chien managed to change his "few" into an effective "many," just as the *Art of War* advocates. Yüeh's forces then easily dominated the battlefield; Wu's survivors fled twenty *li* back into the interior, where they reformed only to suffer another attack and be vanquished. Finally Fu-ch'ai, with ten thousand troops, managed to retreat

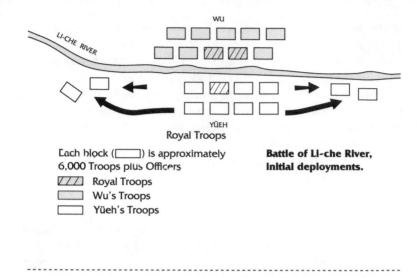

Royal Troops

Each block (□) is approximately 6,000 Troops plus Officers

ZZZ Royal Troops
□ Wu's Troops
□ Yüeh's Troops

Battle of Li-che River, initial deployments.

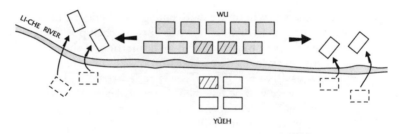

Second Phase:
"Noisy" night crossing by Yüeh's detached forces stimulates Wu's response.

into the stronghold of Wu's capital, where he was then besieged by Kou-chien's army. Thereafter Yüeh assumed full control of all the state's territory and population except for Fu-ch'ai's single enclave.

Over the next five years Yüeh besieged and attacked Fu-ch'ai in his remaining bastion until finally capturing him in 473 B.C., whereupon he opted to commit suicide rather than subsist on a meager fief merely to perpetuate Wu's ancestral sacrifices.[96] With his death the saga concluded and Wu ceased to exist.

In their fatal conflict Yüeh managed to emerge victorious because it utilized every means available to mount a campaign to survive and conquer. Wen Chung plied Fu-ch'ai with treasures and enticements while blinding him through his greedy advisors. Kou-chien nurtured the people; Fan Li structured the army and developed their strategy and tactics. Conversely, Fu-ch'ai focused upon realizing his quest for power; exploited and exhausted the people, both in military activities and in his pursuit of personal pleasure; and was distracted from the real threat by hopes of conquering Ch'i, a vast and powerful northern state. The critical battle at Li-che River was a masterly exer-

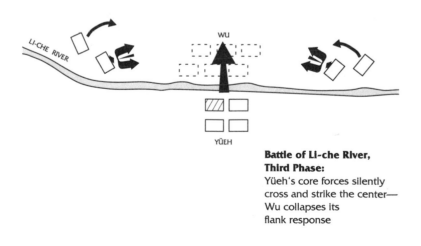

Battle of Li-che River, Third Phase: Yüeh's core forces silently cross and strike the center— Wu collapses its flank response

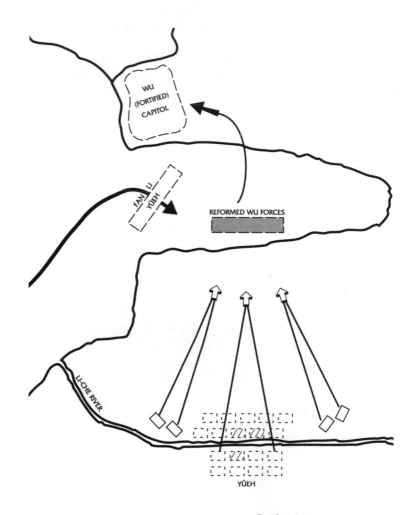

WU
(FORTIFIED)
CAPITOL

FAN LI
YÜEH

REFORMED WU FORCES

LI-CHE RIVER

YÜEH

Battle of Li-che River, Final Phase:
Pincer attack plus center thrust drives Wu back in chaos. Second attack leads to defeat and fleeing to city.

cise in unorthodox tactics, clearly exemplifying the principles found in the *Art of War:* "Attack when they are unprepared, go forth where they will not expect it."[97]

Main
Concepts
in the
Art of War

Sun-tzu's *Art of War*, as transmitted through the ages, consists of thirteen chapters of varying length, each ostensibly focused upon a specific topic. While most contemporary Chinese military scholars continue to characterize the entire work as an organic whole, marked by the logical progression and development of themes from start to finish, obvious relationships between supposedly connected passages are frequently difficult to determine or are simply nonexistent. However, the major concepts generally receive frequent, consistent treatment throughout, largely supporting the attribution of the book to a single figure or well-integrated school of thought.[98]

The military writings recently unearthed from a Han Dynasty tomb include a partial copy of the *Art of War* in essentially its traditional form, together with significant additional material, such as the "King of Wu's Questions."[99] However, the translation that follows has been based upon the heavily annotated classical version because it reflects the understanding and views of the past thousand years, the beliefs upon which government and military officials based their actions in real history. The traditional text has been revised only where the tomb materials resolve otherwise opaque passages or supplement obvious deficiencies, although the impact of such changes on the overall content remains minimal. Significant variations in characters and sentences will also be discussed in notes supplementing the translation.

Because the *Art of War* is remarkably lucid, if compressed and sometimes enigmatic, only a brief introduction to the major concepts, principles, and tactics need be undertaken here. No attempt will be made to exhaustively analyze and systematize all of them, nor will those already discussed in conjunction with Wu's military campaigns be repeated. Each paragraph in the text is self-contained, and should be contemplated in isolation as well as in the context of the chapter. Given the character of the text, we will also forego extensively quoting passages to justify the analysis, although a few critical ones will be introduced to elucidate certain complex concepts, and the latter will also be expanded in the notes. Selected works from the vast secondary literature, including those in Chinese and Japanese, will also be cited in the notes when the authors offer unusual perspectives on the text, advance new interpretations, or provide insightful commentary on problematic sentences.

GENERAL PRINCIPLES

As discussed in the general introduction, by Sun-tzu's era the practice and scope of warfare had evolved sufficiently to endanger the existence of virtually every state, large and small alike. Many had already perished; innumerable ruling families had been extinguished and their peoples subjugated; and others tenuously survived only through adroit political maneuvering and servile submission. Amid the turmoil of the late Spring and Autumn period Sun-tzu felt that mobilizing the nation for war, committing the army to battle, and risking the state's destruction could only be undertaken with the greatest gravity.[100] The very opening words of the *Art of War* stress the critical importance of warfare: "Warfare is the greatest affair of state, the basis of life and death, the Way to survival or extinction. It must be thoroughly pondered and analyzed."[101]

Throughout the book Sun-tzu's approach to employing the army is thoroughly analytical, mandating careful planning and the formulation of an overall strategy before commencing a campaign. The focus of all grand strategy must be the development of a prosperous, contented populace whose willing allegiance to their ruler is unquestioned.[102] Thereafter diplomatic initives can be effected, but military preparations should never be neglected. The primary objective should be to subjugate other states without actually engaging in armed combat, thereby realizing the ideal of complete victory:

> The highest realization of warfare is to attack the enemy's plans; next is to attack their alliances; next to attack their army; and the lowest is to attack their fortified cities.[103] Thus one who excels at employing the military subjugates other people's armies without engaging in battle, captures other people's fortified cities without attacking them, and destroys other people's states without prolonged fighting. He must fight under Heaven with the paramount aim of "preservation." Thus his weapons will not become dull, and the gains can be preserved. This is the strategy for planning offensives.[104]

Whenever possible "victory" should be achieved through diplomatic coercion, thwarting the enemy's plans and alliances, and frustrating his strategy. Only if an enemy threatens the state with military action or refuses to acquiesce without being brutally forced into submission should the government resort to armed combat. Even when exercising this option, every military campaign should focus upon achieving maximum results with minimum risk and exposure, limiting as far as possible the destruction to be inflicted and suffered, fighting with the aim of preservation.[105] Therefore Sun-tzu said:

> Preserving the enemy's state capital is best, destroying their state capital second-best. Preserving their army is best, destroying their army second-best. Preserving their battalions is best, destroying their battalions second-best. Preserving their companies is best, destroying their companies second-best. Preserving their squads is best, destroying their squads second-best. For this reason attaining one hundred victories in one hundred battles is not the pinnacle of excellence. Subjugating the enemy's army without fighting is the true pinnacle of excellence.[106]

In the extant *Art of War* Sun-tzu repeatedly emphasizes the need for rationality and self-control, and stresses the vital necessity to avoid all engagements not based upon extensive, detailed analyses of the situation, the combat options, and one's own capabilities. Detailed calculations were apparently performed in the ancestral temple prior to mobilizing for a campaign, and presumably similar, more specific assessments would be made by the commander before engaging an enemy force in the field.[107] Although undertaken in the ancestral temple, they were not a form of divination (as in previous ages)[108], but were probably based upon quantified estimates that systematically assigned numerical values to the strength of objectively examined aspects for both sides.[109] In chapter one, "Initial Estimations," he states:

> Thus when making a comparative evaluation through estimations, seeking out its true nature, ask:
> Which ruler has the Tao?
> Which general has greater ability?
> Who has gained [the advantages of] Heaven and Earth?
> Whose laws and orders are more thoroughly implemented?
> Whose forces are stronger?
> Whose officers and troops are better trained?[110]
> Whose rewards and punishments are clearer?[111]
> From these I will know victory and defeat.[112]

Furthermore, in chapter four, "Military Disposition," Sun-tzu describes the quantified basis for calculating the force levels necessary to achieve victory:

> Terrain gives birth to measurement; measurement produces the estimation [of forces]. Estimation [of forces] gives rise to calculating [the numbers of men]. Calculating [the numbers of men] gives rise to weighing [strength]. Weighing [strength] gives birth to victory.

Sun-tzu's criteria for tactically analyzing the enemy and battlefield situations may be seen as consisting of some forty paired, mutually defined, interrelated categories that can be abstracted from the text. (This may reflect Taoist thinking about names and their mutual, interrelated definitions, as sometimes claimed, or simply be the product of his own analytical reflection.)[113] Among these are Heaven— Earth;[114] offense—defense; advance—retreat; and unorthodox—orthodox. The comparative state of readiness can be decided by reflecting upon such pairs as hunger—satiety; exhausted—rested; ordered—disordered; fearful—confident; cold—warm; wet—dry; and lax—alert. Whenever such calculations indicate the enemy holds a decided advantage, the general must either avoid him, assume a defensive posture, or conceive and implement tactics that will convert the enemy's superiority into weakness, such as harassing the rested until they become exhausted, as Wu did to Ch'u.

Unlike the incident retold earlier in which the king of Ch'u committed troops over a few mulberry trees, or policies advanced by the Legalists in which military measures are simply another instrument for increasing the wealth and prosperity of the state, Sun-tzu stressed that warfare should not be undertaken unless the state is threatened. Haste, fear of being labeled a coward, and personal emotions such as anger and hatred should never be permitted to adversely influence state and command decision making.[115] The army must not be rashly thrown into an engagement, thrust into a war, or unnecessarily mobilized:

> If it is not advantageous, do not move. If objectives can not be attained, do not employ the army. Unless endangered do not engage in warfare. The ruler cannot mobilize the army out of personal anger. The general can not engage in battle because of personal frustration. When it is advantageous, move; when not advantageous, stop. Anger can revert to happiness, annoyance can revert to joy, but a vanquished state cannot be revived, the dead cannot be brought back to life.[116]

Instead, restraint should be exercised while implementing measures to ensure that the army can not be defeated:

> In antiquity those that excelled in warfare first made themselves unconquerable in order to await [the moment when] the enemy could be conquered. Being unconquerable lies with yourself; being conquerable lies with the enemy.
> Thus one who excels in warfare is able to make himself

unconquerable, but cannot necessarily cause the enemy to be conquerable. Thus it is said a strategy for conquering the enemy can be known but yet not possible to implement.[117]

In Sun-tzu's view employing defensive measures is equally aggressive, ensuring that the army's strength will be sufficient to prevail in situations where other techniques, including deception, can not be effectively implemented. His views are summarized in chapter four, "Military Disposition":

> One who cannot be victorious assumes a defensive posture; one who can be victorious attacks. In these circumstances by assuming a defensive posture, strength will be more than adequate, whereas in offensive actions it would be inadequate.
>
> Those who excel at defense bury themselves away below the lowest depths of Earth. Those who excel at offense move from above the greatest heights of Heaven. Thus they are able to preserve themselves and attain complete victory.

Sun-tzu concludes: "The victorious army first realizes the conditions for victory, and then seeks to engage in battle. The vanquished army fights first, and then seeks victory."[118] Obviously this dictum was directed against those generals who, having assumed the mantle of command, rushed headlong into battle irrespective of the consequences, who fought whenever confronted by an enemy force and thereby endangered not only their own troops, but also the state.[119]

THE COMMANDER'S QUALIFICATIONS

Since the ruler and commander-in-chief control the state's destiny, Sun-tzu discussed their qualifications, variously identifying critical abilities and characteristics, assets and liabilities. Coupled with his assertions regarding the necessary independence of the commander once in the field, they are viewed as providing clear evidence of the rise and presence of the professional general, although such qualities would equally be necessary for any ruler, whether administering the state or serving as his own field commander.[120]

Many of the military and philosophical writings propose ideal combinations of traits, universally giving priority either to courage or wisdom. In the traditional edition of the *Art of War*[121] the first list appears in "Initial Estimations": wisdom, credibility, benevolence, courage, and strictness. Commentators generally emphasize the placement of "wisdom" before courage, although the book does not otherwise discuss any reason for its priority.[122] However, focusing upon wisdom fully accords with the importance bestowed in the book upon calculations, knowledge, and tactical expertise. Conversely, there is no expanded commentary on the role of courage beyond condemning generals committed to dying (because their vainglorious manifestation of courage would bring about the army's destruction).

Abstracting the requisite traits and abilities, and correlating them with the weaknesses specifically mentioned in *The Art of War*, yields the following comprehensive portrait:

STRENGTHS	WEAKNESSES
wisdom	*unenlightened*
knowledge	
credibility	*brutalizes and fears the masses*
strictness	*not strict*
benevolent	*loves the people*[123]
courage	*committed to life*
skillful analyst	*unable to fathom the enemy*
unconcerned by fame	*obsessed with achieving fame for purity*
unconcerned by punishment	
places army first	
tranquil	*easily angered*
obscure	*hasty to act*
upright	*arrogant*
self-disciplined	*weak*
strong commander	*poor commander*
clever/inventive	
all-encompassing talents	

It naturally follows that the absence of a desirable quality or the presence of its opposite must be considered a serious flaw. Astute generals will deliberately seek out and exploit such flaws in an enemy commander, just as the state of Wu did when attacking the vain, greedy, and impulsive Nang Wa. Later military texts such as the *Six Secret Teachings* discuss numerous character deficiencies and exploitable traits, including virtues that have become extreme and therefore unbalanced, in both commanders and rulers, and suggest concrete ways to probe for them and turn them to advantage.[124]

STRATEGY AND TACTICS

Sun-tzu's basic strategy focuses upon manipulating the enemy, creating the opportunity for an easy victory, and then applying maximum power at the appropriate moment. To this end he classifies the types of terrain and their exploitation; advances numerous tactics for probing, manipulating, and weakening the enemy; advocates the employment of both orthodox (*cheng*) and unorthodox (*ch'i*) troops to wrest the victory; and stresses speed and surprise. The enemy is lured into untenable positions with prospects of gain; enervated by being wearied and exhausted before the attack; and penetrated by forces that are suddenly concentrated at vulnerable points. The army should always be active, even when assuming a defensive posture, to create and seize the temporary tactical imbalance of power (*ch'üan*) that will ensure victory.[125] Accordingly, certain situations and configurations of terrain should be avoided, being instead turned to advantage when opportune. Thereafter, the focus can be directed toward realizing the predetermined campaign strategy and implementing appropriate operational and battlefield tactics to defeat the enemy. Avoiding a strong force is not cowardice, but wisdom, for it is self-defeating to fight when and where not advantageous.[126] As Sun-tzu said, "One who knows when he can fight, and when he cannot fight, will be victorious."[127]

The fundamental tactical principle for attacks is "Go forth where they do not expect it, attack where they are not prepared." This principle can only be realized through secrecy in all activities; by complete self-control and strict discipline within the army; and by being unfathomable. The corollary to being unfathomable is seeking out and gaining detailed knowledge of the enemy through all available means, including the rigorous employment of spies. The unvarying rule is never to rely upon the good will of others, nor upon fortuitous circumstances, but guarantee—through knowledge, persistent analysis, and defensive preparation—that the enemy can neither mount a surprise attack nor gain a victory through simple coercion. As Sun-tzu said:

> One who knows the enemy and knows himself will not be endangered in a hundred engagements. One who does not know the enemy but knows himself will sometimes be victorious, sometimes meet with defeat. One who knows neither the enemy nor himself will invariably be defeated in every engagement.[128]

Apart from strongly advocating the use of spies to acquire essential military intelligence,[129] Sun-tzu also emphasized the high price of partial knowledge:

> If I know our troops can attack, but do not know the enemy cannot be attacked, it is only halfway to victory. If I know the enemy can be attacked, but do not realize our troops cannot attack, it is only halfway to victory.
>
> Knowing that the enemy can be attacked, and knowing that our army can effect the attack, but not knowing the terrain is not suitable for combat,[130] is only halfway to victory. Thus one who truly knows the army will never be deluded when he moves, never be impoverished when initiating an action.
>
> Thus it is said if you know them and know yourself, your victory will not be imperiled. If you know Heaven and you know Earth, your victory can be complete.[131]

DECEPTION AND THE FORMLESS

Sun-tzu's military thought has frequently been erroneously identified solely with "deceit and deception" because he advocated employing them to attain military objectives. For this he was often scorned by the literati, but was of course closely followed by later military writers, including most of the *Seven Military Classics*.[132] Although an insightful reading of the *Art of War* will reveal that many of his proposed measures rely on deception for their foundation and implementation, only two explicit statements actually appear in the book. The most famous one is found in chapter one, "Initial Estimations":

> Warfare is the Way (Tao) of deception. Thus although [you are] capable, display incapability to them. When committed to employing your forces, feign inactivity. When [your objective] is nearby, make it appear as if distant; when far away, create the illusion of being nearby.

The second one, from chapter seven, "Military Combat," asserts: "Thus the army is established by deceit, moves for advantage, and changes through segmenting and reuniting." Deceit is of course not practiced as an art or end in itself, contrary to tendencies sometimes prevailing in the modern world. Rather, false measures, feints, prevarications, troop deployments, dragging brush, feigning chaos, and other such acts are all designed to further the single objective of deceiving the enemy so that he will be confused or forced to respond in a predetermined way and thereby provide the army with an exploitable advantage.[133] Warfare must be viewed as a matter of deception, of constantly creating false appearances, spreading disinformation, and employing trickery and deceit. When imaginatively created and effectively implemented, the enemy will neither know where to attack nor what formations to employ, and will accordingly be condemned to making fatal errors.

Apart from measures undertaken within the military itself, "expendable spies" (who "spread disinformation outside the state") should also be employed. Therefore Sun-Tzu advised, "provide our [expendable spies] with [false information] and have them leak it to enemy agents."[134] Naturally their lifespan is limited, for when the ruse is uncovered the expendable spy is normally terminated by the enemy, explaining why they were also termed "dead (or doomed) spies."

Deception, however skillfully practiced, will invariably prove ineffective unless the army can maintain its own plans in secrecy. Although the later military writings more explicitly address the need for secrecy,[135] Sun-tzu stressed that the commanding general should be obscure and unfathomable, never revealing his plans or intentions *even to his own troops:*

> It is essential for a general to be tranquil and obscure, upright and self-disciplined, and able to stupify the eyes and ears of the officers and troops, keeping them ignorant. He alters his management of affairs and changes his strategies to keep other people from recognizing them. He shifts his position and traverses indirect routes to keep other people from being able to anticipate him.[136]

Further on in the chapter Sun-tzu adds: "Direct the masses of the Three Armies as though commanding one man. Press affairs on them, do not explain the purpose to them."[137]

Deception and manipulation are actually aspects of the greater question of form (*hsing*) and the formless. Whenever the army deploys onto the battlefield, its configuration, being immediately apparent, will evoke a reaction in the enemy. Whether the enemy will then modify his original anticipations, vary his tactics, or view the events as confirming a preconceived battle plan depends upon his evaluation of the unfolding situation. In normal circumstances the disposition of the forces quickly betrays the average commander's intentions and methods. Although warfare in this period was not as rigid nor as predictable as in the Early Chou or ancient Western world because segmentation, small unit articulation, and independent movement had all been thoroughly developed by Sun-tzu's time, in general an attack's thrust could still be predicted from the method of deployment.

No doubt realizing that any action will elicit a response and that remaining invisible is impossible, Sun-tzu advanced a theory of what might best be summarized as the "deceptive and formless." While unstated in the *Art of War,* obviously the best way to be unfathomable—that is, to be formless—is to display false appearances to the enemy. By integrating these two principles, a foe can be manipulated and vital secrecy preserved. Many commentators over the centuries failed to realize that the formless is attained through creative deceit and therefore erroneously and artificially isolated the two.

About manifesting forms (*hsing*) to manipulate the enemy Sun-tzu said:

> One who excels at moving the enemy deploys in a configuration (*hsing*) to which the enemy must respond. He offers something that the enemy must seize. With profit he moves them, with the foundation he awaits them.[138]

In chapter six, "Vacuity and Substance" (which contains an extensive discussion on form [*hsing*]), Sun-tzu elucidates two basic principles for effectively waging warfare: attack voids in the enemy and employ substantial force at chosen points. These essential methods have already been witnessed in Wu's attacks on Ch'u, and the important paragraphs from the first half of Sun-tzu's chapter previously cited need not be repeated. However, the conclusion—be formless yourself—bears noting:

> If I determine the enemy's disposition of forces (*hsing*) while I have no perceptible form, I can concentrate [my forces] while the enemy is fragmented. If we are concentrated into a single force while he is fragmented into ten, then we can attack him with ten times his strength. Thus we are many and the enemy is few. If we can attack his few with our many, those whom we engage in battle will be severely constrained.

To fragment an enemy the army must not betray its intentions; secrecy must be maintained. Operating in ignorance, the enemy must inevitably disperse his forces to prepare against thrusts from every direction. As Sun-tzu explains:

> The location where we will engage the enemy must not become known to them. If it is not known, then the positions that they must prepare to defend will be numerous. If the positions the enemy prepares to defend are numerous, then the forces we engage will be few.[139]

In the last paragraphs of the chapter Sun-tzu characterizes the interrelationship of the disposition of force (*hsing*) between the two sides. Certain important principles are buried within these paragraphs: variation is the essence of response; only the commander knows the true configuration behind the visible disposition of force. Sun-tzu observed:

> In accord with the enemy's disposition (*hsing*) we impose measures on the masses that produce victory, but the masses are unable to fathom them. Men all know the disposition (*hsing*) by which we attain victory, but no one knows the configuration (*hsing*) through which we control the victory. Thus a victorious battle [strategy] is not repeated, the configurations (*hsing*) of response [to the enemy] are inexhaustible.

In the very last paragraph the relationship between *shih*, strategic power, and *hsing*, form or disposition of force, is glimpsed. Commentators have sometimes mistakenly understood the concept and nature of this response, believing that once the enemy moves and commits himself, action must then be automatically taken in some fixed or predetermined way. However, Sun-tzu's entire chapter shows that the forms of response, while based upon the enemy's actual disposition and certain unchangeable principles and combat realities, should be freely chosen within essential parameters. As an illustration, an attack on a fixed emplacement might proceed in several ways, depending upon where the enemy is weakest and where he might be anticipating an attack. Flanking forces might be concentrated upon the left or the right; one flank or the other might feign retreat to draw the enemy out, or might concentrate for a deep penetration in order to turn about and attack the rear. Thus while Sun-tzu employs the image of water, the analogy should not be pushed to the extent that there is only one possible flow for a given terrain. Flexibility, as distinguished from the traditional practice of fixed deployment in the Early Chou and seen in the West until recent times, is being stressed. It is decidedly not some form of determinism that is being advocated. Thus he states:

> Now the army's disposition of force (*hsing*) is like water. Water's configuration (*hsing*) avoids heights and races downward. The army's disposition of force (*hsing*) avoids the substantial and strikes the vacuous. Water configures (*hsing*) its flow in accord with the terrain; the army controls its victory in accord with the enemy. Thus the army does not maintain any constant strategic configuration of power (*shih*); water has no constant shape (*hsing*). One who is able to change and transform in accord with the enemy and wrest victory is termed spiritual!

CONFIGURATIONS OF TERRAIN

The recognition that topography is fundamental to military tactics, the classification of terrain types, and the association of basic tactical principles with particular terrains are all generally attributed to Sun-tzu. Even though a cursory examination of the *Tso chuan* will quickly indicate that effective commanders had long been implementing terrain-based tactics, and certain land configurations, such as sinkholes, were commonly known to be fatal to any disposition of forces, Sun-tzu was perhaps the first to study these questions systematically and develop a coherent body of operational principles. The *Art of War* obviously influenced many of the later military writings, particularly the *Six Secret Teachings,* which contains several chapters advancing appropriate tactics for a wide variety of situations.[140]

In his very first chapter Sun-tzu includes terrain (Earth)

among the five major factors in warfare: "Therefore structure warfare according to [the following] five factors, evaluate it comparatively though estimations, and seek out its true nature. The first is termed the Tao, the second Heaven, the third Earth, the fourth generals, and the fifth laws [for military organization and discipline]." He goes on to provide a limited definition of "Earth": "Earth encompasses far or near, difficult or easy, expansive or confined, fatal or tenable terrain." Therefore, one criteria for evaluating the probable victor in any encounter is "Who has gained [the advantages of] Heaven and Earth?"

Everything depends upon terrain because, as previously cited, "terrain gives birth to measurement," leading in turn to determining the forces required and their configuration. As already noted in the discussion of Wu's strategy for attacking Ch'u, military intelligence consists not only of knowledge of the enemy, but also the topography of the invasion route and likely battlegrounds.[141] Consequently, Sun-tzu said:

> Configuration of terrain is an aid to the army. Analyzing the enemy, taking control of victory, estimating ravines and defiles, the distant and near, is the Tao of the superior general. One who knows these and employs them in combat will certainly be victorious. One who does not know these nor employ them in combat will certainly be defeated.[142]

"Nine terrains" are frequently associated with Sun-tzu because that is the title of his famous chapter eleven where the nine appear: dispersive, light, contentious, traversable, focal, heavy, entrapping, encircled, and fatal. However, careful study of the *Art of War* reveals more than twenty distinct configurations of terrain, as well as several specific, deadly land formations such as "Heaven's Well." They are discussed in chapters eight, entitled "Nine Changes"; ten, "Configurations of Terrain"; and eleven, "Nine Terrains."[143] While the terms overlap to some extent, the definitions and associated tactics are never contradictory. Furthermore, the texts remain remarkably clear and explicit even in our era, precluding any need to enumerate or further analyze the various configurations.[144]

Apart from the named configurations Sun-tzu also mentions such problematic obstacles as rivers, wetlands, mountains, marshes, and salt flats. For example, in chapter nine, "Maneuvering the Army," where he correlates four deployments with land features, it states:

> When you cross salt marshes and wetlands, concentrate on quickly getting away from them; do not remain. If you engage in battle in marshes or wetlands, you must stay in areas with marsh grass and keep groves of trees at your back. This is the way to deploy the army in marshes and wetlands.[145]

Although such features are discussed separately, in many cases they may be subsumed under one of the categorical definitions. Those just listed above all fall under "entrapping terrain": "Where there are mountains and forests, ravines and defiles, wetlands and marshes, wherever the road is difficult to negotiate, it is 'entrapping terrain.'"[146]

SPIRIT AND COMMAND

Sun-tzu frequently discusses the essential problem of command: forging a clearly defined organization in control of thoroughly disciplined, well-ordered troops.[147] The critical element is spirit, technically known as *ch'i*, the essential vital energy of life.[148] The concept of *ch'i* is both integral and fundamental to many aspects of Chinese thought, ranging from metaphysics to medicine, science through religion. One popular view believes that the character originally represented the vapors rising from cooking rice, and is thus symbolic of nourishment in every sense.[149] *Ch'i* is the foundation and basis of courage, the vital spirit that is directed by will and intention. When the men are well-trained, rested, properly fed, clothed, and equipped, if their spirits are roused they will fight vigorously. However, if physical or material conditions have blunted their spirit; if there is any imbalance in the relationship between command and troops;[150] or if for any reason they have lost their motivation, they will be defeated.

Conversely, the commanding general must manipulate the situation so as to avoid the enemy when their spirits are strong, such as early in the day, and exploit any opportunity presented by their diminishment, attacking when they no longer have any inclination to fight, such as when about to return to camp. Prolonged warfare can only lead to enervation; therefore, careful planning to guarantee the swift execution of campaign strategy is paramount.[151] Certain situations—such as being thrust onto fatal terrain where a desperate battle must be fought—are conducive to eliciting the army's greatest efforts.[152] Others are debilitating, dangerous, even fatal, and must be scrupulously avoided.[153] Rewards and punishments provide the basis for control, but every effort must be made to foster and maintain the proper attitude of desire and commitment. Accordingly, all detrimental stimuli, such as omens and rumors, must be prohibited.[154]

SHIH: STRATEGIC CONFIGURATION OF POWER

The concept of *shih* (strategic power) figures prominently in both ancient military and Legalist thought, perhaps originating with the former. Although many contemporary monographs on the Legalist thinkers attribute its origin to the philosopher Shen Tao[155] and then trace its appropriation and integration through Han Fei-tzu's systematized thought, studies of *shih* in the military works are just beginning to emerge.[156] Unfortunately, it is a strategic concept whose complexities require a book-length study to resolve a number of fundamental questions, including its definition and character in individual works such as the *Art of War*, where it is used in several, apparently distinct, ways; the evolution of the concept in the military works, and especially the *Seven Military Classics;* whether it and other, related concepts are as technically distinct as frequently assumed, or the earlier stages reflect a rather generalized interchangeability of terms and concepts (such as *hsing*, form, and *shih*, power); and its interrelationship with developments in Legalist thought, and whether the later Military Classics, such as the *Three Strategies,* reflect new dimensions or orientations imposed upon essentially tactical military vocabulary under the influence of newly formulated Legalist views.

A complicating factor is posed by the cryptic nature of many of the texts. Statements and even complete sections are generally brief and often enigmatic, apparently representing only notes or cursive summaries of extensive, complex, systematized thought, most of which has either been lost or was never cohesively formulated in writing.[157] Moreover, the assumption that concepts are used in a consistent and precise way in these early books, while necessary for analytical studies, is not invariably valid, and also needs to be sustained.

The scope of these issues precludes incorporating an intensive examination of the nature and function of *shih* in a book directed to presenting a translation of the *Art of War*. However, a brief characterization of the dimensions of the concept, a short review of previous studies, and an assessment of various translation possibilities remain unavoidable. While we must defer any systematic justification of the terms chosen to translate *shih* and its related concepts, some indication of our reasoning is of course warranted. Most of this discussion will be found compressed into the notes; additional comments briefly explicating the concept within concrete contexts, selectively drawing upon the extensive classical commentaries, will also be found appended to the translations.

A wide variety of terms have been used to translate the term and approximate the concept for the earliest part of the twentieth century until the present. Among those found in the more reliable translations of the *Art of War* and philosophical works that employ *shih* in their discussions are circumstances, energy, latent energy, combined energy, shape, strength, momentum, tactical power, force, authority, influence, power, condition of power, force of circumstances, positional advantage, and purchase.[158]

From the foregoing, coupled with a comparative analysis of the term in the *Art of War,* numerous military writings, and pre-Ch'in philosophical works, it may be concluded that the concept of *shih* entails the idea of advantage resulting from superior position. However, this aspect of positional advantage has perhaps been overemphasized, thereby slighting the essential role the element of mass (the army's forces) fulfills in creating impact. The paradigm example is Sun-tsu's analogy of a log or stone perched atop a hill that, although temporarily stabilized, retains great potential energy. In motion, that energy can be released, and need only be directed to be explosively effective:

> One who employs strategic power commands men in battle as if he were rolling logs and stones. The nature of wood and stone is to be quiet when stable but to move when on precipitous ground. If they are square they stop, if round they tend to move. Thus the strategic power of one who excels at employing men in warfare is comparable to rolling round boulders down a thousand-fathom mountain. Such is the strategic configuration of power [shih].[159]

Consequently, Sun-tzu sought to maneuver the army into a position where it enjoyed such great tactical advantage that the impact of its attack, the impulse of its "strategic configuration of power" (shih), would be like the sudden onrush of water cascading from mountain peaks. Deploying the troops into a suitable configuration (hsing); creating a favorable "imbalance of power" (ch'üan); concentrating forces upon focused targets; exploiting advantages of terrain; and stimulating the men's spirits would all be directed toward this moment, toward this decisive objective.

According to the concepts of modern physics, the momentum that can be developed, and thus the amount of force that can be applied when a rolling stone collides with an object in its path, depends upon the original height; the final speed at the moment of impact (which will have been reduced from the theoretical maximum as it passes over objects and encounters resistance); and its weight. Clearly a stone will transfer less energy at the moment of impact than a much larger boulder, and the total destructive potential is inherently related to the mass of the object.

Thus it appears that two equally important factors are integrated by this concept, and they should therefore be expressed by any translation. First, the strategic advantage conveyed by superior position, and second, the power of the forces involved. ("Power" refers to army's overall capability in all aspects—including endurance, spirit, discipline, equipment, command, and physical condition—rather than strength of numbers alone.) Obviously, as the great commentator Chiang Pai-li noted, strategic advantage has a pronounced temporal character; therefore, it should not be confined to exploiting the advantages of terrain as usually thought.

Strategic advantage is of course *in essence* a comparative term, not an absolute one, although a vast force will possess great power. (In the extreme case the advantages of terrain perhaps become negligible. A minimal force, such as a platoon or company, will represent one extreme, a vast army the other.) Accordingly, we have chosen to translate the term *shih* by "strategic configuration of power," and will use the term throughout except where a different sense, such as shape or circumstances, seems to have been intended. Although "strategic power" is basically an acceptable abridgement, and perhaps adequate in itself, "configuration" will generally be added as a reminder that the power results from configuring the military's armed might in accord with, and to the exploitation of, the terrain in order to gain a strategic advantage. However, when the term is conjoined with others, such as "military" or "army," or the text would read awkwardly, "strategic power" will be employed by itself, with "configuration" understood.

Insofar as two military forces may be described comparatively, there are of course some difficulties, and the question might well be posed, does *shih* exist in the absence of an enemy? Is it inappropriate to refer to the *shih* of an army if the two forces are equally matched, poised across a valley, with both of them, in their static positions, enjoying equal positional advantage relative to a potential battlefield between them and each other? Since Sun-tzu refers to *shih chün*, "strategic power that is equal," it would seem that the term refers to a general evaluation versus terrain, and thus configuration of power, rather than specifically confined to being defined relative to an enemy's position and deployment. (*Ch'üan,* imbalance of power, refers to this relative imbalance of forces.) To facilitate such inquiry and identify occurrences of the term for those who wish to contemplate such issues, "*shih*" will generally be added parenthetically whenever the term is translated.

It should also be noted that *shih* and *hsing* (form), central concepts in the *Art of War,* are also found in an important verse of the *Tao Te Ching,* which may be translated as follows: "The Tao gives them birth, Te [Virtue] nurtures them, things give them form (*hsing*), power (*shih*) completes them."[160]

THE UNORTHODOX AND THE ORTHODOX

The military concepts and applications of the unorthodox (*ch'i*) and orthodox (*cheng*) probably originate with Sun-tzu, although the *Art of War* does not discuss them extensively.[161] Note that the text always orders them as *ch'i/cheng,* unorthodox/orthodox, rather than as prioritized in the West, orthodox/unorthodox. The implications, if any, remain to be explored, although against a background of correctness and uprightness, the choice seems deliberate. The military was generally regarded as *ch'i* (unorthodox), in accord with Lao-tzu's dictum: "With the orthodox govern the state; with the unorthodox employ the army."[162] The later military classics, such as the *Wei Liao-tzu, Six Secret Teachings,* and especially *Questions and Replies,* devote considerable energy to discussing *ch'i* and *cheng* and their employment.[163]

While the subject of unorthodox and orthodox tactics clearly requires an article or book in itself, in essence "orthodox" tactics include employing troops in the normal, conventional, "by the book" expected ways, such as massive frontal assaults, while stressing order and deliberate movement. "Unorthodox" tactics are primarily realized through employing forces, especially flexible ones, in imaginative, unconventional, unexpected ways. Therefore, instead of direct chariot attacks, unorthodox tactics would mount circular or flanking thrusts. Instead of frontal assaults, they would follow indirect routes to stage unexpected, behind-the-lines forays. Their definition is of course dependent upon normal expectation within a particular battlefield context, as well as the enemy's actual anticipations, and therefore they are mutually defining, mutually transforming, and circular in essence.

The extant *Art of War* contains one succinct, critical passage, while the concept's application is visible in the principles and tactics proposed throughout the book:

> In general, in battle one engages with the orthodox and gains victory through the unorthodox. Thus one who excels at sending forth the unorthodox is as inexhaustible as Heaven, as unlimited as the Yangtze and Yellow rivers. What reach an end and begin again are the sun and moon. What die and are reborn are the four seasons.
>
> The notes do not exceed five, but the changes of the five notes can never be fully heard. The colors do not exceed five, but the changes of the five colors can never be completely seen. The flavors do not exceed five, but the changes of the five flavors can never be completely tasted.
>
> In warfare the strategic configurations of power do not exceed the unorthodox and orthodox, but the changes of the unorthodox and orthodox can never be completely exhausted. The unorthodox and orthodox mutually produce each other, just like an endless cycle. Who can exhaust them?[164]

Thus, as explicitly discussed by other military writings, the orthodox may be used in unorthodox ways, while an orthodox attack may be unorthodox when unexpected precisely because it is orthodox; a flanking or indirect assault would thereby be considered normal and therefore orthodox. A frontal feint by a large force, designed to distract or lure an enemy, would also be unorthodox. The concept lends itself to extreme complexities of thought, and has often been misunderstood throughout Chinese history, or even dismissed as simplistic, when it is quite the opposite. However, in essence it remains a descriptive tool for tactical conceptualization, for characterizing and manipulating forces within—and by exploiting—an enemy's matrix of expectations, rather than a transformational mode to be actualized in the concrete reality of men and weapons the way a military formation is deployed. There is nothing mysterious or mystical about *ch'i* and *cheng* and their mutually productive relationship, yet later commentators and strategists sometimes become seriously confused. Under such circumstances, a useful tactical conceptualization becomes an unnecessary obstacle to clear strategic thinking.

The concept's origins remain unclear, although speculation tends to identify it with the conflation of thought that crystallized as Taoism, or as deriving from divinatory practices. The interrelationship of *ch'i* and *cheng* mirrors that of yin and yang, and at least one writer attributes the concept's roots to the yin-yang principles found in the *I Ching*. The orthodox is identified with the firm or hard, while the unorthodox correlates with the soft or yielding.[165] The observation that reversal characterizes the natural world figures prominently in the *Tao Te Ching* traditionally ascribed to the reclusive Lao-tzu. *Cheng* turns into *ch'i*, things revert to their opposites (in complementary, dynamic tension) after reaching their pinnacle, just as yin and yang do.[166]

A better feeling for the range of the terms may be gained by a brief review of scholarly opinion over recent decades. For example, in the introduction to his translation, General Griffith—a highly experienced military officer with expert knowledge of strategy and tactics—states that *cheng* forces engage, or engage and fix the enemy, while *ch'i* forces defeat him, often through flanking and rear attacks.[167] He also characterizes *cheng* forces as the normal or direct, *ch'i* forces as extraordinary or indirect; similarly, as fixing and flanking (or encircling), or again as the "the force(s) of distraction and the force(s) of decision."[168] He goes on to stress that *ch'i* operations are always strange, unexpected, and unorthodox, and notes the reciprocal relationship between *ch'i* and *cheng*. Finally, Griffith adds that the realization of *ch'i* and *cheng* is not confined to tactical levels, but may also be implemented on strategic ones.[169]

The eminent scholar and translator D.C. Lau, in a critical review of Griffith's translation, emphasizes the abstract nature of these two terms, as opposed to invariably identifying them with forces, and suggests that they might best be translated as "straightforward" and "crafty."[170]

Benjamin Wallacker, in a brief, often-cited etymological article, concludes that *cheng* refers to military operations that pin down or "spike" an enemy, while *ch'i* operations are maneuvers that force the enemy off balance, bringing about his defeat. He further speculates that Sun-tzu's "formulations" seem likely to have been derived from experience with cavalry forces. However, this would require revising the date of composition to roughly the dawn of the third century B.C., or pushing back the introduction of cavalry.[171]

In an incisive book (*The Art of Rulership*) Roger T. Ames conceptually translates the terms as "irregular deployments" and "regular deployments."[172] However, "irregular" is perhaps an unfortunate choice, being inherently burdened with adverse military connotations. Extreme order and control are of course necessary to employ forces in *ch'i* maneuvers; therefore Christopher Rand's choice of "extraordinary" and "normal" would seem to represent a better pair.[173]

The Chinese secondary literature on Sun-tzu is overwhelming; however, for *ch'i/cheng* most analysts essentially repeat the definitions found in the *Art of War* and later military writings, emphasizing the realization of these abstract concepts in concrete forces. Flexibility, maneuverability, and swiftness are especially stressed when discussing *ch'i* forces, although they should equally characterize all military units in Sun-tzu's view.[174]

Sun Wu
and the
Art of War

There are three intertwined questions underlying the problem of dating the *Art of War*: Did Sun Wu ever exist? When was the book composed? Was Sun Wu in any way the author, progenitor, or inspiration for the extant work? While these issues have been quietly debated for nearly a thousand years, recent decades have witnessed a new level of intensity as proponents argue fervently for one position or another, frequently on ideological or nationalistic grounds. While a definitive answer is probably unattainable, certain general conclusions can be drawn from the texts and recently recovered tomb materials. Detailed consideration of all the aspects, articles, and evidence would require an extensive monograph; however, some of the larger issues are sufficiently interesting to merit introduction and are therefore summarized below and in the notes.

SUN WU: MAN OR MYTH?

As already noted, skeptics basically question Sun-tzu's existence because his name is never even mentioned in the *Tso chuan,* the primary record of significant events in the Spring and Autumn period. Doubt was first voiced in the Sung dynasty and gained adherents among Confucian-oriented literati with the passage of centuries.[175] However, the absence of his name does not necessarily justify the conclusion that he didn't exist; rather, at most it might indicate he never played a significant role, but still could have been a commander or strategist, and was simply eclipsed by more dramatic figures such as Wu Tzu-hsü. A number of important and generally acknowledged Spring and Autumn period figures do not appear in the *Tso chuan,* but their existence has not been questioned. Therefore traditionalist scholars decry these apparently singular attempts to discredit the proposed progenitor of Chinese military strategy.

The veracity and extent of Sun-tzu's historical achievements have become a burning issue because Sun-tzu's adherents clearly want to identify a famous figure with the *Art of War*, rather than an obscure recluse—however brilliant and perceptive—without visible military experience. The same impulse no doubt underlies assertions that Confucius served as minister in Lu, historical records to the contrary. Taoist and Legalist philosophers need not have participated in reality, but military thinkers, who need credibility, should have, particularly as contemporary strategists such as Fan Li distinguished themselves in Yüeh and other states.

While the *Tso chuan* may be silent, the *Shih chi* and *Wu Yüeh ch'un-ch'iu* both contain versions of the famous training episode with King Ho-lü, as well as several other references and a few additional sentences Sun-tzu may have uttered. In the *Shih chi* these appear in Sun-tzu's own biography; the biography of Wu Tzu-hsü; and the annals of the state of Wu. In the chronicles of King Ho-lü in the *Wu Yüeh ch'un-ch'iu* he is also recorded as participating in two important campaigns, and all these materials are consistent apart from minor additions or omissions. However, the chronicles for the states of Ch'u and Yüeh in the *Shih chi,* even though specifically identifying Wu Tzu-hsü and Po P'i as Wu commanders, do not mention his name, nor do the chronicles of Yüeh in the *Wu Yüeh ch'un-ch'iu.*

Contrary to the absence of Sun-tzu's name in the above noted Ch'u and Yüeh annals, the chronicles of King Ho-lü in the *Wu Yüeh ch'un-chiu* preserve a discussion among Ch'u's ministers that indicates the discontent festering after the state had suffered another defeat at the hands of Wu. They attributed all their problems to the pernicious effects of Fei Wu-chi's machinations, for his behavior had caused the loss of Wu Tzu-hsü and Po P'i to Wu, as well as other talented ministers (such as Fan Li and Wen Chung) to other states. Accordingly, Nang Wa and King Chao mounted an attack against Fei Wu-chi, killing him and exterminating the clan.[176] Although Sun-tzu was never associated with Ch'u, he is identified by the ministers as one of Wu's three troublesome generals.[177]

Sun Wu's name next occurs in Ho-lü's sixth year when the king orders him and Wu Tzu-hsü to mount the counterattack against Ch'u that results in Wu's victory at Yü-chang. Thereafter, Sun-tzu and Wu Tzu-hsü provide joint advice regarding the feasibility of an invasion penetrating as far as the capital of Ying. The record differs somewhat from the one cited earlier:

> In the ninth year the king of Wu addressed Tzu-hsü and Sun Wu: "In the beginning you said that Ying could not be invaded. Now, finally, what about it?"
>
> The two generals replied: "Now warfare that borrows victory in order to complete its awesomeness is not the constant Tao of victory."
>
> The king of Wu asked: "What do you mean?"
>
> The two generals replied: "The army that Ch'u has formed constitutes the strongest enemy under Heaven. Now if we engage their elite vanguard in battle, ten will be lost for every man left alive, and whether your majesty enters Ying will depend on Heaven. We do not dare say it will be certain."
>
> The king of Wu said: "If I want to again suddenly strike Ch'u, what should we do to be successful?"
>
> Wu Tzu-hsü and Sun Wu said: "Nang Wa is greedy and has offended the feudal lords many times, while T'ang and Ts'ai hate him. If you must attack, get T'ang and Ts'ai."[178]

Thereafter the dialogue continues with the generals recounting the story of how Nang Wa detained the two rulers when they failed to satisfy his desires, as previously noted.

Following the conquest of Ying the chronicles describe Wu Tzu-hsü's efforts to avenge his father's death, ending with the following sentences: "Then he ordered Ho-lü to take King Chao's wife as his concubine. Wu Tzu-hsü, Sun Wu, and Po P'i also took as concubines the concubines of Nang Wa and Ssu-ma Ch'eng in order to disgrace Ch'u's ruler and ministers."[179] While it is unlikely that Wu Tzu-hsü "ordered" the king to take such action, the sentence suggests that Sun Wu played a major role and implies that he would also have received substantial rewards from the campaign. In the tenth year the great victory just at the end of the previous year was somewhat mitigated when Wu's armies suffered the two defeats previously described, including a loss resulting from Ch'u's resolute incendiary attack.[180] The text runs:

> Tzu-hsü and the others spoke among themselves: "Even though Ch'u has defeated our secondary force, they still haven't injured us."
> Sun Wu said: "With Wu's shields and halberds I destroyed Ch'u in the west and expelled King Chao. [You] excavated the tomb of King P'ing of Ch'u, cutting and desecrating his corpse. It is already sufficient."
> Wu Tzu-hsü said: "Since the beginnings of the hegemonic kings[181] there has never been a subject who exacted revenge such as this. Let us depart."[182]

The final line of King Ho-lü's chronicles (following his death and the ascension of Fu-ch'ai) largely repeats the evaluation found in Sun-tzu's *Shih chi* biography, but distributes the credit more widely: "At this time Wu, employing the plans of Wu Tzu-hsü, Sun Wu, and Po P'i, destroyed the strong state of Ch'u in the west, overawed Ch'i and Chin in the north, and attacked Yüeh in the south."[183] Po P'i, whose traitorous behavior is graphically portrayed in the chronicles of Fu-ch'ai, thus enjoys remarkably positive treatment.

The only pre-Ch'in books containing any references at all to Sun Wu are *Hsün-tzu* and *Han Fei-tzu*. In the former the Lord of Lin-wu, emphasizing the importance of tactical methods over concerns about the people and their welfare, states: "What the military esteems is seizing advantage; what it practices is change and deception. One who excels at employing the military responds precipitously, distantly, and darkly. No one knows from where he goes forth. When Sun and Wu employed them, they had no enemies under Heaven."[184] In the latter a sentence appears that is also found incorporated in the *Shih chi*: "Within the borders everyone speaks about military affairs. Every family has the books of Sun and Wu stored away, but the army grows weaker. Those who speak about warfare are numerous, but those who bear armor are few."[185] Because both of these statements couple "Sun" with "Wu," some scholars claim that Sun Pin and Wu Ch'i are the intended references, not Sun Wu and Wu Ch'i.[186]

The passages recounted above and earlier comprise all the presently known early materials upon Sun-tzu apart from the tomb fragments to be discussed below. Traditionalist scholars who accept the authenticity and accuracy of the *Shih chi* and *Wu Yüeh ch'un-ch'iu* find little basis for doubting Sun Wu's existence and role, particularly as many *Shih chi* accounts that had been discredited in previous centuries have been largely corroborated by recent archaeological discoveries. However, even though Ssu-ma Ch'ien, the author of the entire work, obviously exercised great diligence in composing his accounts, even frequently including contradictory versions when unable to resolve them, questions remain about what records and materials may have existed in the Former Han after the ravages of wars and centuries, and how reliable they might have remained. Apart from Ssu-ma Ch'ien's own motives and the conceptual matrix he inherently employed to understand and organize events and interpret personalities, over four centuries his primary sources may have undergone editing and drastic revision.[187] Moreover, although the *Wu Yüeh ch'un-ch'iu* is nominally attributed to Chao Yeh, a scholar of the Later Han dynasty active in the second half of the first century A.D., its authenticity has recently been questioned, and it has even been viewed as a romanticized, Yüan dynasty redaction of events from this period.[188] Therefore, even if such doubts are discounted, its accounts can not be used to confirm the veracity of Ssu-ma Ch'ien's source materials, for they may well have been based upon the *Shih chi* itself.

Recently unearthed tomb texts, while initially welcomed as resolving the question of Sun-tzu's existence and the actuality of his interview with King Ho-lü, have only kindled further controversy because each camp interprets their significance in accord with their own viewpoints. However, a set of fragments claimed as comprising the source version for the *Shih chi* account dates at least several decades earlier than Ssu-ma Ch'ien's work.[189] While very badly fragmented, it clearly refers to Sun-tzu and King Ho-lü discussing Sun-tzu's work in thirteen chapters, and also seems to contain a similar account of the training incident. Whether this adds further credence to Ssu-ma Ch'ien's account is uncertain, for an immense gap of three centuries still remains.

However, any possible substantiation of the well-known training episode is particularly important because many doubts have been raised about the propriety, or even possibility, of the ruler allowing his palace women to be employed in such a fashion—as well as whether Sun-tzu could have possibly claimed such power of life and death in a mere exercise.[190] Certainly it was a dramatic gesture, but also one virtually certain to cost him his life. The objection that such a serious matter would have been better tested with a contingent of palace guards can not be easily dismissed.[191] At the same time Sun-tzu represented the new, talented rising class,[192] and Ho-lü had dramatically usurped the throne by having King Liao killed— so it was an age in flux, one in which survival depended upon bold action, and the Confucian emphasis upon propriety had not yet arisen. The role of women in the military also remains unclear, though there are later references to pressing them into service when required.[193]

A second group of bamboo strips (called the "King of Wu's Questions") contains a much more legible record of King Ho-lü questioning Sun-tzu about the state of Chin. This interview, which is fully translated in the section of selected lost materials appended to our translation of the *Art of War,* predicts the sequence in which the ministerial families of Chin would perish from their internecine strife. Since his predictions were not completely accurate, some scholars assume the piece was written by the Sun family after the first few came true, but before their predictions went askew, and therefore in the latter half of the fifth century B.C., or about fifty years after Sun-tzu should have been active.[194] Whether this dating is accepted depends upon the likelihood that Sun-tzu could have accurately predicted the initial events. If they were fairly obvious, as they appear to have been, Sun-tzu himself could have easily foreseen them, particularly after bringing his analytical methods to bear. There is clearly no need to assume he would be completely wrong unless he lived after the fact!

The above then summarizes the main textual materials regarding Sun-tzu and his possible existence. There is an additional tradition regarding his background and family history that developed from the T'ang onward, and has similarly become the focus of fervent debate.[195] The *Shih chi* biography identifies Sun-tzu as a native of Ch'i rather than Wu, and the T'ang reconstruction traces his lineage back to the T'ien clan that had risen to power in Ch'i after the reign of Duke Huan, China's first hegemon. Sun Wu's grandfather, as a reward for military achievement in a campaign against Lü, was granted the surname of "Sun" and apparently enfeoffed at Le-an.[196] While the T'ien clan was among the four major ones energetically contending for power in Ch'i, since they were largely successful (with their allies, the Pao clan) the question arises why Sun Wu would have fled or migrated to Wu, only to remain unknown until befriended by Wu Tzu-hsü. Clearly his family's military background provided him with expertise equally useful to his own clan then immersed in Ch'i's turmoil.

COMPOSITION AND DATING OF THE TEXT

While traditionalists continue to assert that the historical Sun Wu portrayed in the *Shih chi* and *Wu Yüeh ch'un-ch'iu* actually composed the *Art of War*—and often won't even allow for subsequent revisions by his own hand—other scholars have identified numerous historical anachronisms in the extant text encompassing terms, events, technology, and philosophical concepts;[197] emphasized the absence of any evidence corroborating his strategic role in the wars between Wu and Yüeh, as reviewed above; and focused on the disparity between the advanced concepts and nature of large-scale warfare discussed in the *Art of War* and the more limited, primitive battles characteristic of the latter part of the sixth century B.C.[198]

The traditionalist interpretation derives critical support from the numerous *Art of War* passages visible in most other military writings because, it is asserted, such extensive borrowing could only have been possible from the earliest text.[199] Moreover, this widespread copying is thought to provide ample evidence that the *Art of War* was early on considered the most important military treatise, valued far more than any other work, oral or written. The origination of certain analytical concepts, such as terrain classification, is also credited to Sun-tzu; therefore their utilization, by the compilers of the *Ssu-ma Fa,* is thought to prove indisputably Sun-tzu's historical priority rather than the possibility that Sun-tzu benefited from other works.

However, even if the likelihood of later accretions and revisions is disregarded, the traditionalist position still ignores the development and existence of more than two thousand years of warfare and tactics prior to 500 B.C., attributing the virtual creation of military strategy to Sun-tzu alone.[200] The concise, often abstract nature of his passages is cited as evidence that the book was composed at an early stage in the development of Chinese writing, but an equally compelling argument can be advanced that only upon a foundation of extensive battlefield experience and a solid tradition of serious military contemplation could such a philosophically sophisticated style be possible.[201] Basic concepts and common passages would seem to argue for a comprehensive military tradition and evolving expertise, rather than creation *ex nihilo.*

Critics who believe the scope of warfare evident in the *Art of War* far exceeds that which characterized the late Spring and Autumn period focus on Sun-tzu's discussion of the fiscal difficulties and impact of mobilizing a hundred-thousand-man army accompanied by two thousand chariots.[202] In their view, battles in Sun-tzu's era consisted of approximately thirty thousand to forty thousand troops per side, and a few hundred to several hundred chariots per army. (These numbers are consistent with the battle descriptions already excerpted above from the *Tso chuan, Shih chi,* and *Wu Yüeh ch'un-ch'iu.* In comparison, Napoleon had a core force of 72,000 troops at Waterloo, Wellington 68,000.) Moreover, actual battlefield engagements still required only a day; the running series of battles resulting in the conquest of Ying consumed about ten days. While months could be necessary to transport an army deep into enemy territory, prolonged campaigns of such magnitude were still exceptional. Therefore, from their perspective Sun-tzu's discussion of lengthy campaigns and massive armies must reflect the stage of warfare found in the middle of the Warring States period, and not the more primitive Spring and Autumn.[203]

Furthermore, contrary to the nine months required to mount a siege according to the *Art of War,*[204] protracted sieges were unknown in the Spring and Autumn period because cities were small and little fortified. However, in the Warring States period they had become important, strongly fortified economic and strategic centers, and Sun Pin had already categorized them in his own work, *Military Methods,* into worthwhile and defensible objectives. Therefore, unlike in the Spring and Autumn period (as discussed in the general introduction), an invasion force could not simply circumvent them, but had at least to nullify their strategic potential—a task that required specialized equipment, adequate preparation, and great staying power. Accordingly, the *Art of War* is characterized as reflecting Warring States siege warfare rather than Spring and Autumn practices.[205]

Their other criticisms focus on the forms of military organization and Sun-tzu's extensive emphasis on speed and mobility, both seen as more appropriate to infantry than chariot warfare.[206] In addition, the rise of the profession of arms is clearly witnessed in assertions about the commander's necessary independence, and they assert—contrary to our conclusions in the general introduction and above—that rulers did not divorce themselves from the responsibilities of field command until the Warring States.[107] Finally, certain scholars deny that deceit and unorthodox tactics were ever employed in Spring and Autumn conflicts, apparently assuming all engagements were entered only after the two armies had properly arrayed themselves on the field (as they had very early in the period, in the north).[208] This seems quite puzzling since even the historical battle descriptions explored above clearly show the ingenious use of both deception and unorthodox tactics.

While their enumeration of apparent anachronisms is impressive, other reconstructions of the evolution of strategy and warfare reach significantly different conclusions. For example, the increased specialization of officers and troops, the more extensive employment of infantry, and the new emphasis on speed and mobility may all be seen as ongoing changes found in the last years of the Spring and Autumn period.[209] Moreover, assaults on cities in that era were not yet advisable because the economic and strategic rewards were inadequate to repay the efforts. The bronze weapons of the time, being designed for close combat, are also seen as insufficient for undertaking the task, since siege specialization and iron implements had not yet developed. State economies in the period would simply have been incapable of sustaining extensive campaigns, thereby accounting for Sun-tzu's emphasis upon speed rather than duration.[210]

Unmentioned by these scholars but perhaps important, Sun-tzu may simply have employed large, round numbers in his discussion, or late hands may have actively revised the text to accord with the practices of their generation. Also undiscussed is the possible regional character of his observations and theories, reflecting the historical priority of infantry and naval forces in Wu, and tactics designed to accommodate terrain limitations. (However, this equally entails a problem: why are the tactics appropriate to water warfare only minimally discussed in the *Art of War*?) Then most of the above objections would be moot, allowing for the kernal of the work to have been composed by Sun-tzu, and the redaction revised over the years by his family and disciples to reflect evolving developments.

Excluding the now untenable position of those skeptics who dismissed the book as a late fabrication,[211] three major views seem to prevail regarding the composition date for the *Art of War*. The first identifies it with the historical Sun Wu, final compilation occurring shortly after his death in the early fifth century B.C.[212] The second, based upon internal evidence, consigns it to the middle to late Warring States period, or the fourth to third centuries B.C.[213] The third, also founded on internal evidence supplemented by recently discovered texts, places it somewhere in the last half of the fifth century B.C.[214] Since these are issues mainly of interest to specialists, the details are briefly considered in the accompanying footnotes. One additional view remains to be noted: Chang Ch'i-yün's variation on the nonexistence of Sun Wu. Chang advances the intriguing theory that Wu Tzu-hsü is the actual progenitor of the *Art of War,* and that "Sun Wu was probably the name of a book and not a person's name, referring to the military classic transmitted through generations by the Sun family, just like speaking of the Mao recension of the *Shih ching (Book of Odes)*."[215] Chang cites as probable evidence the consignment of Wu's son to the Pao clan in Ch'i, from where Sun Pin later came. Moreover, his son apparently assumed the surname of the Sun clan, and the final version of the *Art of War* would probably have derived from Sun Pin's hand. Of course this was written prior to the discovery of the Lin-i tomb text of the *Art of War,* which contained about one third of the current material, arranged in essentially the same thirteen-chapter format, and fragments of Sun Pin's own work that clearly show technological and tactical advances. The late Chang would probably revise his view, particularly as over the centuries people had conflated the works of the two Suns, rather than viewing them as distinct individuals and authors.

A balanced view—taking into account the evolving nature of warfare, the rising need for military and bureaucratic specialization, the personalities involved, the complexity of the politics, and the fragility of recorded materials—might well conclude that the historical Sun Wu existed, and not only served as a strategist and possibly general, but also composed the core of the book that bears his name. Thereafter the essential teachings were perhaps transmitted within the family or a close-knit school of disciples, being improved and revised with the passing decades, while gradually gaining wider dissemination. The early text may even have been edited by his famous descendant Sun Pin, who also extensively employed its teachings in his own *Military Methods,* and simultaneously made the Sun name even more glorious.

Sun-tzu

The

Art

of

War

in Translation

1

Initial

Estimations[1]

Sun-tzu said:

"Warfare is the greatest affair of state, the basis of life and death, the Way (Tao) to survival or extinction. It must be thoroughly pondered and analyzed.

. . .

"Therefore, structure it according to [the following] five factors, evaluate it comparatively through estimations, and seek out its true nature.[2] The first is termed the Tao, the second Heaven, the third Earth, the fourth generals, and the fifth the laws [for military organization and discipline].

"The Tao[3] causes the people to be fully in accord with the ruler.[4] [Thus] they will die with him; they will live with him and not fear danger.[5]

"Heaven encompasses yin and yang, cold and heat, and the constraints of the seasons.[6]

"Earth encompasses far or near, difficult or easy, expansive or confined, fatal or tenable terrain.[7]

"The general encompasses wisdom, credibility, benevolence, courage, and strictness.

"The laws [for military organization and discipline] encompass organization and regulations, the Tao of command, and the management of logistics.[8]

"There are no generals who have not heard of these five. Those who understand them will be victorious; those who do not understand them will not be victorious.

. . .

"Thus when making a comparative evaluation through estimations, seeking out its true nature, ask:

Which ruler has the Tao?
Which general has greater ability?
Who has gained [the advantages of] Heaven and Earth?
Whose laws and orders are more thoroughly implemented?
Whose forces[9] are stronger?
Whose officers and troops are better trained?
Whose rewards and punishments are clearer?

"From these I will know victory and defeat!

. . .

"If a general follows my [methods for] estimation and you employ him, he will certainly be victorious and should be retained. If a general does not follow my [methods for] estimation and you employ him, he will certainly be defeated, so dismiss him.[10]

. . .

"After estimating the advantages in accord with what you have heard, put it into effect with strategic power (*shih*)[11] supplemented by field tactics that respond to external factors.[12] As for strategic power, [it is] controlling the tactical imbalance of power (*ch'üan*) in accord with the gains to be realized.[13]

. . .

"Warfare is the Way (Tao) of deception.[14] Thus although [you are] capable, display incapability to them. When committed to employing your forces, feign inactivity. When [your objective] is nearby, make it appear as if distant; when far away, create the illusion of being nearby.[15]

. . .

"Display profits to entice them. Create disorder [in their forces] and take them.[16]

"If they are substantial,[17] prepare for them; if they are strong, avoid them.

"If they are angry, perturb them;[18] be deferential to foster their arrogance.[19]

"If they are rested, force them to exert themselves.

"If they are united, cause them to be separated.

"Attack where they are unprepared.

"Go forth where they will not expect it.

"These are the ways military strategists are victorious. They cannot be spoken of in advance.[20]

. . .

"Before the engagement, one who determines in the ancestral temple that he will be victorious has found that the majority of factors are in his favor. Before the engagement one who determines in the ancestral temple that he will not be victorious has found few factors are in his favor.

"If one who finds that the majority of factors favor him will be victorious while one who has found few factors favor him will be defeated, what about someone who finds no factors in his favor?[21]

"If I observe it from this perspective, victory and defeat will be apparent."

2

Waging War

Sun-tzu said:

"In general, the strategy for employing the military [is this]:[22] If there are one thousand four-horse attack chariots, one thousand leather-armored support chariots,[23] one hundred thousand mailed troops, and provisions are transported one thousand *li,* then the domestic and external campaign expenses, the expenditures for advisers and guests, materials such as glue and lacquer, and providing chariots and armor will be one thousand pieces of gold per day. Only then can an army of one hundred thousand be mobilized.

. . .

"When employing them in battle, a victory that is long in coming will blunt their weapons and dampen their ardor.[24] If you attack cities, their strength will be exhausted.[25] If you expose the army to a prolonged campaign, the state's resources will be inadequate.

"When the weapons have grown dull and spirits depressed, when our strength has been expended and resources consumed, then the feudal lords will take advantage of our exhaustion to arise.[26] Even though you have wise generals, they will not be able to achieve a good result.

"Thus in military campaigns I have heard of awkward speed but have never seen any skill in lengthy campaigns. No country has ever profited from protracted warfare.[27] Those who do not thoroughly comprehend the dangers inherent in employing the army are incapable of truly knowing the potential advantages of military actions.

. . .

"One who excels in employing the military does not conscript the people twice or transport provisions a third time.[28] If you obtain your equipment from within the state and rely on seizing provisions from the enemy, then the army's foodstuffs will be sufficient.

"The state is impoverished by the army when it transports provisions far off. When provisions are transported far off, the hundred surnames[29] are impoverished.

"Those in proximity to the army will sell their goods expensively.[30] When goods are expensive, the hundred surnames' wealth will be exhausted. When their wealth is exhausted, they will be extremely hard-pressed [to supply] their village's military impositions.[31]

"When their strength has been expended and their wealth depleted, then the houses in the central plains will be empty.[32] The expenses of the hundred surnames will be some seven-tenths[33] of whatever they have. The ruler's irrecoverable expenditures such as ruined chariots, exhausted horses, armor, helmets, arrows and crossbows, halberd-tipped and spear-tipped [large, movable] protective shields, strong oxen,[34] and large wagons—will consume six-tenths of his resources.

"Thus the wise general will concentrate on securing provisions from the enemy.[35] One bushel of the enemy's foodstuffs is worth twenty of ours; one picul of fodder is worth twenty of ours.

. . .

"Thus what [motivates men] to slay the enemy is anger; what [stimulates them] to seize profits[36] from the enemy is material goods. Thus in chariot encounters, when ten or more chariots are captured, reward the first to get one. Change their flags and pennants to ours; intermix and employ them with our own chariots. Treat the captured soldiers well in order to nurture them [for our use]. This is referred to as 'conquering the enemy and growing stronger.'

. . .

"Thus the army values being victorious; it does not value prolonged warfare. Therefore, a general who understands warfare is Master of Fate for the people, ruler of the state's security or endangerment."

3
Planning
Offensives

謀攻第三

Sun-tzu said:

"In general, the method for employing the military is this: Preserving the [enemy's] state capital is best, destroying their state capital second-best.[37] Preserving their army is best, destroying their army second-best. Preserving their battalions is best, destroying their battalions second-best.[38] Preserving their companies is best, destroying their companies second-best. Preserving their squads is best, destroying their squads second-best. For this reason attaining one hundred victories in one hundred battles is not the pinnacle of excellence. Subjugating the enemy's army without fighting is the true pinnacle of excellence.

. . .

"Thus the highest realization of warfare is to attack the enemy's plans; next is to attack their alliances; next to attack their army; and the lowest is to attack their fortified cities.

"This tactic of attacking fortified cities is adopted only when unavoidable. Preparing large movable protective shields, armored assault wagons, and other equipment and devices will require three months. Building earthworks[39] will require another three months to complete. If the general cannot overcome his impatience but instead launches an assault wherein his men swarm over the walls like ants, he will kill one-third of his officers and troops, and the city will still not be taken. This is the disaster that results from attacking [fortified cities].

"Thus one who excels at employing the military subjugates other people's armies without engaging in battle, captures other people's fortified cities without attacking them, and destroys others people's states without prolonged fighting. He must fight under Heaven with the paramount aim of 'preservation.'[40] Thus his weapons will not become dull, and the gains can be preserved. This is the strategy for planning offensives.

. . .

"In general, the strategy for employing the military is this: If your strength is ten times theirs, surround them; if five, then attack them; if double, then divide your forces.[41] If you are equal in strength to the enemy, you can engage him. If fewer, you can circumvent him. If outmatched, you can avoid him. Thus a small enemy that acts inflexibly[42] will become the captives of a large enemy.

. . .

"The general is the supporting pillar of state. If his talents are all-encompassing, the state will invariably be strong. If the supporting pillar is marked by fissures, the state will invariably grow weak.[43]

. . .

"Thus there are three ways by which an army is put into difficulty by a ruler:[44]

> "He does not know that the Three Armies should not advance but instructs them to advance or does not know that the Three Armies should not withdraw and orders a retreat. This is termed 'entangling the army.'
> "He does not understand the Three Armies' military affairs but [directs them] in the same way as his [civil] administration.[45] Then the officers will become confused.
> "He does not understand the Three Armies' tactical balance of power (*ch'üan*) but undertakes responsibility for command. Then the officers will be doubtful.

"When the Three Armies are already confused and doubtful, the danger of the feudal lords [taking advantage of the situation] arises. This is referred to as 'a disordered army drawing another on to victory.'[46]

. . .

"Thus there are five factors from which victory can be known:[47]

> "One who knows when he can fight, and when he cannot fight, will be victorious.
> "One who recognizes[48] how to employ large and small numbers will be victorious.
> "One whose upper and lower ranks have the same desires will be victorious.

"One who, fully prepared, awaits the unprepared will be victorious.

"One whose general is capable and not interfered with by the ruler will be victorious.

"These five are the Way (Tao) to know victory.

. . .

"Thus it is said that one who knows the enemy and knows himself[49] will not be endangered in a hundred engagements. One who does not know the enemy but knows himself will sometimes be victorious, sometimes meet with defeat. One who knows neither the enemy nor himself will invariably be defeated in every engagement."

軍

形

第

四

4

Military

Disposition[50]

Sun-tzu said:

"In antiquity those that excelled in warfare first made themselves unconquerable[51] in order to await [the moment when] the enemy could be conquered.

"Being unconquerable lies with yourself; being conquerable lies with the enemy.

"Thus one who excels in warfare[52] is able to make himself unconquerable, but cannot necessarily cause the enemy to be conquerable.

"Thus it is said a strategy for conquering the enemy can be known but yet not possible to implement.

. . .

"One who cannot be victorious assumes a defensive posture; one who can be victorious attacks. In these circumstances by assuming a defensive posture, strength will be more than adequate, whereas in offensive actions it would be inadequate.[53]

. . .

"Those who excel at defense bury themselves away below the lowest depths of Earth. Those who excel at offense[54] move from above the greatest heights of Heaven. Thus they are able to preserve themselves and attain complete victory.

"Perceiving a victory that does not surpass what the masses could know is not the pinnacle of excellence. Wrestling victories for which All under Heaven proclaim your excellence is not the pinnacle of excellence.[55]

"Thus lifting an autumn hare cannot be considered great strength; seeing the sun and moon cannot be considered acute vision; hearing the sound of thunder cannot be considered having sensitive ears.

"Those that the ancients[56] referred to as excelling at warfare conquered those who were easy to conquer. Thus the victories of those that excelled in warfare were not marked by fame for wisdom or courageous achievement.[57] Thus their victories were free from errors. One who is free from errors directs his measures toward [certain] victory, conquering those who are already defeated.

. . .

"Thus one who excels at warfare first establishes himself in a position where he cannot be defeated while not losing [any opportunity] to defeat the enemy.

"For this reason, the victorious army first realizes the conditions for victory, and then seeks to engage in battle. The vanquished army fights first, and then seeks victory.

. . .

"One[58] who excels at employing the military cultivates the Tao[59] and preserves the laws; therefore, he is able to be the regulator of victory and defeat.[60]

. . .

"As for military methods:[61] the first is termed measurement; the second, estimation [of forces]; the third, calculation [of numbers of men]; the fourth, weighing [relative strength]; and the fifth, victory.

"Terrain gives birth to measurement;[62] measurement produces the estimation [of forces].[63] Estimation [of forces] gives rise to calculating [the numbers of men]. Calculating [the numbers of men] gives rise to weighing [strength]. Weighing [strength] gives birth to victory.

. . .

"Thus the victorious army is like a ton compared with an ounce, while the defeated army is like an ounce weighed against a ton! The combat of the victorious[64] is like the sudden release of a pent-up torrent down a thousand-fathom gorge. This is the strategic disposition of force (*hsing*)."[65]

兵勢第五

5
Strategic
Military
Power[66]

Sun-tzu said:

"In general, commanding a large number is like commanding a few. It is a question of dividing up the numbers. Fighting with a large number is like fighting with a few. It is a question of configuration and designation.[67]

. . .

"What enable the masses of the Three Armies invariably to withstand the enemy without being defeated are the unorthodox (*ch'i*) and orthodox (*cheng*).[68]

"If wherever the army attacks it is like a whetstone thrown against an egg, it is due to the vacuous and substantial.[69]

"In general, in battle one engages with the orthodox and gains victory through the unorthodox. Thus one who excels at sending forth the unorthodox is as inexhaustible as Heaven,[70] as unlimited as the Yangtze and Yellow rivers.[71] What reach an end and begin again are the sun and moon. What die and are reborn[72] are the four seasons.

"The notes do not exceed five, but the changes[73] of the five notes can never be fully heard. The colors do not exceed five, but the changes of the five colors can never be completely seen. The flavors do not exceed five, but the changes of the five flavors can never be completely tasted. In warfare the strategic configurations of power (*shih*) do not exceed the unorthodox and orthodox, but the changes of the unorthodox and orthodox can never be completely exhausted. The unorthodox and orthodox mutually produce each other, just like an endless cycle.[74] Who can exhaust them?

. . .

"The strategic configuration of power (*shih*) [is visible in] the onrush of pent-up[75] water tumbling stones along. The [effect of] constraints[76] [is visible in] the onrush[77] of a bird of prey breaking the bones of its [target]. Thus the strategic configuration of power (*shih*) of those that excel in warfare is sharply focused, their constraints are precise.[78] Their strategic configuration of power (*shih*) is like a fully drawn crossbow, their constraints like the release of the trigger.

. . .

"Intermixed and turbulent, the fighting appears chaotic, but they cannot be made disordered.[79] In turmoil and confusion, their deployment is circular,[80] and they cannot be defeated.

. . .

"[Simulated] chaos is given birth from control;[81] [the illusion of] fear is given birth from courage; [feigned] weakness is given birth from strength. Order and disorder are a question of numbers; courage and fear are a question of the strategic configuration of power (*shih*); strength and weakness are a question of the deployment [of forces] (*hsing*).

"Thus one who excels at moving the enemy deploys in a configuration (*hsing*) to which the enemy must respond. He offers something that the enemy must seize. With profit he moves them, with the foundation[82] he awaits them.

. . .

"Thus one who excels at warfare seeks [victory] through the strategic configuration of power (*shih*), not from reliance on men. Thus he is able to select men and employ strategic power (*shih*).[83]

. . .

"One who employs strategic power (*shih*) commands men in battle as if he were rolling logs and stones. The nature of wood and stone is to be quiet when stable but to move when on precipitous ground. If they are square they stop, if round they tend to move. Thus the strategic power (*shih*) of one who excels at employing men in warfare is comparable to rolling round boulders down a thousand-fathom mountain. Such is the strategic configuration of power (*shih*)."

虚 實 第 六

6

Vacuity

and

Substance[84]

Sun-tzu said:

"In general, whoever occupies the battleground first and awaits the enemy will be at ease; whoever occupies the battleground afterward and must race to the conflict will be fatigued. Thus one who excels at warfare compels men and is not compelled by other men.[85]

. . .

"In order to cause the enemy to come of their own volition, extend some [apparent] profit. In order to prevent the enemy from coming forth, show them [the potential] harm.

. . .

"Thus if the enemy is rested you can tire him; if he is well fed you can make him hungry; if he is at rest you can move him. Go forth to positions to which he must race.[86] Race forth where he does not expect it.[87]

. . .

"To travel a thousand *li* without becoming fatigued, traverse unoccupied terrain. To ensure taking the objective in an attack, strike positions that are undefended. To be certain of an impregnable defense, secure positions that the enemy will not attack.[88]

"Thus when someone excels in attacking, the enemy does not know where to mount his defense; when someone excels at defense, the enemy does not know where to attack. Subtle! Subtle! It approaches the formless.[89] Spiritual! Spiritual! It attains the soundless. Thus he can be the enemy's Master of Fate.

. . .

"To effect an unhampered[90] advance, strike their vacuities. To effect a retreat that cannot be overtaken, employ unmatchable speed.[91] Thus if I want to engage in combat, even though the enemy has high ramparts and deep moats, he cannot avoid doing battle because I attack objectives he must rescue.

"If I do not want to engage in combat, even though I merely draw a line on the ground and defend it, he will not be able to engage me in battle because we thwart his movements.

. . .

"Thus if I determine the enemy's disposition of forces (*hsing*) while I have no perceptible form,[92] I can concentrate [my forces] while the enemy is fragmented. If we are concentrated into a single force while he is fragmented into ten, then we attack him with ten times his strength. Thus we are many and the enemy is few. If we can attack his few with our many, those who we engage in battle will be severely constrained.

. . .

"The location where we will engage the enemy must not become known to them. If it is not known, then the positions they must prepare to defend will be numerous. If the positions the enemy prepares to defend are numerous, then the forces we will engage will be few. Thus if they prepare to defend the front, to the rear there will be few men. If they defend the rear, in the front there will be few. If they prepare to defend the left flank, then on the right there will be few men. If they prepare to defend the right flank, then on the left there will be few men. If there is no position left undefended, then there will not be any place with more than a few. The few [are the ones] who prepare against others; the many [are the ones] who make others prepare against them.[93]

. . .

"Thus if one knows the field of battle and knows the day of battle, he can traverse a thousand *li* and assemble to engage in combat.[94] If he does not know the field of battle nor know the day for battle, then the left flank cannot aid the right nor the right flank aid the left; the front cannot aid the rear nor the rear aid the front.[95] How much more so when the distant are some tens of *li* away and the near several *li* apart? As I analyze it, even though Yüeh's army is numerous, of what great advantage is it to them for attaining victory?[96] Thus I say victory can be achieved.[97] Even though the enemy is more numerous, they can be forced not to fight.

. . .

"Thus critically analyze them to know the estimations for gain and loss. Stimulate them to know the patterns of their movement and stopping. Determine their disposition of force (*hsing*) to know the tenable and fatal terrain. Probe them to know where they have an excess, where an insufficiency.[98]

"Thus the pinnacle of military deployment approaches the formless. If it is formless, then even the deepest spy cannot discern it or the wise make plans against it.

. . .

"In accord with the enemy's disposition (*hsing*) we impose measures on the masses that produce victory, but the masses are unable to fathom them. Men all know the disposition (*hsing*) by which we attain victory, but no one knows the configuration (*hsing*) through which we control the victory. Thus a victorious battle [strategy] is not repeated, the configurations (*hsing*) of response [to the enemy] are inexhaustible.[99]

. . .

"Now the army's disposition of force (*hsing*) is like water. Water's configuration (*hsing*) avoids heights and races downward. The army's disposition of force (*hsing*) avoids the substantial and strikes the vacuous. Water configures (*hsing*) its flow[102] in accord with the terrain; the army controls its victory in accord with the enemy. Thus the army does not maintain any constant[103] strategic configuration of power (*shih*), water[104] has no constant shape (*hsing*). One who is able to change and transform in accord with the enemy and wrest victory is termed spiritual.[105] Thus [none of] the five phases constantly dominates; the four seasons do not have constant positions; the sun shines for longer and shorter periods; and the moon wanes and waxes."[106]

7
Military
Combat [107]

軍

爭

第

七

Sun-tzu said:

"In general, the strategy for employing the army is this: [From the time] the general receives his commands from the ruler, unites the armies, and assembles the masses, to confronting the enemy and encamping, there is nothing more difficult than military combat. In military combat what is most difficult is turning the circuitous into the straight, turning adversity into advantage.

"Thus if you make the enemy's path circuitous and entice them with profit, although you set out after them you will arrive before them. This results from knowing the tactics[108] of the circuitous and the direct.

. . .

"Thus combat between armies is advantageous; combat between masses is dangerous.[109] If the entire army contends for advantage, you will not arrive in time. If you reduce the army's size to contend for advantage, your baggage and heavy equipment will suffer losses.

"For this reason if you abandon your armor [and heavy equipment][110] to race forward day and night without encamping, covering two days normal distance at a time, marching forward a hundred *li* to contend for gain, the Three Armies' generals will be captured. The strong will be first to arrive, while the exhausted will follow. With such tactics only one in ten will reach [the battle site]. If one contends for gain fifty *li* away, it will cause the general of the Upper Army to stumble, and by following such tactics half the men will reach [the objective]. If you contend for gain at thirty *li*, then two-thirds of the army will reach [the objective].

"Accordingly, if the army does not have baggage and heavy equipment it will be lost; if it does not have provisions it will be lost; if it does not have stores it will be lost.

. . .

Thus one who does not know the plans of the feudal lords cannot prepare alliances beforehand. Someone unfamiliar with the mountains and forests, gorges and defiles, the shape of marshes and wetlands cannot advance the army.

One who does not employ local guides cannot gain advantages of terrain.[111]

. . .

"Thus the army is established by deceit, moves for advantage, and changes through segmenting and reuniting. Thus its speed is like the wind, its slowness like the forest; its invasion and plundering like a fire; unmoving, it is like the mountains. It is as difficult to know as the darkness; in movement it is like thunder.

. . .

"When you plunder a district, divide the wealth among your troops. When you enlarge your territory, divide the profits.[112] Take control of the strategic balance of power (*ch'üan*) and move. The one who first understands the tactics of the circuitous and the direct will be victorious. This is the strategy for military combat.

. . .

"The *Military Administration* states: 'Because they could not hear each other they made gongs and drums; because they could not see each other they made pennants and flags.' Gongs, drums, pennants, and flags are the means to unify the men's ears and eyes. When the men have been unified the courageous will not be able to advance alone, the fearful will not be able to retreat alone. This is the method for employing large numbers.[113]

"Thus in night battles make the fires and drums numerous, and in daylight battles make the flags and pennants numerous in order to change the men's ears and eyes.[114]

. . .

"The *ch'i* of the Three Armies can be snatched away; the commanding general's mind can be seized. For this reason in the morning their *ch'i* is ardent; during the day their *ch'i* becomes indolent; at dusk their *ch'i* is exhausted.[115] Thus one who excels at employing the army avoids their ardent *ch'i* and strikes when it is indolent or exhausted. This is the way to manipulate *ch'i*.[116]

. . .

"In order await the disordered; in tranquility await the clamorous. This is the way to control the mind.

. . .

"With the near await the distant; with the rested await the fatigued; with the sated await the hungry. This is the way to control strength.

. . .

"Do not intercept well-ordered flags; do not attack well-regulated formations.[117] This is the way to control changes.

. . .

"Thus the strategy for employing the military: Do not approach high mountains; do not confront[118] those who have hills behind them. Do not pursue feigned retreats.[119] Do not attack animated troops. Do not swallow an army acting as bait. Do not obstruct an army retreating homeward.[120] If you besiege an army you must leave an outlet.[121] Do not press an exhausted invader. These are the strategies for employing the military."[122]

8
Nine
Changes[123]

九變第八

Sun-tzu said:

"In general, the strategy for employing the military is this. After the general has received his commands from the ruler, united the armies, and assembled the masses:[124]

"Do not encamp on entrapping terrain.[125]
"Unite with your allies on focal terrain.[126]
"Do not remain on isolated terrain.
"Make strategic plans for encircled terrain.
"On fatal terrain you must do battle.[127]
"There are roads that are not[128] followed.[128]
"There are armies that are not attacked.
"There are fortified cities that are not assaulted.[129]
"There is terrain for which one does not contend.[130]
"There are commands from the ruler that are not accepted.[131]

"Thus the general who has a penetrating understanding of the advantages of the nine changes knows how to employ the army. If a general does not have a penetrating understanding of the advantages of the nine changes, even though he is familiar with the topography, he will not be able to realize the advantages of terrain.

"One who commands an army but does not know the techniques for the nine changes, even though he is familiar with the five advantages,[132] will not be able to control men.

. . .

"For this reason the wise must contemplate the intermixture of gain and loss. If they discern advantage [in difficult situations], their efforts can be trusted. If they discern harm [in prospective advantage], difficulties can be resolved.

. . .

"Accordingly, subjugate the feudal lords with potential harm; labor the feudal lords with numerous affairs; and have the feudal lords race after profits.

. . .

"Thus the strategy for employing the army: Do not rely on their not coming, but depend on us having the means to await them. Do not rely on their not attacking, but depend on us having an unassailable position.[133]

. . .

"Thus generals have five dangerous [character traits]:
"One committed to dying can be slain.
"One committed to living can be captured.
"One [easily] angered and hasty [to act] can be insulted.
"One obsessed with being scrupulous and untainted can
    be shamed.
"One who loves the people can be troubled.

"Now these five dangerous traits are excesses in a general, potential disaster for employing the army. The army's destruction and the general's death will invariably stem from these five, so they must be investigated."[134]

行軍第九

9

Maneuvering

the

Army

Sun-tzu said:

"As for deploying the army and fathoming the enemy:

"To cross mountains follow the valleys, search out tenable ground,[135] and occupy the heights. If the enemy holds the heights, do not climb up to engage them in battle. This is the way to deploy an army in the mountains.[136]

"After crossing rivers[137] you must distance yourself from them. If the enemy is fording a river to advance, do not confront them in the water. When half their forces have crossed, it will be advantageous to strike them. If you want to engage the enemy in battle, do not array your forces near the river to confront the invader but look for tenable ground and occupy the heights. Do not confront the current's flow.[138] This is the way to deploy the army where there are rivers.

"When you cross salt marshes and wetlands, concentrate on quickly getting away from them; do not remain. If you engage in battle in marshes or wetlands, you must stay in areas with marsh grass and keep groves of trees at your back. This is the way to deploy the army in marshes and wetlands.[139]

"On level plains deploy on easy[140] terrain with the right flank positioned with high ground to the rear, fatal terrain to the fore, and tenable terrain to the rear. This is the way to deploy on the plains.

"These four [deployments], advantageous to the army, are the means by which the Yellow Emperor conquered the four emperors.[141]

. . .

"Now the army likes heights and abhors low areas, esteems the sunny (yang) and disdains the shady (yin). It nourishes life and occupies the substantial.[142] An army that avoids the hundred illnesses is said to be certain of victory.[143]

. . .

"Where there are hills and embankments you must occupy the yang side, keeping them to the right rear. This is to the army's advantage and [exploits the natural] assistance of the terrain.

. . .

"When it rains upstream, foam appears.[144] If you want to cross over, wait until it settles.

. . .

"You must quickly get away from deadly configurations of terrain such as precipitous gorges with mountain torrents, Heaven's Well,[145] Heaven's Jail,[146] Heaven's Net,[147] Heaven's Pit,[148] and Heaven's Fissure.[149] Do not approach them. When we keep them at a distance, the enemy [is forced to] approach them. When we face them, the enemy [is compelled to] have them at their rear.

. . .

"When on the flanks the army encounters ravines and defiles, wetlands with reeds and tall grass, mountain forests,[150] or areas with heavy, entangled undergrowth, you must thoroughly search them because they are places where an ambush or spies would be concealed.[151]

. . .

"If [an enemy] in close proximity remains quiet, they are relying on their tactical occupation of ravines.[152] If while far off they challenge you to battle, they want you to advance [because] they occupy easy terrain to their advantage.

. . .

"If large numbers of trees move, they are approaching. If there are many [visible] obstacles in the heavy grass, it is to make us suspicious.[153] If the birds take flight, there is an ambush. If the animals are afraid, [enemy] forces are mounting a sudden attack.

. . .

"If dust rises high up in a sharply defined column, chariots are coming. If it is low and broad, the infantry is advancing. If it is dispersed in thin shafts, they are gathering firewood. If it is sparse, coming and going, they are encamping.

"One who speaks deferentially but increases his preparations will advance. One who speaks belligerently and advances hastily will retreat.

"One whose light chariots first fan out to the sides is deploying [for battle].[154]

"One who seeks peace without setting any prior conditions is [executing] a stratagem.

"One whose troops race off but [who] deploys his army into formation is implementing a predetermined schedule.

"One [whose troops] half advance and half retreat is enticing you.

. . .

"Those who stand about leaning on their weapons are hungry. If those who draw water drink first, they are thirsty. When they see potential gain but do not know whether to advance, they are tired.

. . .

"Where birds congregate it is empty. If the enemy cries out at night, they are afraid. If the army is turbulent,[155] the general lacks severity. If their flags and pennants move about, they are in chaos. If the officers are angry, they are exhausted.

. . .

"If they kill their horses and eat the meat, the army lacks grain.[156] If they hang up their cooking utensils and do not return to camp, they are an exhausted invader.[157]

. . .

"One whose troops repeatedly congregate in small groups here and there, whispering together, has lost the masses. One who frequently grants rewards is in deep distress. One who frequently imposes punishments is in great difficulty. One who is at first excessively brutal and then fears the masses is the pinnacle of stupidity.[158]

. . .

"One who has emissaries come forth with offerings wants to rest for a while.

. . .

"If their troops are aroused and approach our forces, only to maintain their positions without engaging in battle or breaking off the confrontation, you must carefully investigate it.

. . .

"The army does not esteem the number of troops being

more numerous for it only means one can not aggressively advance.[159] It is sufficient for you to muster your own strength, analyze the enemy, and take them. Only someone who lacks strategic planning and slights an enemy will inevitably be captured by others.

. . .

"If you impose punishments on the troops before they have become attached, they will not be submissive. If they are not submissive, they will be difficult to employ. If you do not impose punishments after the troops have become attached, they cannot be used.[160]

. . .

"Thus if you command them with the civil[161] and unify them through the martial, this is what is referred to as 'being certain to take them.'[162]

. . .

"If orders are consistently implemented to instruct the people, then the people will submit. If orders are not consistently implemented to instruct the people, then the people will not submit. One whose orders are consistently carried out has established a mutual relationship with the people."

地形第十

10
Configurations
of
Terrain

Sun-tzu said:

"The major configurations (*hsing*) of terrain are accessible, suspended, stalemated, constricted, precipitous, and expansive.

"If we can go forth and the enemy can also advance, it is termed 'accessible.' In an accessible configuration, first occupy the heights and yang [side], and improve the routes for transporting provisions. Then when we engage in battle, it will be advantageous.

"If we can go forth but it will be difficult to return, it is termed 'suspended.'[164] In a suspended configuration, if they are unprepared go forth and conquer them. If the enemy is prepared and we sally forth without being victorious, it will be difficult to turn back and [is] not advantageous.

"If it is not advantageous for us to go forth nor advantageous for the enemy to come forward, it is termed "stalemated."[165] In a stalemated configuration, even though the enemy tries to entice us with profit, we do not go forth. Withdraw [our forces] and depart.[166] If we strike them when half the enemy has come forth, it will be advantageous.

"As for constricted configurations, if we occupy them first we must fully deploy throughout them in order to await the enemy.[167] If the enemy occupies them first and fully deploys in them, do not follow them in. If they do not fully deploy in them, then follow them in.

"As for precipitous configurations,[168] if we occupy them we must hold the heights and yang sides to await the enemy. If the enemy occupies them first, withdraw [our forces] and depart. Do not follow them.

"As for expansive configurations, if our strategic power (*shih*) is equal,[169] it will be difficult to provoke [them to] combat. Engaging in combat will not be be advantageous.

"Now these six are the Tao of terrain. Any general who undertakes responsibility for command cannot but investigate them.

"Thus there are [six types of ill-fated] armies: running [off], lax, sinking, crumbling, chaotic, and routed. Now these six are not disasters brought about by Heaven and Earth but by the general's errors.

"Now if, when their strategic power (*shih*) is equal, one attacks ten, this is called 'running [off].'[170]

"If the troops are strong but the officers are weak, it is termed 'lax.'

"If the officers are strong but the troops weak, it is termed 'sinking.'

"If the higher officers are angry and insubordinate, engaging the enemy themselves out of unrestrained anger while the general does not yet know their capability, it is termed 'crumbling.'

"If the general is weak and not strict, unenlightened in his instructions and leadership; the officers and troops lack constant [duties]; and their deployment of troops into formation is askew, it is termed 'chaotic.'

"If the general, unable to fathom the enemy, engages a large number with a small number, attacks the strong with the weak while the army lacks a properly selected vanguard, it is termed 'routed.'.

"Now these six are the Tao of defeat. Any general who undertakes responsibility for command cannot but investigate them.

. . .

"Configuration of terrain is an aid to the army. Analyzing the enemy, taking control of victory, estimating ravines and defiles, the distant and near, is the Tao of the superior general.[171] One who knows these and employs them in combat will certainly be victorious. One who does not know these or employ them in combat will certainly be defeated.

. . .

"If the Tao of Warfare [indicates] certain victory, even though the ruler has instructed that combat should be avoided, if you must engage in battle it is permissible. If the

Tao of Warfare indicates you will not be victorious, even though the ruler instructs you to engage in battle, not fighting is permissible.

"Thus [a general] who does not advance to seek fame, nor [fail to retreat] to avoid [being charged with the capital] offense of retreating, but seeks only to preserve the people and gain advantage for the ruler is the state's treasure.

.   .   .

"When the general regards his troops as young children, they will advance into the deepest valleys with him. When he regards the troops as his beloved children, they will be willing to die with him.[172]

"If they are well treated but cannot be employed, if they are loved but cannot be commanded, or when in chaos they cannot be governed, they may be compared to arrogant children and cannot be used.

.   .   .

"If I know our troops can attack, but do not know the enemy cannot be attacked, it is only halfway to victory. If I know the enemy can be attacked, but do not realize our troops cannot attack, it is only halfway to victory.

"Knowing that the enemy can be attacked, and knowing that our army can effect the attack, but not knowing the terrain is not suitable for combat, is only halfway to victory. Thus one who truly knows the army will never be deluded when he moves, never be impoverished when initiating an action.

"Thus it is said if you know them and know yourself, your victory will not be imperiled. If you know Heaven and know Earth, your victory can be complete.[173]

11

Nine

Terrains

Sun-tzu said:

"The strategy for employing the military is [this]: There is dispersive terrain, light terrain, contentious terrain, traversable terrain, focal terrain, heavy terrain, entrapping terrain, encircled terrain, and fatal terrain.[174]

"When the feudal lords fight in their own territory, it is 'dispersive terrain.'[175]

"When they enter someone else's territory, but not deeply, it is 'light terrain.'[176]

"If when we occupy it, it will be advantageous to us while if they occupy it, it will be advantageous to them, it is 'contentious terrain.'[177]

"When we can go and they can also come, it is 'traversable terrain.'[178]

"Land of the feudal lords surrounded on three sides such that whoever arrives first will gain the masses of All under Heaven is 'focal terrain.'[179]

"When one penetrates deeply into enemy territory, bypassing numerous cities, it is 'heavy terrain.'[180]

"Where there are mountains and forests, ravines and defiles, wetlands and marshes, wherever the road is difficult to negotiate, it is 'entrapping terrain.[181]

"Where the entrance is constricted,[182] the return is circuitous, and with a small number they can strike our masses, it is 'encircled terrain.'[183]

"Where if one fights with intensity he will survive but if he does not fight with intensity he will perish, it is ' fatal terrain.'[184]

. . .

"For this reason on dispersive terrain do not engage the enemy.

"On light terrain do not stop.

"On contentious terrain do not attack.[185]

"On traversable terrain do not allow your forces to become isolated.

"On focal terrain unit and form alliances [with nearby feudal lords.][186]
"On heavy terrain plunder for provisions.
"On entrapping terrain move [through quickly].[187]
"On encircled terrain use strategy.[188]
"On fatal terrain engage in battle.

. . .

"In antiquity those who were referred to as excelling in the employment of the army were able to keep the enemy's forward and rear forces from connecting; the many and few from relying on each other; the noble and lowly from coming to each other's rescue; the upper and lower ranks from trusting each other; the troops to be separated, unable to reassemble, or when assembled, not to be well-ordered.[189] They moved when it was advantageous, halted when it was not advantageous.

. . .

"If I dare ask, if the enemy is numerous, disciplined, and about to advance, how should we respond to them? I would say, first seize something that they love for then they will listen to you.

. . .

"It is the nature of the army to stress speed; to take advantage of the enemy's absence; to travel unanticipated roads; and to attack when they are not alert.

. . .

"In general, the Tao of an invader is that when one has penetrated deeply [into enemy territory], the army will be unified, and the defenders will not be able to conquer you.

. . .

"If one forages in the fertile countryside, then the Three Armies will have enough to eat. If you carefully nurture them and do not [over-]labor them, their *ch'i* will be united and their strength will be at maximum.

. . .

"When you mobilize the army and form strategic plans, you must be unfathomable.

. . .

"Cast them into positions from which there is nowhere to go and they will die without retreating. If there is no escape from death, the officers and soldiers will fully exhaust their strength.

.   .   .

"When the soldiers and officers have penetrated deeply into [enemy territory], they will cling together. When there is no alternative, they will fight.

.   .   .

"For this reason even though the soldiers are not instructed, they are prepared; without seeking it, their cooperation is obtained;[190] without covenants they are close together; without issuing orders they are reliable. Prohibit omens, eliminate doubt so that they will die without other thoughts.[191]

.   .   .

"If our soldiers do not have excessive wealth, it is not because they detest material goods. If they do not live long lives,[192] it is not because they abhor longevity. On the day that the orders are issued the tears of the soldiers who are sitting will soak their sleeves, while the tears of those lying down will roll down their cheeks. However, if you throw them into a hopeless situation, they will have the courage of Chu or Kuei.

.   .   .

"Thus one who excels at employing the army may be compared to the *shuaijan* [snake]. The *shuaijan* is found on Mt. Ch'ang. If you strike its head the tail will respond; if you strike its tail the head will respond. If you strike the middle [of the body][193] both the head and tail will react. If I dare ask, can we make the army like the *shuaijan,* I would say we can. For example, the people of Wu and Yüeh hate each other; but if, when fording a river in the same boat they encounter severe wind, their efforts to rescue each other will be like the left and right hands.

.   .   .

"For this reason fettering the horses[194] and burying the chariot wheels are inadequate to rely on [to prevent the soldiers from fleeing.]. Unify their courage to be as one through the Tao of administration. Realize the appropriate employment of the hard and soft[195] through the patterns of terrain.

. . .

"Thus one who excels at employing the army leads them by the hand as if they were only one man, so they cannot avoid it.

. . .

"It is essential for a general to be tranquil and obscure, upright and self-disciplined, and able to stupefy the eyes and ears of the officers and troops, keeping them ignorant.[196] He alters his management of affairs and changes his strategies to keep other people[197] from recognizing them. He shifts his position and traverses indirect routes to keep other people from being able to anticipate him.

. . .

"At the moment the general has designated with them, it will be as if they ascended a height and abandoned their ladders. The general advances with them deep into the territory of the feudal lords and then releases the trigger.[198] He commands them as if racing a herd of sheep—they are driven away, driven back, but no one knows where they are going.

. . .

"Assembling the masses of the Three Armies, casting them into danger, is the responsibility of the general.

. . .

"The nine transformations of terrain—the advantages deriving from contraction and expansion, the patterns of human emotions—must be investigated.[199]

. . .

"In general, the Tao of the invader is [this]:[200]

"When the troops have penetrated deeply, they will be unified, but where only shallowly, they will [be inclined to] scatter.

"When [the army] has left the state, crossed the [enemy's] border, and is on campaign, it is 'isolated terrain.'

"When the four sides are open [to others], this is 'focal terrain.'

"When you have advanced deeply, it is 'heavy terrain.'

"If you have penetrated only shallowly, it is 'light terrain.'

"If you have strongholds behind you and constrictions before you, it is 'encircled terrain.'

"If there is no place to go, it is 'fatal terrain.'[201]

"For this reason on dispersive terrain I unify their will.

"On light terrain I have them group together.

"On contentious terrain I race our rear elements forward.[202]

"On traversable terrain I focus on defense.[203]

"On focal terrain I solidify our alliances.[204]

"On heavy terrain I ensure a continuous supply of provisions.[205]

"On entrapping terrain I [speedily] advance along the roads.

"On encircled terrain I obstruct any openings.[206]

"On fatal terrain I show them that we will not live.

. . .

"Thus it is the nature of the army to defend when encircled;[207] to fight fervently when unavoidable; and to follow orders when compelled [by circumstances].

. . .

"For this reason one who does not know the plans of the feudal lords cannot forge preparatory alliances. One who does not know the topography of mountains and forests, ravines and defiles, wetlands and marshes cannot maneuver the army. One who does not employ local guides will not secure advantages of terrain. One who does not know one of these four or five cannot [command] the army of a hegemon or a true king.[208]

. . .

"Now when the army of a hegemon or true king attacks a great state, their masses are unable to assemble. When it applies its awesomeness to the enemy, their alliances cannot be sustained. For this reason it does not contend with any alliances under Heaven.[209] It does not nurture the authority (*ch'üan*) of others under Heaven. Have faith in yourself, apply your awesomeness to the enemy. Then his cities can be taken, his state can be subjugated.[210]

. . .

"Bestow rewards not required by law, impose exceptional governmental orders. Direct the masses of the Three Armies as though commanding one man. Press affairs upon them, do not explain the purpose to them. Compel them with [prospects for] profit, but do not inform them about the [potential] harm.

. . .

"Cast them into hopeless situations and they will be preserved; have them penetrate fatal terrain and they will live. Only after the masses have penetrated dangerous [terrain] will they be able to craft victory out of defeat.

. . .

"The prosecution of military affairs lies in according with and [learning] in detail the enemy's intentions.[211] If one then focuses [his strength] toward the enemy, strikes a thousand *li* away, and kills their general, it is termed 'being skillful and capable in completing military affairs.'

. . .

"For this reason on the day the government mobilizes the army close the passes, destroy all tallies, and do not allow their emissaries to pass through. Hold intense strategic discussions[212] in the upper hall of the temple in order to bring about the execution of affairs.

. . .

"If the enemy opens the door, you must race in.

. . .

"[Attack] what they love first. Do not fix any time for battle, assess and react to the enemy in order to determine the strategy for battle.

. . .

"For this reason at first be like a virgin [at home]; later—when the enemy opens the door—be like a fleeing rabbit. The enemy will be unable to withstand you."

火

攻

第

十

二

12
Incendiary[213]
Attacks

Sun-tzu said:

"There are five types of incendiary attack: The first is to incinerate men, the second to incinerate provisions, the third to incinerate supply trains, the fourth to incinerate armories, and the fifth to incinerate formations.[214]

  • • •

"Implementing an incendiary attack depends on the proper conditions. Equipment for incendiary attack should be fully prepared before required. Launching an incendiary attack has its appropriate seasons, igniting the fire the proper days. As for the seasons, it is the time of the dry spell; as for the day, when the moon is in *chi, pi, i,* or *chen.* When it is in these four lunar lodges, these are days the wind will arise.

  • • •

"In general, in incendiary warfare you must respond to the five changes of fire:

"If fires are started within [their camp], then you should immediately respond [with an attack] from outside.

"If fires are ignited but their army remains quiet, then wait; do not attack.

"When they flare into a conflagration, if you can follow up, then do so; if you cannot, then desist.

"If the attack can be launched from outside without relying on inside [assistance], initiate it at an appropriate time.

"If fires are ignited upwind, do not attack downwind.

  • • •

"Winds that arise in the daytime will persist; those that arise at night will stop.

  • • •

"Now the army must know the five changes of fire in order to defend against them at the astrologically appropriate times. Thus using fire to aid an attack is enlightened, using water to assist an attack is powerful. Water can be used to sever, but cannot be employed to seize.[215]

. . .

"Now if someone is victorious in battle and succeeds in attack but does not exploit the achievement, it is disastrous, and his fate should be termed 'wasteful and tarrying.' Thus it is said the wise general ponders it, the good general cultivates it.

. . .

"If it is not advantageous, do not move. If objectives cannot be attained, do not employ the army. Unless endangered do not engage in warfare. The ruler cannot mobilize the army out of personal anger. The general cannot engage in battle because of personal frustration. When it is advantageous, move; when not advantageous, stop. Anger can revert to happiness, annoyance can revert to joy, but a vanquished state cannot be revived, the dead cannot be brought back to life.

"Thus the unenlightened ruler is cautious about it, the good general respectful of it. This is the Tao for bringing security to the state and preserving the army intact."

13
Employing
Spies [216]

用間第十三

Sun-tzu said:

"When you send forth an army of a hundred thousand on a campaign, marching them out a thousand *li,* the expenditures of the common people and the contributions of the feudal house will be one thousand pieces of gold per day.[217] Those inconvenienced and troubled both within and without the border, who are exhausted on the road or unable to pursue their agricultural work, will be seven hundred thousand families.

"Armies remain locked in a standoff for years to fight for victory on a single day, yet [generals] begrudge bestowing ranks and emoluments of one hundred pieces of gold and therefore do not know the enemy's situation.[218] This is the ultimate inhumanity. Such a person is not a general for the people, an assistant for a ruler, or the arbiter of victory.

. . .

"The means by which enlightened rulers and sagacious generals moved and conquered others, that their achievements surpassed the masses, was advance knowledge.

"Advance knowledge cannot be gained from ghosts and spirits, inferred from phenomena, or projected from the measures of Heaven, but must be gained from men for it is the knowledge of the enemy's true situation.

. . .

"Thus there are five types of spies to be employed: local spy, internal spy, turned spy [double agent], dead [expendable] spy, and the living spy. When all five are employed together and no one knows their Tao, this is termed "spiritual methodology." They are a ruler's treasures.

"Local spies—employ people from the local district.

"Internal spies—employ their people who hold government positions.

"Double agents—employ the enemy's spies.

"Expendable spies—are employed to spread disinformation outside the state. Provide our [expendable] spies [with false information] and have them leak it to enemy agents.[219]

"Living spies—return with their reports.

"Thus of all the Three Armies' affairs[220] no relationship is closer than with spies; no rewards are more generous than those given to spies, no affairs are more secret than those pertaining to spies.

   . . .

"Unless someone has the wisdom of a Sage, he cannot use spies; unless he is benevolent and righteous, he cannot employ spies; unless he is subtle and perspicacious, he cannot perceive the substance in intelligence reports. It is subtle, subtle! There are no areas in which one does not employ spies.

   . . .

"If before the mission has begun it has already been exposed, the spy and those he informed should all be put to death.

   . . .

"In general, as for the armies you want to strike, the cities you want to attack, and the men you want to assassinate, you must first know the names of the defensive commander, his assistants, staff, door guards, and attendants. You must have our spies search out and learn them all.

   . . .

"You must search for enemy agents who have come to spy on us. Tempt them with profits, instruct and retain them. Thus double agents can be obtained and employed. Through knowledge gained from them, you can recruit both local and internal spies. Through knowledge gained from them, the expendable spy can spread his falsehoods, can be used to misinform the enemy. Through knowledge gained from them, our living spies can be employed as times require.

"The ruler must know these five aspects of espionage work. This knowledge inevitably depends on turned spies; therefore, you must be generous to double agents.

   . . .

"In antiquity, when the Yin arose, they had I Chih in the

Hsia. When the Chou arose, they had Lü Ya [the T'ai Kung] in the Yin.[221] Thus enlightened rulers and sagacious generals who are able to get intelligent spies will invariably attain great achievements. This is the essence of the military, what the Three Armies rely on to move."

竹簡佚文

Tomb

Texts

and

Lost

Writings

A NUMBER of works preserve fragments and even passages that apparently derive from the *Art of War* or are otherwise identified with Sun-tzu's thought. Whether they were deliberately excised; simply dropped out of the text at an early date; constitute supplementary materials originating with Sun-tzu after he composed the thirteen section *Art of War* to capture King Ho-lü's interest; or are simply subsequent expansions by members of his school remains heavily debated. Much of the material is redundant or so brief as to be unimportant. However, the *T'ung tien* contains thirteen highly relevant passages on configurations of terrain with correlated battle tactics. Although they strongly resemble those found in the *Wu-tzu* and especially the *Six Secret Teachings,* they may have originally been formulated by Sun-tzu himself. However, their question and reply format implies a composition date subsequent to that for the *Art of War.* While claims that they record actual questions posed by the king cannot be summarily dismissed, frequent references to the cavalry forces that would not appear for generations require later revisions. Probably these passages stem from Sun-tzu's school of thought, being formulated by distant students and simply projected back into history. Issues similar to those raised by the question of Sun-tzu's existence and the authenticity of the *Art of War* equally plague these "lost materials" and the newly recovered tomb writings.

The most important and coherent passages from among the recovered bamboo slips and the *T'ung tien* are translated here: the first, termed "Nine Configurations," restates material from chapters eight ("Nine Changes"), ten "Configurations of Terrain"), and eleven ("Nine Terrains"). It is followed by the recovered bamboo strip version called "Four Changes" since the latter is generally thought to belong to "Nine Terrains." Two supplementary passages we entitled "Two Questions" from the *T'ung tien* continue the thread, and the section concludes with the tomb text called the "King of Wu's Questions." While several additional bamboo texts have been recovered from the Lin-i and other tombs, they are less immediately accessible and relevant to the study of Sun-tzu's thought, and are left to appropriately annotated articles.

Nine
Configurations[1]

(Passages from the *T'ung tien*)

The king of Wu asked Sun Wu: "On 'dispersive terrain,' the officers and troops are thinking of their families.[2] As we cannot engage in battle with them, we must solidly defend our positions and not go forth. If the enemy attacks our small cities; plunders our fields; prevents us from gathering firewood; blocks our major roads; and awaits our emptiness and depletion to urgently advance and attack, what should we do?"

Sun Wu replied: "When the enemy has deeply penetrated our capital region, putting numerous fortifications and cities behind them, their officers and men regard the army as their family, are focused in their intentions, and lightly enter into battle.[3] [On the contrary] our troops are in their native state; they feel secure on their territory and embrace life. Therefore in battle formation they are not firm, when they engage in battle they are not victorious. We should assemble the people and gather the masses; collect the foodstuffs, livestock, and cloth; defend the walled cities and prepare [to defend] the passes; and dispatch light troops to sever their supply routes. If they are not able to provoke us into battle; their provisions fail to arrive; and there's nothing in the countryside that they can plunder, their Three Armies will be in difficulty.[4] Take advantage of the situation to entice them, and then we can be successful.

If we want to engage in battle in the countryside we must rely upon the strategic configuration of power. Utilize ravines to establish ambushes.[5] Lacking ravines, we must conceal ourselves in the weather, darkness, dusk, and fog, going forth where they will not expect it, suddenly striking their indolent forces. Then we will achieve results."

The king of Wu asked Sun Wu: "Suppose we have reached 'light terrain' and have just entered the enemy's borders.[6] Our officers and men are thinking of turning back. It's hard to advance, but easy to withdraw. We do not yet have ravines and defiles behind us, and the Three Armies are fearful. The commanding general wants to advance, the officers and troops want to retreat, so above and below are of different minds. The enemy is defending his walled cities and fortifications, putting his chariots and cavalry in good order. Some occupy positions to our fore, others strike our rear. What should we do?"

Sun Wu replied: "When we have reached 'light terrain' the officers and men are not yet focused because their task is entering the border, not waging battle. Do not approach his famous cities nor traverse his major roads. Feign doubt, pretend confusion. Show him that we are about to depart. Then initially select elite cavalry to silently enter their territory and plunder their cattle, horses, and other domestic animals. When the Three Armies observe that they were able to advance they will not be afraid. Divide our superior soldiers and have them secretly prepare ambushes. Should the enemy come up, strike without hesitation; if they do not come up, then abandon the ambushes and depart."

He also said "Suppose the army has entered the enemy's borders. The enemy solidifies his fortifications without engaging in battle. Our officers and troops are thinking of returning home, but [even] if we want to retreat it would also be difficult.[7] This is referred to as 'light terrain.' We should select elite cavalry to establish ambushes on the strategic roads. When we withdraw the enemy will pursue us; when they come up, strike them."

The king of Wu asked Sun Wu: "On 'contentious terrain' suppose the enemy arrives first, occupies the strategic positions and holds the advantageous ones with selected troops and well-trained soldiers.[8] Some of them go forth, others assume defensive positions, thereby being prepared against our unorthodox tactics. What should we do?"

Sun Wu replied: "The rule for fighting on 'contentious terrain' is that one who yields will gain, while one who fights will lose. If the enemy has gained a position, then be careful not to attack it. Draw him away by pretending to go off. Set up flags, beat the drums, and move swiftly toward what he loves. Drag wood to raise clouds of dust, befuddle his ears and eyes. Divide up our superior troops, secretly placing them in ambush. The enemy will certainly come forth to rescue [the endangered target]. What others want we will give them; what they abandon we will take. That is the Way (Tao) to fight for land [they occupy] first.

If we arrive first and the enemy uses this strategy, then select fierce troops to solidly defend our position. Have our light troops pursue [the enemy's feigned departure], splitting some off to set up ambushes in the ravines and defiles. If the enemy turns about to fight, the troops in ambush on the flanks should rise up. This is the Way (Tao) to achieve complete victory."

The king of Wu asked Sun Wu: "If on 'traversable terrain' where movement is easy we are about to isolate the enemy and we want to ensure he cannot advance, we must order our cities along the border to improve their defensive preparations, thoroughly sever all open roads, and secure the blockades at the passes.[9] Suppose we have not planned for it beforehand, while the enemy has already made such preparations. They will be able to advance, but we will not be able to go forth. If our numbers are moreover equal, what then?"

Sun Wu replied: "Since we cannot go forth but they can come up, we should split off some troops and conceal them. Our defenders should appear at ease and lax. Display incapability, and the enemy will definitely arrive. Establish ambushes, conceal ourselves in the grass, and go forth where he doesn't expect it. Then we can be successful."

The king of Wu asked Sun Wu: "On 'focal terrain' one values being first. If the road is far and we mobilize after the enemy, even though we race our chariots and gallop our horses we will not be able to arrive first. What then?"

Sun Wu replied: "[Focal terrain is] territory bordered by three states with roads open in the four directions. If we and the enemy oppose each other, while on the side there are other states, then one who would be referred to as 'first' must dispatch polite emissaries with generous gifts, to make alliances with the neighboring states. Establish friendly relations with them and secure their favor. Then even though our troops arrive after the enemy, the masses [of the region] will already be allied with us. With picked soldiers and well-trained troops they will block the advantageous positions and occupy them. They will sustain our military affairs and make our provisions substantial. Order our chariots and cavalry to go in and out with an attitude of respectful anticipation. We will have the support of the masses, while the enemy will have lost its partisans. The armies of the feudal states, like the horns of an ox,[10] thundering the drums will attack en masse. The enemy will be startled and terrified, and no one will know what they ought to do."

The king of Wu asked Sun Wu: "Suppose we have lead the troops deep into 'heavy terrain,' bypassing a great many places so our supply routes are cut off or blocked.[11] Suppose we want to return home but can not get past their strategic configuration of power. If we want to forage on the enemy's land and maintain our troops without loss, then what should we do?"

Sun Wu replied; "Whenever we remain on heavy terrain the officers and troops will readily be courageous. If the supply routes are no longer open, then we must plunder to extend our provisions. Whatever the lower ranks obtain in grain or cloth must all be forwarded to the top, and those that collect the most will be rewarded. The warriors will [no longer] think about returning home.

If you want to turn about and go forth, urgently make defensive preparations. Deepen the moats and raise the ramparts, showing the enemy our determination to remain indefinitely. The enemy will suspect we have an open route somewhere, and will remove themselves from the critical roads. Then we can order our light chariots to sally forth silently, the dust flying up, using the cattle and horses as bait. If the enemy goes forth, beat the drums and follow him. [Prior to this] secretly conceal some warriors in ambush, setting the time with them so that our forces within and without can launch a coordinated attack. The enemy's defeat can then be known."

The king of Wu asked Sun Wu: "Suppose we enter 'entrapping terrain'—mountains, rivers, ravines, and defiles.[12] The road is difficult to follow; we have been on the move for a long time and the troops are tired. The enemy lies before us, and is ambushing our rear. His encampment occupies a position to the left, while they defend against our right.[13] His superior chariots and skilled cavalry are pressing us on a constricted road. What then?"

Sun Wu replied: "First have the light chariots advance about ten *li* so that they and the enemy are observing each other. When our [main army] has reached their ravines and defiles, deploy some to go to the left, others to the right, while the commanding general conducts observations in all directions. Select vacuities and seize them, then have all our forces converge together on the road, stopping only when tired."

The king of Wu asked Sun Wu: "Suppose we have entered 'encircled terrain,' so that before us there is a strong enemy, and to our rear precipitous and difficult ground.[14] The enemy has severed our supply lines, and is taking advantage of our moving disposition. If they beat their drums and yell but do not advance—in order to observe our capability—what should we do?"

Sun-Wu replied: "On 'encircled terrain' it is appropriate to block up all the openings, showing the troops that there is no place to go. Then they will regard the army as their family; the multitude will be of one mind; and the strength of the Three Armies will be united. Furthermore, steam food for several days, not displaying any fire or smoke, thus creating the appearance of decay, confusion, paucity of numbers, and weakness.[15] When the enemy sees us their battle preparations will certainly be light.

Exhort and incite our officers and troops, cause their anger to be aroused. Assume formation, deploying our superior troops in ambush in the ravines and defiles to the left and right. Beat the drums and go forth. If the enemy opposes us, fervently strike them, concentrating on breaking through. Fight in the front, consolidate in the rear, and set our flanks out to the left and right."

[The king of Wu] again asked: "Suppose the enemy is surrounded by our forces. They lie in ambush and make deep plans. They display enticements to us, they tire us with their pennants, moving all about as if in confusion. We do not know how to deal with this. What should we do?"

Sun Wu replied: "Have a thousand men take up pennants, divide up, and block off the strategic roads. Have our light troops advance and try to provoke the enemy. Deploy our battle arrays but do not press them. Intercept them, but do not go off. This is the art of defeating stratagems."

The king of Wu asked Sun Wu: "Suppose our army has gone out beyond the borders, and our forces are arrayed in front of the enemy. The enemy's forces arrive in great number, encircling us several layers deep. We want to suddenly burst out but all four sides are blocked.[16] If we want to encourage our officers and incite our masses of troops, have them risk their lives and crush the encirclement, then how should we do it?"

Sun Wu replied: "Make the moats deeper and the ramparts higher, showing that we are making preparations to defend our position. Be quiet and still, without moving, to conceal our capability. Announce orders to the Three Armies to feign hopelessness. Kill your cattle and burn the [supply] wagons to feast our warriors. Completely burn all provisions, fill in the wells, level the stoves, cut off your hair, cast aside your caps, completely eliminate all thoughts of life, have no further plans.[17] When the officers are determined to die, then have them polish their armor and sharpen their blades. When their *ch'i* has been united and their strength as one, some should attack the two flanks, thundering the drums and yelling fervently. The enemy will also become frightened, and no one will know how to withstand us. Elite troops and detached units should urgently attack their rear. This is the Way (Tao) by which to lose the road and seek life. Thus it is said that 'one who is in difficulty but doesn't make plans is impoverished; one who is impoverished and doesn't fight is lost.'"

The king of Wu also asked: "What if we surround the enemy?"

Sun Wu replied: "Mountain peaks and valley confines that are difficult to traverse are referred to as the '[means to] impoverish invaders.'[18] The method for attacking them is to set our troops in ambush in dark and concealed places. Open a road for [the enemy] to depart, show them a path for flight.[19] When they are seeking life and escaping [from death] they certainly won't have any will to fight. Then we can strike them; even if they are numerous they will certainly be destroyed."

The *Art of War* also states: "If the enemy is on 'fatal terrain,' the *ch'i* of his officers and troops will be courageous. If we want to strike him the strategy is to [seemingly] accord with him and not resist. Secretly guard against his advantageous positions. Sever his supply routes. If you are afraid that he has unorthodox troops concealed that have not been observed, have our bowmen and crossbowmen guard against his positions."

Four Changes[20]

(Tomb Text)

[. . . . . There are roads that are not followed; there are armies that are not attacked]; there are fortified cities that are not assaulted; there is terrain for which one does not contend; there are orders[21] from the ruler [which are not implemented[22]].

As for the roads that are not followed: when we enter [enemy territory] shallowly, then affairs to the fore will not be known. When we enter deeply, then advantages to the rear can not be consolidated. If we move then it will not be advantageous; if we remain still then we will be imprisoned. In such cases do not follow them.

As for armies that are not attacked: our two armies have intercepted each other and encamped. We estimate[23] that our strength is sufficient to destroy their army and capture their general. [However], if we estimate it from a long-range perspective, there are [those who excel in] unorthodox strategic power and skillful tactics among them, and the army . . . . . general. In such cases, even though the army can be attacked, do not attack it.

As for fortified cities that are not assaulted: We estimate that our strength is sufficient to seize it. If we seize it, it will not be of any advantage to the fore; if we gain it we will not be able to protect it at the rear.[24] If our strength [equals?] theirs, the city certainly will not be taken. If, when we gain the advantages of a forward (position) the city will then surrender by itself, while if we do not gain such advantages (the city) will not cause harm to the rear—in such cases, even though the city can be assaulted, do not assault it.

As for terrain that is not contested: in mountain valleys where the water [flow?] is unable to sustain life[25] . . . . . empty. . . . . In such cases do not contend for it.

As for orders of the ruler which are not implemented: if the ruler's orders are contrary to these "four changes," then do not implement them. . . . . Implement. . . . . Affairs . . . . . changes, then he knows how to employ the military.

Two
Questions

(Passages Preserved in the *T'ung-tien*)[26]

The king of Wu asked Sun Wu: "The enemy is courageous and unafraid, arrogant and reckless. His soldiers are numerous and strong. What should we do?"

Sun Wu said: "Speak and act submissively in order to accord with their intentions.[27] Do not cause them to comprehend [the situation], and thereby increase their indolence. In accord with the enemy's shifts and changes, submerge [our forces] in ambush to await [the moment]. Then do not look at their forward motion, nor look back to their rearward movement, but strike them in the middle. Even though they are numerous, they can be taken. The Tao for attacking the arrogant is to not engage their advance front."

The king of Wu asked Sun Wu: "The enemy is securely holding the mountains and ravines, occupying all the advantageous positions.[28] Their provisions are also sufficient. [Even though] we challenge them they do not come forth. They take advantage of cracks [in our defenses] to raid and plunder. What should we do?"

Sun Wu said: "Segment and deploy our forces to defend the strategic points; exercise vigilance in preparations, do not be indolent. Deeply investigate their true situation, secretly await their laxity. Entice them with profit, prevent them from gathering firewood. When they have not gained anything in a long time, they will inevitably change by themselves. Wait until they leave their strongholds; seize what they love. [Even though] the enemy forcibly occupies precipitous passes, we will still be able to destroy them."

King of Wu's Questions

(Tomb Text)[29]

The king of Wu asked Sun-tzu: "When the six generals[30] divide up and occupy Chin's territory, who will perish first? Who will be solid and successful?"

Sun-tzu said: "The Fan and Chung-hang clans[31] will be the first to perish."

"Who will be next?"

"The Chih clan will be next."

"Who will be next?"

"The Han and Wei will be next. The Chao have not lost their ancient laws, so the state of Chin will revert to them."

The king of Wu asked: "May I hear the explanation?"

Sun-tzu said: "Yes. The Fan and Chung-hang clans, in regulating their fields, take eighty paces as the length and one hundred sixty paces as the breadth,[32] and impose taxes of one fifth [of the produce] on them. The fields [under administration][33] are narrow, the warriors attached [to the fields] numerous. [Because] they impose a tax of one-fifth, the ducal house is rich. The ducal house is rich, the attached warriors are numerous. The ruler is arrogant, the ministers extravagant. They hope for achievement and frequently engage in warfare. Thus I say they will perish first.

"[The Chih, in regulating their fields, take ninety paces as the length and one hundred eighty paces as the breadth, and impose taxes of one fifth on them. The fields under administration are narrow, the attached warriors numerous. Because they impose a tax of one-fifth, the ducal house is rich.][34] The ducal house is rich, the attached warriors numerous. The ruler is arrogant, the ministers extravagant. They hope for achievement and frequently engage in warfare. Thus the Chih will be next after the Fan and Chung-hang.

"The Han and Wei, in regulating their fields, take a hundred paces for the length and two hundred paces for the breadth, and impose taxes of one fifth on them. The lands under administration are narrow, the attached warriors are numerous. Taxing them at one fifth, the ducal house is rich. The ruler is arrogant, the ministers extravagant. They hope for achievement and frequently engage in warfare. Thus I say Han and Wei will be next after the Chih.

"The Chao, in regulating their fields, take a hundred and twenty paces for the length and two hundred forty paces for the breadth. The duke does not impose any taxes on them.[35] The ducal house is poor, their attached warriors few. The ruler is frugal, the ministers [respectful] and they thereby govern a rich populace. Thus I say it is a solid state. The state of Chin will revert to them."

The king of Wu said: "Excellent." The Tao of the true king . . . [must be] to generously love his people."

Notes
to the
General
Introduction
and
Historical
Background

Abbreviations Used in the Notes

(See also the lists at the beginning of the notes of The Art of War translation.)

AA	*Acta Asiatica*
AM	*Asia Major*
BIHP	*Bulletin of the Institute of History and Philology*
BMFEA	*Bulletin of the Museum of Far Eastern Antiquities*
BSOAS	*Bulletin of the School of Oriental and African Studies*
CC	*Chinese Culture*
CCCY	*Chin-chu chin-i editions*
EC	*Early China*
GSR	*Grammata Serica Recensa (Bernhard Karlgren, BMFEA 29 [1957])*
HJAS	*Harvard Journal of Asiatic Studies*
JAOS	*Journal of the American Oriental Society*
JAS	*Journal of Asian Studies*
JCP	*Journal of Chinese Philosophy*
JNCBRAS	*Journal of the North Central Branch, Royal Asiatic Society*
JRAS	*Journal of the Royal Asiatic Society*
KK	*K'ao-ku Hsüeh-pao*
MS	*Monumenta Serica*
PEW	*Philosophy East and West*
TP	*T'oung Pao*
WW	*Wen-wu*
LTCC WCCS	*Liu-t'ao chih-chieh,* in *Ming-pen Wu-ching Ch'i-shu chih-chieh,* vol. 2, (Shih-ti chiao-yü ch'u-pan-she, Taipei, 1972).
LT CS	K'ung Te-ch'i, *Liu-t'ao ch'ien-shuo* (Chieh-fang-chün ch'u-pan-she, Peking, 1987).
TKLT CCCY	Hsü Pei-ken, *T'ai Kung Liu-t'ao chin-chu chin-i* (Shang-wu yin-shu-kuan, Taipei, 1976).
TKLT WCHC	*T'ai Kung Liu-t'ao,* in *Ch'ung-k'an Wu-ching hui-chieh* (Chung-chou Ku-chi ch'u-pan-she, Cheng-chou, 1989).

References to various volumes in the *Seven Military Classics* are to our Westview translation: Ralph D. and Mei-chün Sawyer, *The Seven Military Classics of Ancient China,* Westview Press, Boulder, 1993. Titles are abbreviated as follows:

Art of War	*Sun-tzu's Art of War*
Ssu-ma Fa	*The Methods of the Ssu-ma*
Questions and Replies	*Questions and Replies between T'ang T'ai-tsung and Li Wei-kung*
Three Strategies	*Three Strategies of Huang Shih-kung*
Six Secret Teachings	*T'ai Kung's Six Secret Teachings*

1. The Confucius (551–479 B.C.) of the *Analects* demands courage and resoluteness in the practice of righteousness and requires that his disciples always do what is appropriate. He cultivated the six arts, which included chariot driving and archery, and in other texts refers to the terrible visage of the righteous man when he dons his armor. He also indicated that the *chün-tzu,* or perfected man, does not compete, which was taken by later Confucians as evidence that conflict and warfare are inappropriate for civilized men. Other early Confucians, such as Mencius (371–289 B.C.) and Hsün-tzu (a Confucian of the late Warring States period who wrote extensively on military affairs), were cognizant of the inescapable necessity of wars and armies. Only after several centuries, as the Confucians became further removed from the pristine spirit of their founder and the realities of the early context, did the tendency toward pacificism, or (perhaps more correctly) the *civil,* emerge and gain ascendancy. This is a complex topic that requires an extensive separate analytic work.

2. The dates assigned to the Spring and Autumn and the Warring States periods vary somewhat depending on the writer's predelictions. The *Ch'un ch'iu,* or *Spring and Autumn Annals,* which chronicles events from 722 to 481 B.C., was traditionally held to have been edited didactically by Confucius and was one of the essential *Five Classics.* (Confucius no doubt used the work for educational purposes and may have emended it to some extent, but he cannot be considered the compiler or editor in any real sense.) The *Tso chuan,* purportedly a commentary to the *Spring and Autumn Annals* but in actuality a self-existent work that portrays the period in considerable detail, covers the years 722 to 468 B.C. (or 464 B.C.; opinion seems to vary). The *Intrigues of the Warring States* contains some material from the early fifth century B.C., but it basically records the people and events of the period 403–221 B.C., when the Ch'in officially assumed the mantle of imperial rule. Thus the Spring and Autumn period should refer to 722–481 B.C. and the Warring States era to 403–221 B.C., traditional dates that are adopted herein. However, there is also considerable logic to dating the Spring and Autumn period from the movement of the Western Chou capital to the east in 771 B.C. and extending the Warring States period to cover the interval between the end of the *Tso chuan* material and 403 B.C. This gives dates such as those Herrlee G. Creel adopts in *The Origins of Statecraft in China* (University of Chicago Press, Chicago, 1970, p. 47): 770–464 and 463–222 B.C.

3. Lord Shang (died 338 B.C.), although much reviled by Confucian tradition, had great impact in reforming the laws and institutions of the state of Ch'in. Among his important contributions were imposing stringent laws; advocating and implementing a severe but certain system of rewards and punishments; restricting the conferring of rank to military achievements; organizing the entire populace as well as the military into groups of five and ten, thereby creating a dual-purpose, mutual guarantee system that facilitated immediate conscription; and eliminating the boundary paths between fields, making land a salable commodity. (Some of these reforms may have had antecedents, including those involving the military. For example, see Fu Shao-chieh, *Wu-tzu chin-chu chin-i,* Shang-wu yin-shu-kuan, Taipei, 1976, p. 17.) The remnants of Lord Shang's book have been translated by J.J.L. Duyvendak as *The Book of Lord Shang* (Arthur Probsthain, London, 1928; reprint, University of Chicago Press, 1963).

4. Han Fei-tzu (died 233 B.C.), a famous Legalist and former disciple of Hsün-tzu (298–238 B.C.), left an extensive treatise which has been translated in full by W. K. Liao (*The Complete Works of Han Fei-tzu,* 2 vols., Arthur Probsthain, London, 1959 [reprint of 1939 edition]), and as selections by Burton Watson (*Han Fei-tzu; Basic Writings,* Columbia University Press, New York, 1964.)

5. "Virtue," although encompassing the basic meaning of moral virtue, was the object of much complex thought in ancient China and came to have numerous nuances and technical meanings, including "power" and "potency." Some of these are discussed briefly in the footnotes to the translations. In general, "Virtue" (capitalized) is used to translate the term *te* whenever the transcendent dimensions are critical—when the cultivation of *te* (virtue) leads to Virtue, which is synonymous with moral achievement and the inner power that accompanies it. Within the context of Taoist texts and to a certain extent military writings influenced by them, the term *te* indicates inner potency or power—generally as contrasted with and distinguished from the moral and ethical realm because the artificial constraints of rites, morals, and ethics were anathema to most Taoist-oriented thinkers (neo-Taoism and eclectic works excepted). A specialized body of literature has developed in recent years, due partly to the discovery of previously unknown manuscripts; these writings offer various conceptualizations and systematizations under the rubric of "Huang-Lao" thought, although there is by no means universal accord that these trends constitute a school or an affiliation. Specialists are no doubt aware of them, but the general reader may find Arthur Waley's classic comments on the term *te* in his introduction to *The Way and Its Power* (Grove Press, New York, 1958), or D. C. Lau's thoughts in his translation of the *Tao Te Ching* (Chinese University Press, Hong Kong, 1982) of interest. Also see the notes to the introduction to the *Art of War* for further discussion and sources, and Aat Vervoorn's article "Taoism, Legalism, and the Quest for Order in Warring States China," *JCP* 8 (September 1981): 303–24.

Throughout we translate *te* as "virtue" when it refers to morals and ethics and as "Virtue" when it connotes the attainment of a special status—with inherent power—through the cultivation of virtue, which is not unlike the original meaning of *virtus.* The questions of its transcendent dimensions, relationship to potency, and metaphysical realization in warfare command must be left to another book and the studies of experts.

6. Every "civilized" dynasty, including the Shang, appears to have exploited "barbarian"—defined by reference to the dynasty's own self-perceived level of civilization—peoples against other, similar peoples. In many cases they were even settled in the frontier regions, just within state borders, and shouldered the burden of dynastic defense. However, this first appeared as an articulated policy in the Han era and was symptomatic of the steppe-sedentary conflict. Discussions may be found in Owen Lattimore, *Inner Asian Frontiers of China* (Beacon Press, Boston, 1962); Yü Ying-shih, *Trade and Expansion in Han China* (University of California Press, Berkeley, 1967); and Sechin Jagchid and Van Jay Symons, *Peace, War, and Trade Along the Great Wall* (Indiana University Press, Bloomington, 1989).

7. This discussion of the Shang is based on standard Western texts and monographs, such as Kwang-chih Chang's *Shang Civilization* (Yale University Press,

New Haven, 1980) and Cheng Te-k'un's *Shang China* (Heffer, Cambridge, 1960), supplemented by the normal range of articles from specialist journals, such as *Early China* and *Wen wu*, and the following classic works: Sun Lin, *Hsia Shang shih-kao* (Wen-wu ch'u-pan-she, Peking, 1987), and Tuan Chen-mei, *Yin-hsü k'ao-ku-shih* (Chung-chou ku-chi ch'u-pan-she, Honan, 1991). They are listed in the bibliography under the sections for historical materials.

8. A major point of contention is whether slaves were used solely for domestic work and perhaps occasional agricultural activities or whether the entire Shang edifice was based on the systematic use and exploitation of a slave class of agricultural workers. Depending on whether a Marxist or another synthetic framework is employed, the evidence is defined and interpreted differently. However, it appears that enslaved prisoners and their descendants were found largely in domestic work rather than agriculture.

9. In the Shang and Chou dynasties, the presence of the lineage's ancestral temple virtually constituted the defining feature of a capital city. Naturally, various deities, spirits, and animistic forces were also worshipped, depending on the period, state, and beliefs of the time. The ruler's ancestral temple always played a critical role in prewar discussions and in prebattle ceremonies, as is evident in the *Seven Military Classics*.

10. In the past decade a number of lengthy, minutely detailed articles based on historical records, recently recovered bronze inscriptions, calendrical reconstructions, and celestial phenomena have discussed the probable date for Chou's conquest of the Shang. The traditionally held date of 1122 B.C. proposed by the Han dynasty scholar Liu Hsin has been invalidated emphatically by David Pankenier's proof that the rare five-planet conjunction recorded in the *Bamboo Annals* actually occurred on May 28, 1059 B.C. (See David W. Pankenier, "Astronomical Dates in Shang and Western Zhou," *EC* 7 [1981–82], pp. 2–5.) Various other dates previously proposed—such as 1111, 1075 (T'ang Lan), 1027, 1025, and 1023 (Bernhard Karlgren)—have also been discarded. Current arguments, based on essentially the same evidence—including the critical five-planet conjunction—variously supplemented or interpreted, produce three theories: Pankenier's January 20, 1046 B.C. (Pankenier, "Astronomical Dates," pp. 2–37, in particular p. 16); David S. Nivison's January 15, 1045 B.C. (originally proposed in his article "The Dates of Western Chou," *HJAS* 43 [December 1983]: 481–580), and 1040 (according to his note revising the *JAS* article published almost simultaneously in *Early China* [EC 8 (1982–83), pp. 76–78]); and Edward Shaughnessy, who supports Nivison's first date of January 15, 1045 (see "'New' Evidence on the Zhou Conquest," *EC* 6 [1980–81], pp. 57–79, and "The 'Current' *Bamboo Annals* and the Date of the Zhou Conquest of Shang," *EC 11–12* [1985–87], pp. 33–60, especially p. 45). Chou Fa-kao also supports the 1045 date in a Chinese review article ("Wu Wang k'e Shang te nien-tai wen-t'i," in *Li-shih Yü-yen Yen-chiu-so chi-k'an* [*BIHP*] 56, no. 1 [1985], Taipei, pp. 5–41). Because 1045 B.C. appears well-founded, it is adopted herein. However, for further discussions, see Chang, *Shang Civilization*, pp. 15–19; Creel, *The Origins of Statecraft in China*, pp. 487–91, who suggests accepting the traditional date of 1122 B.C. even though acknowledging it may be inaccurate; Tung Tso-pin, "Hsi-Chou nien-li-p'u," *BIHP* 23 (1951), pp. 681–760; Ch'ü Wan-li, "Hsi-Chou shih-shih kai-shu," *BIHP* 42 (1971),

pp. 775–802; Jung Men-yüan, "Shih-t'an Hsi-Chou chi-nien," *Chung-hua wen-shih lun-ts'ung* 1 (1980), pp. 16–20; Ho Yu-ch'i, "Chou Wu-wang fa-Chou te nien-tai wen-t'i," *Chung-shan Ta-hsüeh hsüeh-pao* 1 (1981), pp. 64–70; and Edward L. Shaughnessy, "On the Authenticity of the *Bamboo Annals*," *HJAS*, 46 (June 1986): 149–80.

11. The casting of massive ritual cauldrons, some weighing several hundred pounds, and the production of bronze weapons required hundreds of skilled artisans engaged in coordinated activity.

12. It is well-known that in the plains area of central China—the locus of the Shang dynasty—the soft yellowish earth can easily be dug with a sharpened wooden stick or other nonmetallic object. Naturally, agricultural efficiency improves with metal plows and hoes, but they were not essential and were rarely, if ever, used in the Shang era. (See Chang, *Shang Civilization*, p. 223; Hsu and Linduff, *Western Chou Civilization*, pp. 75 and 353; and T. R. Treger, *A Geography of China*. [Aldine, Chicago, 1965], pp. 50–51.) A contrary view is taken by the traditionalist Ch'en Liang-tso in a lengthy, detailed review of the archaeological evidence. He concludes that the Shang already had bronze agricultural implements, which were used concurrently with those made of inexpensive materials such as stone and bone. Moreover, in his view, these implements were employed extensively throughout the Chou period until they were finally displaced by iron in the Warring States era. (See Ch'en Liang-tso, "Wo-kuo ku-tai te ch'ing-t'ung nung-chü," *Han-hsüeh yen-chiu* vol. 2, no. 1 [June 1984]: pp. 135–166; vol. 2, no. 2 [December 1984]: 363–402.)

13. Rice, which requires wet cultivation, originated in the south and was little grown in Shang central areas. For general discussions of agriculture in China, see *Science and Civilisation in China*, vol. 6, part 2, *Agriculture*, by Francesca Bray, (Cambridge University Press, Cambridge, 1984); Kwang-chih Chang, ed., *Food in Chinese Culture*, (Yale University Press, New Haven, 1977); and E. N. Anderson, *The Food of China* (Yale University Press, New Haven, 1988).

14. The enormous numbers of animals used in the almost continuous sacrifices, which went to feed the priestly caste and the nobility, is cited as evidence that cattle and other animals must have been raised. Cf. Chang, *Shang Civilization*, pp. 142–45, 230.

15. See ibid., pp. 195–96. The king's wives are also recorded as having commanded troops and as having personal forces.

16. Cf. Cheng Te-k'un, *Shang China*, pp. 208–12; Chang, *Shang Civilization*, p. 249. The total number in the army during wartime is sometimes estimated at thirty thousand (Cheng, *Shang China*, p. 210), which would be many measures smaller than the number of troops reported as having engaged in the battle of Mu-yeh. This suggests that the more limited figures apply only to the early to middle Shang era—perhaps with significant expansion later—as well as overstatement.

17. See Fan Yuzhou, "Military Campaign Inscriptions from YH 127," *BSOAS* vol. 52, no. 3 (1989): pp. 533–48; and David N. Keightley, who cites the extensive nature of the king's travels in "The Late Shang State," in *The Origins of Chinese Civilization* (University of California Press, Berkeley, 1983), pp. 552–55.

18. A later term, the Three Armies (*san chün*), was used constantly to refer to

a campaign army. Whether it originates with these three divisions (*san shih*) or was simply an organizational creation (such as for upper, middle, and lower) is not clear. (Cf. Chin Hsiang-heng, "Ts'ung chia-ku pu-ts'u yen-chiu Yin Shang chün-lü-chung chih wang-tsu san-hsing san-shih," *Chung-kuo wen-tzu* 52 [1974], pp. 1–26; and the material on military organization that concludes the introduction.)

19. A basic distinction in the Shang and Early Chou was made between the people who dwelled within the *kuo*, the "state," and those who lived outside it. At this time a state was essentially a city fortified by surrounding walls, with the privileged class residing within its protective confines. The city dwellers furnished the warriors, whereas those outside the walls were not required to serve or were merely conscripted as menial support (if they were not alien peoples under the control of the *kuo*). This distinction declined as the scope of warfare eventually expanded in the Spring and Autumn period. (See, for example, Hsü Hsi-ch'en, "Chou-tai ping-chih ch'u-lun," *Chung-kuo-shih yen-chiu* 4 [1985], pp. 4–5.)

20. On warfare objectives, see Yang Hung, *Chung-kuo ku-ping-ch'i lun-ts'ung*, Ming-wen shu-chü, Taipei, 1983, p. 8. Although agriculturally based and accordingly prosperous, the Shang ruling house required vast riches to distribute to the nobility, whether directly or indirectly (through allowing them to retain the plunders of war). Because the Shang domain was extensive and the nobility counted in the tens of thousands of families, it was rather voracious. For example, in one battle the Shang reportedly took thirty thousand prisoners (see Chang, *Shang Civilization*, p. 194).

21. Among the peoples particularly chosen for sacrifice were the Ch'iang, from whose Chiang clan many of the principal wives of the Chou royalty came. The T'ai Kung, adviser to Kings Wen and Wu of the Chou, was also of Ch'iang origin. It seems possible that the Shang's enmity toward the Ch'iang drove them to an alliance with the Chou, although this is not known. See E. G. Pulleyblank, "The Chinese and Their Neighbors in Prehistoric and Early Historic Times," in *The Origins of Chinese Civilization*, pp. 420–21; Chang, *Shang Civilization*, p. 249.

22. In the Shang and probably the Early Chou, weapons were generally stored in government armories and were distributed only when required for military campaigns. (See Yen I-p'ing, "Yin Shang ping-chih," *Chung-kuo wen-tzu*, NS 7 [1983], p. 39.) This reflected the considerable cost of weapons and diffused any threat of an armed political revolt against the ruling family. Furthermore, because of the cost factor, some researchers believe conscripted infantrymen were generally not furnished with serious weapons until the infantry grew in significance and less expensive iron weapons became available. For example, see Chung-kuo chün-shih-shih Pien-hsieh-tsu, *Chung-kuo chün-shih-shih*, vol. 4; *Ping-fa* (Chieh-fang-chün ch'u-pan-she, Peking, 1988), p. 2.

23. The dagger-ax derives its name from the daggerlike blade horizontally affixed near the top of a long wooden shaft, but it is primarily a hooking weapon. Wounds are inflicted by swinging down and pulling forward, with the curved knifelike blade cutting in and hooking the enemy (rather than delivering a crushing, chopping blow directly into the soldier as an ax blade would. The ancients also had axes, but their role seems to have been limited and perhaps largely ceremonial.) See Chou Wei, *Chung-kuo ping-ch'i shih-kao* (Ming-wen

shu-chü, Taipei, 1980), pp. 64–88; Hayashi Minao, *Chūgoku In-shū jidai no buki* (Kyoto Daigaku Jimbun Kagaku Kenkyūsho, Kyoto, 1972), pp. 3–96; Lao Kan, "Chan-kuo shih-tai te chan-cheng fang-fa," *BIHP* 37 (1967): pp. 53–57; and Shih Chang-ju,"Hsiao-t'un Yin-tai te ch'eng-t'ao ping-ch'i," *BIHP* 22 (1950): pp. 59–65. A number of specialized articles have discussed this indigenous weapon, including Ma Heng, "Ko chi chih yen-chiu," *Yenching hsüeh-pao,* no. 5 (1929): pp. 745–53; Kuo Pao-chün, "Ko chi yü-lun," *BIHP,* 5, no. 3 (1935): pp. 313–26; and Li Chi, "Yü-pei ch'u-t'u ch'ing-t'ung kou-ping fen-lei t'u-ch'ich," *BIHP* 22 (1950): pp. 1–31.

24. The spear was already extant in Shang times and no doubt dates back to the neolithic period. Shang spears boasted bronze spearheads (as well as those made of other materials, such as stone and bone), but with the development of iron technology, iron tips appeared by the Warring States period. In addition, the longer spears suited to use with the chariot (and thus also employed by infantry) in the Shang and Early Chou tended to be too unwieldy for infantrymen and consequently were shortened somewhat in the Warring States period. Conversely, the blades tended to become longer and sharper in the early Spring and Autumn period and continued to undergo similar modifications thereafter. For detailed discussions, in addition to references listed in the bibliography, see Chou Wei, *Chung-kuo ping-ch'i shih-kao,* pp. 98–102; and Hiyashi Minao, *Chūgoku In-Shū jidai no buki,* pp. 97–130.

25. The bow was already a major part of the Shang warrior's arsenal and was generally carried by the chariot commander. Composite bows appeared early, increasing in complexity, size, and strength over the centuries with improvements in bonding and crafting technology. Various materials, including bamboo, were employed and were matched for greatest composite strength under tension. In the Shang era wooden shafted arrows generally mounted bronze points, although bone, stone, and other materials were also employed. However, bronze continued to prevail even after iron had generally appeared in the Warring States. For an overview and detailed discussions, see Hiyashi Minao, *Chūgoku In-Shū jidai no buki,* pp. 243–99 (on bows) and pp. 321–74 (on arrows); Yoshida Mitsukuni (who also discusses cross-bows), "Yumi to ōyumi," *Tōyōshi kenkyū* 12, no. 3 (1953): pp. 82–92; and the classic report and analysis of Shih Chang-ju, "Hsiao-t'un Yin-tai te ch'eng-t'ao ping-ch'i," pp. 25–44 (on the bow) and pp. 44–54 (on arrows).

26. See the last part of the introduction for an annotated discussion of the development and history of armor in ancient China.

27. In recent years there have been a number of claims for widespread use of bronze swords in the Early Chou, such as Hsu and Linduff, *Western Chou Civilization,* p. 81. However, although the innovative horizon for many weapons and technological achievements continues to be pushed earlier and earlier with each new discovery, it would seem these would best be termed daggers rather than swords, both in length and function. See the last part of the introduction for an annotated discussion of the sword's history and some of the issues surrounding it.

28. "Chien-hsüan," *Lü-shih ch'un-ch'iu* (CCCY edition, Shang-wu yin-shu-kuan, Taipei, 1985), p. 204. Although claims that the Hsia had chariots are generally discounted, such assertions continue to be made, including in the recent PRC publication *Chung-kuo chün-shih-shih,* vol. 4 *Ping-fa,* p. 5.

29. See the last part of the introduction for an annotated discussion of the introduction and history of the chariot in China.

30. See the discussion of military organization in the last part of the introduction for further information and references.

31. The *Ssu-ma Fa* discusses the practice and objectives of holding such hunts, and they are mentioned in a number of the other *Seven Military Classics* as well as in the *Tso chuan* and the "Ta Ssu-ma" section of the *Chou li*. (See the translator's introduction and notes to the *Ssu-ma Fa* translation for further information.) Also see *Ping-fa*, pp. 32–33; Yen I-p'ing, "Yin Shang ping-chih," p. 40; and Hsü Hsi-ch'en, "Chou-tai ping-chih ch'u-lun," p. 10.

The difficulty in attaining the required chariot skills and their expense are cited by some historians as the critical factors that made the rise of infantry units inevitable. Conscripts, whatever their class origin, simply could not be trained in the time available. For example, see Yang K'uan, "Ch'un-ch'iu Chan-kuo-chien feng-chien te chün-shih tsu-chih ho chan-cheng te pien-hua," *Li-shih chiao-hsüeh* 4 (1954), p. 12.

32. One tradition asserts that the Chou were descendants of the Hsia, whereas modern scholars such as K. C. Chang postulate that the peoples of the "Three Dynasties" were culturally and racially alike but politically distinct. (See K. C. Chang, "Sandai Archaeology and the Formation of States in Ancient China: Processual Aspects of the Origins of Chinese Civilization," in *The Origins of Chinese Civilization*, ed. David N. Keightly, pp. 495–521; and Chang, *Shang Civilization*, pp. 348–55.)

33. The Chou's "barbarian" origin was generally recognized in antiquity, and the *Shih chi* explicitly records Tan Fu—the Chou progenitor—as deliberately abandoning nomadic ways after his people resettled with him in the south to avoid conflict with other barbarians. (See the "Chou Annals.")

34. King Chou of the Shang was persuaded by opulent bribes not only to release the future King Wen from detainment but also to name him "Lord of the West." Under this title he was entrusted with responsibility for defending Shang's flank and thereby afforded an excellent pretext for developing and exercising his own military powers.

35. It is generally thought that speed, mobility, and surprise marked the Chou campaign, with the chariot playing a key role. However, there are dissenting views, such as Hsu and Linduff (*Western Chou Civilization*, p. 88), who consider other factors more important, such as the effective deployment of infantry, longer swords, and superior armor (see Hsu and Linduff, p. 81).

36. According to the *Shih chi*, the Shang had a one-hundred-thousand-man campaign army in the south, which could have amounted to a third or more of their total available forces and perhaps included some of their best units. King Chou of the Shang compounded his difficulties by ignoring repeated warnings about the potential danger posed by the Chou and notice of their actual advance. (Numbers from this period are extremely unreliable and should only be understood as indicative of comparative size.)

37. Because the antiquity of the *Six Secret Teachings* is almost universally denied, it seems possible that this revolutionary impulse may have been directed toward the imperial Ch'in by writers very late in the Warring States period. Their

hatred of the brutal Ch'in would account for the ferocity of the policies, with such fervor being envisioned in the heroes of the ancient Chou as they gambled everything to overturn the vile despot. Whether the combatants observed any civilizing rites (such as in the early Spring and Autumn period) in the centuries prior to the battle at Mu-yeh is doubtful, but the traditional view assumes that they did.

38. See Hsü Pei-ken, *Chung-kuo kuo-fang ssu-hsiang-shih*, pp. 291–93. The Chou dynasty ruled in part through its avowed policy of cultural acculturation, transforming the diverse people within its domain through gradual assimilation while absorbing and integrating new characteristics themselves. The concept of the Central States and the Hua-Hsia identity arose with them, although the surviving states in the Warring States period still retained distinctive regional personalities and characteristics. For a general discussion, see Cho-yun Hsu and Katheryn M. Linduff, *Western Chou Civilization* (Yale University Press, New Haven, 1988), chapters 4–6.

39. Historical materials from the Chou period and thereafter, such as the *Shih chi*, were clearly influenced by the effective propaganda efforts of the Chou both prior and subsequent to the conquest. Their vile portrait of the evil Shang ruler was amplified by later writers—especially the Confucians—for didactic purposes, although not without an occasional dissenting voice (for example, Tzu Kung, *Analects* XIX:20). This is not to deny that the Shang oppressed the people or that King Chou of the Shang was not a villain. Rather, it should simply be understood that the Chou's self-portrait depicting the cause of Virtue as naturally attracting allies and politically dominating the realm was underpinned in actuality by extensive military achievements and persuasive power.

40. The Shang's triumph over King Chieh, the last evil ruler of the Hsia, was traditionally portrayed in terms similar to those describing the Chou's conquest of the Shang, but much simplified. King T'ang—the founder of the Shang dynasty—cultivated his Virtue, pursued benevolent policies, and garnered his strength on the fringe of the Hsia empire until finally engaging in a decisive battle. There was even a sagely counterpart to the T'ai Kung, the famous minister I Yin, who may have created the indirect striking tactics that proved successful for the Shang. (See Hsü Pei-ken et al., *Chung-kuo li-tai chan-cheng-shih*, 18 vols. [Li-ming, Taipei, 1976], revised edition, vol. 1, pp. 49–53, and also the early chapters of the *Shang shu* [Book of Documents]. The *Shang shu* also portrays Shang dynasty kings acting as strong supporters of virtue and as punitive agents against the unrighteous.)

41. Although the parameters of the dynastic cycle postulate an essentially continuous decline in the power of the imperial house, with allowances for temporary resurgences, recently discovered historical materials indicate that the Shang kings continued to be vigorous monarchs, mounting military expeditions and conducting tours of inspection throughout the years. Even though the last ruler—who is recorded as having been enthroned for more than sixty years—considerably debauched the image of the king, earlier kings, such as Wu Ting, were both effective and powerful.

42. The archetypal seductress played an extensive but tragic role throughout Chinese history, with several infamous examples bringing the imperial house to ruin. Even the less famous seductresses were constant sources of tension because

the almighty emperors—despite having numerous consorts, concubines, and other ladies in waiting—were easily persuaded by their favorites to grant state favors and administrative or military power to their own relatives, thereby weakening the imperial house and creating sources of dissension. The displacement of an old consort by a new beauty or the replacement of an heir also caused interminable strife and intrigue.

43. *Shih chi*, "Shang Annals," translated from *Shih-chi chin-chu*, vol. 1 (Shang-wu yin-shu-kuan, Taipei, 1979), p. 94.

44. Hou (ruler) Chi (millet) was one of the legendary deified figures traditionally credited with creating China's culture and civilization. He is identified particularly with agricultural developments, such as the domestication of wild grains, and is recorded in the "Chou Annals" as having been appointed minister of agriculture by Emperor Shun.

45. "Chou Annals," *Shih-chi chin-chu*, vol. 1, p. 101. It should be noted that the Chou were already powerful before this confrontation with the other barbarians; therefore, the traditional account is obviously highly simplified.

46. Hsü Pei-ken, *Chung-kuo kuo-fang ssu-hsiang-shih*, pp. 274–75.

47. For further discussions of Shang-Chou relations, see Hsu and Linduff, *Western Chou Civilizaton*, pp. 41–49; and Herrlee G. Creel, *The Origins of Statecraft in China* (University of Chicago Press, Chicago, 1970), pp. 57–69.

King Wu Ting of the Shang is recorded as having conducted military campaigns against the Chou before they descended to the Wei River valley. Chi Li apparently acted on behalf of the Shang against troublesome tribes from the northwest quarter before being perceived as too great a threat himself. The fact that the Shang could command and imprison both Chi Li and King Wen is testimony to their regional power and the Chou's continued submission, even though Shang rulers could not completely control the outer quarters. Because both Chi Li and King Wen were married to Shang princesses and members of the Shang nobility also appear to have married women from the Chou royal house, marriage relations were another aspect of their political policies.

48. His detention is variously said to have lasted anywhere from one to six or seven years. During this period he reputedly devoted himself to serious contemplation, ordering the sixty-four hexagrams of the *I ching* and appending the Judgments—activities befitting a future cultural legend. (The texts for the individual hexagram lines are attributed to the duke of Chou, one of his sons, and Confucius is closely identified with the book as well.) His reign, which began when he was fifty, is recorded in the *Shih chi* as having lasted fifty-five years; he died nine years after being released by the Shang. However, such great longevity (which he apparently shared with the T'ai Kung and the evil King Chou) is extremely problematic, particularly in an age in which people had short life expectancies. For discussions of the Shang and Chou chronologies, see, among others, David N. Keightley, "The *Bamboo Annals* and the Shang-Chou Chronology," *HJAS*, 38, no. 2 (1978): 423–38; Edward J. Shaughnessy, "On the Authenticity of the *Bamboo Annals*," *HJAS* 46, no. 1 (1986): 149–80; Chou Fa-kao, "Chronology of the Western Chou Dynasty," *Hsiang-kang Chung-wen Ta-hsüeh Chung-kuo Wen-hua Yen-chiu-so hsüeh-pao* 4, no. 1 (1971): 173–205; Ch'ü Wan-li, "Shih-chi Yin-pen-chi chi ch'i-t'o chi-lu-chung so-tsai Yin-Shang

shih-tai te shih-shih," *Taiwan Ta-hsü wen-shih-che hsüeh-pao* 14, no. 11 (1965): 87–118; Jung Meng-yüan, "Shih-t'an Hsi-Chou chi-nien," *Chung-hua wen-shih lun-ts'ung* no. 1, (1980): 1–21; Ch'ü Wan-li, "Hsi-Chou shih-shih kai-shu," *BIHP* 42 (1971): 775–802; Tung Tso-pin, "Hsi-Chou nien-li-p'u," *BIHP* 23 (1951): 681–760; and Ho Yu-ch'i, "Chou Wu-wang fa-Chou te nien-tai wen-t'i," *Chung-shan Ta-hsüeh hsüeh-pao*, no. 1, (1981); 64–70.

49. Several Chinese military historians have stressed the importance of the location because it exposed them to constant military challenges. Not only did the Chou train for and mount military campaigns against their enemies, but they were also forced always to be prepared instantly to ward off sudden incursions. Their leaders, including the king, personally supervised them in the fields and directed their responses to such military emergencies. This experience nurtured unity, a strong spirit, and an unflinching commitment to battle. It also symbolizes the farmer-soldier ideal later bureaucrats felt characterized the practices of antiquity and came to be cited frequently whenever they sought to disparage the need for professional military men and studies. (However, as discussed in the general introduction, it should be remembered that at this time the nobility rather than the peasants were the active members of the fighting forces.) See, for example, Hsü Pei-ken, *Chung-kuo kuo-fang ssu-hsiang-shih*, p. 276.

50. Career military men turned historians, such as Hsü Pei-ken, see the long preparatory period as not just providing the time necessary to cultivate Virtue and slowly develop the economic basis for a powerful state with a satisfied populace but also as being the minimum interval required to create—in accord with the Tai Kung's strategy—the revolutionary military weapons that would permit the Chou to effect radical new strategies against their vastly superior enemies. General Hsü is a particularly strong advocate of the chariot's decisive importance at Mu-yeh, the first battle in which it was employed en masse. Based on his estimates, the Chou could probably not have constructed more than a score of chariots per year—particularly armored ones—and at least three thousand horses had to be bred and trained. Charioteers also had to become practiced in the requisite individual skills and coordinated in integrated battle tactics. Furthermore, a large number of bronze weapons had to be manufactured; thus the Chou became more skilled in metalworking techniques and developed their own styles of weapons. (See Hsü Pei-ken, *Chung-kuo kuo-fang ssu-hsiang-shih*,pp. 284–86, and *T'ai kung Liu-t'ao chin-chu chin-i* [Shang-wu yin-shu-kuan, Taipei, 1976], pp. 14–26.)

51. The T'ang imperial family's military heritage was particularly strong, and the early emperors valued the martial as much as or perhaps more than the civil. Therefore, they sanctioned the creation of separate, increasingly professional military forces and the establishment of a state temple honoring the T'ai Kung as an exemplary military figure and the progenitor of military studies. Confucians, who tended to denigrate the T'ai Kung as merely a military man rather than recognizing him as a Sage like Confucius or the duke of Chou (despite historical records attesting to his unremitting promotion of essentially Confucian virtues), continually opposed such efforts. In their view the civil—the *li*—and concepts of virtue are all that should be required to govern well and tranquilize the realm. (They repeatedly cited Confucius' statement that he never studied military affairs [*Analects* XV:1] but ignored his famous assertion [preserved in his *Shih chi* biog-

raphy] that both the civil and martial are necessary.) Eventually, they succeeded in having the state cult dismantled, although the T'ai Kung unofficially continued to be a patron figure for centuries. This unrealistic outlook no doubt greatly contributed to China's military weakness throughout the centuries, despite the empire's vast resources, technological achievements, and powerful administrative organization. (For an extensive discussion, see D. L. McMullen, "The Cult of Ch'i T'ai-kung and T'ang Attitudes to the Military," *T'ang Studies* 7 [1989]: 59–103; and T'ao Hsi-sheng, *Ping-fa san-shu,* pp. 1–4.)

52. Conceptually, the *Six Secret Teachings* falls into the late Warring states' philosophical milieu and contains extensive material that appears to expand Sun-tzu's ideas. Among the most important "borrowed" concepts are unorthodox tactics; the characteristics and role of the general; manipulating *ch'i;* and identifying tactics appropriate to various configurations of terrain. All of these are substantially advanced over the earlier cited precursors, and may reflect the state of warfare in the third century B.C. Furthermore, the book frequently mentions advanced weapons, such as the crossbow and sword, and devotes entire chapters to cavalry and infantry tactics. While these may have been added by later generations, it seems likely the present text reached final form about the middle to late Warring States period. (An extensive discussion may be found in the introduction and notes to our translation of the *Six Secret Teachings* in the *Seven Military Classics.*) The issue of borrowing and priority is complex: many passages in the various *Seven Military Classics* are similar, even identical. (This is particularly true of the *Six Secret Teachings, Wu-tzu,* and *Art of War.*) The majority may in fact simply represent discussions of essential topics in a common conceptual language, perhaps based on textual materials or traditions apart from the extant writings upon which contemporary studies must focus. For example, the *Art of War* may be terse and abstract because Sun-tzu benefited from an embryonic text of the *Six Secret Teachings* and was an astute student of military thought. The absence of conceptual and textual borrowing would probably be more remarkable than its presence because it would indicate highly segmented and strictly preserved schools of tactics and strategy.

53. The tradition of Chi'i military studies requires a separate work; however, a brief discussion is found in the footnotes to the introductory section of the *Ssu-ma Fa.* (Also see T'ao Hsi-sheng, *Ping-fa san-shu* [Shih-huo ch'u-pan-she, Taipei, 1979], pp. 1–5, and "Chan-lüeh yüan-li yü ko-ming fan-kung te tao-lu," in *Ping-fa san-shu,* pp. 1–9; Hsü Pei-ken, *Chung-kuo kuo-fang ssu-hsiang-shih* [Chung-yang wu-kung-ying-she, Taipei, 1983], pp. 282–84.)

54. This appears to be Hsü Pei-ken's position at various points in the introduction to his modern Chinese translation, *T'ai Kung Liu-t'ao chin-chu chin-i* (see pp. 6–7, 18, and 31. Also see his *Chung-kuo kuo-fang ssu-hsiang-shih,* p. 283.) Most of the military writings cited in note 71 below adhere to this view (for example, Li Chiu-jui, *Chung-kuo chün-shih ssu-hsiang-shih,* pp. 101–02).

The question of accretion and loss is too complex to be considered within the scope of a note. However, in his "Treatise on Literature" included in the dynastic history of the Former Han (written in the Later Han), Pan Ku noted three writings associated with the T'ai Kung: "Plans" in 81 sections; "Words," or "Sayings," in 71 sections; and "Military," or "Weapons," in 85 sections, for a very large total of 237 sections. The present *Six Secret Teachings* only contains 60 sections or chapters, although many possible remnants are scattered about in other works. Even though a partial text has been recovered from a Han tomb, textual reductions and losses apparently continued after the Han dynasty as well. (Compare the *Ch'ün-shu chih-yao* and also Wang Chung-min, *Tun-huang ku-chi hsü-lu* [Shang-wu yin-shu-kuan, Peking, 1958], p. 150. Also see Gustav Haloun, "Legalist Fragments, Part 1: Kuan-tsi 55 and Related Texts," *AM* NS 2, no. 1 [1951–52]: 85–120.) Hsü Pei-ken, who studied the text extensively for at least two decades, has speculated about the possible fate of these books. First, the military writings perhaps formed the basis for the *Six Secret Teachings*, although some more general, historically oriented materials have been included. The chapters in "Plans" may have become the essence of the *Yin-fu ching*, another work associated with his name, which is traditionally thought to have been handed down eventually through Kuei Ku-tzu to Su Ch'in. Finally, the remaining work, "Words"—which may have been a record of his pronouncements while he was ruler of Ch'i—could have been preserved by Ch'i state historians and passed down within the state to ultimately comprise the basis of the *Three Strategies of Huang-shih Kung*. (This reconstruction is not generally accepted by Western scholars. For details, see Hsü Pei-ken, TKLT CCCY, pp. 27–31.)

55. According to the *Lü-shih ch'un-ch'iu*, he was a *shih* (lowest rank of noble) of the Eastern I people. Ch'iang people with the Chiang surname apparently were early allies of the Chou after an even earlier period of conflict.

Recent scholars have questioned the veracity of the T'ai Kung's eastern origin. Yang Yün-ju, for example, noting the Chiang clan's early marriage relations with the Chou, concludes that both the Chiang and the Chou were originally members of the northwest barbarian peoples and that the Chiang did not venture eastward until after the Chou conquest. See "Chiang-hsing te min-tsu ho Chiang T'ai-kung te ku-shih," in *Ku-shih pien*, ed. Ku Chieh-kang, vol. 2 (Shang-hai ku-chi, Shanghai, 1982; original copyright 1930), pp. 113–17.

56. In all the stories about the T'ai Kung found in the various Warring States and later writings, he is invariably portrayed as old, retired, and poor. For example, the *Shuo yüan* frequently uses his late, meteoric rise to power after an undistinguished life to illustrate that talent and merit alone are inadequate unless one meets the proper moment. One passage states, "When Lü Wang was fifty he sold food in Chi-chin; when he was seventy he butchered cows in Chao-ko; so if when he was ninety he commanded the army for the Son of Heaven, it was because he met King Wen." (*Shuo-yüan* CCCY, p. 581, and an additional reference on p. 562.) His "lands were inadequate to repay the cost of the seeds, (the yield from) his fishing inadequate to repay the cost of the nets, but for governing All under Heaven he had more than enough wisdom." (*Shuo-yüan* CCCY, p. 569.) "He was an old fellow whose wife had put him out, who had worked as a butcher's assistant in Chao-ko and as an inn employee in Chi-chin who welcomed guests." (*Shuo-yüan* CCCY, p. 234.) In the *Han-shih wai-chuan* he is laboring as a boatman when he encounters King Wen. This incident is translated in James R. Hightower, *Han shih wai chuan* (Harvard University Press, Cambridge, 1952), pp. 140–42.

57. The term "hegemon" does not appear until centuries after the events recorded in this biography, thus suggesting the dialogue is a late fabrication.

58. The story about how the T'ai Kung received his name is more than a little

dubious; however, completely satisfactory explanations are lacking. He was apparently known by several names, perhaps depending on the recorder's perspective and location. "T'ai Kung" should refer to his enfeoffment as king of Ch'i and thus the state's official progenitor. "Lü" in "Lü Wang" probably refers to his place of origin, whereas Wang may have been his personal name; this is also the case for "Lü Shang." "Shih," in "Shih Shang-fu," perhaps referred to his command position, "T'ai Shih," rather than to his role as preceptor (shih) to Kings Wen and Wu. "Shang-fu," or "Father Shang," may be an honorific reference from the two kings toward their army's commander in chief or perhaps their strategist-adviser. (See Yang Yün-ju, "Chiang-hsing," pp. 109–12.)

59. The Shih chi biography states he was appointed as a shih, which generally means "commander" but can also include didactic functions, as in "preceptor" or "teacher." Clearly, the T'ai Kung's role was far more encompassing and was related more to strategy than command. Historical references apart from the Shih chi do not record him as being commander in chief (normally a role the Chou king should personally have filled), but he seems to have commanded a force at the battle of Mu-yeh and led the initial charge to instigate the conflict. (See the "Chou Annals" in the Shih chi. Also note his superior role in the command of forces securing the area after the conquest in the I-Chou shu.)

Traditional sources indicate that subsequently, King Wu married the T'ai Kung's daughter and that she became one of the ten great ministers of his reign. (See Wei Ju-lin, Chung-kuo li-tai ming-chiang chi ch'i yung-ping ssu-hsiang [Chung-yang wen-wu kung-ying-she, Taipei, 1981], p. 2.)

60. The practice of traveling about to seek receptive rulers on whom to exercise one's persuasion is identified with the Warring States period and should be considered anachronistic. However, he may have traveled about in disguise, trying to perceive a single opportunity, or he may simply have been exceptional.

61. Mencius twice mentions that the T'ai Kung dwelled on the coast of the Eastern Sea to avoid King Chou (Mencius, IVA: 14, VIIA:22) and also refers to him and San-i Sheng as having known King Wen (Mencius, VIIB:38). The Hsin shu mentions him "coming from the sea coast to give his allegiance" (Hsin shu, 10:9B).

62. Because the concept of unorthodox (ch'i) stratagems is attributed primarily to Sun-tzu, it is interesting to note the Shih chi's appraisal of the T'ai Kung's achievements in this regard.

63. For a brief discussion of ch'üan, see note 125 to the translation.

64. These conquests and alliances secured their base of operations and allowed them to expand toward the Shang domain. For further discussion, see Hsu and Linduff, Western Chou Civilization, pp. 89–92.

65. This very famous sentence is cited repeatedly by the T'ai Kung's detractors to support their contention that Virtue alone, rather than the Tai Kung's despicable machinations, was enough to win the empire for the Chou.

66. Whether "Tsang-ssu" refers to a green, nine-headed river animal (originally based on a rhinoceros?) and is being invoked as a spirit to lend power to the oath or scare the men or refers to an officer for the boats is the subject of speculation.

67. The question has frequently been raised as to why King Wu did not immediately lead an attack on the Shang, particularly when he could have capitalized on

the element of surprise. Various explanations have been offered, among them that King Wu felt his strength and preparations were still insufficient or that perhaps he had not expected such an overwhelming response and had neither supplies nor plans to support an attack. (Although concrete plans could have been formulated in the intervening two years, little more could have been done to dramatically alter the balance of forces.) Other suggestions include General Hsü's belief that the Chou did not bring their chariots to the assembly but concealed them for explosive use in the actual engagement and that this rally represented a sort of dress rehearsal. King Chou's minions certainly reported the events in detail, including King Wu's public acknowledgment— despite startling support to the contrary— that a subject should not attack his ruler. This sustained King Chou's complacency and arrogance—the "Shang Annals" indicate his disdain for any Chou threat to his power and his certainty that he would continue to enjoy the sanction of Heaven—and set the stage for the next meeting, which was then similarly regarded. King Wu thus was able to advance swiftly by an indirect southern route (fording the frozen river in an area supposedly well-known to the T'ai Kung who, according to one source, had sold rice there) and approach the capital before King Chou could muster all his forces and recall his expeditionary forces in the south. (See Hsü Pei-ken, *Chung-kuo kuo-fang ssu-hsiang-shih*, pp. 285–86, and *Chung-kuo li-tai chang-cheng-shih*, vol. 1, pp. 74–76; and the statements attributed to King Chou in the "Shang Annals.")

68. The murder of Pi-kan and other events (such as the high officials fleeing to Chou with the sacrificial musical instruments) no doubt precipitated the king's decision to attack Shang.

The T'ai Kung's rejection of bad weather and ill portents is remarkable for an age obsessed with such beliefs. In his view, even though he claimed the Mandate of Heaven, how could the signs be auspicious for a ruler about to attack his sovereign? (Note that this incident, with additional dialogue, also appears in the *Han-shih wai-chuan*. See Hightower's translation, *Han shih wai chuan*, pp. 89–90.)

Although the T'ai Kung was obviously daring and resolute, some scholars have cited such statements as evidence that this material is fabricated because such pragmatic, unmystical views were not common until the Warring States period, when the military classics began to reject the influence of portents and signs. However, although there are serious doubts about the veracity of the details, this opinion perhaps too conveniently assumes a nonexistent homogeneity of thought and recklessly denies the possibility of the exceptional.

69. The "Shang Annals" records the manner of the king's death rather differently: "On *chia-tzu* King Chou's troops were defeated. King Chou raced back in and mounted the Deer Tower. He clothed himself in his treasures and jade, went into the fire and died. King Wu of the Chou subsequently chopped off Chou's head, hanging it up with a white pennon" (*Shih-chi chin-chu*, vol. 1, p. 96). The *I-Chou shu* account in the "Shih-fu" chapter similarly records that King Chou immolated himself, whereas in the "Chou Annals" King Wu symbolically shoots King Chou with three arrows, then decapitates him.

70. The nine great bronze cauldrons symbolized imperial authority, and possessing them was deemed a matter of great consequence in establishing dynastic power and legitimacy.

71. An analysis and discussion of the battle of Mu-yeh merits a separate chapter. Among the many unresolved questions, perhaps the most important concerns the relative strength of the respective forces. According to the *Shih chi* and some other accounts, the Shang fielded seven hundred thousand men, whereas the Chou only had three hundred chariots, three thousand Tiger Guards, and forty-five thousand armored soldiers. The number for the Shang is extremely suspect and is subject to various explanations: It may be a general expression of size; an error for what should be seventy thousand or one hundred seventy thousand; or the total troops of the entire Shang forces, including all their allies—many of whom were already committed in other areas. The numbers for the Chou seem more reasonable but in fact may only refer to their core forces without including those of their allies. (Clearly, however, the forces of the Chou were vastly outnumbered by those of the Shang.) Depending on the source consulted, the actual battle either required little expenditure of forces—with the Shang troops offering minimal resistance to their king's morally superior enemy—or the carnage flooded the fields with blood. (Both the *Shang shu* and the *Shih chi* assert that the Shang troops "inverted their weapons" and otherwise offered little resistance.) The *I-Chou shu* lists 177,779 killed and 310,230 captured as a result of the entire campaign, which are astounding figures. (For brief discussions, see Edward L. Shaughnessy, "'New' Evidence on the Zhou conquest," pp. 57–61.)

Notwithstanding the above evidence, the actual battle appears to have quickly turned into a rout and have ended within a few hours of the initial clash. Among the factors favoring the Chou was their commitment to the cause and consequent great fighting spirit, in contrast to the apparently reluctant, despondent Shang troops. The Chou forces were thoroughly trained and prepared, whereas the Shang were said to be deficient in both respects. The Chou unleashed an initial charge of one hundred elite stalwarts, headed by the T'ai Kung, and immediately followed with a chariot attack that moved swiftly across the plains. The combined effect both startled and terrified the Shang troops, who had not previously encountered massed chariot assaults. (Skeptics, however, such as Hsu and Linduff [*Western Chou Civilization,* pp. 81–88] believe superior infantry played the critical role and that the chariots were unimportant.) King Chou reportedly turned and fled, and his command immediately disintegrated. Because the Chou had strongly publicized (through charges possibly similar to those in the *Shang shu*) that King Chou—rather than the people—was the designated enemy, any compulsion to fight on the part of the Shang was seriously undermined. The battle and choice of battlefield were forced on the Shang because the Chou had crossed to the south—avoiding the bulwark of standing Shang defenses—and swiftly advanced. Finally, the Chou had prepared in secret, established a series of power bases, and either neutralized or gained the allegiance of states and peoples along the attack route and around the Shang. Although the Shang had obviously engineered their own self-destruction by alienating the people and eliminating effective administrators, the Chou may also have used many of the measures advocated in the Cultural Warfare chapter of the *Six Secret Teachings* to further subvert them. For general discussions of these factors, see Chang Shao-sheng and Liu Wen-ch'an, eds., *Chung-kuo ku-tai chan-cheng t'ung-lan,* 2 vols.

(Ch'ang-cheng ch'u-pan-she, Peking, 1985), pp. 7–10; Li Chen, *Chung-kuo li-tai chan-cheng shih-hua* (Li-ming, Taipei, 1985,) pp. 13–19; Hsü Pei-ken, *Chung-kuo kuo-fang ssu-hsiang-shih*, pp. 282–90, and *Chung-kuo li-tai chan-cheng-shih*, vol. 1, pp. 71–84.

72. Being in accord with local customs while still influencing the people is one of the keystones of the T'ai Kung's military thought and is consonant with post-conquest Chou policies. Its wisdom was proven subsequently by numerous historical incidents, including military disasters.

73. These measures are all associated historically with the state of Ch'i and with its heritage of Legalist thought.

74. King Wu died about two years after the conquest, providing an opportunity for his brothers—in alliance with the Shang prince who was retained in heavily circumscribed, essentially symbolic power—to revolt. The duke of Chou together with the duke of Shao and possibly the T'ai Kung required three years to subdue the dissident peoples.

75. This charge appears in the *Tso chuan*. Cf. Legge, *The Chinese Classics: The Ch'un Ts'ew with The Tso Chuen*, vol. 5, pp. 139–40.

76. "Expansive" should probably be understood as outgoing, energetic, active.

77. "The Hereditary House of Ch'i T'ai Kung," *Shih chi, chüan* 32, translated from *Shih-chi chin-chu*, vol. 3, pp. 1502–06, 1535.

78. The authenticity of *Shang shu* chapters is much debated; the consensus is that some portions may be early Chou material but that the bulk represents later composition.

79. See, for example, Edward L. Shaughnessy, "'New' Evidence on the Zhou Conquest," pp. 60–61.

80. See Sarah Allan, "The Identities of Taigong Wang in Zhou and Han Literature," *MS*. 30 (1972–73), pp. 57–99. Allan concludes that the T'ai Kung commanded the forces in the famous battles and was also accorded a special status in ritual affairs that was essentially equal to that of the royal clan members (p. 67). Her conclusion is based in part on early *Book of Odes* verses, which she notes as the only Western Chou references to the T'ai Kung (p. 59). However, Shaughnessy's article has proven the authenticity of the "Shih-fu" chapter of the *I-Chou shu* (which is not mentioned in Allan's article), and additional contemporary evidence shows that the T'ai Kung commanded troops and was entrusted with critical security operations. (See Shaughnessy, "'New' Evidence on the Zhou Conquest," pp. 57, 67. Also see Ku Chieh-kang, "I-Chou-shu 'Shih-fu' p'ien chiao-chu hsieh-ting yü p'ing-lun," *Wen-shih* 2 [1963]: 1–42. Ku similarly concludes that the "Shih-fu" chapter is an authentic record and provides glosses on the passage referring to the T'ai Kung on pp. 6–7 of his article. It should also be noted that Allan's article states that the authentic historical material always refers to the T'ai Kung as "Shih Shang-fu" ("Taigong Wang," p. 60). However, in the *I-Chou shu* he is referred to as "T'ai Kung Wang," and in the first chapter of the recently discovered bamboo strips of the *Six Secret Teachings* he is called "Lü Shang." (See Lo Fu-i, "Lin-i Han-chien kai-shu," *WW*, 1974: 2, p. 33.)

81. Allan, "Taigong Wang," pp. 68–72. The Chiang, as previously discussed, were allies of the Chou and furnished troops in the decisive battles. (Unfortunately, this explanation is not entirely satisfactory because it fails to account ade-

quately for the T'ai Kung's early, apparently menial status—one hardly befitting an important ally. Allan suggests that the motif of recognition may underlie these legends (see discussion, pp. 89–98), and it is an important theme in Chinese thought. For example, see Eric Henry, "The Motif of Recognition in Early China," *HJAS*, 47, no. 1 (1987): 5–30; and Ralph D. Sawyer, *Knowing Men* (Kaofeng, Taipei, 1979). Henry only mentions the T'ai Kung in a footnote.

82. It need hardly be mentioned that all of the contemporary military historians in both Taiwan and the People's Republic of China whose works have been cited in the notes above not only accept the fact of the T'ai Kung's existence but also attribute the major strategic and command role to him. Accordingly, they tend to see his thoughts as being largely preserved in the *Six Secret Teachings*, even though they have either been much revised over the centuries or were actually composed at a later date. (Western scholars, such as Hsu and Linduff, generally tend to ignore him altogether, although in his *Origins of Statecraft* [pp. 343–344] Creel posits his authenticity.)

References to the T'ai Kung are found throughout pre-Han writings—such as *Mencius*, Sun-tzu's *Art of War*, *Hsün-tzu*, *Han Fei-tzu*, *Lü-shih ch'un-ch'iu*, *Huai-nan tzu*, *Kuo yü* and *Shuo yüan*. Extensive dialogues attributed to the T'ai Kung and King Wu also appear in the *Shuo yüan*, and several pages of quotations are preserved in the *T'ung tien*. That his historical authenticity has been doubted seems remarkable and perhaps symbolizes much about the nature of thought in China.

83. See Edward L. Shaughnessy, "'New' Evidence on the Zhou Conquest," pp. 66–67.

84. Herrlee G. Creel's classic work, *The Origins of Statecraft in China*, still contains the most extensive reconstruction and discussion of these measures as well as of the Chou military. However, also see Hsu and Linduff, *Western Chou Civilization*.

85. See Hsu and Linduff, *Western Chou Civilization*, pp. 113–19; and Tu Cheng-sheng, "Lüeh-lun Yin i-min te tsao-yü yü ti-wei," *BIHP* 53 (December 1982): 661–709.

86. For a discussion of the meaning of "army" in this period, see the section entitled Military Organization at the end of the introduction.

87. See Cho-yün Hsü's extensive analysis, *Ancient China in Transition* Stanford University Press, Stanford, 1965).

88. See the translator's introduction and notes to the *Ssu-ma Fa* translation. The emphasis on discipline and concerted action evident throughout the *Seven Military Classics* reflects this shift from the noble days of chariot warfare. For additional discussion of the code of chivalry and its inevitable decline, see Frank A. Kierman, Jr., "Phases and Modes of Combat in Early China," in *Chinese Ways in Warfare*, ed. Franz A. Kierman, Jr., and John K. Fairbank (Harvard University Press, Cambridge, 1974), pp. 27–66.

89. This incident, as recorded in the *Tso chuan* for the first year of Duke Chao, has historical importance because it shows the "barbarian" enemy fighting solely as infantrymen rather than mounted on horses or from chariots. In addition, the Chou's realization of the limitations of chariot warfare is clearly shown by the necessity they felt to abandon their own chariots and engage the enemy in con-

fined valley terrain. The reluctance of at least one high official to relinquish his honored position as a charioteer and descend to the status of a foot soldier (for which he was summarily executed) also illustrates the prevailing attitude even this late in the Spring and Autumn period. (See Legge's translation of the incident, *The Chinese Classics:* vol. 5, *The Ch'un Ts'ew with The Tso Chuen* [Oxford University Press, Oxford, 1872; [reprinted Chin-hsüeh shu-chü, Taipei, 1968], p. 579.) Wei Shu initiated the conversion and formulated a plan whose effectiveness was augmented by its deceptiveness. To confuse the enemy he deployed the combined chariot and accompanying infantry forces in an unusual, unbalanced formation, provoking the enemy's laughter and ridicule—until the Chin forces sprang into action and routed them. "Be deceptive" was a dictum clearly in the minds of commanders in this era, a century or two before Sun-tzu's *Art of War*. (For further discussion and analysis, see *Ping-fa,* p. 36, and the *Wu-pei-chih* 53, pp. 22B–24B.) As the infantry expanded, officers from the nobility were assigned to command them, and rank was granted to everyone—regardless of status—for military achievement. Consequently, the status of the foot soldier improved dramatically, and although the old attitudes (which disdained foot assignment against the prestige of being assigned to the chariot) were never completely erased, their amelioration marked a significant change (see *Ping-fa,* p. 58).

It should be noted that chariots were not employed at this time in such peripheral southeastern states as Wu and Yüeh. Initially, this might have been because of ignorance and unsuitable terrain, but even after they were taught the skills of chariot driving and the tactics of warfare deployment, these and several other states fielded only infantry units. (For further discussion, see Tu Cheng-sheng, "Chou-tai feng-chien chieh-t'i-hou te chün-cheng hsin-chih-hsü," *BIHP* 55 no. 1 [1984]: 74–75, 82–89; *Ping-fa,* p. 58; Yang K'uan, "Ch'un-ch'iu Chan-kuo-chien," p. 11; and Yang Hung, *Chung-kuo ku-ping-ch'i,* p. 126.)

90. Another weapon, the *chi,* probably began to appear in some numbers around this time. The *chi,* or "spear-tipped dagger-ax," differed from the dagger-ax in one formidable aspect: It had a metal point at the top of the shaft to allow thrusting and stabbing. With the addition of this spear tip, the weapon could be used for an initial stabbing thrust, but if the target were missed, it could be pulled back or swung to catch the enemy with the knifelike horizontal blade. In the early stages it was probably made from two separate bronze parts, which were secured to a pole; this has prompted some archaeologists to argue that the *chi* has a longer history than is generally acknowledged. (After the wooden shaft had completely disintegrated, the two parts, which would be found separately, would be misinterpreted as having come from two weapons—a dagger-ax and a spear—rather than being parts of an integrated, composite one.) However, it appears that the *chi* was primarily a foot soldier's weapon, perhaps developed to better equip them to attack chariots; thus it grew in popularity as infantry forces were augmented. In Shang tombs only *ko* (halberds, dagger-axes) are found, whereas Han excavations yield only *chi,* or spear-tipped dagger-axes. In the thousand years between the demise of the Shang and the flourishing of the Han, *chi* were probably created in the early Chou or Spring and Autumn periods, gradually becoming more popular until proliferating in the Warring States era. For detailed discussions, see Kuo Pao-chün, "Ko chi yü-lun," pp. 313–26; Kuo Mo-jo, *Yin*

Chou ch'ing-t'ung-ch'i ming-wen yen-chiu, (Jenmin ch'u-pan-she, Shanghai, 1954), pp. 172–86; Ma Heng, "Ko chi chih yen-chiu," pp. 745–53; Chou Wei, *Chung-kuo ping-ch'i shih-kao,* pp. 88–98; and Hayashi Minao, *Chūgoku In-Shū jidai no buki,* pp. 10–13 and 78–96.

In an article examining a multiple-blade *chi* excavated from a Warring States tomb, Sun Chi concludes that this sort of weapon was probably wielded by charioteers against foot soldiers and thus represented a response to the growth of infantry forces and their mounting threat to the chariot. (The attachment of knife blades to the wheel hubs served a similar function, as his article discusses on p. 83.) This implies further questions about the evolution of the *chi*—whether it was developed for infantrymen or for chariot-mounted warriors contending with other chariots or infantrymen—to which answers are unavailable. See Sun Chi, "Yu-jen ch'e-wei yü to-ko-chi," *WW,* 1980: 12, pp. 83–85.

91. See the last part of the introduction for details and also note 100 below.

92. Some of these qualifications are recorded in *Hsün-tzu,* the *Wu-tzu,* and itemized in the *Six Secret Teachings.*

93. The Seven Strong States at the start of the Warring States period, as identified by Liu Hsiang's classic list, were Ch'i, Yen, the Three Chin (Han, Chao, Wei), and the newly powerful, originally peripheral states of Ch'u and Ch'in. Wu and Yüeh, two other so-called barbarian states, also emerged as significant forces.

94. The *Ssu-ma Fa* discusses the distinctions that mark the form and spirit of the civilian and military realms and advises against their becoming confused or intermixed. Most of the *Seven Military Classics* discuss the qualifications necessary for generalship, reflecting the rising concern with professionalism and a turning away from the preoccupation with moral qualifications found in the *Tso chuan.* Ironically, in earlier times the Shang and Chou kings as well as the local vassal lords not only governed their respective realms but also commanded the army and exercised supreme military power. Over time they became divorced from the complexities of battle. Further discussion will be found in the introduction to the *Art of War* translation.

95. Strategic points, such as passes and major road intersections, were increasingly guarded and fortified. The northern states, such as Yen and Chao, sought to diminish the mobility of mounted nomadic forces by creating static defense systems ("walls") along their lengthy, exposed borders. See Yang K'uan, "Ch'un-ch'iu Chan-kuo-chien feng-chien te chün-shih tsu-chih ho chan-cheng te pien-hua," p. 12. Also note Arthur Waldron's work on "walls"; "The Problem of the Great Wall of China," *HJAS* 43, no. 2 (1983): 643–63; and *The Great Wall of China: From History to Myth* (Cambridge University Press, Cambridge, 1990).

96. See Yang Hung, *Chung-kuo ku-ping-ch'i,* pp. 140–41; and *Ping-fa,* pp. 78–89. The Mohists were famous for their doctrine of not making distinctions in one's love for his fellow man. Under the direction of Mo-tzu (fl. 479–438 B.C.)—their founder and leader—they actively practiced their doctrine of opposing warfare, rushing to aid the defense of the besieged. See Robin D. S. Yates, "Siege Engines and Late Zhou Military Technology," in *Explorations in the History of Science and Technology in China,* ed. Li Guohao et al., (Shanghai Chinese Classics Publishing House, Shanghai, 1982), pp. 409–51, for a discussion of the technology that appeared in this period. For the medieval period, which includes

the T'ang (the era of the *Questions and Replies*), see Herbert Franke, "Siege and Defense of Towns in Medieval China," in *Chinese Ways in Warfare*, pp. 151–94.

97. Although early Chinese compound bows were extremely powerful, crossbows provided dramatically more formidable firepower; their strength and effective killing range generally increased over the centuries as their mechanisms were perfected. The earliest type was probably hand-cocked, using only arm strength. More powerful versions required leg strength, and the strongest used a rope attached to the waist to pull the sling back. (See Hsü Chung-shu, "I-she yü nu," pp. 435–38.) By the end of the Warring States period, crossbows had come into extensive use, although their strategic value was probably not exploited fully until the Han dynasty. Hand-held crossbows, which fired two bolts simultaneously, and repeating models (as well as repeating double-bolt models) dating from the Warring States period have now been excavated, reflecting the crossbow's technological sophistication and importance. (See Ch'en Yüeh-chün, "Chiang-ling Ch'u-mu ch'u-t'u shuang-shih ping-she lien-fa-nu yen-chiu," *WW*, 1990: 5, pp. 89–96.) Larger, winch-powered models mounted on chariots or carriages, also capable of shooting multiple bolts, are described in the *Six Secret Teachings* and are discussed in the translation. (Also see Robin D.S. Yates, "Siege Engines and Late Zhou Military Technology," pp. 432–43.)

Tradition holds that the Yellow Emperor invented the crossbow, and Hsü Chung-shu, analyzing linguistic evidence, strongly believes that both the bow and crossbow are indigenous developments dating from pre-Shang times. (See Hsü Chung-shu. "I-she yü nu chih su-yüan chi kuan-yü tz'u-lei ming-wu chih k'ao-shih," pp. 417–18, 438.) However, Hsü's classic view not withstanding, based on textual references and other linguistic evidence it appears the crossbow probably originated outside the central states area of China, perhaps in Ch'u or the southwest. (See Jerry Norman and Tsu-lin Mei, "The Austroasiatics in Ancient South China: Some Lexical Evidence," *MS* 32 [1976]: 293–94; Yang Hung, *Ku-ping-ch'i*, pp. 143–44; and Ch'en Yüeh-chün, "Lien-fa-nu," p. 96.) Remnants of crossbows with bronze trigger mechanisms have been found in tombs from the middle Warring States period, prompting scholars such as Kao Chih-hsi to argue for a much earlier (indigenous) invention—probably in the Spring and Autumn period—using wooden components. (See Kao Chih-hsi, "Chi Ch'ang-sha, Ch'ang-te ch'u-t'u nu-chi te Chan-kuo-mu—chien-t'an yu-kuan nu-chi, kung-shih te chi-ke wen-t'i," *WW*, 1964: 6, pp. 41–44. Also see Ch'en Yüeh-chün, "Lien-fa-nu," p. 96. Note that as of this writing, no pre-Warring States crossbows have been discovered. See Hayashi's Minao's extensive, although dated, summary, *Chūgoku In-Shū jidai no buki*, pp. 301–30.) The first recorded tactical use appears to have been at the battle of Ma-ling in 341 B.C., as depicted in the *Shih-chi* and the text of the Sun Pin's *Ping-fa*. The *Spring and Autumn Annals of Wu and Yüeh* also contain numerous references to crossbows, but truly extensive employment probably began with the Han, who exploited their superior firepower and range.

98. See the last part of the introduction for an annotated discussion of the cavalry in Chinese history.

99. The speed and mobility of the cavalry in all but the most impenetrable forests and marshes allowed the development of unorthodox tactics (*ch'i*) versus orthodox (*cheng*) methods. Although infantry forces can also be employed in

unorthodox ways, an essential aspect of the unorthodox is its unexpectedness, its exploitation of surprise, for which the cavalry is ideally suited. Sun-tzu is generally credited with advancing the idea of the unorthodox, and it is extensively discussed and expanded in the *Questions and Replies* (based on actual employment by T'ang T'ai-tsung and General Li in decisive battles when they were struggling to establish the T'ang). The *Six Secret Teachings* also analyzes the relative methods for employing infantry, chariot, and cavalry forces.

100. Iron was used extensively for the agricultural implements—generally manufactured and distributed under government monopoly—during the Warring States period. The Japanese scholar Sekino Takeshi has advanced the idea that cheap, readily available, mass-produced iron swords provided Ch'in's conscripted infantry forces their great killing power. (Cf. Sekino Takeshi, "Chūgoku shoki bunka no ikkōsatsu—dōtestsu katoki no kaimei ni yosete," *Shigaku zasshi*, 60 [October 1951]: 867–907.) However, others strongly dispute his contention for a variety of reasons. First, the sword had always been a weapon of the nobility and was generally carried by officers rather than ordinary infantrymen. (Cf. Noel Barnard, "Did the Swords Exist," *EC* [1978–79], pp. 62–63.) They would naturally have preferred the familiar elegance of the bronze weapon over the cruder iron sword. Second, bronze swords were probably still superior to early iron versions in the hands of the skilled warrior, and complex metal-working technology (such as layering with different alloys) produced very sharp, fine weapons. Third, few iron swords have been unearthed—even from the famous tombs of Ch'in Shih-Huang-ti, where most of the warriors are armed with bronze rather than iron weapons. (Cf. Noel Barnard, "Did the Swords Exist," p. 63; David N. Keightley, "Where Have All the Swords Gone?" *EC* 2 [1976], pp. 31–34.) Thus several scholars have concluded that the Han era marks the true ascension of iron weapons, with the bronze sword becoming an anachronism thereafter. For a dissenting view, see Li Xueqin, "Iron Objects," in *Eastern Zhou and Qin Civilizations* (Yale University Press, New Haven, 1985), pp. 315–29, who notes that China had cast iron, wrought iron, and steel by the Warring States era, which suggests a long prehistory in the Spring and Autumn period.)

101. See Wu Ch'i's biography in the translator's introduction to the *Wu-tzu*.

102. The battle of Ma-ling is apparently the first recorded conflict in which crossbows were employed. (There are also different versions regarding who exercised ultimate command—P'ang Chüan, who may have been killed at the earlier battle, or the imperial prince, who sallied forth with the home defense forces. General P'ang's character flaws and rashness were frequently cited by Chinese military analysts as evidence of the need for a constellation of virtues in any supreme commander.)

103. The complex process of analyzing language, concepts, and historical events to create a systematic textual chronology has been both complicated and simplified by the writings discovered in various tombs in recent decades. The detailed textual studies of Ch'ing dynasty scholars, although valuable for understanding the texts themselves, have led to conclusions that must now be reexamined and revised. (Discussions of the provenance of the individual *Seven Military Classics* are found in each introduction. For a general discussion, see Robin D. S. Yates, "New Light on Ancient Chinese Military Texts," *TP* 74 [1988]; 211–48.)

104. See Hayashi Minao, "Chūgoku sen-Shin jidai no basha," *Tōhō Gakuhō* 29 (1959); p. 225.
105. Cf. Edward L. Shaughnessy, "Historical Perspectives on the Introduction of the Chariot into China," *HJAS*, 48, no. 1 (1988): p. 190.
106. Cf. ibid., pp. 192, 208.
107. Cf. Cheng Te-k'un, *Chou China* (W. Heffer & Sons, Ltd., Cambridge, 1963), pp. 265–72.
108. Cf. Stuart Piggott, "Chariots in the Caucasus and in China," *Antiquity* 48 (1974): pp. 16–24.
109. Cf. Shih Chang-ju, "Yin-hsü tsui-chin chih chung-yao fa-hsien," *Chung-kuo k'ao-ku hsüeh-pao*, no. 2 (1947): p. 20.
110. See, among others, Shaughnessy, "Historical Perspectives," p. 198.
111. Cf. Ku Chieh-kang and Yang Hsiang-k'uei, "Chung-kuo ku-tai ch'e-chan k'ao-lüeh," *Tung-fang tsa-chih* 34, no. 1 (1937): pp. 52–53; and also the descriptions in the *Six Secret Teachings*.
112. Cf. Shaughnessy, "Historical Perspectives," pp. 199, 213–21; Herrlee G. Creel, *The Origins of Statecraft in China* (University of Chicago Press, Chicago, 1970); p. 271; and Hayashi, "Basha," p. 278.
113. Cf. Ku and Yang, "Ch'e-chan," pp. 39–54.
114. Cf. Shaughnessy, "Historical Perspectives," p. 217; for Creel's doubts about barbarians employing chariots, see *Statecraft*, p. 266.
115. Cf. Cheng, *Chou*, p. 266; Kawamata Masanori, "Higashi Ajia no kodai sensha to Nishi-Ajia," *Koshi Shunjū* 4 (1987), pp. 38–58; for a dissenting opinion, see Shih Chang-ju, "Yin-shü," p. 22.
116. See Ku and Yang, "Ch'e-chan," p. 49.
117. Cf. ibid., p. 44; and Shaughnessy, "Historical Perspectives," pp. 224–25.
118. Cf. Creel, *Statecraft,* pp. 262–69.
119. Cf. Yang Hung, "Ch'e-chan-yü chan-ch'e," *WW*, 1977: 5, pp. 82–90 (also incorporated into his book, *Chung-kuo ku-ping-ch'i lun-ts'ung* [Wen-wu ch'u-pan-she, Peking, 1980]).
120. Cf. Shaughnessy, "Historical Perspectives," pp. 222–23.
121. See Yang Hung, *Ku-ping-ch'i*, p. 126; Li Xueqin, *Eastern Zhou and Qin Civilizations* (Yale University Press, New Haven, 1985), pp. 198, 272.
122. See Creel, *Statecraft*, pp. 256–62.
123. Cf. Yang Hung, *Ku-ping-ch'i*, p. 100.
124. Cf. Creel, *Statecraft*, note 61, pp. 262–63.
125. Shaughnessy, "Historical Perspectives," p. 227.
126. See Shih, "Yin-shü," pp. 21–22.
127. Cf. Chan Li and Chou Shih-ch'ü, "Shih-t'an Yang-chia-wan Han-wu ch'i-ping-yung," *WW*, 1977: 10, pp. 22.
128. E. G. Pulleyblank, "Tribe and State: Prehistoric and Historic Times," in *The Origins of Chinese Civilization*, ed. David N. Keightley (University of California Press, Berkeley, 1983), p. 450.
129. W. Perceval Yetts, "The Horse: A Factor in Early Chinese History," *Eurasia Septentionalis Antiqua 9* (1934): p. 236.
130. These passages are discussed in the footnotes to the translations. For a summary of the current view, including comments on Sun Pin's brief statements,

see Chauncey S. Goodrich, "Riding Astride and the Saddle in Ancient China," *HJAS* 44, no. 2 (1984): pp. 220–81.

131. Pulleyblank, "Tribe and State," p. 450.

132. See Yang Hung, *Ku-ping-ch'i*, pp. 28–29.

133. See Yetts, "The Horse," pp. 231–36; Herrlee G. Creel, "The Role of the Horse in Chinese History," in Creel, *What is Taoism and Other Studies in Chinese Cultural History* (University of Chicago Press, Chicago, 1970), pp. 160–86; and Friedrich Hirth, "The Story of Chang K'ien, China's Pioneer in Western Asia,' *JAOS* 37 (1917): pp. 89–116.

134. See Chan and Chou, "Han-mu," pp. 26–27.

135. A summary based primarily on Yang Hung, *Ku-ping-ch'i*, pp. 4–96; Chou Wei, *Chung-kuo ping-ch'i shih-kao* (Ming-wen shu-chü, Taipei, 1980), pp. 169ff; and Albert E. Dien, "A Study of Early Chinese Armor," *Artibus Asiae* 43 (1981–82): 5–66.

136. See, among many others, Yang Hung, *Ku-ping-ch'i*, p. 93; Noel Barnard, "Did the Swords Exist," *EC*, no. 4 (1978–79): p. 62; Kuo Yü-kou, "Yin Chou te ch'ing-tung wu-ch'i," *KK*, 1961: 2, pp. 114–15; and Max Loehr, "The Earliest Chinese Swords and the Akinakes," *Oriental Art* 1 (1948): pp. 132–36.

137. Cf. Barnard, "Did the Swords Exist," p. 62.

138. T'ung En-cheng, "Wo-kuo Hsi-nan ti-ch'ü ch'ing-t'ung-chien te yen-chiu," *KK*, 1977: 2, pp. 35–55. Also see Cho-yun Hsu and Katheryn M. Linduff, *Western Chou Civilization* (Yale University Press, New Haven, 1988), pp. 77–81.

139. Yang Hung, *Ku-ping-ch'i*, pp. 125–26.

140. Cf. Chou Wei, *Chung-kuo ping-ch'i shih-kao*, pp. 88–98.

141. Cf. Yang Hung, *Ku-ping-ch'i* p. 126.

142. See Kwang-chih Chang, "The Chinese Bronze Age: A Modern Synthesis," in Wen Fong, ed., *The Great Bronze Age of China* (Knopf, New York, 1980), p. 45; Chang, *Chung-kuo ch'ing-t'ung shih-tai* (Chung-wen Ta-hsüeh ch'u-pan-she, Hong Kong, 1982), p. 13.

143. Cf. Emma C. Bunker, "The Steppe Connection," *EC* 9–10 (1983–85): pp. 72–73.

144. See Loehr, "The Earliest Chinese Swords," pp. 132–42.

145. Cf. Chou Wei, *Chung-kuo ping-ch'i shih-kao*, pp. 112–16.

146. See Yang Hung, *Ku-ping-ch'i*, p. 129.

147. Hayashi Minao, *Chūgoku In-Shū jidai no buki* (Kyoto Daigaku Jimbun Kagaku Kenkyūsho, Kyoto, 1972), pp. 199–236.

148. Chou Wei, *Chung-kuo ping-ch'i shih-kao*, pp. 109–57. The number of articles that have appeared in PRC archaeological publications since 1970 is too great to list in detail.

149. Tu Cheng-sheng, "Chou-tai feng-chien chieh-t'i-hou te chün-cheng hsin-chih-hsü—pien-hu ch'i-min te yen-chiu chih-erh," *BIHP* 55, no. 1 (1984): p. 75.

150. Yang K'uan, "Ch'un-ch'iu Chan-kuo-chien feng-chien te chün-shih tsu-chih ho chan-cheng te pien-hua," *Li-shih chiao-hsüeh*, no. 4 (1954): pp. 7–8.

151. For discussion, see K. C. Chang, *Shang Civilization* (Yale University Press, New Haven, 1980), pp. 195–96; Hsu and Linduff, *Western Chou Civilization*, p. 85.

152. Cf. Yen I-p'ing, "Yin-Shang ping-chih," *Chung-kuo wen-tzu*, NS 7 (1983):

24–28; and *Chung-kuo chün-shih-shih,* vol. 4: *Ping-fa* (Chieh-fang-chün ch'u-pan-she, Peking, 1988), pp. 7–13.

153. Cf. Yen I-p'ing, "Yin-Shang ping-chih," p. 38.

154. Hsu and Linduff, *Western Chou Civilization,* p. 164.

155. Lao Kan, "Chan-kuo shih-tai te chan-cheng fang-fa," *BIHP* 37 (1967): p. 48.

156. Chin Hsiang-heng, "Ts'ung chia-ku pu-ts'u yen-chiu Yin Shang chün-lü-chung chih wang-tsu san-hsing san-shih," *Chung-kuo wen-tzu* 52 (1974): pp. 7B–14A; and *Ping-fa,* p. 14. Chin believes *chün* represents an expansion of *shih* and that the Chou only used the term *shih.*

157. Tu Cheng-sheng, "Hsin-chih hsü," p. 78.

158. Cf. ibid., pp. 75, 78.

159. See *Ping-fa,* pp. 15–25, for a discussion of basic deployment principles. Additional comments are found in the footnotes to the translations.

160. Cf. Yen I-p'ing, "Yin-Shang ping-chih," p. 24. A decade-based system is found in the *Wei Liao-tzu.*

161. For Western terms, see John I. Alger, *Definitions and Doctrine of the Military Art* (Avery Publishing Group, Wayne, N.J.), p. 1985.

162. Cf. Chang, Shang Civilization, p. 195.

163. See Lao Kan, "Chan-kuo shih-tai," p. 47.

164. See Tu Cheng-sheng, "Hsin-chih-hsü," p. 92. The term designates the armies of the left, center, and right; but when more than three armies are fielded, then it refers to the left and right flanks and the center force, depending on how they are integrated and commanded.

165. Yang K'uan, "Ch'un-ch'iu pien-hua," p. 11; Chin Hsiang-heng, "San-hsing san-shih," p. 9A.

166. Cf. Hsü Hsi-ch'en, "Chou-tai ping-chih ch'u-lun," *Chung-kuo-shih yen-chiu,* no. 4 (1985): 4–6; Chang, *Shang Civilization,* pp. 161–65.

167. Cf. Hsü, "Chou-tai ping-chih," pp. 6–8; and Yang K'uan, "Ch'un-ch'iu pien-hua," pp. 8–10.

168. See Tu Cheng-sheng, "Hsin-chih-hsü," p. 74.

Notes
to the
Introduction

Abbreviations and basic texts

SS AS	Amano Shizuo, *Sonshi, Goshi* (Meiji Shoin, Tokyo, 1972).
SS AY	Asano Yuichi, *Sonshi* (Kodansha, Tokyo, 1986).
SS HT	Hosokawa Toshikazu, *Sonshi, Goshi* (Gakken kenkyūsha, Tokyo, 1982).
SS NT	Nakatani Takao, *Sonshi* (Kyoikusha, Tokyo, 1987).
SS TY	Tadokoro Yoshiyuki, *Sonshi* (Meitoku shuppansha, Tokyo, 1970).
ST CCCY	Wei Ju-lin, *Sun-tzu chin-chu chin i* (Shang-wu yin-shu-kuan, Taipei, 1972).
ST SCC	*Sun-tzu shih-chieh-chueh* (Shih-chieh shu-chü, Taipei, 1984).
ST WCHC	*Sun-tzu* in *Ch'ung-k'an Wu-ching hui-chieh* (Chung-chou ku-chi ch'u-pan-she, Cheng-chou, 1989).
STPF CS	Wu Ju-sung, *Sun-tzu ping-fa ch'ien-shuo* (Chieh-fang-chün ch'u-pan-she, Peking, 1983).
STPF HC	Chün-k'o-yüan chan-cheng li-cheng-pu, ed., *Sun-tzu ping-fa hsin-chu* (Chung-hua shu-chü, Peking, 1981).
STPF SY	Chu Chün, *Sun-tzu ping-fa shih-i* (Hai-ch'ao ch'u-pan-she, Peking, 1980).
STPF TC	Wei Ju-lin, *Sun-tzu ping-fa ta-ch'uan* (Li-ming, Taipei, 1970).
STPF WC	Wang Chien-tung, *Sun-tzu ping-fa* (Chih-yang ch'u-pan-she, Taipei, 1989).
SWTCC WCCS	*Sun Wu-tzu chih-chieh*, in *Ming-pen Wu-ching Ch'i-shu chih-chieh*, vol. 1 (Shih-ti chiao-yü ch'u-pan-she, Taipei, 1972).
WYCC	*Wu Yüeh ch'un-ch'iu*, SPKY ed. (Shih-chieh shu-chü, Taipei, 1967).

1. During the T'ang dynasty—and perhaps much earlier—numerous editions of the *Art of War* (and other military writings) were introduced into Japan along with other books and aspects of Chinese culture and religion. Apparently the book was widely studied, and influenced several notable figures. The most accessible brief history of the text and its influence in Japan is found appended to Griffith's translation of the *Art of War* cited in note 3, below, pp. 169–78. Several articles have also appeared in the collected volume *Sun-tzu hsin-t'an—Chung-wai hsüeh-che lun Sun-tzu*, ed. Ch'en Chi-k'ang (Chieh-fang-chün ch'u-pan-she, Peking, 1990): "*Sun-tzu ping-fa* tsai jih-pen-te ch'uan-po yüan-liu chi i-pu ku-pen *Sun-tzu ping-fa* te tsai-fa-hsien" (by Kao Tien-fang, Ch'en P'eng, and Wang Yen-yü), pp. 338–51, and "Ch'ien-t'an *Sun-tzu ping-fa* tsai jih-pen li-tai chan-cheng, ch'ing-pao kung-tso-chung te tung-yung" (by Chou Hong-chin and Yü Ch'üan-ting), pp. 352–58.

Over the centuries there have been numerous Japanese translations of varying quality, including both scholarly renditions and extremely simplified popular editions—even comic-book versions—in this century. Many popularly oriented works adapting and exploiting Sun-tzu's thoughts in remarkably diverse human endeavours have also appeared. The more serious select and discuss important principles for guiding action and behavior in human relations and business; multivolume audio-cassette versions have even been prepared for self-study while commuting or driving. While numerous Japanese translations and derivative publications have been consulted for our translation, they will be noted only where differing significantly from the traditional Chinese commentary to the text.

2. Lionel Giles, trans., *Sun-tzu on the Art of War* (Luzac and Co., London, 1910).

3. Samuel B. Griffith, *The Art of War* (Oxford University Press, London, 1963). Griffith also supplements the translated text with selected materials from the most important traditional commentaries.

4. For example, Thomas Cleary's *The Art of War* (Shambala Publications, Boston, 1988). The introduction contains a discussion of the *Art of War* as a Taoist book, and the translation incorporates extensive quotations from the commentaries.

5. For example, see Li Ling in *Hsü Wei-shu t'ung-k'ao*, pp. 1614–17; Ch'i Ssu-ho in *Hsü Wei-shu t'ung-k'ao*, pp. 1598–99; and Chang Hsin-ch'eng, *Wei-shu t'ung-k'ao*, vol. 2, pp. 797–800. The absence of Sun Wu's name and accomplishments in the *Tso chuan*, well noted for portraying Wu's events in comparative detail, is often considered fatal to any claim of historicity. However, a few scholars argue that many persons and events pivotal to the history of various minor states went unrecorded, so in this regard Sun-tzu should not be considered remarkable. (For further discussion, see the section at the end of the introduction on the question of Sun-tzu's existence.)

For its realistic approach (employing spies and deception) designed to ensure the state's survival, the *Art of War* was also vehemently condemned by Confucian literati throughout late Chinese history, as well as by numerous Westerners early in this century. (They unfortunately displayed the same attitude as Secretary of State Stimson in his unimaginable quashing of code-breaking activities in a hostile world.) Sun Wu's existence and role, as well as the book itself, were accordingly viewed as late fabrications, unworthy of consideration except by the morally reprehensible.

6. Sun Wu and Sun Pin's connected biographies in the *Shih chi, chüan* 65, are translated by Griffith in his introduction (*The Art of War,* pp. 57–62) and may also be found in most other translations.

7. Wu Tzu-hsü, largely credited with the major role in Wu's ascendancy, became the subject of a popular cult and numerous stories because of his achievements and perverse execution. (See David Johnson, "The Wu Tzu-hsü *Pien-wen* and Its Sources," *HJAS* 40.1, [June 1980]: pp. 93–156; [December 1980]: *HJAS* 40.2, pp. 465–505.) The fact that Sun tzu is not mentioned in the *Tso chuan* is sometimes justified by pointing out that Wu Tzu-hsü was such a dominant figure, as well as Sun-tzu's direct superior, that he simply eclipsed Sun-tzu when credit for Wu's military success was apportioned. (Cf. Wei Ju-lin, ST CCCY, p. 5.) His biography is translated and analyzed in our introduction.

8. In Sun-tzu's *Shih chi* biography, Po P'i is referred to as Po Hsi. (The character for *hsi* appears on the left side of *p'i,* and therefore the *Shih chi* version would seem to have picked up an abbreviated writing.) However, as most of the other writings that will be excerpted for analysis call him "Po P'i," for convenience Po P'i will be used throughout. All other important people will be treated similarly.

9. According to most writings, Sun Wu was a native of Ch'i, as will be discussed in the introduction. Chao Yeh either had conclusive evidence available to him, or lacked a basis for attributing his origins to another state.

10. Ch'i Ssu-ho, among others, doesn't believe Sun-tzu would have ever been allowed to commandeer palace women to illustrate his theories of military discipline, nor that the execution of the two captains would have been understood as proving anything. He therefore views the entire episode as an exaggeration. (See *Hsü Wei-shu t'ung-k'ao,* p. 1598.) Wu Ju-sung believes the incident illustrates Sun-tzu's fundamental teaching that a general, once in command of the army, does not accept orders from the ruler, rather than any lesson about discipline, in accord with his particular understanding of Sun-tzu's major contribution being the isolation and characterization of the professional general. (STPF CS, p. 3. Also see the discussion on Sun-tzu and the text later in the introduction.)

11. This and similarly worded phrases appear frequently in the *Seven Military Classics,* as well as in the *Art of War*. Essentially a quotation from the *Tao Te Ching,* it is generally taken as evidence of Taoist influence upon military thought. However, perhaps this single saying was simply adopted by various military strategists because of their sobering experience in actual warfare, without reference to, or acceptance of, any other aspects of philosophical Taoism.

12. *Wu Yüeh ch'un-ch'iu, chüan* 4, "Ho-lü nei-chuan." (The translation follows the SPKY edition reprinted as *Wu Yüeh ch'un-ch'iu* [hereafter WYCC] [Shih-chieh shu-chü, Taipei, 1967], vol. 1, pp. 31–33A.) The biography continues with an important passage in which Sun-tzu advises the king not to press further attacks against Ch'u because the people are already exhausted. While his name is mentioned several more times in the chapter, except in a single case where he briefly offers tactical advice, it is always coupled with Wu Tzu-hsü. Insofar as the *Wu Yüeh ch'un-ch'iu* is attributed to the first century A.D., nearly two centuries after the *Shih chi,* it is not considered reliable evidence for Sun-

tzu's activities. However, recent PRC popular military histories frequently contain biographies of Sun-tzu based upon such remote material (including many late Warring States and Ch'in period writings), reconstructed in some detail. For example, see Ch'en Wu-t'ung and Su Shuang-pi, *Chung-kuo li-tai ming-chiang*, 2 vols. (Honan jen-min ch'u-pan-she, Honan, 1987), vol. 1, pp. 13–18. Virtually every modern edition and translation cites the *Shih chi* biography and assumes Sun-tzu's authenticity, although the *Chung-kuo ku-tai chan-cheng t'ung-chien* (Ch'ang-cheng ch'u-pan-she, Peking, 1988), pp. 74–81, never even mentions his name in the account of the war between Wu and Yüeh.

13. Sun-tzu's origins will be discussed at the end of the introduction in the section on the question of Sun-tzu's existence.

14. The monumental issue of the relationship between Taoist and military thought in antiquity, including questions of origins, modification of concepts, and direction of influence, obviously requires a voluminous study in itself. Many secondary works in Chinese contain at least brief ruminations on the subject, but almost all of them tend to treat it simplistically and ineffectually. (Hsü Wen-chu's chapter entitled "Sun-tzu ho Lao-tzu ssu-hsiang pi-chiao," found in his book *Sun-tzu yen-chiu* [Kuang-tung ch'u-pan-she, Taipei, 1980], pp. 192–208, is an exception.) In the West, Christopher Rand has initiated the analytical effort with an intriguing, if complex article providing a conceptual framework for dissecting the various approaches to certain felt problems. (See "Chinese Military Thought and Philosophical Taoism," *Monumenta Serica* 34 [1979–80]: 171–218, and "Li Ch'üan and Chinese Military Thought," *HJAS* 39.1 [June, 1979]: 107–37.) Insofar as it is impossible to compress a meaningful, comparative presentation of Taoist ideas and military thought into a few pages of closely packed footnotes, we have opted to introduce appropriate comments at relevant points in the translation and introductory material. (Ch'en Ch'i-t'ien's *Sun-tzu ping-fa chiao-shih* [Chung-hua shu-chü, Taipei, 1955; reprint of 1944 ed.] contains a succinct analysis of the major philosophical schools' attitudes toward warfare that corrects some general misimpressions found throughout Chinese history. [See pp. 231–51.] Kagakuraoka Masatoshi's article "Sonshi to Roshi" [*Toho shukyo* 37 (April, 1971): 39–50] is among the earliest focusing on this issue.)

15. WYCC, vol. 1, p. 46A.

16. Based upon the *Shih chi* account, Wu Ju-sung believes the historical Sun-tzu was active in Wu, despite intrigues and treachery, for roughly thirty years, from 512 to 482 B.C. (See STPF CS, p. 4.) Chan Li-po suggests a more limited period, 512 to 496. ("Lüeh-t'an Lin-i Han-mu chu-chien Sun-tzu ping-fa," WW 1974: 12, p. 15.)

17. *Tung-Chou lieh-kuo-chih* (Shih-chieh shu-chü, Taipei, 1973), vol. 3, chapter 77, pp. 720–21.

18. For a discussion of the Early Chou and such campaigns, see Herrlee G. Creel, *The Origins of Statecraft in China* (University of Chicago Press, 1970), pp. 233 ff.

19. Wu apparently launched the first seaborne invasion in Chinese history, attacking Ch'i in 485 B.C. (See Chang Ch'i-yün, *Chung-hua wu-ch'ien-nien shih* [hereafter *Wu-ch'ien-nien shih*] [Chung-kuo Wen-hua Ta-hsüeh, Taipei, 1961], vol. 3, p. 88.)

20. For a discussion, see the section of "swords" at the end of the general introduction.

21. Including many small states that claimed royal Chou ancestors. (See San-chün Ta-hsüeh, *Chung-kuo li-tai chan-cheng-shih* [hereafter abbreviated by title] [Li-ming wen-hua, Taipei], vol. 2, p. 6, and *Wu-ch'ien-nien shih*, vol. 3, p. 71.) Creel attributes the origination of the *hsien* (district) system to Ch'u, particularly as it would have facilitated imposing central government administration on annexed territory. (See Herrlee G. Creel, "The Beginnings of Bureaucracy in China: The Origins of the *Hsien*," *Journal of Asian Studies* 23 (1964): 155–84.)

22. For a translation of the *Tso chuan* accounts of the battle of Ch'eng-p'u, see Watson, *The Tso chuan* (hereafter *Tso chuan*) (Columbia University Press, New York, 1989), pp. 50–64. The battle is also discussed by Frank Kierman in *Chinese Ways in Warfare*, eds. Frank A. Kierman and John K. Fairbank (Harvard University Press, 1974), pp. 47–56, and in *Chung-kuo li-tai chan-cheng-shih*, vol. 1, pp. 171–78.

23. The duke of Shen was among the many nobles and ministers felled by amorous desires, in this case coming into conflict with the ruler. Ch'u's losses were turned to great advantage by both Wu and Yüeh.

24. As Wan Chiu-ho points out, in 584 B.C. the year preceding the duke's visit, Wu mounted a campaign that traveled a thousand *li* and attacked the minor state of T'an, defeating it. Wu's growing power inevitably nominated it as a plausible candidate to counter Ch'u's threats. See Wan Chiu-ho, "Po-chü-chih-chan yü Huang-ch'ih-chih-hui," *Hsien-ch'in, Ch'in-Han-shih fu-k'an* 1992: 8, p. 56.

25. See the general introduction for the history and problems of chariot employment.

26. King T'ai is also known as Tan Fu (Tan-fu), the Ancient Duke already encountered in the general introduction as the progenitor of the Chou dynasty. T'ai-po, his son, supposedly went to the barbarian area of Wu to avoid ascending the throne. Since King Wu established the Chou when he defeated the Shang and was descended from T'ai-po's younger brother, in theory the Chou had to be ritually deferential to the state of Wu. See WYCC, *chüan* 1, I:1–5; *Shih chi, chüan* 31 ("The Hereditary House of Wu T'ai-po"); and Chang Ch'i-yün *Wu-ch'ien-nien shih*, vol. 3, p. 82.

27. Chang Ch'i-yün suggests short hair was necessary for people constantly in water, while their tattoos were designed to frighten water creatures. See *Wu-ch'ien-nien shih*, vol. 3, p. 82.

28. *Chung-kuo li-tai chan-cheng-shih*, vol. 2, pp. 8–14.

29. Ibid., p. 14.

30. Ibid., pp. 5–6, 9–18.

31. Ibid., p. 18. Floating downstream to engage an enemy obviously requires far less energy than mounting a campaign against the current. Consequently, Ch'u's forces should have been both rested and more numerous (considering that their journey would be much faster, and fewer supplies would have to be carried). The comparative advantage of engaging from a downstream position, or arrayed along the bank, would seem to be a question of tactics plus the strength of the current.

32. Nurturing the people and eliminating evil are fundamental domestic poli-

cies advocated in many of the *Seven Military Classics*, including the *Six Secret Teachings*, and such philosophical works as *Mencius* and the *Lü-shih ch'un-ch'iu*. Conducting punitive expeditions against those who brutalize and exhaust their people and who indulge in extravagance and licentiousness was morally sanctioned from the Chou's conquest of the Shang onward, as previously discussed.

33. Chapter 3, "Planning Offensives."

34. Chapter 8, "Nine Changes."

35. Chapter 6, "Vacuity and Substance."

36. *Chung-kuo li-tai chan-cheng-shih*, vol. 2, pp. 21–23. In Sun-tzu's era omens and magical thought still retained the power to frighten the troops and depress their morale. The later military classics, including the *Wu-tzu* (in which Wu Ch'i describes conditions in which an attack can be made *without divining about the prospects*), generally warn against allowing baleful influences in camp, and many specifically deny the potency of signs, omens, and indications. Sun-tzu mentions that prior knowledge can not be gained through divination and interpreting signs, but only through spies (chapter 13, "Employing Spies"), but otherwise is silent. However, an enemy perturbed and disspirited provides an opportunity to exploit a weakness in their *ch'i*, in accord with Sun-tzu's principles.

37. Military activities being associated with yin—the dark, negative—a moonless night signified yin proceeding to its extremity. Since extremes are inherently unstable, and the cycle is about to revert, with yang beginning to ascend as the new moon makes its appearance, military affairs would be extremely risky, unpredictable, and probably fated to failure.

38. "Wu Tzu-hsü lieh-chuan," *chüan* 66, the *Shih chi*. The translation is based upon Ma T'e-ying, *Shih chi chin-chu* (Shang-wu yin-shu-kuan, Taipei, 1979), vol. 4, pp. 2213–22. The biography is also included in Burton Watson's *Records of the Historian: Chapters from the Shih chi of Ssu-ma Ch'ien* (Columbia University Press, New York, 1969), pp. 16–29, and has previously been translated by R. C. Rudolph ("The Shih chi biography of Wu Tzu-hsü," *Oriens Extremus* 9 (1962): 105–20.)

39. The "woman of Ch'in" was a royal princess, the ruler's younger sister. The marriage was no doubt designed to establish or secure some minimal relationship between the two "barbarian" states on either side of Ch'u.

40. Ts'ai was a small state originally north of Ch'u, later annexed by them. It had a strong martial tradition, and the ruler's support figured prominently in the victorious invasion by which Wu reached Ch'u's capital of Ying.

41. "Great affairs" normally refer to revolutionary acts—in particular, the ousting of a debauched and oppressed ruler.

42. The text obviously suffers from disruptions that the Grand Historian did not resolve. "Each escaped alone" is interpolated.

43. In later versions of the story, the boatman commits suicide by drowning himself so as to forever preserve Wu's secret.

44. Other versions describe an encounter with a peasant woman who provides him with food and then drowns herself as well.

45. Chuan Chu, who had concealed the murder weapon—a dagger—in a fish, thereby immediately established his name for all time. His story is preserved in the *Shih chi* collective biography "The Assassins."

46. Po P'i apparently benefited from Wu Tzu-hsü's aid because Wu, blinded by his desire for revenge against Ch'u, apparently misread Po's character. (WYCC, vol. 1, pp. 15b–17a.) Hsi Yüan was Po Chou-li's son.

47. Both rulers, as will be discussed later, had been detained by Nang Wa for refusing to cater to his desires.

48. See the discussion that follows later in the introduction for a quotation.

49. This was essentially an appeal for solidarity among the descendants of the Chi and Chiang clans—the royal families of the Chou—who had emigrated centuries ago to nominally establish numerous minor Chou states along the Han River. Wu claims that Ch'u had destroyed all of them.

50. This event, whether actual or not, is generally dated to 500 B.C.

51. Or possibly his finger. (The translation of "toe" follows Tu Yü's commentary to the *Tso chuan*. Under Duke Ting's fourteenth year, in recounting the battle between Wu and Yüeh, the *Tso chuan* states "Ling Ku-fu attacked Ho-lü with a halberd. He injured Ho-lü's toe and got his shoe." Tu notes that Ho-lü's big toe was severed, and Yang adds that the term for big toe, *chiang chih*, also meant "middle finger" in antiquity. Since *chih*, the word found in the *Shih chi* biography, can mean either toe or finger, other translations often employ "finger." See Yang Po-chün, *Ch'un-ch'iu Tso-chuan-chu* (Chung-hua shu-chü, Peking, 1990), vol. 4, p. 1596.

52. The Announcement appears in the *Shu ching*, better known as the *Book of Documents*. For the context, see Legge's classic translation: *The Shoo King, The Chinese Classics*, vol. 3, book 7, "Pwan-kang."

53. Another example of Wu Tzu-hsü's failure to evaluate men properly. Even King Ho-lü is quoted as saying that "Fu-ch'ai is stupid and not benevolent." (See WYCC, vol. 1, pp. 44B–46B.)

54. While much of the *Shih chi* follows the *Tso chuan* closely, other parts are clearly based upon different sources and materials. The degree to which his source materials may have been altered and embellished, or even "creatively supplemented," over time is difficult to determine. Because only a brief space is devoted to most people, they tend to have an archetypal cast and be characterized by just a few phrases. However, officials such as Fei Wu-chi—who destroyed men and even forged the king's orders—hardly need more development.

55. See note 23, above.

56. Especially in such military classics as the *Six Secret Teachings* and the *Three Strategies*.

57. See chapter 15, "Civil Offensive," *T'ai Kung's Six Secret Teachings* in *The Seven Military Classics of Ancient China*, pp. 56–57.

58. In chapter 7, "Military Combat," Sun-tzu states: "When you plunder a district, divide the wealth among your troops. When you enlarge your territory, divide the profits." Common practice was of course to seize whatever was mobile; the later military classics stress not harming local inhabitants, destroying fields and buildings, or seizing the enemy's wealth as part of their psychological doctrine and good moral practice.

59. *Chung-kuo li-tai chan-cheng-shih*, vol. 2, p. 41.

60. The *Tso chuan*, Duke Chao, thirtieth year.

61. Chapter 7, "Military Combat."

62. The system of five made the Squad of five, including its leader, the basic organizational unit. While methods for employing the Squad of five are found in most of the military writings, one of the clearest expositions, with the rules and regulations, is found in chapters 14 and 16 of the *Wei Liao-tzu,* entitled "Orders for the Squad of Five" and "Orders for Binding the Squad of Five." (See *Seven Military Classics,* pp. 263–65, and the section on military organization in the introduction. Lord Shang's exposition on employing the unit of five is found in his chapter "Within the Borders." For a translation see J.J.L. Duyvendak, *The Book of Lord Shang* (University of Chicago Press, 1963; reprint of original edition, 1928), pp. 294–303.

63. *Chung-kuo li-tai chan-cheng-shih,* vol. 2, p. 34. The number of chariots associated with the army is unclear. In the *Tso chuan* record of the campaign to Ying, one of Nang Wa's advisers urges quick action because Ch'u's chariots, partially employing leather, could not withstand the moisture of the river area, whereas those of Wu could (See *Tso chuan,* Duke Ting, fourth year.) It is unlikely they would have been ferried up the Huai River, although the southern force probably employed them to a greater degree.

64. The ideal commander was thought to be a man who, eschewing the privileges of rank, shared hardships and the travails of ordinary military life with his men. Such behavior bonded his troops to him, and also allowed hm to know their limits and endurance. Wu Ch'i, as portrayed in his biography in the *Shih chi,* exemplified the true genereral, and descriptions much in his mold are found in several of the military classics.

65. Duke Chao of Ts'ai had presented a fur garment and a jade pendant to the ruler, keeping similar ones for himself. Duke Ch'eng of T'ang had arrived with two unusual horses. In both cases they refused to relinquish them to Nang Wa, thereby incurring his enmity. While the incident is recorded in the *Tso chuan* (Duke Ting, third year), it is also recounted by Sun-tzu and Wu Tzu-hsü when explaining to King Ho-lü why Ch'u had become vulnerable. (WYCC, vol. 1, pp. 37–38).

66. Chin, which headed the alliance of numerous northern states, was actually afraid to initiate military action against Ch'u, and in the end no real coercive pressure was applied apart from the specter of a threatening alliance. According to the *Wu Yüeh ch'un-ch'iu,* their release was due to the rulers' ministers presenting alternative gifts sufficiently dazzling that Nang Wa released them. (WYCC, vol. 1, pp. 37B–38)

67. *Chung-kuo li-tai chan-cheng-shih,* vol. 2, p. 32.

68. Chapter 6, "Vacuity and Substance."

69. The summaries and analyses found in two works are particularly useful for studying this campaign: Ch'ang Ch'i-yün's *Chung-hua Wu-ch'ien-nien shih* (Chung-kuo Wen-hua Ta-hsüeh, Taipei, 1963), vol. 3, p. 87, and that by the Armed Forces University, *Chung-kuo li-tai chan-cheng-shih,* vol. 2, pp. 29–50. Wan Chiu-ho's article "Po-chü-chih-chan yü Huang-ch'ih-chih-hui," *Hsien-Ch'in, Ch'in-Han-shih fu-k'an* 1992: 8, pp. 56–62, also contains a similar analysis. Material relating to the battles is translated by Burton Watson in the *Tso chuan,* pp. 180–90.

70. See *Tso chuan,* Duke Ting, fourth year.

71. Chapter 11, "Nine Terrains." Naturally the wise general can also exploit this tendency in his men, and in the same chapter Sun-tzu advocates casting them

onto fatal ground to attain their maximum effort: "Cast them into hopeless situations and they will be preserved; have them penetrate fatal terrain and they will live."

72. *Tso chuan*, Duke Ting, fifth year.

73. Ibid. He is quoted somewhat differently in the *Shih chi* (*chüan* 31, "The Hereditary House of T'ai-po of Wu"), where Fu-kai exclaims: "The king has already subordinated the army to me. The army takes advantage to be foremost, so how can I wait!"

74. Chapter 10, "Configurations of Terrain."

75. Chapter 3, "Planning Offensives."

76. Cf. Chang Ch'i-yün, *Chung-hua wu-ch'ien-nien-shih*, vol. 3, p. 87.

77. The title of king is anachronistic because he had not yet returned to Wu to usurp the throne. That it was not corrected by the original recorders is puzzling.

78. The *Tso chuan*, Duke Ting, fourth year.

79. Chapter 11, "Nine Terrains."

80. Chapter 7, "Military Combat."

81. Chapter 9, "Maneuvering the Army."

82. Chapter 11, "Nine Terrains."

83. Chapter 7, "Military Combat." (Also see the notes to the translation.)

84. Chapter 2, "Waging War."

85. Chapter 7, "Military Combat."

86. Chapter 7, "Military Combat." (Also found in chapter 11, "Nine Terrains.")

87. In addition to the accounts found in the *Tso chuan*, *Wu Yüeh ch'un-ch'iu*, and *Shih chi* (such as "The Hereditary House of Kou-chien, King of Yüeh"), the discussion that follows is also based on *Chung-kuo li-tai chan-cheng-shih*, vol. 2., pp. 52–76; *Wu-ch'ien-nien shih*, vol. 3, pp. 89–92, 94–104; and Wan Chiu-ho, "Po-chü-chih-chan yü Huang-ch'ih-chih-hui," *Hsien-Ch'in, Ch'in-Han-shih fu-k'an* 1992: 8, pp. 59–61.

88. Apparently King Fu-ch'ai became so enthralled with the women of Yüeh that Po P'i was virtually able to mesmerize him into dooming himself and his state. Beautiful women were used throughout the period as an offensive weapon, generally to befuddle a ruler or gain power over a minister. Apart from any question of moralizing, licentiousness and effective rule were known to be mutually incompatible. Many examples of the tactical exploitation of beautiful women may be found in the *Seven Military Classics*.

89. Chapter 12, "Incendiary Attacks." On the other hand, arguments that a benevolent ruler extends mercy to his enemies were well known, although increasingly ignored with the passage of time, and proved a formidable obstacle to Wu Tzu-hsü.

90. Exactly in the manner prescribed by the T'ai Kung in chapter 15 of the *Six Secret Teachings*.

91. In chapter 1, "Initial Estimations," Sun-tzu said: "Be deferential to foster their arrogance." In order to weaken his enemy, King Kou-chien encouraged them to undertake massive, distant campaigns, just as Sun-tzu advised.

92. *Chung-kuo li-tai chan-cheng-shih*, vol. 2, pp. 66–68.

93. Chapter 6, "Vacuity and Substance." Also see chapter 6 in general on the

methods for manipulating men and attaining the objective of "compelling others."

94. Chapter 6, "Vacuity and Substance."

95. Ibid.

96. Just as the Chou had allowed the state of Shang to retain the small fief of Sung, to perpetuate their sacrifices to their ancestors.

97. Chapter 1, "Initial Estimations."

98. The *Art of War* is classified by the *Han shu* under the subcategory of "*ping ch'üan mou,*" roughly "military (imbalance of) power and planning." (See note 125 below for a brief discussion of *ch'üan; shih,* with which it is closely related, is analyzed later in the introduction and in note 158.) *Ch'üan* is frequently identified with expediency, with military measures that stress volatile tactics, swiftness, and indirection to achieve their aims. Books in this category are aptly described as follows: "[Experts in] *ch'üan* and *mou* preserve the state with the orthodox (*cheng,* the upright), and employ the army with the unorthodox (*ch'i*). Only after first estimating [the prospects for victory] do they engage in warfare. They unite the disposition of troops (*hsing*) and strategic power (*shih*), embrace yin and yang, and utilize [those skilled in] technology and the crafts." Other works included in this section are Sun Pin's *Military Methods* and the *Wu-tzu,* books by Lord Shang and the T'ai Kung having been deleted from the original *Ch'i lüeh* listing. (Cf. Robin D. S. Yates, "New Light on Ancient Chinese Military Texts: Notes on their Nature and Evolution, and the Development of Military Specialization in Warring States China,"*T'oung Pao* 74 [1988]: 214–24.)

99. The bamboo-slip edition discovered at Lin-i comprises slightly more than one third of the present *Art of War,* arranged in thirteen sections with many chapter headings identical to those in the current text. While some discrepancies in extant traditional versions (such as found in the *Ten Commentaries* edition and the *Seven Military Classics* edition) have long been noted, they are essentially the same as—although of course more extensive than—the Lin-i reconstructed text. Additional material uncovered in the tomb, including a brief conversation recorded between the king of Wu and Sun-tzu (generally felt to be reasonably authentic record of their initial interview) perhaps sustains the opinion that the original form of the *Art of War* was thirteen sections, as recorded in the *Shih chi,* and suggests that Ssu-ma Ch'ien employed materials now lost when writing the Suns' biography. (The bamboo-slip edition, of course, only proves that this particular version existed prior to, or at least early in, the Han dynasty. Scholars continue to argue about the further implications, including whether the section now entitled "King of Wu's Questions" provides evidence for Sun Wu's existence and the early origin of the text, as will be discussed in our introductory section on the question of Sun-tzu's existence.) For a brief English overview, see Robin Yates, "New Light," pp. 211–20.

Among the most important original reports on the excavation and contents of this tomb, including the recovered texts, are the following: "Shantung Lin-i Hsi-Han-mu fa-hsien *Sun-tzu ping fa* ho *Sun Pin ping-fa* teng chu-chien te chien-pao," *WW* 1974: 2, pp. 15–21; Hsü Ti, "Lüeh-t'an Lin-i Yin-chüeh-shan Han-mu ch'u-t'u te ku-tai ping-shu ts'an-chien," *WW* 1974: 2, pp. 27–31; Lo Fu-i, "Lin-i Han-chien kai-shu," *WW* 1974: 2, pp. 32–35 and Chan Li-po, "Lüeh-t'an Lin-i

Han-mu chu-chien *Sun-tzu ping-fa*," *WW* 1974: 12, pp. 13–19. (Chan Li-po points out several instances in which the bamboo-slip edition's reading is completely opposite the present text. In some sentences this radically alters the meaning, resolving otherwise contorted and opaque constructions. These will be cited in the notes to the translation, together with other views, such as those of Chu Chün.) Also see Li Ling's summary reprinted in *Hsü Wei-shu t'ung-kao,* pp. 1605–08.

100. Wu Ju-sung emphasizes Sun-tzu's dictum that warfare is the greatest affair of state, as distinguished from the Shang-Chou tradition identifying both sacrifice and warfare as the sole important matters. Wu feels that Sun-tzu's view reflects the new reality emerging late in the Spring and Autumn period, and the clash of economic interests between the newly landed class and the old nobility that had monopolized military power and authority. (See STPF CS, pp. 9–12.)

101. Chapter 1, "Initial Estimations."

102. The *Art of War,* while expressing the basic view found throughout the *Seven Military Classics* that the state must always be prepared for warfare and nurture adequate material welfare, advocates keeping the people essentially ignorant and manipulating them in battle like sheep. Accordingly, some scholars (particularly in the PRC) have concluded that the author lived some after the rise of early Legalist thought—such measures being characteristic of that approach—and even termed him a Legalist strategist. See, for example: Tsun Hsin, "*Sun-tzu ping-fa* te tso-che chi ch'i shih-tai," *WW* 1974: 12, pp. 22–24; Ch'i Ssu-ho in *Hsü Wei-shu t'ung-k'ao,* p. 1603; Li Ling in *Hsü Wei-shu t'ung-k'ao,* p. 1613; and Chan Li-po, "Lüeh-t'an Lin-i Han-mu chu-chien *Sun-tzu ping-fa,*"*WW* 1974: 12, pp. 14–15. Keeping the people simple and ignorant is also a pronounced doctrine in the *Tao Te Ching*. However, see the translation notes to chapter 11.

103. See the discussion on sieges in the last section of the introduction where the question of internal evidence for dating the text is raised. Also note the inclusion of tomb text material on cities in the chapter entitled "Nine Changes" in the translation.

104. Chapter 3, "Planning Offensives."

105. See the notes to the translation for a discussion of these objectives. The late Spring and Autumn period, marking the transition from limited-scale, somewhat formal warfare (with reputedly general adherence to codes of behavior) to the unlimited carnage and brutality of the Warring States period, was supposedly still affected by doctrines of humane conduct. That is, some thinkers felt that campaigns that deliberately minimize the damage and suffering inflicted upon the enemy would not only be more in accord with concepts of virtue (and the casting out of the evil), but also lessen the enemy's opposition and undermine his will to fight. In contrast, as Sun-tzu noted, brutal attacks would force the enemy to mount a pitched defense, knowing that they would all perish if vanquished. Less intense opposition would invariably result in fewer losses for one's own side. It is, of course, always possible that this policy reflected a deliberate reaction to the carnage of the later period, such as the *Three Strategies* perhaps does. Barbarian armies were identified with the opposite policy of striking terror in those under attack: failing to surrender early on would result in total annihilation.

106. Chapter 3, "Planning Offensives."

107. The final paragraph of the chapter summarizes the role and importance of the process: "Before the engagement, one who determines in the ancestral temple that he will be victorious has found that the majority of factors are in his favor. Before the engagement one who determines in the ancestral temple that he will not be victorious has found few factors are in his favor."

108. Sun-tzu's materialistic concept of Heaven, and his opposition to consulting omens, are seen by Wu Ju-sung as evidence of a new attitude and approach, in contradistinction with the old concepts held by the Chou nobility and the earlier Shang. (See STPF CS, p. 18.) However, yin-yang and such other concepts as five-phase theory, which also appear in the *Art of War*, thereafter developed into an influential school of thought, apparently affecting military theory and even command practices, although being condemned in such other *Seven Military Classics* as the *Six Secret Teachings* and the *Wei Liao-tzu*.

109. Cf. D. C. Lau, "Some Notes on the *Sun-tzu*," *BSOAS* 28 (1965): 331–32, and Hsü Wen-chu, *Sun-tzu yen-chiu* (Kuang-tung ch'u-pan-she, Taipei, 1980), pp. 168–69.

110. Although Sun-tzu's biography suggests training should be one of his strong points, unlike in the later military writings there is no mention of methods for training and instruction. However, he observes that disorder in the troops, as well as rebellious troops whose general applied punishment before they had become emotionally attached, would provide opportunities to be exploited. (The subject of military training is focused upon in such chapters as "Teaching Combat" [*Six Secret Teachings*]; "Controlling the Army" [*Wu-tzu*]; "Orders for Restraining the Troops" [*Wei Liao-tzu*]; and Book II of *Questions and Replies*.)

111. Although Sun-tzu offers little commentary, the systematic implementaton of rewards and punishments, as well as their psychology, is the focus of much discussion in the later writings. For example, see "Rewards and Punishments" and "The General's Awesomeness" in the *Six Secret Teachings*, and numerous chapters in the *Wei Liao-tzu*.

112. Altogether some eight factors (counting advantages of Heaven and Earth separately) should have relative estimates assigned to them. No doubt some comparative weighting system had to be employed because advantages of Earth might have been deemed more important than force strength. Some of these factors are detailed in the text.

113. See T'an Ching-wu, *Sun-tzu ping-fa tsui-hsin-chieh*, (self-published, Taipei, 1981; rev. ed.), pp. 25–27 for an extensive list.

114. Heaven is usually interpreted as encompassing climate, the seasons, and weather. Earth, discussed further in the introduction, includes advantages of terrain (such as favorable position, or ability to take advantage of ravines or trap an enemy in a valley), a secure water supply, grass, freedom from dampness, and similar factors.

115. Sun-tzu's discussion of the general's critical qualities is viewed as evidence that professional commanders had already appeared on the historical stage, displacing personal field command by hereditary rulers. (Cf. STPF SY, p. 12.) Further confirmation is provided by his insistence that the ruler should not interfere with the commander once the latter has assumed the mantle of authority and ventured forth, as illustrated by the famous incident from his

biography, and the origin of such problems (discussed in chapter 3, "Planning Offensives.")

116. Chapter 12, "Incendiary Attacks."

117. Chapter 4, "Military Disposition."

118. Sun-tzu also said: "Those that the ancients referred to as excelling at warfare conquered those who were easy to conquer. Thus the victories of those that excelled in warfare were not marked by fame for wisdom or courageous achievement. Thus their victories were free from errors. One who is free from errors directs his measures toward [certain] victory, conquering those who are already defeated."

119. Some generals no doubt felt invincible, others that they had no alternative but to fight given their likely condemnation by an impatient ruler. One of the ten errors that mark generals in the *Six Secret Teachings* is "being hasty and impatient." (See chapter 19, "A Discussion of Generals.")

120. See the general introduction for a discussion of the shift in command from ruler to professional general.

121. In the tomb text it also appears first; however, all the following characters have been lost.

122. Many of the other military writings stress that wisdom—embracing not only basic mental acuity but also tactical planning and analytical skills, knowledge, and the ability to abstract lessons from experience—outweighs courage in importance. The general must be courageous, but courage does not predominate. The dangers of courage untempered by other qualities, including wisdom, were much remarked upon in most of the *Seven Military Classics*. For example, in "A Discussion of Generals" (*Six Secret Teachings*) five talents are identified: "What we refer to as the five talents are courage, wisdom, benevolence, trustworthiness, and loyalty. If he is courageous he cannot be overwhelmed. If he is wise he cannot be forced into turmoil. If he is benevolent he will love his men. If he is trustworthy he will not be deceitful. If he is loyal he will not be of two minds." Among the "ten errors" is "being courageous and treating death lightly" because "one who is courageous and treats death lightly can be destroyed by violence." (*Seven Military Classics*, p. 62.) Other lists of vital characteristics are found in the *Wu-tzu* (chapter 4, "The Tao of the General")—awesomeness, virtue, benevolence, and courage; and the *Three Strategies of Huang Shih-kung,* Book I—pure, quiet, controlled, accepts criticism, judges disputes, attracts and employs men, selects and accepts advice, knows the customs of states, able to map mountains and rivers, discern defiles and difficulties, and control military authority. Similarly, he can't be troubled, greedy, or arrogant.

123. In chapter 8, "Nine Changes," in remarking upon dangerous traits in generals, Sun-tzu said: "One who loves the people can be troubled." The T'ai Kung mentions "being benevolent but unable to inflict suffering" as a fatal error in generals because "he can be worn down" ("A Discussion of Generals," the *Six Secret Teachings.*)

124. One such list in the *Six Secret Teachings* is cited in note 122 above. A fundamental principle was to attack weakness and flaws in enemy commanders; Wu Ch'i was particularly noted for probing the enemy to discover the commander's ability. See chapter 2 of the *Wu-tzu*, "Evaluating the Enemy."

125. *Ch'üan* is a difficult term to isolate and precisely define, and the classical commentators assign a wide range of meanings to it. Virtually everyone agrees it anciently referred to the "weight of a steelyard," and thus meant "to weigh." (Cf. Kalgren, *Grammata Serica Recensa*, entry 158/O.) A. C. Graham, for example, with reference to its use in the Mohist classics, defines it as the "weighing" (of benefit and harm)," and "'positional advantage' used for leverage" (*Disputers of the Tao*, pp. 145, 157, 209, 164). Duyvendak notes it implies the "deciding influence and authority" (*The Book of Lord Shang*, p. 260, note 1). Other translators assign a wide range of equivalents, such as "power," "authority," "circumstances," and "expediency." (See, for example, Rickett, *Kuan Tzu*, p. 45, where he notes its closenesss to *shih*, suggests the translation of "political power," and comments that it can also refer to whatever might be expedient.) The classical Chinese commentators tend to stress the sense of weighing, of balancing forces, as well as its meaning of "authority." However, *ch'üan* is also set off against *cheng*—that is, it is the "expedient" (associated with the exercise of power, particularly military power) compared with the "upright," the "orthodox," or the "correct," the measures of proper government and the civil. (See, for example, T'ao Hsi-hseng, *Ping-fa san-shu* [Shih-huo ch'u-pan-she, Taipei, 1979], pp. 5–6.) Its origins are frequently associated with the philosopher Shen Pu-hai, about whom Herrlee G. Creel has written a brief monograph: *Shen Pu-Hai: A Chinese Political Philosopher of the Fourth Century B.C.* (University of Chicago Press, 1974).

In some usages, the simple equivalent of "authority" is clearly adequate; however, in others the term appears to refer to the strategic imbalance of power, or the strategic advantage obtained from such imbalance, and will therefore be translated as "strategic (im)balance of power." (A discussion on the term "power" follows in the introduction.)

126. Note that Wu Ju-sung believes it is not generally recognized that the *Art of War*, just as some Taoist writings, discusses means and methods for wresting victory with a small force, and fewer numbers. (See STPF CS, p. 17.)

127. Chapter 3, "Planning Offensives."

128. Ibid.

129. In chapter 13, "Employing Spies," Sun-tzu points out the burdens and suffering imposed on the people by warfare, concluding: "Armies remain locked in a standoff for years to fight for victory on a single day, yet [generals] begrudge bestowing ranks and emoluments of one hundred pieces of gold and therefore do not know the enemy's situation. This is the ultimate inhumanity. Such a person is not a general for the people, an assistant for a ruler, or the arbiter of victory."

130. This is the justification for employing scouts and local guides, and otherwise buying or gaining true intelligence of the terrain and its features.

131. Chapter 10, "Configurations of Terrain."

132. Employing deceit and being deceptive are constant themes in the *Seven Military Classics,* as may immediately be seen from the number of entries in the index. In addition to advocating their employment on the battlefield, *Questions and Replies* also views them as important for preserving the secrecy of military doctrine. (See Book 1.)

133. Creating a localized imbalance in power (*ch'üan*).

134. Chapter 13, "Employing Spies."

135. For example, Books 1 and 2 of the *Three Strategies of Huang Shih-kung;* chapter 17, "Three Doubts," and chapter 26, "The Army's Strategic Power," in the *Six Secret Teachings.*

136. Chapter 11, "Nine Terrains." Later in the chapter Sun-tzu adds: "When you mobilize the army and form strategic plans, you must be unfathomable."

137. Chapter 11, "Nine Terrains." He also said: "At the moment the general has designated with them, it will be as if they ascended a height and abandoned their ladders. The general advances with them deep into the territory of the feudal lords and then releases the trigger. He comands them as if racing a herd of sheep— they are driven away, driven back, but no one knows where they are going."

138. Chapter 5, "Strategic Military Power." In "Vacuity and Substance," he states: "In order to cause the enemy to come of their own volition, extend some [apparent] profit. In order to prevent the enemy from coming forth, show them the [potential] harm."

139. Chapter 6, "Vacuity and Substance."

140. Virtually the last half of the lengthy *Six Secret Teachings*—that is, the Tiger, Leopard, and even much of the Canine Secret Teaching—is devoted to tactical discussions centered upon various configurations of terrain and battlefield situations. Whether the *Wu-tzu* borrowed from the *Art of War* or was based upon common military knowledge and Wu Ch'i's own observations and experience remains to be determined. The main discussion is found in chapter 5, "Responding to Change."

141. Thus the information provided to Wu by minority peoples and such states as Ts'ai and T'ang proved essential.

142. Chapter 10, "Configurations of Terrain."

143. The tomb texts include a brief fragment entitled "Configurations of Terrain, II," and "Four Changes." The latter has been incorporated into our translation; the former is basically worthless.

144. Many of the configurations relate not to specific terrain features but to the degree an invasion force has penetrated enemy territory.

145. Chapter 9, "Maneuvering the Army." Similar admonitions are found in the *Six Secret Teachings* and *Wu-tzu* regarding entrapping terrain.

146. Chapter 11, "Nine Terrains."

147. This is the basis for segmenting and combining, for effecting battlefield tactics.

148. The military thinkers all understood the difficulty of forcing men to enter battle and engage in combat, of compelling them to kill other men. (Sun-tzu observes it is anger that motivates them to do so.) They identified *ch'i* as the component whose development and surge made such actions possible. Sun-tzu was perhaps the first to recognize and describe the critical role of spirit and courage in battle, although the other *Seven Military Classics* and some of the early philosophical writings consider ways to develop, manipulate, and ensure the proper combative spirit. Among the philosophers, Mencius is famous for his cultivation of "overflowing *ch'i*" (II:A2), although his conception differed significantly from the military thinkers.

The definitions, dimensions, and dynamics of *ch'i* are quite complex, entailing both metaphysical and psychological aspects. This extremely important concept still lacks a serious monograph in English, although it is touched upon in a number of places in Needham's *Science and Civilisation in China*. There are significant works and numerous articles in Chinese and Japanese, the best of which are Ononzawa Seiichi, Fukunaga Mitsuji, and Yamanoi Yu, eds., *Ki no shisō* (Tokyo Daigaku shuppansha, Tokyo, 1978), and Kuroda Genji, *Ki no kenkyū* (Tokyo Bijustsu, Tokyo, 1977).

149. For example, one version states: "Ch'i, Vapor, the *ch'i* or fumes rising from fermenting rice; ether, breath, air" (G. D. Wilder and J. H. Ingram, *Analysis of Chinese Characters*, 2d ed. (College of Chinese Studies in China, Shanghai, 1934, p. 18). This is a popular as opposed to an etymological view, and probably derives from the fragrant vapors rising from cooking or steaming rice. (The modern character is written with a component part that means "rice.") The actual origins are obscure and a matter of much speculation, looking to observations of natural phenomena, such as vapors and clouds, for possibilities. The character seems to have appeared late in the Spring and Autumn, becoming frequent in the Warring States.

150. In chapters 9 and 10 Sun-tzu notes a number of circumstances in which disharmony and other problems marking disunity and the loss of hierarchical order affect the army.

151. The pernicious effects of prolonged campaigns (which exhaust the people, depress the men's spirits, and destroy cohesion) were clearly observed by Sun-tzu, leading to his emphasis upon avoiding them.

152. As previously discussed in connection with Fu-kai's avoidance of pressing his foe too fervently during their invasion of Ch'u. This view also appears in many other writings, including the *Ssu-ma Fa* (chapter 5, "Employing Masses"). Conversely, the nature of the general's task in nurturing the proper forms of courage and commitment, the *ch'i* necessary to fight, was also well understood and prominently discussed. For example, in chapter 4 of the *Ssu-ma Fa* ("Strict Positions") it states: "When men have minds set on victory, all they see is the enemy. When men have minds filled with fear, all they see is their fear." Warriors oblivious to death would be capable of anything. (The example of how one man, committed to dying, is able to frighten a thousand in the marketplace is sometimes cited. For example, see "Discussion of Regulations" in the *Wei Liao-tzu*.)

153. Suspended, stalemated, constricted, and precipitous configurations all entail the potential for defeat. Especially dangerous configurations such as Heaven's Furnace and Heaven's Well virtually doom any force trapped within them. However, dispersive and light terrains present psychological problems, for the men are not united nor inclined to fight.

154. Most of the military writings warn against the debilitating influence of rumors and omens. In "Nine Terrains" Sun-tzu advised: "Prohibit omens, eliminate doubt so that they will die without other thoughts." Similar expressions are found in Book 2 of the *Three Strategies of Huang Shih-kung;* Book 3 of *Questions and Replies;* and chapter 1, "Heavenly Offices," in the *Wei Liao-tzu*.

155. A shadowy figure who lived in the fourth century B.C., and to whom the *Shen-tzu* is nominally attributed.

156. Among the best are Wang Pang-hsiung, *Han Fei-tzu te che-hsüeh* (Tung-ta t'u-shu, Taipei, 1977), pp. 165–79; Hsieh Yün-fei, *Han Fei-tzu hsi-lun* (Tung-ta t'u-shu, Taipei, 1980), pp. 95–100; and Wu Hsiu-ying, *Han Fei-tzu chiu-i* (Wen-

shih-che ch'u-pan-she), pp. 86–91. Roger Ames essentially initiated the study of *shih* as a primary, discrete concept with a lengthy chapter in *The Art of Rulership* (University of Hawaii, Honolulu, 1983), pp. 65–107, entitled "*SHIH* (Strategic Advantage/Political Purchase)."

157. The development of private books may have largely coincided with the rise of specialist military studies. See, for example, Yates, "New Light," pp. 218–19, and the discussion on the authenticity of the *Art of War* at the end of the introduction. For general background—although military books are not discussed—consult Burton Watson's early work *Early Chinese Literature* (Columbia University Press, New York, 1962); T. H. Tsien, *Written on Bamboo and Silk* (University of Chicago Press, 1962); and *Science and Civilisation in China: Chemistry and Chemical Technology*, vol. 5, part 1, *Paper and Printing* (Cambridge University Press, Cambridge, England, 1985).

158. Giles (see note 2, above) tends to be severely criticized for his mistranslation and misunderstanding of the *Art of War*, although not always justifiably. His English equivalents for *shih* include "circumstances," "energy," "latent energy," "combined energy," "shape" (where the usage is synonymous with *hsing*, "shape" or "form"), and "strength," as well as simply eliding the term by not translating it. None of them seem particularly appropriate, although "latent energy" characterizes situational potential more accurately in several contexts.

General Griffith, a highly qualified military officer with extensive wartime experience and expert knowledge of strategy and tactics as well as their conceptions and precise vocabulary, also employs a number of distinct, context-dependent terms. (Note that he is generally criticized by D. C. Lau for lacking consistency in his terminology, but the sense of this term definitely varies within the *Art of War*. In a rather critical review of Griffith's translation, Lau discusses several of the main ideas and problems of the text. See "Some Notes on the *Sun Tzu*," BSOAS 28 (1965): 317–35. Lau's views, while preliminary, are important to understanding the text, and are taken into account in the translation.) These include "circumstances," "situation" (including at least once where it seems highly inappropriate), "momentum," "strength," and "tactical power" (which merits serious consideration as an equivalent for *shih*). He also offers a valuable footnote to the title of the fifth chapter: "*Shih*, the title of this chapter, means 'force,' 'influence,' 'authority,' 'energy.' The commentators take it to mean 'energy' or 'potential' in some contexts and 'situation' in others" (*Art of War*, p. 90). In contrast, for his recent translation (see note 4) Cleary selected "force of momentum," "formation," "conditions," and "forces."

The concept appears in the *Book of Lord Shang* and the *Kuan-tzu*, both probably (for the most part) dating to somewhat after the *Art of War*. For the former, Duyvendak, in *The Book of Lord Shang* (University of Chicago, Chicago, 1963; reprint of 1928 ed.) translates the term as "condition," "power," and "condition of power," with the following note: "power would really express better the sense of what is meant. Power, that is, which relies on the general condition and trend of things, as an abstract idea, and well distinguished from brute force" (p. 98; also see his general discussion, pp. 97–100.) Rickett, in his new translation of the *Kuan-tzu* (*Guanzi*, Princeton University Press, Princeton, 1985), vol. 1, employs "circumstances," "situation," "force of circumstances," and "authority" derived from a specific position or situation" (see pp. 45, 58–59). He also notes that *ch'üan*, discussed separately, refers to "whatever is expedient under varying circumstances" (p. 45) and cites a passage from the *Han chi* that defines the temporal nature of *shih* (p. 81–82). Other translations include (with reference to *Han Fei-tzu*) Graham's "power-base" and sometimes just "power." He expands upon it as "a situation of strength, or on occasional weakness, in relation to circumstances, for example strategic position on the battlefield" (*Disputers of the Tao* [Open Court, LaSalle, 1989], p. 278). Also Christopher Rand's "circumstantial power" ("Chinese Military Thought and Philosophical Taoism," p. 174); Yates, "positional advantage" ("New Light," p. 224.); and Burton Watson's "advantageous circumstances" (*Hsün-Tzu: Basic Writings* [Columbia University Press, New York, 1963], p. 57 and elsewhere). D. C. Lau, despite his incisive criticism, does not offer either a definition or translation for it in his review article.

Roger Ames's chapter devoted to *shih* traces the concept's evolution from the military thinkers Sun-tzu and Sun Pin through its adoption by the Legalists and into later, eclectic texts, such as the *Huai Nan-tzu*, providing extensive material and careful analysis. After noting the various meanings (and close relationship with the term for form, *hsing*), he summarizes his findings as follows: "In the *Sun Tzu*, then, the term *shih* has at least three dimensions of meaning: (1) "circumstances" or "conditions"; (2) "physical disposition" in connection with the deployment of troops; and (3) occupation of a superior position and access to the potential advantages it confers" (*The Art of Rulership*, p. 68). Because of the apparently close connection between the concept and the strategic advantage derived from occupation of superior positions, Ames elects to employ the interesting, if perhaps somewhat unknown term "purchase." As his analysis and arguments are well documented and readily available, it is only necessary to note that he consciously discards "power" and "force" as too vague, believing that "*shih* usually refers to something quite different from the actual strength required to accomplish something" (page 222, note 11).

159. Chapter 5, "Strategic Military Power." Sun-tzu also said: "The strategic configuration of power [is visible in] the onrush of pent-up water tumbling stones along."

160. Verse 51.

161. Ch'i Ssu-ho, whose views are summarized in the last part of our introduction (on the authenticity of the text), does not believe unorthodox tactics were employed prior to, or even during, Sun-tzu's time—contrary to our conclusions both there and earlier in the introduction.

162. Verse 57.

163. Much of the *Questions and Replies* focuses on elucidating the complexities of the unorthodox and orthodox, providing useful insights. The frequency of the topic throughout the *Seven Military Classics* precludes meaningful expansion here. (Refer to the index of our translation for a comprehensive listing.)

164. Chapter 4, "Military Disposition."

165. See Hsiao T'ien-shih, *Sun-tzu chan-cheng-lun* (Tzu-yu ch'u-pan-she, Taipei, 1983; reprint of 1942 ed.), pp. 197–99.

166. Cf. Hsü Wen-chu, *Sun-tzu yen-chiu* (Kuang-tung ch'u-pan-she, Taipei,

1980), pp. 206–08. Hsü observes that while Sun-tzu speaks about the mutually productive relationship of *ch'i* and *cheng*, he emphasizes the unorthodox. Also see Kaguraoka, "Sonsi to Roshi," especially pp. 44–46.

167. See Griffith, *The Art of War,* pp. 34–35.

168. See ibid., p. 42.

169. See ibid., p. 43.

170. D. C. Lau, "Some Notes on the *Sun-tzu,*" pp. 330–31.

171. See "Two Concepts in Early Chinese Military Thought," *Language* 42, no. 2 (1966): 295–99. However, see our general introduction for a discussion on the first introduction and subsequent slow diffusion of the cavalry in China.

172. *The Art of Rulership* (University of Hawaii, Honolulu, 1983), p. 68.

173. See "Chinese Military Thought," p. 118. As Sun-tzu stated: "[Simulated] chaos is given birth from control; [the illusion of] fear is given birth from courage; [feigned] weakness is given birth from strength" (chapter 5, "Strategic Military Power").

174. For example, see the anonymous Ming dynasty work *Ts'ao-lu ching-lüeh,* reprinted as *Chung-kuo ping-hsüeh t'ung-lun* (Li-ming, Taipei, 1986), pp. 107–10, and Hsiao T'ien-shih, *Sun-tzu chan-cheng lun,* pp. 197–99. In the Ming dynasty Chao Pen-hsüeh noted that very few generals excelled at employing the unorthodox (*Sun-tzu-shu chiao-chieh yin-lei* [Chung-hua shu-chü, Taipei; reprint, 1970], p. 79).

175. Several famous Sung dynasty scholars voiced skepticism: Ou-yang Hsiu, Mei Sheng-yü, Ch'en Chen-sun, Kao Ssu-sun, and particularly Yeh Shih, with whom the position became identified. See Ch'i Ssu-h'o, "Sun-tzu chu-tso shih-tai k'ao" (hereafter "Sun-tzu shih-tai"), *Yen-ching hsüeh-pao,* no. 26 (1939): 176.

176. The need for Nang Wa and King Chao to take concerted action indicates the strength of the Fei clan and the growing power of the great families in the late Spring and Autumn period.

177. In the T'ang another theory suddenly appeared that identified Sun-tzu's ancestors as having come from Ch'u. See Chou Wei-yen's summary of these possibilities, "Sun Wu ku-li Le-an tsai-chin 'Hui-min shuo' te-nan ch'eng-li," *Chung-kuo-shih yen-chiu* 1991: 3, p. 139.

178. WYCC, vol. 1, p. 32A.

179. Ibid., p. 41A. Note that in "The Hereditary House of Wu T'ai-po" in the *Shih-chi* (*chüan 31*), both Po P'i and Wu Tzu-hsü are recorded as whipping the king's corpse.

180. See Duke Ting, fifth year, the *Tso chuan.* Ch'u's leadership experienced dissension over employing an incendiary attack against Wu because their own dead still lay exposed in the intervening fields and would also be burned. However, realists prevailed, arguing that if the state proved victorious (rather than being extinguished), the spirits could thereby continue to receive sacrifices and should be pleased. (For a translation, see Watson, *The Tso chuan,* p. 187.)

181. The term "hegemonic kings" arose only late in the Warring States period after numerous state rulers had proclaimed themselves kings. (In the Spring and Autumn period the Chou king had retained at least nominal royal prestige, while only the rulers of the new peripheral states such as Wu and Yüeh had the audacity to style themselves kings.) With this proliferation the most powerful Warring

States monarchs then sought to distinguish themselves further, giving rise to the title "hegemonic king." The term's appearance in the *Art of War* is therefore cited by Ch'i Ssu-ho as evidence of a late Warring States composition date. (See "Sun-tzu shih-tai," pp. 184–85.) Note that our translation (chapter 11, "Nine Terrains"), however, treats the term as two individual referents, "hegemons and true kings," the latter being distingiushed from the former by their righteousness, because the bamboo-strip (tomb text) edition has *"wang pa"*—"kings and hegemons." (If the tomb text preserves the original order, Ch'i Ssu-ho's justification evaporates.)

182. WYCC, vol. 1, pp. 42B–43A.

183. Ibid., p. 46A.

184. Chapter 15, "Discussion of the Military," *Hsün-tzu chi-chieh* (Shih-chieh shu-chü, Taipei, 1974), pp. 176–77.

185. Chapter 49, "Five Vermin," *Han Fei-tzu chi-chieh* (Shih-chieh shu-chü, Taipei, 1969), p. 347.

186. See "Sun-tzu shih-tai," pp. 179–80. Sun Pin, a descendant of Sun-tzu, was a brilliant strategist whose achievements have been dramatically preserved in the *Shih chi* and essentially corroborated by the Lin-i texts. His work, entitled *Ping-fa*, is best translated as *Military Methods* to distinguish it from Sun-tzu's work of the same name. Although early bibliographic data indicated the existence of two distinct works, Sun Pin's book was apparently lost by the end of the Han, and confusion arose as to which Sun actually penned the traditonally transmitted text of the *Art of War*. (A separate, otherwise unknown chapter on cavalry has been preserved in the *T'ung tien*.) Numerous modern Chinese and Japanese translations have already appeared; preliminary reports appeared in *Wen wu* in 1974 with further explications thereafter, and are largely contained in the articles cited in note 99, above.

187. For a discussion of Ssu-ma Ch'ien's life and work, see Burton Watson, *Ssu-ma Ch'ien: Grand Historian of China* (Columbia University Press, New York, 1957). A voluminous secondary literature on Ssu-ma Ch'ien and the *Shih chi* exists in Asian languages; a concise introduction in Chinese is Liu Wei-shih, *Ssu-ma Ch'ien yen-chiu* (Kuo-li pien-shih-kuan, Taipei, 1975).

188. The *Wu Yüeh ch'un-ch'iu* was traditionally attributed to the reclusive scholar Chao Yeh, who was active in the late first century A.D. nearly two centuries after the *Shih chi* was written. The book contains much material deemed extraneous by serious scholars (including reports about spiritual swords and geomantic traditions), and it has often been characterized as a romanticized depiction of the period, bordering on a novel. However, Chao had an impeccable reputation as a scholar; was known for his detailed knowledge of the period in question and the histories of Wu and Yüeh; and is said to have dwelled in retirement for perhaps twenty years on K'uai-chi mountain, where King Kou-chien had fled after being thrashed by Wu in his early days. Whether he had local records or other materials available to him cannot be completely ruled out. However, how much of the extant work is actually by his hand and how much is later revision—or even fabrication—especially by Yüan dynasty commentators, is also problematic.

189. See Ch'ang Hung, "Tu Lin-i Han-chien-chung *Sun Wu chuan*, KK 1975: 4, pp. 210–12. Despite various claims, the fact of its preexistence does not neces-

sarily mean Ssu-ma Ch'ien saw this version, particularly as it was unearthed from a private tomb rather than preserved in an imperial library.

190. Ch'i Ssu-ho, among others, doesn't believe Sun-tzu would have ever been allowed to commandeer palace women to illustrate his theories of military discipline, nor that the execution of the two captains would have been understood as proving anything. He therefore views the entire episode as an exaggeration. (See "Sun-tzu shih-tai," p. 178.) Wu Ju-sung believes the incident illustrates Sun-tzu's fundamental teaching that a general, once in command of the army, does not accept orders from the ruler, rather than any lesson about discipline, in accord with his particular understanding of Sun-tzu's major contribution being the isolation and characterization of the professional general (STPF CS, p. 3).

191. A few hundred soldiers from the palace guard or a similar contingent would certainly have been more readily employed, and more likely candidates, being accustomed to military discipline. However this would miss the point of the entire episode—to test Sun-tzu's theories with people previously unexposed to such rigors. In the *Shih chi* it is the king himself who inquires whether the test could be conducted with palace women, rather than Sun-tzu boldly suggesting it. Perhaps he suggested them precisely because they would be weak, spoiled, and, due to their privileged position, unlikely to cooperate in such a farcical exercise.

192. Ch'ang Hung's analysis of the fragments leads him to conclude that the episode probably occurred, and is in fact a manifestation of the class conflict between the old nobility and the rising economic (landlord) class. In his view Suntzu was compelled to take such dramatic action in order to impose the "rule of law" on the old nobility. See Ch'ang Hung, "Tu Lin-i Han-chien-chung *Sun Wu chuan*," pp. 211–12.

193. Ch'ang Hung draws attention to Shang Yang's plans to have the ablebodied women comprise one of three armies and employ them to defend cities against invasion and siege. See Ch'ang Hung, ibid, p. 212. This is discussed in "Military Defense" in the *Book of Lord Shang*, where old men and women are also to be combined to compose another army. These armies are kept rigorously separated so as to prevent complex emotional effects from arising and undermining the defenders' morale and commitment. For a translation see J.J.L. Duyvendak, *The Book of Lord Shang* (University of Chicago Press, 1963; reprint of ed.), pp. 248–52. In chapter 6 of the *Wei Liao-tzu*, "Tactical Balance of Power in Defense," there is also a reference to women defending the parapets. (See Sawyer, *Seven Military Classics*, p. 253.) Finally, see the introduction, where the role of women generals in the Shang and Eary Chou is noted.

194. Wu Shu-p'ing, "Ts'ung Lin-i Han-mu chu-chien *Wu-wen* k'an Sun Wu te Fa-chia ssu-hsiang," *WW* 1975: 4, pp. 6–13.

195. A typical reconstruction following this line is found in the popular work *Chung-kuo li-tai ming-chiang*, 2 vols., Ch'en Wu-t'ung and Su Shuang-pi, eds. (Honan jen-min ch'u-pan-she, Honan, 1987), vol. 1, pp. 14–16. Its authenticity is naturally denied, being a reconstruction eight centuries after Ssu-ma Ch'ien found himself unable to be any more specific in tracing Sun-tzu's lineage than identifying him as a "man of Ch'i." See, for example, "Sun-tzu shih-tai," p. 189.

196. Several articles have discussed the location of the Sun family's original "home town." For example, see Chou Wei-yen, "Sun Wu ku-li Le-an tsai-chin

"Hui-min shuo" te nan-ch'eng-li," *Chung-kuo-shih yen-chiu* 1991: 3, pp. 139–45; Huo Yin-chang and Wu Ju-sung, "Sun-tzu ku-li "Hui-min shuo" pu-k'o tung-yao," *Chung-kuo-shih yen-chiu* 1991: 3, pp. 146–57; Li Tsu-te, "Sun-tzu ku-li 'Le-an' shuo chih-i," *Chung-kuo-shih yen-chiu* 1992: 2, pp. 35–39; and Ch'en Han-p'ing, "Sun Wu ku-li t'an-t'ao chih-i," *Chung-kuo-shih yen-chiu* 1992: 2, pp. 40–51. Also see Ch'en Chi-kang, ed., *Sun-tzu hsin-t'an—Chung-wai hsüeh-che lun Sun-tzu* (Chieh-fang-chün ch'u-pan-she, Peking, 1990): "Sun Wu ku-li k'ao-i" (Wu Ju-sung, Ch'en Ping-ts'ai), pp. 245–61; "Sun Wu ku-li k'ao-ch'a" (Wang Ping-ch'en), pp. 262–66; and "Hui-min-hsien chien-chih yen-ko k'ao-lüeh" (Liu P'ei-jan), pp 267–71.

197. For example, see Ch'i Ssu-ho, "Sun-tzu shih-tai," pp. 184–86. Both subsequent historical events and later concepts are noted within the *Art of War*. Among the former are references to Su Ch'in in some editions (and the tomb text), while the development of the five-phase theory (as now explicated by the Lin-i text entitled "The Yellow Emperor Conquers the Red Emperor"), necessary to understand one passage, should be counted among the latter. (See Li Ling's excerpted comments in *Hsü Wei-shu t'ung-k'ao*, ed. Cheng Liang-shu, 3 vols., [Hsüeh-sheng shu-chü, Taipei, 1984], pp. 1606–7. Also see Ch'ü Wan-li, *Hsien-Ch'in wen-shih tzu-liao k'ao-pien* (Lien-ching, Taipei, 1985), pp. 433–35; and Chang Hsin-ch'eng, *Wei-shu t'ung-k'ao*, 2 vols. [Shang-wu yin-shu-kuan, Taipei, 1970; reprint of 1939 ed.], vol. 2, pp. 797–801.) Other examples are discussed below and in the notes to the translation.

198. See the notes below accompanying the summary discussion that follows.

199. See, for example, Cheng Liang-shu's analysis of the terms, concepts, and passages borrowed from Sun-tzu in two relatively early works, Sun Pin's *Military Methods* and the *Wei Liao-tzu*, in *Hsü Wei-shu t'ung-k'ao*, pp. 1617–25. A study of the actual passages quoted or otherwise incorporated in the other *Seven Military Classics* requires a monograph in itself. They are particularly extensive in the *Six Secret Teachings,* although some question remains whether many of them did not also preexist the *Art of War* or might have been derived from an early kernal text of the *Six Secret Teachings*. These issues are considered to some extent in our translation of the *Seven Military Classics of Ancient China*.

200. Wu Ju-sung, in the introduction to his *Ch'ien-shuo,* briefly notes some important military events historically predating Sun-tzu (see p. 14). A quick reading of the *Tso chuan* up to the conquest of Ying will also yield numerous battles and a variety of tactics, all suggestive of principles and concepts already well known among commanders and military thinkers in his era. (For a convenient study, see Chu Pao-ch'ing, *Tso-shih ping-fa* [Shanhsi jen-min ch'u-pan-she, 1991].) In the *Art of War* Sun-tzu also quotes from now lost, preexisting military works.

201. The question of the *Art of War*'s placement within a fairly continuous evolution of written styles is also the subject of debate. For example, Li Ling (*Hsü Wei-shu t'ung-k'ao*, pp. 1613–14) and Robin D. S. Yates ("New Light on Ancient Chinese Military Texts: Notes on their Nature and Evolution, and the Development of Military Specialization in Warring States China," *T'oung Pao* 74 [1988]: 218–19) view the text as somewhat advanced over the basic verbatim, summary format of the *Analects,* with some conjoined passages and a logical division of top-

ics, but less so than Sun Pin, and far less than Hsün-tzu and other philosophers of the late Warring States period. They tend to note its similarities with the *Mo-tzu's* style, and Yates also believes many of the connectives are later additions, provided in an attempt to integrate the text. Yates suggests a date of approximately 453–403 B.C. with later additions, while Li Ling ascribes the book to a somewhat later time, roughly the middle of the Warring States period. (Yates also advances the thought that the military works were perhaps the first private books to appear in China.) However, Ch'i Ssu-ho and others, concurring with the general view that private books did not really appear until the Warring States period, observe that Sun Wu should have been approximately contemporaneous with Confucius, yet the language and presentation is more sophisticated than is characteristic of this early period. Ch'i believes that Lord Shang and Wu Ch'i initiated the first books, followed by Sun Pin and others, and that the *Art of War* represents the confluence of Confucius' theory of kingship, Lao-tzu's concepts of nonaction and unorthodox/orthodox, and Mo-tzu's defensive strategies. He therefore concludes it is not the work of a single person, but rather evolved over a considerable period, being composed in the middle to late Warring States period. (See "Sun-tzu shih-tai," pp. 186–88.)

202. Sun-tzu extensively discusses the efforts required to mobilize a 100,000-man campaign army in chapter 2, "Waging War," as a prelude to asserting two main points: warfare is the greatest affair of state, and provisions need to be seized from the enemy. The key passage runs: "If there are a thousand four-horse chariots, a thousand leather armored support chariots, a hundred thousand mailed troops, and provisions are transported a thousand *li,* then the domestic and external campaign expenses, the expenditures for advisors and guests, materials such as glue and lacquer, and providing chariots and armor will be a thousand pieces of gold per day. Only then can an army of a hundred thousand be mobilized." (Also note the reference to "advisors," clearly exemplified by Sun-tzu and Wu Tzu-hsü, but claimed by some critics as not being found in the Spring and Autumn period.)

203. See Ch'i Ssu-ho, "Sun-tzu shih-tai," pp. 180–82; and Li Ling in *Hsü Wei-shu t'ung-k'ao,* pp. 1608–10. The *Wei Liao-tzu* states in chapter 3: "Who led a mass of a hundred thousand and no one under Heaven opposed him? Duke Huan. Who led a mass of seventy thousand and no one under Heaven opposed him? Wu Ch'i. Who led a mass of thirty thousand and no one under Heaven opposed him? Sun-tzu." The text goes on to indicate army size in the middle to late Warring States period: "Today among the armies led by commanders from the various feudal states there is not one that does not reach a mass of two hundred thousand men." Duke Huan of Ch'i, the first hegemon, reigned from 685 to 634 B.C.; therefore most scholars discount the accuracy of a hundred-thousand-man army, although Ch'i was a powerful military state. It might also be remembered that the Shang dynasty purportedly had several hundred thousand men under arms at the time of its destruction.

204. Discussed in chapter 3, "Planning Offensives." The essential paragraph runs: "The tactic of attacking fortified cities is adopted only when unavoidable. Preparing large movable protective shields, armored assault wagons, and other equipment and devices will require three months. Building earthworks will require another three months to complete. If the general can not overcome his

impatience, but instead launches an assault wherein his men swarm over the walls like ants, he will kill a third of his officers and troops, and the city will still not be taken. This is the disaster that results from attacking [fortified cities]." The development of assault and siege equipment progressed rapidly in the Warring States period. For a general introduction, see the works of Robin D. S. Yates listed in the bibliography.

205. See Ch'i Ssu-ho, "Sun-tzu shih-tai," pp. 182–84.

206. See Li Ling in *Hsü Wei-shu t'ung-k'ao*, p. 1610. Also see *Wei-shu t'ung-k'ao*, vol. 2, pp. 797–801; *Hsien-ch'in wen-shih tzu-liao k'ao-pien*, pp. 424–25; and Murayama Makoto, "Sonbu to Sonbin" in *Chugoku no meishō to sambō* (Shinjimbutsu, Tokyo, 1991), pp. 88–91.

207. For example, see Ch'i Ssu-ho, "Sun-tzu shih-tai," p. 184.

208. *Hsü Wei-shu t'ung-k'ao*, p. 1612.

209. See, for example, Wu Ju-sung, STPF CS, pp. 8–12.

210. See Tsun Hsin, "*Sun-tzu ping-fa* te tso-che chi ch'i shih-tai," *WW* 1974: 12, pp. 20–24. The *Six Secret Teachings* and the *Wei Liao-tzu* also consider tactics for siege warfare, while Mo-tzu and his followers are famous for developing and implementing defensive techniques, some of which are preserved in the *Mo-tzu*.

211. Skeptics abound from the Sung dynasty onward. Some, based upon Tu Fu, accused Ts'ao Ts'ao (the first known commentator) of butchering the text; others doubted Sun-tzu's existence, or felt the work must be a later forgery. (See citations in note 5, above.) Their skepticism was in part based upon the *Han shu* bibliographical notation of a *Sun-tzu* in eighty-two *pien* (sections or chapters), despite the *Shih chi* reference to thirteen sections, giving rise to the charges against Ts'ao Ts'ao. The discovery of the bamboo-slip edition in the tomb at Lin-i in 1972, while comprising only a third of the present edition, at least conclusively proves the book existed in roughly current form early in the Han dynasty. Ch'ü Wan-li and others therefore suggest that the thirteen-section work had to be complete before Sun-tzu's interview with the king of Wu, for the king remarks upon this number, and the additional sections, if thirteen is not an outright error, probably comprised materials such as found at Lin-i, including further dialogues between the king and Sun-tzu. (See *Hsien-Ch'in wen-shih tzu-liao k'ao-pien*, pp. 433–44. For further fragmentary materials, including possible evidence for a sixteen-section version of the text, see "Ta-t'ung Shang-sun-chia sai Han-chien shih-wen," *WW* 1981: 2) Later notations describe the Sun-tzu in three *chüan* or rolls, indicating the difficulty of reconstructing textual lineages with such obscure materials.

212. Cheng Liang-shu, after studying both traditional and newly recovered materials, concludes that the *Shih chi* account is basically accurate, and the *Art of War* was probably composed between 496 and 453 B.C. (See *Hsü Wei-shu t'ung-k'ao*, pp. 1617–26.)

213. See, for example, Ch'i Ssu-ho, who consigns it to the late Warring States period (*Hsü Wei-shu t'ung-k'ao*, pp. 1598–1605).

214. Yates, for example, accepts the view (based upon internal evidence in comparison with historical events) that the text was composed between 453 and 403 B.C. (See "New Light," pp. 216–19.)

215. Ch'ang Ch'i-yün, *Chung-hua wu-ch'ien-nien shih* (Chung-kuo Wen-hua

Ta-hsüeh, Taipei, 1961), vol. 3, p. 92. Ch'i Ssu-ho hypothetically advances the thought that "Sun Wu" might refer to the book's authorship among the Sun family, the term *"wu"* being added to indicate someone exceptionally skilled in the martial arts such as "employing the military." See Ch'i Ssu-ho, "Sun-tzu shih-tai," p. 188.

Notes
to the
Translation

Abbreviations and basic texts

SS AS   Amano Shizuo, *Sonshi, Goshi* (Meiji Shoin, Tokyo, 1972).

SS MM   Murayama Makoto, *Sonshi, Goshi* 3rd. ed., Tokuma Shoten, Tokyo, 1986).

SS AY   Aasno Yuichi, *Sonshi* (Kodansha, Tokyo, 1986).

SS HT   Hosokawa Toshikazu, *Sonshi, Goshi* (Gakken kenkyūsha, Tokyo, 1982).

SS NT   Nakatani Takao, *Sonshi* (Kyoikusha, Tokyo 1987).

SS TY   Tadokoro Yoshiyuki, *Sonshi* (Meitoku shuppansha, Tokyo, 1970).

ST CCCY   Wei Ju-lin, *Sun-tzu chin-chu chin-i* (Shang-wu yin-shu-kuan, Taipei, 1972).

ST SCC   *Sun-tzu shih-chia-chu* (Shih-chieh shu-chü, Taipei, 1984).

ST WCHC   *Sun-tzu* in *Ch'ung-k'an Wu-ching hui-chieh* (Chung-chou ku-chi ch'u-pan-she, Cheng-chou, 1989).

STPF CS   Wu Ju-sung, *Sun-tzu ping-fa ch'ien-shuo* (Chieh-fang-chün ch'u-pan-she, Peking, 1983).

STPF HC   Chün-k'o-yüan chan-cheng li-cheng-pu, ed., *Sun-tzu ping-fa hsin-chu* (Chung-hua shu-chü, Peking, 1981).

STPF SY   Chu Chün, *Sun-tzu ping-fa shih-i* (Hai-ch'ao ch'u-pan-she, Peking, 1990).

STPF TC   Wei Ju-lin, *Sun-tzu ping-fa ta-ch'uan* (Li-ming, Taipei, 1970).

STPF WC   Wang Chien-tung, *Sun-tzu ping-fa* (Chih-yang ch'u-pan-she, Taipei, 1989).

SWTCC WCCS   *Sun Wu-tzu chih-chieh*, in *Ming-pen Wu-ching Ch'i-shu chih-chieh*, vol. 1 (Shih-ti chiao-yü ch'u-pan-she, Taipei, 1972).

WYCC   *Wu Yüeh ch'un-ch'iu*, SPKY edition (Shih-chieh shu-chü, Taipei, 1967).

Insofar as the *Art of War* has been the most studied of the *Seven Military Classics*, numerous editions and commentaries are readily available, with additional modern works appearing annually. Therefore, in general only a single reference or two—if any—is provided for the commentators' views. Scholars with expertise in the relevant languages can easily refer to the passages in such standard works as the *Shih-chia chu, Shih-i-chia chu*, or those listed in the abbreviations at the beginning of the notes. While notes will be added to many passages, they will not repeat material already discussed in the introduction.

The discovery of the Han dynasty bamboo slips (hereafter abbreviated BS) has occasioned close scrutiny of the traditionally transmitted texts, including the Sung/Ming *Seven Military Classics* edition. However, although many contemporary scholars uncritically accept the BS as preserving the original text of the *Art of War*, many questions remain. A more balanced view is provided by Chu Chün and is cited in the notes as appropriate. Variations in meaning caused by character differences are also noted, but not simple differences caused by the presence or absence of connectives or particles or minor inversions in textual order. Furthermore, given the fragmentary nature of the text, phrases and sentences missing in the BS are not cited unless they radically affect the meaning. Important fragments and "lost passages" will also be cited as appropriate.

1. "Estimations" in the sense of objectively estimating the relative strength and weakness of oneself and the enemy for a series of factors. Although twelve such factors are discussed in this chapter, as noted in the translator's introduction there are several tens of paired factors that could be employed equally well in making such determinations.
The character translated as "estimations"—*chi*—also has the meaning "plans," leading some to translate the title as "Initial Plans," or "First Plans."
2. It is frequently assumed that the factors to be compared are the seven enumerated several paragraphs below because the five that immediately follow are already subsumed under "structure it according to [the following] five factors" (cf. ST SCC, p. 2; and STPF CS, p. 30). However, it seems clear that the "five factors" define the domain for comparative calculations.
Historically, some commentators did not accept the addition of "affairs" following the world "five," the correctness of which has been sustained by the BS, which also lack "factors." (Cf. Ch'en Ch'i-t'ien, *Sun-tzu ping-fa chiao-shih* [Chung-hua shu-chü, Taipei, 1955], p. 65.) Chu Chün (STPF SY, pp. 2–3) believes "factors" should not be excised, despite its absence in the BS.)
3. Not the metaphysical Tao of the Taoists but the Tao of government, understood as legal and administrative measures and policies. Liu Yin (SWTCC WCCS, vol. 1, p. 2A) understands it in terms of the usual array of Confucian virtues. However, Kuan Feng has observed that the concept is never made explicit in the *Art of War*. See Kuan Feng, "Sun-tzu chün-shih che-hsüeh ssu-hsiang yen-chiu," *Che-hsüeh yen-chiu*, no. 2 (1957): p. 72.
4. The character translated as "ruler"—*shang*—may also be understood as "superiors," and the commentators espouse both possibilities. Although Liu Yin is somewhat ambivalent (SWTCC WCCS, vol. 1, p. 2A), the translation follows STPF CS, p. 30; and SS AS, p. 26.

5. "Thus" is added from the bamboo slips, although it is implied in any case. The BS conclude the sentence with the phrase "the people will not deceive/contravene him" rather than the traditional "not fear danger." However, Chu Chün believes the traditional reading is preferable (STPF SY, p. 3). Note that the term "deceive" also occurs in the famous sentence somewhat later: "Warfare is the Tao of deception."

Commentators who stress the Legalism in Sun-tzu's thought understand the sentence as "they will die for him, they will live for him." They especially cite Sun-tzu's directive to the commanding general to manipulate his troops in combat like sheep, keeping them ignorant (cf. STPF CS, pp. 30–34). Although Sun-tzu does not advocate positive measures directed to fostering the people's welfare—such as are found in the other *Military Classics*—he does discuss gaining the allegiance of the masses before they can be employed, not impoverishing them, and the importance of benevolence in a commander. Most scholars thus have understood the ideal as being exemplified historically by King Wu of the Chou, who had garnered the willing support of the people. (For further discussion, see Wu Shu-p'ing, "Ts'ung Lin-i Han-mu chu-chien *Wu-wen* k'an Sun Wu te Fa-chia ssu-hsiang," *WW*, 1975: 4, pp. 6–13.)

6. The BS add: "according with and going contrary to, [the basis of] victory in warfare." Neither STPF CS nor STPF SY includes it. (STPF HC, p. 150.)

7. Terrain classification is one of the keystones of Sun-tzu's strategic analysis, as will become clear from the extensive materials in Chapters eight, ten, and eleven (where these terms are further defined). His insights were studied and expanded by Sun Pin as well as many later thinkers.

The BS add "high or low" at the start of the classifications (STPF SY, p. 3).

8. These terms are variously understood by the commentators. "The Tao of command" may refer to the exercise of command or to the establishment of military hierarchy, the chain of command. "Management of logistics" probably encompasses everything from the types and nature of the army's equipment to the provision and management of that equipment in campaigns. (For summaries, see SS AS, p. 27; STPF SY, pp. 9–10; and ST SCC, p. 8.)

Wu Ju-sung also equates the "laws" with the last four items in the series of questions for comparative evaluation: the implementation of laws and orders, strong forces, well-trained officers and troops, and clear rewards and punishments (See STPF CS pp. 37–38.

9. "Forces" could also be translated as "weapons and masses" rather than understood as "army masses" or "infantry and masses." However, "masses" emphasizes the contrast with the next criterion for evaluation, the trained "officers and troops" (cf. STPF SY, p. 11; STPF CS, p. 30).

10. Ch'en Hao early interpreted this passage as referring to Sun Wu himself staying or leaving, rather than retaining or dismissing a general. In addition, he identifies the "general" as the king of Wu, because he frequently commanded the army himself, and interprets Sun-tzu's statement as a barb to gain employment (SWT SCC, pp. 11–12. Cf. SS AS, p. 34). However, "retaining him" as a translation seems more reasonable than the sense of remaining with him.

Liu Yin (SWTCC WCCS, I:6B) makes an odd distinction between the first "general" in the sentence, which he believes refers to the Grand General in his consultations with the ruler, and the second general, which he sees as referring to any subordinate general appointed to implement the chosen strategy (also see STPF SY, p. 12).

11. Liu Yin believes this should refer to the subordinate generals entrusted with field command, "listening to the estimations" and resulting plans (SWTCC WCCS, vol. 1, p. 6), but others believe it refers to the king of Wu—the "you" in the translation (cf. SS AS, p. 35; ST SCC, p. 12). *Shih* is discussed in the introductory notes.

12. This is also understood as "outside the normal realm of tactics," using the unorthodox (cf. ST SCC, p. 12; SS AS, p. 36).

13. The imbalance of power should be created with the objective of facilitating and attaining the "gains to be realized." Merely creating an imbalance of power would be pointless, and such an imbalance is already inherently dependent on the advantages one possesses (cf. STPF SY, pp. 13–14, for a similar view and an example). *Ch'üan* is discussed in the introductory notes.

14. The term "deception" here inadequately conveys both the positive and negative aspects of the matter. We prefer to translate as "deception and artifice" because much craft is involved in not only concealing appearance, which is the simplest form of deception, but also in creating false impressions. Although all the military writings exploit deceit and deception, Sun-tzu's statement is the most explicit formulation of the principle.

The fourteen sentences that follow should be understood as tactical principles flowing from this realization. They are also believed to reflect or to be a distillation of tactical experience gained through combat situations in the Spring and Autumn period (STPF CS, pp. 39–40). Many have already been analyzed in the introductory overview on the conflict between Wu and Ch'u.

15. Translators often take this as "when you are nearby make it appear as if you are distant," but this would clearly be contrary to reality. It would be impossible for the enemy not to know—through reconnaissance and observation—an army's actual position, although attempts were initiated routinely to diminish the accuracy of such perceptions (such as by dragging brush and increasing or reducing the number of cook fires at night). More likely the position to which the army is about to move, an objective that is about to be attacked, is intended as translated (following Liu Yin, SWTCC WCCS, vol. 1, p. 9A. Compare ST SCC, p. 14). Chu Chün notes this might also be understood temporally, as immediate future and some distant time (STPF SY, p. 14).

16. Two readings of these laconic sentences are possible. The critical question is whether the first term in each of them and the several that follow below should be read in the light of the Tao of Warfare and thus as explications of craft and deception and ways to manipulate the enemy, as Sun-tzu discusses extensively, or simply as a series of individual items. In the latter case, it is possible that they were simply conjoined here—rather than being the product of Sun Wu's systematic analysis—from preexisting rubrics about military action. It is tempting to read them all in parallel, with the first term always describing an aspect of the enemy and the second an action to be applied, but in our opinion the imposition of such parallelism—which is frequently invalid even for two phrases within a single short sentence—is too artificial.

Accordingly, for the first sentence, one reading would be that "If the enemy [desires] profit, entice them"—understanding "with the prospect of profit," which is somewhat redundant. The translation emphasizes the active approach because we should assume that armies will generally move for tactical advantage. At the same time we must remember that a frequently discussed (and readily exploitable) flaw in some commanding generals is greed.

For the second sentence, two additional renderings are variously suggested: "If they are disordered, seize them," and "Show [apparent] disorder [in your own forces] and seize them." The commentators cite a number of historical examples in support of the latter, but the former has adherents as well, and decisive evidence for a definitive reading is lacking. (Measures such as enticing them with profits, sowing rumors, and fostering their licentiousness would all cause the sort of disorder that could easily be capitalized on.) The translation follows Liu Yin. (SWTCC WCCS, vol. 1, p. 9B. Cf. ST SCC, p. 15. Also note the extensive analysis, with examples of these and the following sentences, in Tzu Yü-ch'iu, ed., *Mou-lüeh k'u* [Lan-t'ien ch'u-pan-she, Peking, 1990], pp. 70–76.)

The term "take them" is said to indicate an easy victory rather than a difficult conflict (cf. ST SCC, p. 15).

17. The "substantial" and the "vacuous" (or empty) form a correlative pair that is closely identified with Sun-tzu's thought, although the terms may have predated him. One of his fundamental principles is exploiting voids, weaknesses, fissures, and vacuities. The opposite, the "substantial" (*shih*)—corresponding roughly to strong, well-organized, disciplined, expertly commanded, entrenched forces—is generally to be avoided rather than attacked with ineffectual and wasteful frontal assaults. (Wang Chien-tung, STPF WC, p. 31, notes the phrase can also be understood as "be substantial and prepare for them," although this appears less appropriate.) The theme of chapter 6 is "Vacuity and Substance."

18. The military thinkers generally advocate fostering and exploiting anger because it blinds the general to the realities of the battlefield and takes away the troops' judgment. Consequently, suggestions that *jao* means "avoid them" are probably not accurate, even though Sun-tzu does recommend avoiding an army when it is at the peak of its fervor. (An alternative translation would be 'anger and perturb them.") However, note that in chapter 2 Sun-tzu also states, "what [motivates men] to slay the enemy is anger."

19. Again, two readings are possible, the alternative being "if they are humble/lowly, make them arrogant" (cf. Tau, ed., *Mou-lüeh k'u,* pp. 71–73; STPF SY, p. 15). The translation follows Liu Yin, SWTCC WCCS, vol. 1, pp. 10B–11A. Logically, if they are "humble" they already lack combative spirit, and it would be foolish to raise their anger to no purpose. (On the other hand, they may also simply be restrained and composed.)

20. The text appears to suggest the general cannot transmit or divulge his determinations with regard to these factors before the battle. However, it may also entail the idea that they cannot be rigidly or arbitrarily determined before the situation develops. Commentators embrace both views (cf. ST SCC, pp. 20–21; STPF CS, p. 31).

21. The procedure for strategic analysis in the ancestral temple apparently assigned relative values to the various factors, including those discussed in this

chapter. D. C. Lau (see "Some Notes on the *Sun-tzu*," pp. 331–32) suggests that counting sticks were used for each factor and then the totals taken. Some form of relative weighing was probably used because certain factors would be more significant than others, and a simple total is probably misleading. (The translation follows Liu Yin. Also compare STPF CS, p. 31; Ch'en's *Chiao-shih,* pp. 72–73; Kuan Feng's comments on the various factors in "Sun-tzu chün-shih che-hsüeh ssu-hsiang yen-chiu," pp. 71–75; and Yü Tse-min, "Shih-hsi Chung-kuo ku-tai te chan-lüeh, kai-nien," in *Ping-chia shih-yüan* ed. Chün-shih Li-shih Yen-chiu-hui [Chün-shih k'o-hsüeh ch'u-pan-she, Peking, 1990], vol. 2, pp. 221–26.) Giles errs in understanding "no points" as simply failing to perform any strategic calculations.

22. D. C. Lau ("Some Notes on the *Sun-tzu*," pp. 321–25) has pointed out that initial phrases in Sun-tzu passages are often captions or summaries. The five-character phrase introducing this section appears to be one of these; however, others are less clear. Traditionally, such introductory captions have simply been made the subject of a sentence, understanding a term such as "requires" to bridge the subject and its expansion (cf. ST CCCY, p. 86; STPF WC, p. 52; and STPF CS, p. 42). Our translations generally adopt Lau's insight wherever captions apparently precede material of any length.

23. Sun-tzu refers to "leather-armored" support chariots, and it is commonly assumed that leather was the main component for armoring chariots, being flexible and easily made to conform to the desired shape. Multiple layers of lacquer would further protect the already toughened hides, preserving them from the ravages of weather. At the start of the *Wu-tzu* Wu Ch'i observes to Marquis Wen: "Your leather armored chariots block the doors; their wheels are covered and the hubs protected." However, when Nang Wa (previously discussed in the introduction) decided precipitously to change his course of action, it was in part because Wu's chariots were wood, while their own chariots used leather and were therefore thought to be in danger of deteriorating from the dampness of the wetland area. (The *Tso chuan,* Duke Ting, fourth year: "Hei, of Wu-ch'eng, addressed Tzu-ch'ang, 'Wu employs wood, but we use leather so we can not long endure. It would be better to quickly engage in battle.'")

24. Griffith (*The Art of War,* p. 73) and some modern Chinese editions (such as STPF WC, p. 53) insert a character meaning "to value" or "esteem" in this sentence, citing (in Griffith's case) the *Seven Military Classics* edition, However, neither the latter nor the ST SCC edition contains it; Liu Yin merely uses it in his commentary explaining the passage (cf. SWTCC WCCS, vol. 1, p. 15A; and ST SCC, p. 23). The *Ssu-ma Fa* observes: "In general, in battle one endures through strength, and gains victory through spirit. One can endure with a solid defense, but will achieve victory through being endangered. When the heart's foundation is solid, a new surge of *ch'i* will bring victory. With armor one is secure; with weapons one attains victory." ("Strict Positions," pp. 138–39.)

25. This and similar sentences, as discussed in the translator's introduction, are cited as evidence for the undeveloped state of offensive and siege warfare and the relative economic unimportance of cities.

26. Extensive military campaigns invariably create a vacuum that can be readily exploited. Yüeh and Ch'in capitalized upon Wu's "vacuity" when Ho-lü's forces

penetrated Ch'u's interior as far as Ying, and Yüeh later struck when King Fu-ch'ai ventured north to Yellow Pond (as discussed in the introduction).

27. It was frequently asserted that any state that constantly engaged in warfare would simply exhaust itself and, irrespective of its victorious record, ultimately be vanquished. Wu Ch'i said: "Now being victorious in battle is easy, but preserving the results of victory is difficult. Thus it is said that among the states under Heaven that engage in warfare, those that garner five victories will meet with disaster; those with four victories will be exhausted; those with three victories will become hegemons; those with two victories will be kings; and those with one victory will become emperors. For this reason those who have conquered the world through numerous victories are extremely rare, while those who thereby perished are many" ("Planning for the State," *Wu-tzu*, p. 208).

28. This sentence has various interpretations. Generally, it is agreed that the campaign should be won with only a single mobilization and conscription, which would be reasonably possible given the nature and still-limited scope of warfare in Sun-tzu's era (cf. STPF SY, pp. 27–28). Not transporting provisions a third time is understood in two distinct ways: The army is provisioned only once—when about to depart—and thereafter it must plunder and forage, securing provisions on the march and in the field. Moreover, when the troops return they are not reprovisioned (cf. SWTCC WCCS, vol. 1, p. 16B). A second, more common, and more logical interpretation holds that they are provisioned at the commencement of the campaign and supplied again on returning after recrossing the state's borders but must fend for themselves when in the field (cf. ST SCC, pp. 26–27; and SS AS, p. 54).

29. As noted in the general introduction, in the Early Chou period the "hundred surnames" were essentially the members of the aristocracy, the free men. As time passed and their status declined, they lost their privileged status and became the common people. The usage of the term in Sun-tzu reflects a period when the earlier meaning was becoming eclipsed but the term was probably not yet simply equivalent to "common people." From the context it is apparent that the hundred surnames farm the land, have the material wealth to pay taxes, and have the leisure to fulfill military obligations. Because the *Art of War* specifically uses this term, it is distinguished from terms that mean "the people" or the "common people" in the translation.

30. The bamboo slips have "market" for "army," with the phrase reading "the market nearby" ("the army" then being understood).

31. Military expeditions thus impose heavy direct and indirect burdens on the populace. Under the military taxation system (imposed in varying degrees and different forms) in Sun-tzu's era, hamlets and villages—depending on their classification, acreage tilled, and population—had to provide men to serve in the military effort and furnish weapons, equipment, and draft animals. If they could not obtain the weapons and supplies from their own inventory or stock, they had to be purchased. Moreover, the cost of such items for the village's own use concurrently escalated, depleting everyone's financial resources. Thus wartime inflation would strike them especially hard. (For further commentary, see Liu Yin, SWTCC WCCS, vol. 1, p. 17B; Ch'en, *Chiao-shih*, pp. 78–79; and STPF WC, p. 64.)

Most of the military writings stress the need for economic prosperity, for attaining a high level of material welfare within the state. The *Wei Liao-tzu*, written significantly later, further emphasizes the need for markets and commerce, for by then market cities could sustain much of the state's military effort. (See "Martial Plans," pp. 254–55.)

32. The BS are somewhat different, reading "They will exhaust their strength on the central plains, while in the interior their houses will be empty" (cf. STPF SY, p. 30). The term for "empty" is actually the much stronger term "vacuous," or "void."

33. The BS have "six-tenths" rather than "seven-tenths."

34. The term translated as "large oxen" is literally "village oxen." The meaning seems to have originated with the reported practice of having each village of sixteen "well-fields" (with eight families to each of the latter) raise one ox, which presumably remained the ruler's property. It would be employed for military purposes when required. This might explain how such oxen were viewed as expenditures from the ruler's treasury rather than as a tax contribution from the people (cf. SWTCC WCCS, vol. 1, p. 17B; and SS AS, p. 55).

35. While foraging on enemy terrain proved important in Wu's campaigns against Ch'u—and probably in every invasion in antiquity—many of the military thinkers advised against plundering, foraging, or allowing destructive behavior in order to minimize the resistance being faced. As this would concomitantly increase the logistical burden, such restraint was probably observed infrequently.

36. "Profits," understood as profits for the state. However, the term also means "advantage," as in military advantage, and the sentence could equally well be understood as "What [stimulates them] to seize advantage from the enemy is material goods." Wang Hsi views this sentence as referring simply to the establishment of rewards as incentives because "If you cause the masses to covet profits and take them for themselves, then perhaps they will violate the constraints and [military] discipline" (ST SCC, p. 31).

37. The translation follows Liu Yin's commentary on the *Seven Military Classics* and expresses the traditional viewpoint—namely, that preserving the enemy's state is the primary objective; destroying it is only second best. This accords with Sun-tzu's overall emphasis on speedily wresting victory and subjugating one's enemies without engaging in battle if at all possible. (Modern Chinese commentators cite the example of Germany nourishing its rancor and hatred subsequent to World War I until militarily reasserting itself in World War II. See, for example, STPF WC, pp. 76–83.)

However, D. C. Lau ("Some Notes on the *Sun-tzu*," pp. 333–35) argues that the sentence should be translated as "It is best to preserve one's own state intact; to crush the enemy's state is only a second best." Although he advances a cogent argument, the traditional understanding appears more appropriate. Whether from a Confucian, Taoist, or Legalist perspective, the idea of gaining victory while inflicting the least amount of damage on the enemy is generally fundamental. Except perhaps when blindly exacting revenge, all commanders seek to minimize their own losses while maximizing the gains that can be realized. Occupying a thoroughly devastated state was never espoused by any ancient Chinese military thinker, although scorched earth policies were prominently exploited by "barbarian" tribes later in Chinese history, and mass slaughter accompanied by wartime rampages that resulted in the wholesale destruction of cities did characterize the late Warring States period.

38. Unit force levels are discussed at the end of the general historical introduction.

39. These earthworks are variously identified as mounds for overlooking and assaulting the city and as protective walls that allow the besiegers shielded movement outside the city's walls, beneath potentially withering fire (cf. STPF SY, p. 44).

40. This continues the thought of the first passage because a ruler whose objectives include "preserving" others is more likely to be welcomed by the populace. (It also accords with the Confucian ideal of King Wu, previously noted.)

41. Following Liu Yin, SWTCC WCCS, vol. 1, pp. 24B–25A; and SS AS, p. 74. D. C. Lau ("Some Notes on the *Sun-tzu*," p. 320) believes this sentence refers to dividing the enemy, which is equally possible. However, with double strength, as Liu Yin (following Ts'ao Ts'ao) notes, one can mount a frontal assault with one part to fix them and then employ a flanking (i.e., unorthodox) attack to overwhelm them. This understanding also seems more congruent with the next sentence, which still allows for engaging the enemy if you are merely equal in strength. Forcing the enemy to divide his troops is a hallmark of Sun-tzu's thought. By dividing one's forces to launch a secondary front, the enemy would be forced to respond or face the loss of his other position. Thus he would also have to divide his forces, thereby accomplishing Sun-tzu's objective. (See Tu Yu's commentary and also the divergent views in ST SCC, p. 44, and Chu's analysis, STPF SY, pp. 47–49. The passage is also analyzed in Book I of *Questions and Replies,* where Li Ching concurs with Ts'ao Ts'ao's explanation of dividing into two—one force being orthodox, one unorthodox.) The question of how to employ disproportionate numbers—particularly when outnumbering the enemy—is discussed in virtually every military classic. Sun Pin (particularly in "Eight Formations" and "Ten Questions") and Wu-tzu generally advocate segmenting one's forces (and later reconcentrating) to strike the enemy more effectively. However, a fragment in Sun Pin's chapter "Questions of King Wei" states: "If one is double the enemy, stop and do not move, be full and await them, only then . . ."

42. Such as by assuming a desperate position to fight to the death or mounting a defense when flight would be appropriate.

43. This thought is echoed in several of the military writings, suggesting that they all postdate the rise of the profession of arms, and that tactical thought evolved with the appearance of professional generals. The various texts unanimously agree on the absolute need for the general to be a man of strong character and diverse abilities.

44. Apart from differences in tactical knowledge, experience, and viewpoint between the ruler and his commanding general, presumably the major problem in Sun-tzu's era would arise from communication difficulties. It would be difficult for the ruler to have even general knowledge of the potential battlefield and the enemy's forces, and impossible for him to react to an evolving situation given that the most cryptic information would require hours to relay by signal fires (if available), and days or weeks by other methods.

Sun Pin's *Military Methods* frequently asserts the need for the general to be independent and free of the ruler's interference in order to achieve victory. The chapter entitled "Selecting the Troops" also stresses the need for the general to be loyal, implying that by his time (a century after Sun-tzu) generals had become more powerful than the ruler, and therefore posed as serious a threat to the monarch's house as to enemy states.

45. As discussed in the translator's introduction, Sun-tzu is writing after the early rise of the professional commander and the increasing estrangement of many rulers from field command. The distinction between the forms of administration, discipline, and temperament appropriate to the civil and the martial is more pronounced in the other *Military Classics,* such as the *Ssu-ma Fa.* (For discussion, see the introductory section to the translation.) However, even here Sun-tzu is already warning of the dangers posed by inappropriately intermixing them.

Some editions have *ssu*—"direct" or "manage"—rather than *t'ung*—"the same as"—which resolves a somewhat awkward passage. However, both the Sung and Ming editions have *t'ung,* which can be understood as translated. (The next sentence also contains "same as [the civil]," which has been left untranslated because it can also be understood as the ruler uniting the authority for the joint command in his own hands. Cf. STPF SY, pp. 51–52; and STPF CS, p. 47. Also note the explanations in SS AS, pp. 79–80.)

46. Doubt and disorder are generally identified in the military writings as key opportunities for exploitation. For example, Wu-tzu said: "If the enemy approaches in reckless disarray, unthinking; if their flags and banners are confused and in disorder; and if their men and horses frequently look about, then one unit can attack ten of theirs, invariably causing them to be helpless." ("Evaluating the Enemy," p. 213).

47. In "Evaluating the Enemy" Wu Ch'i isolates eight circumstances in which victory is certain and the enemy should be attacked immediately, and six in which it should not be attacked. Other works (such as Sun Pin's chapter entitled "The General's Losses") offer similar criteria for evaluating the possibilities of victory.

48. The BS have *chih,* "to know" or "to understand," rather than "recognizes."

49. The BS read "Thus, in warfare, one who knows them (the enemy) and knows himself . . ."

50. The BS contain two versions of this chapter, the second basically somewhat shorter than the first.

51. "Unconquerable" rather than "invincible" because the latter tends to connote a permanence inappropriate to fluctuating battlefield conditions. The invincible are never conquerable, whereas an army—due to its disposition, exploitation of terrain, and other factors—may be temporarily unconquerable.

52. The BS lack "in warfare."

53. Contrary to our usual practice, in this case the translation is based on the Han bamboo text rather than the traditional *Seven Military Classics.* The latter has perturbed commentators because of its apparent inconsistency with Sun-tzu's thought and the logical development of the paragraph. The traditional text simply reads: "If one defends then he is [or will be] insufficient; if he attacks then he will [have] a surplus." This is understood by commentators such as Liu Yin to mean that one defends *because* his strength is inadequate and attacks because his force is more than abundant (cf. SWTCC WCCS, vol. 1, p. 30). However, this contorts

the grammar because it requires that the term be reversed: "If insufficient one defends" (cf. ST SCC, p. 56; STPF CS, p. 59. Also note Chu Chün's balanced appraisal, STPF SY, pp. 58–59).

54. The phrase "One who excels at offense" does not appear in the BS. The sentences would then be elided to read: "One who excels at defense buries himself away below the lowest depths of Earth and moves from above the greatest heights of Heaven." There are also unimportant, minor variations in the BS versions (cf. STPF CS, pp. 60–61; STPF SY, p. 60).

55. The pinnacle of excellence is more subtle, more spiritual than the visible and the spectacular. Reaction should be muted because they are confounded.

56. The BS lack "the ancients."

57. From the two BS versions, the original sentence apparently read: "Thus the battles of those who excelled did not have unorthodox victories, nor fame for wisdom, nor courageous achievements of courage" (cf. STPF CS, pp. 58–59; STPF SY, p. 60).

58. The BS have "Thus one who excels cultivates the Tao."

59. "Tao" is variously explained by the commentators as referring to such Confucian virtues as benevolence and righteousness—implemented to attract the people—or the military principles essential to being unconquerable. Cf. SWTCC WCCS, vol. 1, p. 32B; ST SCC, pp. 61–62.

60. The BS have *cheng*—"upright," "to rectify," "to regulate"—instead of *cheng*—"government." However, as Chu Chün notes, the former could have been a loan for the latter because the two were somewhat interchangeable at that time. He therefore rejects the emendation suggested by the bamboo slips. The translation reflects the traditional text, but with the character for government understood as "regulator," rather than following commentaries that read it as "government" and produce a translation that reads "Therefore he is able to conquer defeated governments" (cf. STPF CS, p. 59; STPF SY, pp. 60–61; and ST SCC, pp. 61–62).

61. The caption for this sentence, literally "military *fa*," is considered to be a book title by Tadokoro Yoshiyuki (SSTY, p. 118) and Ch'en Ch'i-t'ien (*Chiao-shih*, p. 105), translatable as the "Art of Methods." This is the same title as the *Art of War* (which is best translated as "Military Methods," but we have adopted the traditional rendering). *Fa* encompasses the meanings of "laws" and "methods," with the latter more appropriate here. Rather than the title of a preexistent book or section of a work (which is also referred to in several other military classics), it should be understood as the fundamental methods for warfare, the measures that then follow (cf. STPF SY, p. 61; SS AS, p. 104). In the BS only the term *fa* appears, but Chu Chün retains "military methods" (STPF SY, p. 61).

62. "Measurement" is generally understood by the commentators as referring not only to the extent and dimensions of the terrain but also its classification according to the categories advanced in the various chapters that follow.

63. "Estimation" is variously described as referring to types of forces suitable for segments of the terrain, such as crossbowmen for the hills, or the quantities of materials required to sustain the battle. All these terms are not otherwise discussed in the *Art of War*, and their referents thus remain a matter of speculation.

64. The BS add "weighing" and "the people" to the traditional text, producing

"weighing the victory of a combative people." Although this is accepted by Wu Ju-sung (STPF CS, p. 58), Chu Chün appears correct in opting for the traditional text (and thereby avoiding an awkward grammatical construction). CF. STPF SY, p. 61.

65. As D. C. Lau has pointed out ("Some Notes on the *Sun-tzu*," pp. 332–33), the use of *hsing* (shape, configuration) here is nearly identical to *shih* (strategic power).

66. The BS merely have *Shih*, "Strategic Power," for the title.

67. The terms translated as "configuration" and "designation" are *hsing*—"form" or "shape"—and *ming*—"name." Within the context of Sun-tzu's thought, the first seems to indicate the form or configuration of forces, as in formations and standard deployments. The second appears to refer to naming the units, designating them in some fashion—such as by flags with specific symbols. However, the earliest commentary, which is by the great general Ts'ao Ts'ao, equated *hsing*/form with flags and *ming*/name with gongs and drums. Liu Yin and others extrapolate on this thought, but some scholars—such as Tu Mu—identify *hsing* with deployments and *ming* with flags (see SWTCC WCCS, vol. 1, p. 35; ST SCC, pp. 66–67; STPF CS, pp. 67–68; and Wang Chien-tung's overview, STPF, WC, pp. 144–46). Robin D. S. Yates ("New Light," pp. 220–22), based on his extensive research on the *Mo-tzu*, believes both terms refer to flags and that the historically and philosophically significant term *hsing-ming* originates with the military thinkers. For an early discussion of *hsing-ming*—often translated as "performance and title"—as well as the issue of which character is appropriate for the term *hsing*, see Herrlee G. Creel, "The Meaning of *Hsing-ming*," reprinted in *What is Taoism* (University of Chicago Press, Chicago, 1970), pp. 79–91.

68. For "invariably" the BS have "entirely/altogether." (Cf. STPF CS, p. 65; and STPF SY, p. 74. Chu Chün [STPF SY] does not accept the revision.)

Unorthodox (*ch'i*) and orthodox (*cheng*) are discussed in the notes to the translator's introduction. An intriguing view is also advanced by Kuan Feng, equating the orthodox with movements designed to realize advantage and the unorthodox with actions that turn disadvantageous situations into advantageous ones (See "Sun-tzu chün-shih che-hsüeh," pp. 81–82. There are extensive discussions of the unorthodox and orthodox and their realization in concrete tactics throughout the military classics, including the *Six Secret Teachings* (especially the chapter entitled "The Unorthodox Army"), *Wu-tzu*, Sun Pin's *Military Methods, Questions and Replies*, and even the *Ssu-ma Fa* (although the concept and unorthodox tactics presumably did not exist at the traditionally ascribed time of composition).

69. See note 17 for an explanation of the vacuous and substantial.

70. The BS have "Heaven and Earth" rather than just "Heaven."

71. The BS have "rivers and seas" or "Yellow River and the seas" rather than the "Yangtze and Yellow rivers."

72. The Sung and Ming editions have *keng* rather than *fu*. Although Sun-tzu does not continue the explicit comparison, all the commentators make it clear that the unorthodox and orthodox are mutually related just like these further examples of cyclic phenomena (SWTCC WCCS, vol. 1, p. 36B; ST SCC, p. 69). This theme appears in Sun Pin's text in the last chapter, entitled "The Unorthodox and Orthodox."

73. Although the character *pien,* "change," has generally been translated as "transformation," we have opted to preserve the (possibly artificial) distinction between *pien* ("change") and *hua* ("transformation") throughout our translation of the *Seven Military Classics.* As a tentative basis for employing "change" rather than "transformation," it might be observed that musical notes are not transformed in substance when producing new sounds, only changed in effect. Similarly, the composition of a military force is untransformed when its employment is changed from orthodox to unorthodox. However, this is a topic that requires further study, and an illuminating paper by Nathan Sivin should appear coincident with the publication of this book.

74. The BS version is slightly different; it lacks the character *shun* but adds another *huan,* so it would read: "The unorthodox and orthodox in circle [fashion] mutually produce each other, just like an endless circle" (cf. STPF CS, p. 65 and STPF SY, p. 75).

75. The BS lack "pent-up" or "accumulated" water. Most translators use the term "torrent" to describe the flow, but the essential idea in the Sung/Ming edition is that water has been restrained and has accumulated and then—when suddenly released—flows violently, turbulently, carrying even stones along. (This is not to deny that some very swift currents can tumble stones, but the pent-up water image is more appropriate to the idea of potential power unleashed and is used in many other military writings—perhaps quoted from Sun-tzu—in this fashion.)

76. The term translated as "constraints" is *chieh,* commonly used to indicate constraints or measures imposed on troops. The term lacks a satisfactory English rendering because it encompasses the concepts of "control," "timing," and "measure." The commentators generally agree it refers to the modulation of both time and space. Sun-tzu apparently intends "constraints" to encompass the deliberate structuring of actions to ensure that the timing is precise and that the impulse of strategic power is imparted at the proper moment to the objective at a critical position. When the target is moving, such as a bird or an enemy, controlling action to attain this objective becomes more difficult. The final stage should be kept short so as to minimize the enemy's ability to avoid the onslaught or effect countermeasures, as Sun-tzu states below. Liu Yin notes it also refers to the control or measurement of strength so that the objective will be reached and not missed. (SWTCC WCCS, vol. 1, p. 37B. Also see ST SCC, pp. 71–72; ST CCCY, p. 124; and SS AS, pp. 119–20.)

77. The same term as for the "onrush" of the water, although "to attack" is clearly assumed.

78. Literally, "short." Whether in a temporal or spatial dimension, briefness is synonymous with precision and effectiveness.

79. It is a basic principle in the military classics that only an army that is thoroughly disciplined and well-trained in segmenting and reforming can maintain order within the swirl of battle. To effect unorthodox tactics, to create the facade of chaos, requires the greatest discipline. (This topic is intensively discussed in the first two books of *Questions and Replies.*)

80. The meaning of the circular formation has stimulated voluminous commentaries. Essentially, the army seems to be involuntarily compressed into a circular formation and is therefore vulnerable. However, such a formation presents

no exposed points or positions yet offers the possibility of numerous fixed deployments and the employment of both orthodox and unorthodox tactics through unfolding. Consequently, in some views it is chosen deliberately rather than forced on the army to allow flexibility while creating the similitude of difficulty and apparent defeat (cf. SWTCC WCCS. vol. 1, p. 38A; ST SCC, pp. 72–75).

81. The translation follows Liu Yin's commentary, understanding the sentence as expressing some bases for practicing the art of deception (SWTCC WCCS, vol. 1, p. 38A). However, there are other possible frames of reference for "Chaos is given birth from control," among them that one's own troops may become chaotic despite being well controlled. This might result from overcontrol, lack of flexibility, too fragile an organization, a shift in battlefield conditions, or laxity in maintaining discipline and organization (cf. ST SCC, pp. 74–76; STPF SY, p. 84; SS AS, pp. 122–23).

82. "Foundation," following the Sung/Ming text. However, many other texts—including the BS and the SCC—have "troops," which most modern commentators feel is correct. "Foundation" presumably refers to the general's well-disciplined, well-organized army, so indirectly it means "forces." (Cf. SWTCC WCCS, vol. 1, p. 39A; ST SCC, p. 78; STPF SY, p. 75. Wu Ju-sung retains *pen*, "foundation," and translates it as "heavy forces." STPF CS, p. 67.)

83. Liu Yin comments: "Thus one who excels at warfare seeks (victory) through the certain victory of the army's strategic power, not through reliance on untalented men. Thus he is able to select the talented among men and entrust them with strategic power" (SWTCC WCCS, vol. 1, p. 39B). Although many others follow Liu Yin's thoughts, a second line of commentary observes that by relying on strategic power, men can be employed according to their talents in the quest for victory. Within the context of surpassing power, even the timid will become assertive and perform their roles—something rewards, punishments, and the laws may not be able to accomplish. Furthermore, men will not be forced to attempt actions they are unable to perform (cf. ST SCC, pp. 79–80; SS AS, p. 127; STPF SY, pp. 86–87).

84. The chapter is so named because key paragraphs advance the concept of striking and exploiting any voids or weaknesses in the enemy's deployment. The substantial should always be avoided rather than confronted. (In the BS, the title characters are reversed: "Substance and Vacuity.")

85. Controlling others, rather than being controlled by others, is one of Suntzu's fundamental principles, and many of his tactical measures are devoted to appropriately manipulating the enemy (as already discussed in the introduction).

86. The *Seven Military Classics* edition reads "Go forth to places he will not race to," whereas the ST SCC edition emends the "not" to "must" (cf. SWTCC WCCS, vol. 2, pp. 2B–3A; ST SCC, p. 87). D. C. Lau also supplies a perceptive note on the error of this emendation ("Some Notes on the *Sun-tzu,*" p. 321), but the recovered bamboo text indicates the original reading is "must," and collateral evidence appears in the "T'ai-p'ing yü-lan" (hereafter TPYL) quotation. (However Chu Chün prefers the traditional text. See STPF SY, pp. 90–91, 96.) This coheres well with the preceding sentence, and the traditional text has been altered accordingly. Also note that some commentators and translators would understand the traditional sentence as "Go by way of places he will not race to."

87. Because this sentence does not appear in the bamboo text, some modern commentators view it as a later, inappropriate accretion (see STPF CS, p. 78). However, these coupled sentences are frequently quoted in other military works and have an inherent parallelism that tends to suggest their correctness (cf. SS AS, p. 134).

88. STPF CS, based on the BS, emends "will not attack" to "must attack" (STPF CS, p. 73). There is also collateral evidence for this reading in the TPYL. However, "will not attack" accords with the chapter's trend of thought, particularly in light of such sentences below as "When someone excels at defense the enemy does not know where to attack" and "If I do not want to engage in combat, even though I merely draw a line on the ground and defend it, they will not be able to engage me in battle because we thwart his movements." If the defense is impregnable, the enemy will be deterred from foolishly attacking and uselessly expending his forces. (Cf. STPF SY, p. 91; SS AS, pp. 137–38; and ST SCC, pp. 88–89.) Wu Ju-sung notes that tacticians of Sun-tzu's generation valued defense over offense, although his text accepts the BS version "must attack" (see STPF CS, pp. 77–78).

89. Formless, "not hsing," having no form or discernible configuration.

90. The BS have "an advance which is unresponded to" rather than "unhampered" (or "not repulsed").

91. There are two differences in the BS: "stopped" for "pursued" and "distance" for "speed." Thus it would read "To effect a retreat that cannot be stopped, employ unreachable distance." These are variously accepted or rejected by modern commentators. (Cf. STPF CS, p. 73; STPF HC, pp. 91–92; and the traditional commentaries, ST SCC, pp. 90–91.)

92. This sentence has occasioned rather divergent views. Although the translation reflects the chapter's progression, another possibility is understanding the "hsing chih" at the beginning of the sentence in a causative sense, as causing them to betray their form (STPF SY, p. 99). A radically different view—expressed by Liu Yin, among others—suggests that through the employment of unorthodox and orthodox tactics, one creates and displays a deceptive form or disposition to the enemy while actually being formless (SWTCC WCCS, vol. 2, p. 5B). Others simply interpret it as displaying a form to the enemy (see STPF CS, p. 75; ST SCC, p. 93; and SS AS, p. 144).

In the BS the sentence begins with "Thus those who excel at command . . ."

93. Note that D. C. Lau also understands the sentence in this way, as do several commentators. Cf. "Some Notes on the Sun-tzu," pp. 329–30.

94. The BS invert the sequence of "field of battle" and "day of battle" and also lack the character for "Assemble."

95. The sequence of left/right and front/rear is reversed in the BS.

96. Presumably a comment directed to the king of Wu by Sun-tzu. However, Chang Yü comments that "I" is an error for Wu, the State's name (which seems unlikely). SWTCC WCCS, vol. 2, p. 8A; ST SCC, p. 97.

97. The BS have "solely" or "monopolized" for "achieved." Accordingly, "Thus I say victory can be monopolized."

98. Wu Ch'i suggested the following concrete method for probing an unknown enemy: "Order some courageous men from the lower ranks to lead some light

shock troops to test him. [When the enemy responds] they should concentrate on running off instead of trying to gain some objective. Then analyze the enemy's advance, whether their actions—such as sitting and standing—are in unison and their organization well preserved; whether when they pursue your retreat they feign being unable to catch you, or when they perceive easy gain they pretend not to realize it. A commander like this may be termed a 'wise general.' Do not engage him in battle." Obviously a disordered response, which Wu Ch'i also describes, indicates a "stupid general" ("The Tao of the General," p. 219. Essentially the same passage appears in "The Questions of King Wei" in Sun Pin's 'Military Methods).

99. Predictability means having form; therefore, repeating previously successful tactical methods would completely contradict Sun-tzu's principle of being formless. Through flexibility and variation the configuration of response attains the inexhaustible.

100. The BS have "move/moving" rather than "configuration." Because "configuration" is used consistently throughout the chapter, it seems preferable.

101. The BS have "victory" rather than "configuration."

102. Again the BS have "move" rather than "flow." (Chu Chün, among others, prefers the traditional text. See STPF SY, p. 93.)

103. The BS have "complete," so the phrase would be translated as "completed (fixed) configuration of power."

104. The BS lack "water," so the last part of the sentence would also describe the army.

105. The BS only have "transform" rather than "change and transform" and also lack "wrest victory."

106. The BS have two characters at the end, shen yao—perhaps an additional comment by an unknown hand with the meaning "Spiritual Essentials." The last sentence (about the five phases, four seasons, and sun and moon) appears to be a later comment. Deleting it would eliminate one of the standard justifications cited for the lateness of the text.

107. The title does not refer to actual combat but to achieving the conditions that make contention possible. The main themes are therefore the considerations of rapid versus measured advance; exploitation and avoidance of terrain and obstacles; and the critical element of ch'i, the army's spirit.

108. "Tactics" or "plans," but also the same character as "estimations" and therefore suggestive of comparatively valuing the effects of various routes.

109. The translation follows the Military Classics edition (SWTCC WCCS, vol. 2, p. 14B). However, other editions (such as the ST SCC, p. 106; STPF CS, p. 81; STPF SY, p. 109) and the BS all have the character for "army" (chün) rather than "masses" (chung), so both parts read in parallel: "Thus combat between armies can be advantageous; combat between armies can be dangerous." Both readings are congruent with the chapter's content because fighting with an undisciplined mass is dangerous, whereas it is the nature of warfare to entail both gain and loss.

110. Following STPF WC, p. 215, and SS AS, p. 169. They literally "roll up their armor" and presumably leave it behind with the baggage train so as to allow greater foot speed. (Heavy equipment is implied from the sentences below, which all couple the baggage and heavy equipment.)

111. A principle thoroughly understood by Wu in its campaigns against Ch'u.

112. In the *Art of War* and the *Ssu-ma Fa*, the concept of plundering and then dividing the spoils among the troops remains evident. In contrast, the later *Military Classics* strongly advocate a policy of neither harming the general populace nor seizing their possessions.

113. Wu Ch'i states: "Now the different drums, gongs, and bells are the means to awe the ear; flags and banners, pennants and standards the means to awe the eye; and prohibitions, orders, punishments, and fines the means to awe the mind ("The Tao of the General," *Wu-tzu*, p. 218).

114. Night battles did not commence until late in the Spring and Autumn period and were not common because the confusion wrought by the darkness made the results uncertain. The exact reason for multiplying the numbers of flags and fires is a subject of debate among the commentators: It was done either to ensure that their effect as tools for communication and signaling literally overwhelmed the soldiers or (and possibly as well as) to confuse the enemy by confronting it with a myriad stimuli (cf. SWTCC WCCS, vol. 2, pp. 19B–20; ST SCC, pp. 117–18). In "Certain Escape" the T'ai Kung advises: "Make your fires and drums numerous, and [attack] as if coming out of the very ground or dropping from Heaven above" (*Six Secret Teachings*, p. 81). A similar passage appears in "Ten Formations," chapter 16 of Sun Pin's *Military Methods*. Wu Ch'i said: "In general it is the rule of battle that during daylight hours the flags, banners, pennants, and standards provide the measure, while at night the gongs, drums, pipes, and whistles provide the constraints" ("Responding to Change," *Wu-tzu*, p. 219).

In the BS, this passage immediately follows the quotation from the *Military Administration* (STPF CS, p. 81).

115. Following D. C. Lau's gloss on *kuei* ("Some Notes on the Sun-tzu," p. 320).

116. The concept and manipulation of *ch'i* have already been briefly discussed in the introduction. They are fundamental topics in the military writings; each thinker proposes different methods for attaining courage, for developing the *ch'i* necessary in the soldiers. A separate monograph on the psychology of *ch'i* in battlefield contexts would be required to fully address the subject, which might well be summarized by a passage from the *Wei Liao-tzu*: "Now the means by which the general fights is the people; the means by which the people fight is their *ch'i*. When their *ch'i* is substantial they will fight; when their *ch'i* has been snatched away they will run off" ("Combat Awesomeness," p. 247). The ideal was to nurture warriors oblivious to death, who would therefore fight with invincibility and awesome power. The image of a warrior committed to death is found in several writings, sometimes placed in a marketplace, at others—as in the *Wu-tzu*—in the woods. Wu Ch'i said: "Now if there is a murderous villain hidden in the woods, even though one thousand men pursue him they all look around like owls and glance about like wolves. Why? They are afraid that violence will erupt and harm them personally. Thus one man oblivious to life and death can frighten one thousand" ("Stimulating the Officers," p. 223). In the *Wei Liao-tzu* it states: "If a warrior wields a sword to strike people in the marketplace, among ten thousand people there will not be anyone who does not avoid him. If I say it is not only that one man is courageous, but that the ten thousand are unlike him, what is the reason?

Being committed to dying and being committed to seeking life are not comparable" ("Discussion of Regulations," p. 245. For other important passages and further discussion, consult the text and index to the *Seven Military Classics*).

Sun Pin's *Military Methods* also contains an important chapter on *ch'i*, the first part of which describes the process of attaining the requisite levels as the time for battle approaches: "When you form the army and assemble the masses [concentrate upon stimulating their *ch'i*.] When you once again move out and reassemble the army, concentrate upon ordering the soldiers and sharpening their *ch'i*. When you approach the border and near the enemy, concentrate upon honing their *ch'i*. When the day for battle has been set, concentrate upon making their *ch'i* decisive. When the day for battle is at hand, concentrate upon expanding their *ch'i*" ("Expanding Ch'i," the *Military Methods*). While the chapter is fragmented, it clearly elucidates the methods for nurturing and realizing these *ch'i* levels in the troops, providing the most explicit and systematic psychological analysis found in any of the military writings.

117. Or "majestic formations."

118. The BS have *ni*—"go against," "go contrary to"—rather than *ying*—"to meet," "to confront." This reading is also preferred by Chu Chün (STPF SY, p. 112).

119. The feigned retreat was apparently one of the most common ruses employed in antiquity. By suddenly extending an irresistible "bait," an army's flight could entice the enemy's troops into enthusiastically breaking their ranks and engaging in an increasingly disordered pursuit—only to painfully discover they had fallen prey to unorthodox tactics. The *Six Secret Teachings* states: "Distant observation posts and far-off scouts, explosive haste and feigned retreats are the means by which to force the surrender of walled fortifications and compel the submission of towns" ("The Unorthodox Army," p. 71. Note the objective: attacking fortified cities). The difficulty of course lies in determining what is a true retreat (presumably terror and flight would be indicative), what mere deception. For example, the T'ai Kung observed: "Whenever the cavalry penetrates the ranks of the enemy but does not destroy their formation so that the enemy feigns flight, only to turn their chariots and cavalry about to strike our rear—this is a situation in which the cavalry will be defeated" ("Cavalry in Battle," p. 103). Accordingly the *Ssu-ma Fa* observed: "In antiquity they did not pursue a fleeing enemy too far or follow a retreating army too closely. By not pursuing them too far, it was difficult to draw them into a trap; by not pursuing so closely as to catch up, it was hard to ambush them" ("Obligations of the Son of Heaven," p. 129).

Li Ching and T'ang T'ai-tsung discussed Sun-tzu's passage and the nature of feigned ("unorthodox") retreats: "The T'ai-tsung said: 'Whenever an army withdraws can it be termed unorthodox?' Li Ching said: 'It is not so. Whenever the soldiers retreat with their flags confused and disordered, the sounds of the large and small drums not responding to each other, and their orders shouted out in a clamor, this is true defeat, not unorthodox strategy. If the flags are ordered, the drums respond to each other, and the commands and orders seem unified, then even though they may be retreating and running, it is not a defeat and must be a case of unorthodox strategy'" (*Questions and Replies*, p. 323).

120. The *Art of War* is a laconic text, and principles are advanced without any

qualifying constraints or circumstances. "Not obstructing a retreating army" is a typical example because Sun-tzu also advises against losing opportunities or failing to exploit victories. When an enemy has been compelled to retreat, his discipline, strength, deployment, and similar factors must all be considered in determining whether to bottle him up and press for surrender, or permit a retreat that may produce even greater disorder and thus an even easier opportunity. Wu-tzu, in analyzing the opportune circumstances for attacking an enemy, said: "When they have lost the critical moment and not followed up on opportunities, they can be attacked" (*Wu-tzu*, p. 213). (Unlike the *Three Strategies* or *Six Secret Teachings*, the *Art of War* never suggests implementing policies of compassion.)

121. To weaken their will and avoid stimulating any resolve to fight to the death. The BS have "leave an outlet"; the Ming text has "must/outlet," the "leave" being understood. (Cf. STPF SY, p. 112, for Chu's rejection of the Ming edition.)

122. Liu Yin notes that this last paragraph is apparently repeated from the next chapter. However, only the Ming edition has the passage in the next chapter as well, where it is apparently an accidental accretion.

The BS have "masses/large numbers" for "military."

123. Chapter titles in the extant editions of the ancient classics have frequently been appended by later hands—whether compilers, subsequent authors adding material, or commentators. Many were simply drawn from the first few words of the chapter, others from a salient sentence within it; therefore, they may be largely unrelated to the chapter's overall subject matter. "Nine Changes" forces the commentators to somehow justify "changes" because the chapter's admonitions against certain courses of action on particular terrains do not constitute changes. For example, Chang Yü asserts that the chapter refers to employing the expedient—the "unusual" rather than the "normal"—in these situations, but his view lacks justification. Although the concept of flexible response is critical to Sun-tzu's tactics, it hardly seems to be the topic of this chapter. Others—including Liu Yin—suggest the chapter is badly mangled, and because the BS preserve only about forty words, they offer little help. In addition, the BS fragments lack a title. Finally, "nine" may simply be used here as a cognomen for "many" or "numerous," such as "Nine Heavens" (STPF SY, pp. 128–29). A minority view holds that "nine" might also be an error for "five" because five terrains are discussed (see SWTCC WCCS, vol. 2, pp. 24–25; ST SCC, p. 131; SS AS, pp. 194–95; and STPF CS, pp. 89–91).

124. This repeats the formula used previously to introduce the topic. Five classifications of terrain follow, all of which also appear in subsequent chapters in similar descriptive lists—frequently with definitions. Although some notes are provided below, also refer to chapters 10 and 11 for further explication. (For additional discussion of the terms together with a full translation of the relevant lost material on terrain classification from the *Art of War* that is preserved in the *T'ung-tien* and other texts, see the supplementary section of tomb fragments and lost passages that follows the *Art of War* translation.)

125. "Entrapping terrain" is traditionally understood as low-lying ground, perhaps surrounded by hills or mountains and characterized by bodies of water such as marshes or swamps. It is thought to be land that can be inundated, possibly by heavy rains or by breaking restraining banks (as was done in China in World

War II) and consequently involves heavy slogging for the chariots and men. However, there is considerable disagreement as to its defining characteristics (See STPF SY, pp. 125–26; ST CCCY, p. 165; ST SCC, p. 131). The *Six Secret Teachings,* among other works, discusses the dangers posed by similar terrain in chapter 58. The BS have *fan*—"overflow" or "inundate"—rather than *p'i,* which means "subvert(ed)" or "defeated." Chu Chün prefers the original because the scope is wider and is capable of encompassing any terrain through which passage is difficult (STPF SY, pp. 125–26). There is another, nearly identical character *i,* which means "bridge" or "embankment"; its existence raises further, although unexplored, possibilities.

126. "Focal" terrain (following Griffith's apt term) is defined in chapter 11 as "land of the feudal lords surrounded on three sides such that whoever arrives first will gain the masses of All under Heaven." The characters literally mean "terrain where highways intersect"; therefore, narrowly defined it would be land that is accessible from several directions over prepared roads.

127. Several sentences follow in the Ming edition of the *Seven Military Classics* that have been duplicated erroneously from other sections. Neither the Sung dynasty edition of the *Seven Military Classics* nor other editions—such as the SCC—contain them, and they are therefore omitted here.

128. Emending "can" to "not," following the Sung edition and the tomb fragments entitled "Four Changes." (Cf. ST SCC, pp. 132–33, and the translation in the fragments section.)

129. Note that this is not a categorical injunction not to attack fortified cities. Rather, there are *some* or *certain* cities that should not be attacked. Avoiding siege warfare has perhaps been overemphasized in Sun-tzu just because he stressed the wasted resources involved in mounting a lengthy effort.

130. With this sentence there are already nine principles.

131. Wu Ju-sung notes that in the so-called "lost" fragments from the bamboo slips, the following sentences appear: "There are orders from the ruler which are not implemented. If the ruler orders anything contrary to these four, then do not implement it." "Four" refers to the last four in the series (see STPF CS, pp. 89–91). The "Nine Changes" would therefore be encompassed by the series listed prior to the strong statement about not accepting certain orders from the ruler, which is consonant with the view of commentators such as Wang Hsi, rather than being an arbitrary number (cf. STPF CS, pp. 89–91; ST SCC, p. 131; STPF WC, p. 254).

132. "Five advantages" is found in almost all editions, including the Sung and Ming, and is generally understood as referring to the advantages of the first terrains characterized at the start of this chapter. However, there may be errors in the characters because the "five" are not advantageous but rather are disadvantageous terrains, and much circumlocution is required to convert them to "advantage." One suggestion is that this should read "advantages of terrain"—the advantages and terrains, however, remaining unspecified. (See ST CCCY, p. 164; and SS AS, pp. 201–3. Compare ST SCC, pp. 136–37.)

133. Being prepared, rather than having to depend upon circumstances and perhaps the good will of others, was a fundamental aspect of the military thinkers' grand strategy. For example, the *Ssu-ma Fa* states: "Even though a state may be

vast, those who love warfare will inevitably perish. Even though calm may prevail under Heaven, those who forget warfare will certainly be endangered" ("Benevolence the Foundation," p. 126). Much of the first third of the *Six Secret Teachings* is similarly devoted to the theme of enriching the people and the country so as to be materially prepared to wage warfare when necessary. Fortuitously, at their stage in the evolution of weapons, the tools of crafts, agriculture, and hunting could still be employed in warfare without any great disadvantage, and their good maintenance was advocated as part of a preparatory strategy. (See chapter 30, "Agricultural Implements.")

134. As discussed in the introduction, exploiting character flaws and emotional weaknesses in the enemy's commanding general was viewed as critical for successfully effecting battlefield tactics. The *Six Secret Teachings* devotes a chapter to enumerating the strengths and weaknesses of generals, citing, for example, the results of certain flaws: "One who is courageous and treats death lightly can be destroyed by violence. One who is hasty and impatient can be destroyed by persistence. One who is greedy and loves profit can be bribed. One who is benevolent but unable to inflict suffering can be worn down. One who is wise but fearful can be distressed. One who is trustworthy and likes to trust others can be deceived. One who is scrupulous and incorruptible but does not love men can be insulted. One who is wise but indecisive can be suddenly attacked. One who is resolute and self-reliant can be confounded by events. One who is fearful and likes to entrust responsibility to others can be tricked" (Chapter 19, "A Discussion of Generals," pp. 63–64).

In "The Tao of the General" Wu Ch'i states: "Now the commanding general of the Three Armies should combine both military and civilian abilities. The employment of soldiers requires uniting both hardness and softness. In general when people discuss generalship they usually focus on courage. However, courage is but one of the general's many characteristics because the courageous will rashly join battle with the enemy. To rashly join battle with an enemy without knowing the advantages and disadvantages is not acceptable" (*Wu-tzu*, p. 217). In the same chapter Wu-tzu provides several examples of exploitable flaws.

The most extensive list of requisite characteristics is found in the recently recovered *Military Methods* of Sun Pin. In "Selecting the Troops" he asserts that trust, loyalty, and daring are essential, the second no doubt reflecting the powerful status of the professional commander in his time. In "The General's Righteousness" he states that a general must be righteous (because righteousness is the foundation for severity and, in turn, awesomeness), benevolent, virtuous, trustworthy (or credible), and wise. In "Eight Formations" he advises that the general needs sufficient wisdom, courage, and (understanding of) the Tao (of warfare). Finally, in two chapters entitled "The General's Defeats" and "The General's Loses" he enumerates some twenty character flaws, weaknesses, behavioral errors, and pernicious conditions in the army that result in defeat, including: greed, arrogance, overconfidence, self-reliance, indecisiveness, dilatoriness, laxness, and perversity.

135. Literally, "espy life"—generally understood as "look for tenable ground," terrain that can be fought on or defended. Some commentators identify it with the yang side, the side looking toward the sun (facing south or east). (Cf. SWTCC WCCS, vol. 2, p. 35A; ST SCC, pp. 144–45; STPF WC, pp. 273–74.)

136. The *Six Secret Teachings* analyzes the tactics for mountain warfare in a number of places, and focuses on them in such chapters as the "Crow and Cloud Formations in the Mountains." The other military classics also discuss such terrain considerations, but are less focused.

137. Sun-tzu rarely discusses the military problems posed by water—streams, rivers, lakes—no doubt reflecting an early heritage of plains warfare. As the scope of conflict expanded, the problems entailed in fording rivers, crossing wetlands, and negotiating lakes grew enormously, stimulating the development of naval forces in the southeast. Accordingly, the later military classics address these concerns somewhat extensively. (The character translated as "rivers"—*shui* rather than *ch'uan*—originally a graph of running water, can refer to rivers or to bodies of water in general. Because Sun-tzu speaks about the current's direction, rivers appear to be intended here.)

138. This is understood as meaning that armies should not assume positions downstream from an enemy because of such potential dangers as being inundated by suddenly released flood waters or felled by drinking water drawn from a poisoned river (see SWTCC WCCS, vol. 2, p. 36A; ST SCC, p. 147).

139. The problems posed by wetlands and marshy terrain (also termed "entrapping" terrain by Sun-tzu later in the text) must have been well known to every military commander, and they are duly noted in virtually all the military writings, including Sun Pin's *Military Methods*. For example, see "Responding to Change" in the *Wu-tzu*, and the "Crow and Cloud Formation in the Marshes" and "Battle Chariots" in the *Six Secret Teachings*.

140. Presumably, terrain easy for chariots to negotiate and for supply wagons to cross.

141. Fragments recovered from the Han tomb (as well as materials in the *Shih chi*) briefly summarize the Yellow Emperor's conquest over the other four (evil) emperors, striking each in turn in his associated quarter (that is, the Black Emperor in the north, the White Emperor in the west, and so on). This conflict, which is denied vigorously by the Confucians, was popularly understood as marking the (mythological) inception of military conflict and strategy in China. See "Lin-i Yin-ch'üeh-shan Han-mu ch'u-t'u *Sun-tzu ping-fa* ts'an-chien shih-wen," *WW*, 1974: 12, p. 12

142. Life-supporting terrain is obviously ground that has sunlight, grass for the animals, brush and trees for firewood, and especially potable water. Liu Yin and others equate the "substantial" with high ground (SWTCC WCCS, vol. 2, p. 38A. Cf. ST SCC, p. 150, and STPF SY, pp. 142–43).

143. The BS lack "is said to be certain of victory," so the sentence is read as being linked with the start of the next passage (cf. STPF SY, p. 137).

144. Chu Chün points out that observing the presence of bubbles or foam on the river, which indicates rain upstream, exemplifies Sun-tzu's approach to analyzing and fathoming the enemy and battlefield situations. From the bubbles one can deduce that it has rained and can anticipate a surge in the river's flow and level. Such a surge could prove disastrous for an army encamped too close to the shore or caught suddenly in midstream (STPF SY, p. 137).

145. Although the commentators differ somewhat on the details of this and the following dangerous, natural configurations of terrain—several of which are con-

crete cases of Sun-tzu's more general classifications—their defining characteristics are clear (cf. SWTCC WCCS, vol. 2, pp. 38B–39A; ST SCC, pp. 151–53). They and many others are discussed by Sun Pin as well in "Treasures of Terrain."

Heaven's Well is so named because it is a significant depression, such as a valley, surrounded on four sides by hills or mountains. It is dangerous because the runoff of rainwater from unexpected storms can inundate the lowlands.

146. Heaven's Jail is a valley with steep hills or mountains on three sides. Forces that carelessly enter it can easily be bottled up, unable to ascend the sides to escape.

147. Heaven's Net refers to any area of extensive, dense growth—including heavy forests or dense vegetation (including junglelike growth of underbrush and vines) that will obstruct the passage of vehicles or entangle the men.

148. Heaven's Pit refers to an area characterized by soft, probably muddy terrain, perhaps marked by wetlands, that will mire both men and vehicles.

149. Heaven's Fissure refers to terrain that suggests a fissure in the earth. Therefore, it encompasses long, narrow passages constrained by hills or forests from which an enemy might advantageously dominate the passage.

150. The BS have "small forests," or woods.

151. The BS have "which could conceal hidden (forces)" right after "entangled undergrowth" and "places of evildoers" at the end of the sentence. (Neither the STPF CS nor the STPF SY takes notes of these.)

152. The occupation of ravines was of particular interest to the classical strategists (as evidenced by material in both the *Six Secret Teachings* and *Wei Liao-tzu*); this is generally seen as indicating weakness and the need to avail oneself of advantages of terrain.

153. Easily visible obstacles have been made deliberately detectable in order to create the suspicion of ambush or the emplacement of entangling devices and thereby beguile the ordinary commander to divert his forces to the enemy's advantage.

154. Presumably, to define the field of battle and pre-position for the infantry advance.

155. They lack military discipline, grumble and move about, are noisy, and obey orders reluctantly.

156. The translation follows the *Seven Military Classics* edition. Other editions (cf. ST SCC, pp. 161–62) are somewhat different, combining this and the following sentence to read: "If they feed grain to the horses and eat meat while the army does not hang up its cooking utensils nor return to camp, they are an exhausted invader."

157 These are all signs that they are preparing to launch a desperate attack; otherwise, they would need the horses and draft animals as well as their cooking utensils. (In chapter 11 Sun-tzu advises breaking the cooking utensils and similar measures to dramatically impress on the soldiers the hopelessness of their situation and increase their determination for a last-ditch engagement.)

158. The commander, through his ill-conceived measures, has lost control over them and fears they will revolt. (Excessive rewards and punishments are symptoms of a breakdown in discipline and loss of authority.)

159. This sentence probably refers to one's own troops. That is, it is not impor-

tant that you be more numerous than the enemy because if you are not, you merely have to conceive good tactical measures. The BS lack "esteem," which accordingly is understood. "Aggressively" or "in martial fashion" (*wu*) is thought here to refer to actions taken without basis, manifesting bravado without forethought (cf. ST SCC, pp. 164–65; STPF SY, p. 147).

160. This passage is cited in a discussion in Book 2 of *Questions and Replies*, wherein the greater question of the importance and role of punishments is raised. (Also note Sun Pin's chapter, "The Questions of King Wen.")

161. Another dimension to the civil-martial relationship.

162. Generally translated as "certain victory" or "certain conquest," the characters do not contain "victory/conquer." Rather, this is the term encountered previously for easily seizing the enemy (see note 16 above).

163. Configurations (*hsing*) of terrain, with their tactical implications. Unfortunately, the configurations are named rather than defined; parts of the text have apparently been lost, and none are preserved in the BS. Each configuration correlates the topography with the basic maneuvers possible in the situation on the assumption that two armies are confronting each other. (A fragment entitled "Configurations of Terrain, II," was found in the tomb but is virtually worthless.)

164. "Suspended," or "hung up." Although the text seems simple enough, there is a hidden question of perspective that the commentators have not noticed. If the situational analysis refers to the army's present position, when it goes forth it will not be able to return. Accordingly, the terrain it initially occupied would best be termed "irrecoverable." From the perspective of the position to which it advances, it becomes "hung up." Presumably, the "suspended configuration" encompasses both the initial and final positions across the terrain. (Cf. ST SCC, pp. 169–70; STPF SY, p. 154; SS AS, p. 246; and STPF CS, p. 105.)

165. "Stalemated" describes the tactical situation, although the exact character is *chih*—"branch," or "to support." Both sides are supported, so they are in a stalemate. The commentators suggest a lengthy standoff (cf. ST SCC, p. 170).

166. This might also be understood as to "draw off (our forces) to make them (i.e., the enemy) depart." That is, by withdrawing one *compels* the enemy to depart from his entrenched, advantageous position. Withdrawing one's forces and departing is the means through which the enemy's departure is accomplished in either case, but the conclusion—of stimulating them to movement—is implicit in the text translation and is necessary for the next sentence—striking when the enemy is half out.

167. "Constricted" configurations are generally described as extensive mountain valleys. Others also identify them with river or lake crossings. (Cf. SWTCC WCCS, vol. 2, p. 48B; STPF SY, p. 154; STPF CS, p. 106; and ST SCC, p. 171.) Furthermore, the commentators generally understand the sentence as referring to occupying the mouth; however, there is no textual reason to so restrict it because the sentence simply advises to "fully" occupy it. (By leaving the entrance unobstructed, enemy forces can be lured into the killing zone created by deploying forces on both sides throughout the valley, as in several famous historical battles.)

168. "Precipitous," invoking the image of steep mountain gorges or ravines ("ravines" being the translation in other contexts). It is difficult terrain to traverse;

therefore, occupying the heights is paramount. (Cf. SWTCC WCCS, vol. 2, p. 48B, STPF SY, p. 154; ST SCC, pp. 171–72.)

169. Following Liu Yin, taking "strategic power being equal" as an additional condition. (See SWTCC WCCS, vol. 2, p. 49a. Cf. STPF CS, p. 106.)

170. The odds are so insurmountable that any sort of direct attack can only result in failure and the retreat of the forces so foolishly flung at the enemy (SWTCC WCCS, vol. 2, p. 49B).

171. Following SWTCC WCCS and ST SCC. The *T'ung-tien* has "estimating the fullest extent of the difficult and easy, advantageous and harmful, distant and near" (cf. ST SCC, p. 176; and Lau, "Some Notes on the *Sun-tzu*," p. 328). "Ravines" is the same character translated previously as "precipitous" for the configurations of terrain.

172. Here—unlike the earlier passage, which is open to some interpretation—the text clearly means "with" rather than "for" him (refer to note 5 above).

173. Following the Sung, Ming, and SCC editions. However, some others have "inexhaustible" rather than "complete" (cf. STPF SY, p. 153; SS AS, pp. 261–62).

174. The nine terrains analyzed in this chapter appear in two sequences, with some variation. In addition, some of the terms appeared previously in chapters 8 and 10; others are new but apparently overlap with earlier configurations. This suggests that essential materials have been lost, the text has been corrupted, or the concepts were in a state of flux and not yet rigidly defined.

175. Following Giles and Griffith, who use the appropriate term "dispersive." The commentators generally understand "dispersive" as referring to the tendency of the men, while fighting within their native state, to be thinking of their homes and families and to be inclined to return there. Consequently, they are neither unified nor aroused to a fighting spirit. (Cf. SWTCC WCCS, vol. 2, p. 56A; ST SCC, p. 182; and STPF SY, p. 168.) Note that later in the chapter the commander must unify their will on dispersive terrain (before invading enemy territory), and Sun-tzu also advises against engaging the enemy on dispersive terrain. This was perhaps a strategy designed to vitiate an invader's strength before engaging him in battle.

176. Apparently, the soldiers still do not regard the enterprise too seriously and continue to think about home and family. Because it remains relatively easy to withdraw but dangerous to forge ahead, it is termed "light" terrain. (Cf. SWTCC WCCS, vol. 2, p. 56Aa; STPF SY, p. 168; and ST SCC, p. 183. Griffith uses "frontier," Giles "facile.")

177. This is ground for which one contends, therefore "contentious" terrain. (Giles also translates as "contentious," Griffith as "key ground," and it is unquestionably a strategic point.) The configurations of terrain previously warned against in the last chapter are probably prime objectives under this category because of their great tactical potential if they can be seized and exploited. (Cf. ST SCC, p.. 183–84; STPF SY, p. 169.)

178. In chapter 10 this is termed "accessible" terrain. Army movement is unhampered.

179. Following Griffith's apt term, "focal." Presumably, this is territory in which major highways intersect and is accessible to major powers on various sides. Its occupation is the key to controlling vast territory. (See note 126 above, where the term first appears. Also compare ST SCC, p. 185; and STPF SY, p. 170.)

180. Griffith translates as "serious." This term contrasts with "light terrain," the severity of their situation now being clearly apparent to the soldiers. Their minds are unified, their courage united. (Cf. SWTCC WCCS, vol. 2, p. 57A; and ST SCC, pp. 185–86.) Chu Chün sees the critical element as the cessation of food supplies, with the soldiers suddenly having to forage and plunder to sustain themselves, as stated slightly later in the chapter. This weighs heavily on them (STPF SY, pp. 170–71).

181. This seems to also encompass Heaven's Pit and Heaven's Net. The term is first discussed in chapter 8.

182. "Constricted" is the same term as that used for one of the configurations in chapter 10. (It can also mean a "gorge.")

183. The term for "encircled" can also be translated as "besieged" in other contexts and clearly carries such implications (see ST SCC, p. 186). The emphasis here is on the necessity to pass through a narrow opening or along a narrow passage, which constrains the flow of men and materials and thereby makes them vulnerable to being surrounded and attacked by even a small force.

184. Sun-tzu consistently advocates exploiting "ground of death" because when troops are deployed on it, the situation forces them to fight valiantly. The commentators think it would be terrain with solid obstacles to the front—such as mountains—and water to the rear, preventing a withdrawal. (Cf. ST SCC, pp. 187–88; and STPF SY, pp. 171–72.)

185. If you cannot occupy it first, do not attack an entrenched enemy. (SWTCC WCCS, vol. 2 p. 58A; and ST SCC, p. 189.)

186. In chapter 8 it states, "Unite with your allies on focal terrain."

187. In chapter 8 it states, "Do not encamp on entrapping terrain."

188. Chapter 8: "Make strategic plans for encircled terrain."

189. Some commentators take this as referring to "uniting with the enemy in battle." However, the general import of the paragraph does not restrict the techniques strictly to combat measures.

190. There is disagreement over what is actually obtained without being sought (cf. ST SCC, p. 187).

191. The importance of omens and measures for minimizing their impact are considered in most of the military writings. When the Chou dynasty arose it claimed to have witnessed appropriate omens confirming it had received the Mandate of Heaven, although the T'ai Kung (in the *Six Secret Teachings*) emphasizes human suffering as the true sign. (In his biography, translated in the introduction, he is also recorded as ignoring ominous portents and dismissing any need for divination. However, he included three astrologers for the army's central staff to interpret such signs—and perhaps thereby eliminate doubt.) Among the indications of probable victory he cites: "If the Three Armies have been startled a number of times, the officers and troops no longer maintaining good order; they terrify each other [with stories about] the enemy's strength; they speak to each other about the disadvantages; they anxiously look about at each other, listening carefully; they talk incessantly of ill omens, a myriad of mouths confusing each other; they fear neither laws nor orders and do not regard their general seriously—these are indications of weakness" (The Army's Indications,' p. 73). In the *Wu-tzu* one of the eight conditions "in which one engages in battle without performing divination" is: "the army has

been out in the field for an extended period; their food supplies are exhausted; the hundred surnames are resentful and angry; and numerous baleful portents have arisen, with the superior officers being unable to quash their effects" ("Evaluating the Enemy," p. 212). The *Wei Liao-tzu* condemns superstitious practices, but the *Ssu-ma Fa* directs itself to suggesting measures to counteract omens: "Whenever affairs are well executed they will endure; when they accord with ancient ways they can be effected. When the oath is clear and stimulating the men will be strong, and you will extinguish [the effects] of baleful omens and auspicious signs. The Tao for eliminating baleful omens is as follows: One is called righteousness. Charge [the people] with good faith, approach them with strength, establish the foundation [of kingly government], and unify the strategic power of All under Heaven. There will not be any men who are not pleased, so this is termed 'doubly employing the people.' Another is called [advantages conferred by] the strategic balance of power. Increase the [enemy's excesses], seize what he loves. Then acting from without, we can cause a response from within" ("Determining Rank," p. 136).

192. The BS have "deaths" instead of "lives," but the difference is ignored by the STPF CS and STPF SY.

193. This phrase, which is implicit in any case, appears in the BS.

194. Following Chao Pen-hsüeh, *Sun-tzu-shu chiao-chieh yin-lei*, vol. 2, p. 36B. Liu Yin (SWTCC WCCS, vol. 2, pp. 64B–65A) cites one commentator who emends the character translated as "fetter" to "release," understanding the sentence to refer to "releasing the horses."

195. Some commentators incorrectly equate "hard and soft" with "strong and weak." The two pairs are clearly distinguished in the *Military Classics*. For example, the *Three Strategies* declares: "The *Military Pronouncements* states: 'If one can be soft and hard, his state will be increasingly glorious! If one can be weak and strong, his state will be increasingly illustrious! If purely soft and purely weak, his state will inevitably decline. If purely hard and purely strong, his state will inevitably be destroyed'" ("Superior Strategy," p. 293. The hard and soft also appear in Sun Pin's *Military Methods*).

196. Literally, "keeping them stupid." Chu Chün believes this merely refers to preserving all plans in total secrecy rather than being a policy to keep the soldiers stupid (STPF SY, p. 176).

197. Especially the enemy.

198. Analogous with releasing the trigger of a cocked crossbow. In some editions, such as the ST SCC (p. 203), the following sentence appears: "They burn their boats and smash their cooking pots."

199. This sentence also appears in the fragment entitled "Configuration of Terrain, II."

200. This paragraph again discusses the nine types of terrain, but from the perspective of acting as an invader. Some commentators believe it is redundant or erroneous, but others—such as the modern military historian General Wei Ju-lin—stress the difference between principles for general combat and those for invading another's territory (see ST CCCY, p. 222–24).

201. The BS are somewhat different: "If you have strongholds behind you and the enemy before you, it is 'fatal terrain.' If there is no place to go, it is 'exhausted terrain.'"

202. Some commentators take this as referring to the enemy's rear, but the context of the preceding statements indicates it should refer to actions taken with regard to one's own army. (CF. STPF CS, p. 115; and STPF WC, p. 370.) The BS have "I will cause them not to remain."

203. The actions to be taken for four of the terrains are somewhat reversed in the BS. In this case the BS have the conclusion to the next sentence: "I solidify our alliances."

204. The BS have "I focus on what we rely on."

205. The BS have "I race our rear elements forward."

206. Liu Yin explains this as meaning that the general closes off any openings deliberately offered by the enemy to lure his forces out of their encirclement (SWTCC WCCS, vol. 2, p. 69A). Leaving such an opening was a common way to keep the defenders from mounting a last-ditch, pitched defense. (Both the *Six Secret Teachings* and the *Wei Liao-tzu* discuss this technique.)

207. The BS preface the sentence with a fragment that apparently means "It is the nature of the feudal lords. . . ."

208. Reading *pa wang* as two distinct terms rather than "hegemonic king" (cf. STPF CS, p. 115).

209. This is sometimes understood as not contending with others to form alliances, which would miss the main point of the passage.

210. Note that here Sun-tzu advises the proper basis for "taking cities," further countering the overemphasis upon not attacking cities.

211. This sentence is somewhat problematic. Most of the commentators interpret it in the light of Sun-tzu's policy of being deceptive, and in fact the character for "details" might also be an error for a similar character meaning "to deceive." Thus they understand it as "accord with and pretend to follow the enemy's intentions." (Cf. SWTCC WCCS, vol. 2, p. 73A; ST SCC, p. 212.) The translation essentially follows STPF SY, p. 184. Wu Ju-sung (STPF CS, p. 115) understands it as simply finding out the details of the enemy's intentions.

212. Literally, "grind (it out)" in the temple, which presumably means somberly work out the plans and estimations. The SCC text has "incite" rather than "grind." (SWTCC WCCS, vol. 2, pp. 73B–74A; ST SCC, p. 214. Compare STPF SY, p. 183.)

213. Although incendiary attacks are recorded in the *Tso chuan*, among the *Seven Military Classics* the principles for employing fire are little discussed. Only two chapters focus upon it: Sun-tzu's "Incendiary Attacks," which centers on offense, and the T'ai Kung's "Incendiary Warfare," which elucidates defensive techniques (thus suggesting that incendiary attacks must have been more extensively employed in the period than recorded in the *Tso chuan* and other writings). In Sun Pin's *Military Methods,* incendiary warfare is briefly discussed in "Ten Formations."

214. The fifth objective is variously interpreted as shooting flaming arrows into an encampment, burning their weapons, or attacking their formations, as translated (cf. ST SCC, p. 218).

215. While the dangers posed to an army encamped or deployed on low-lying terrain are noted by several writers, there is virtually no discussion in the *Seven Military Classics* about employing water as an offensive weapon. In the campaigns between Wu and Ch'u, King Ho-lü employed water at least once to flood the forces

of the minor state of Hsü, suggesting that diverting streams was part of their offensive repertoire, as should be expected for a water-logged state (See the *Tso chuan*, Duke Chao, thirtieth year. The commentators note that this is the first recorded use of such methods.) Perhaps such engagements provided the experiential basis for Sun-tzu's statement.

216. The *Art of War* was much vilified by hypocritical Confucian literati for advocating the employment of spies. However, most of the military writings acknowledged, if not stressed, the need for spies to obtain vital military intelligence. The T'ai Kung includes officers who act as spies on the general command staff; Wu Ch'i mentions their employment in several contexts in the *Wu-tzu*; and many texts speak about the need to block out spies. (For the latter see "Superior Strategy" in the *Three Strategies*; "The Source of Offices" in the *Wei Liao-tzu*; and even Sun-tzu, who stressed the impenetrability of the formless against the "deepest spy" near the end of chapter 6, "Vacuity and Substance.")

217. The second mention of a campaign army with a force level of a hundred thousand men. Subsequently Sun Pin refers to force levels in the "hundreds of thousands" ("Distinction of Guest and Host," the *Military Methods*).

218. Although this lengthy standoff is cited as evidence that the *Art of War* was composed well after Sun-tzu's era, it should be noted that the actual conflict only requires a day—certainly consonant with the century before Sun-tzu. Of course he is speaking comparatively about extremes for illustrative purposes, but it may also be the case that the standoff is between states rather than actual field armies.

219. When the deceit is discovered, they are murdered or executed.

220. The BS have "relationship" rather than "affairs."

221. The BS add "Shuai Shih-pi in the Hsing. When Yen arose, they had Su Ch'in in Ch'i." Because Su Ch'in was active in the second half of the fourth century B.C.—almost two centuries after Sun Wu presumably advanced his tactics—this is obviously a later accretion.

Notes
to the
Tomb
Texts
and
Lost
Writings

1. The nine configurations that follow, excerpted from the *T'ung tien* compiled by Tu Yu in the eighth century A.D., are thought to comprise material preserved from the 82-chapter version of the *Art of War* apparently still extant in the Han dynasty. (See note 211 to the introduction.) The translation generally follows Sun Hsing-yen's convenient summary in the *Sun-tzu shih-chia-chu* (Shih-chieh shu-chü, Taipei, 1984), pp. 4–6, with occasional corrections based on the *T'ung tien* (*chüan* 159). The different configurations, together with their recommended tactics, should be read in conjunction with chapter 11, "Nine Terrains"; the essential sentences will be found in the notes below. A number of similar situations—contained in the *Six Secret Teachings,* the *Wu-tzu,* and Sun Pin's *Military Methods* (especially "Ten Questions")—will be cited to facilitate further study.

2. Sun-tzu states: "When the feudal lords fight in their own territory it is 'dispersive terrain.'" As for the appropriate tactics: "On dispersive terrain do not engage the enemy," and "On dispersive terrain I unify their will" (chapter 11, "Nine Terrains").

3. The invading enemy, having penetrated deeply, finds itself on Sun-tzu's "deep," "isolated," or even "fatal terrain." According to Sun-tzu's psychology of *ch'i,* circumstances force them to be courageous; they are constantly prepared to fight. (Also see "Explosive Warfare" in *Six Secret Teachings.*)

4. This is the complementary situation to the last one contained in this section.

5. Ravines were deemed critical to establishing ambushes, holding terrain, stopping an enemy, and attacking superior numbers. Sun Pin states: "What causes difficulty for the enemy is ravines" ("The Questions of King Wei"). The T'ai Kung states: "Valleys with streams and treacherous ravines are the means by which to stop chariots and defend against cavalry," and "Holding defiles and narrows is the means by which to be solidly entrenched" (chapter 27, "The Unorthodox Army," *Six Secret Teachings).*

6. Sun-tzu states: "When they enter someone else's territory, but not deeply, it is 'light terrain,'" and notes that "when the troops have penetrated deeply, they will be unified, but where only shallowly, will [be inclined to] scatter." As for the appropriate tactics: 'On light terrain I have them group together," and "On light terrain do not stop" (chapter 11, "Nine Terrains"; also see "Approaching the Border" in *Six Secret Teachings*).

7. This sentence, abstracted from Ho T'ing-hsi's commentary, has perhaps inadvertently dropped the interrogative format. The first part was probably framed as a question by the king of Wu, while the second part, starting right after the footnote with "This is referred to," was probably Sun-tzu's reply.

8. Sun-tzu states: "If when we occupy it, it will be advantageous to us, while if they occupy it, it will be advantageous to them, it is 'contentious terrain.'" As for the appropriate tactics: "On contentious terrain I race our rear elements forward," and "On contentious terrain do not attack" (chapter 11, "Nine Terrains").

9. Sun-tzu states: "When we can go and they can also come, it is 'traversable terrain.'" As for the appropriate tactics: "On traversable terrain I focus on defense," and "On traversable terrain do not allow your forces to become isolated" (chapter 11, "Nine Terrains").

10. The term "horns of an ox" is generally translated simply as "the flanks." In this case, however, the original image is strong and appropriate.

11. Sun-tzu states: "When one penetrates deeply into enemy territory, bypassing numerous cities, it is 'heavy terrain.'" As for the appropriate tactics: "On heavy terrain I ensure a continuous supply of provisions," and "On heavy terrain plunder for provisions" (chapter 11, "Nine Terrains"; also see "Movement and Rest," "Gongs and Drums," "Severed Routes," "Strong Enemy," and "Martial Enemy," all of which discuss situations of deep penetration in the *Six Secret Teachings*).

12. Sun-tzu states: "Where there are mountains and forests, ravines and defiles, wetlands and marshes, wherever the road is difficult to negotiate, it is "entrapping terrain.'" Sun Pin states: "Five types of terrain are conducive to defeat: gorges with streams; [valleys]; river areas; marshes; and salt flats" ("Treasures of Terrain"). The tactics appropriate to entrapping terrain: "On entrapping terrain I speedily advance along the roads," and "On entrapping terrain move through quickly" (chapter 11, "Nine Terrains"). And, "Do not encamp on entrapping terrain" (chapter 8, "Nine Changes"). The problems posed by water for an invasion army are discussed in several of the chapters of the *Six Secret Teachings*, such as "Certain Escape" and "Planning for the Army."

13. Sun Pin states: "Neither the army nor any formation should attack to the front right. Establish your perimeter to the right; do not establish your perimeter to the left" ("Treasures of Terrain").

14. Sun-tzu states: "Where the entrance is constricted, the return is circuitous, and with a small number they can strike our masses, it is 'encircled terrain.'" Separately, he also notes: "If you have strongholds behind you and constrictions before you, it is 'encircled terrain.'" As for the appropriate tactics: "On encircled terrain I obstruct any openings," and "On encircled terrain use strategy" (chapter 11, "Nine Terrains"). And "make strategic plans for encircled terrain" (chapter 8, "Nine Changes"; the chapter entitled "Urgent Battles" in the *Six Secret Teachings* addresses a similar situation).

15. Manipulating the cookfires—which would of course be readily observable to an enemy even at a distance—was a common ruse effectively employed by Sun Pin and others.

16. This situation resembles one discussed by the T'ai Kung in "Certain Escape" in the *Six Secret Teachings*.

17. All measures commonly found in the military writings designed to convince the soldiers that there is no hope, that death is the only way.

18. Most of the military writings advocated using mountain heights and constricted valleys to put the enemy into difficulty. For example, see "Crow and Cloud Formation in the Mountains," "Divided Valleys," and the "Few and the Many" in the *Six Secret Teachings*, and "Responding to Change" in the *Wu-tzu*.

19. Sun-tzu said: "If you besiege an army you must leave an outlet" (chapter 7, "Military Combat").

20. As discussed in translation notes 123, 131, and 132, the recovered bamboo slips contain a section entitled "Four Changes" that is thought by some scholars to be Sun-tzu's own elucidation of the initial paragraph of chapter 8, "Nine Changes." While the first few sentences are identical with the last five in the traditional Sun-tzu text, in our opinion the expansion that follows is commentary rather than original text that inadvertently dropped out. Whether it stems from

Sun-tzu's hand or a later member of his school remains a matter of dispute; however, the style and tone seem closer to Sun Pin's *Military Methods*, the *Wu-tzu*, or even the *Six Secret Teachings*, and the passages therefore probably postdate the extant text of the *Art of War*. Accordingly we have consigned them to a supplementary section rather than integrating them into the main translation.

The title has been appended by the compilers of the bamboo-strip redaction, any original one having been inscribed on a now-missing strip. The text has appeared and been discussed in a number of articles, including "Lin-i Yin-ch'üehshan Han-mu ch'u-t'u *Sun-tzu ping-fa* ts'an-chien shih-wen," *WW* 1974: 12, pp. 11–12.

21. "Orders" (*ling*) as distinguished from "commands" or "edicts" (*ming*), the later appearing in the extant Sun-tzu.

22. "Implemented" as distinguished from "accepted" in the extant *Art of War*.

23. "Estimate" in the sense of carefully calculate, as in the first chapter, "Initial Estimations."

24. Reading "rear" in parallel with the sentences that follow, on the assumption that the army would continue to press forward. However, the clause may also be translated: "If we gain it we will not be able to defend it later."

25. Valleys with strong streams could pose problems of passage and fording, as well as flooding. (For example, see "Planning for the Army" in the *Six Secret Teachings*.). However, an area with inadequate water supplies would quickly put the men and horses in difficulty.

26. The translation follows Sun Hsing-yen, *Sun-tzu shih-chia-chu* (Shih-chieh shu-chü, Taipei, 1984), p. 7. The first question-and-reply sequence is found in *chüan* 152, the second set in *chüan* 159 of the *T'ung tien*.

27. Nurturing arrogance in an enemy so inclined was another fundamental principle of the ancient military strategists. For example, in "Initial Estimations" Sun-tzu states: "If they are angry, perturb them; be deferential to foster their arrogance."

28. About mountains Sun-tzu said: "To cross mountains follow the valleys, search out tenable ground, and occupy the heights. If the enemy holds the heights, do not climb up to engage them in battle" (chapter 9, "Maneuvering the Army").

29. The name inscribed on the first strip is "Wu Inquires"; however, as it is the king of Wu who is specified in the first sentence, we have translated the title as the "King of Wu's Questions." The translation follows the text reproduced in Wu Shup'ing, "Ts'ung Lin-i Han-mu chu-chien *Wu-wen* k'an Sun Wu te Fa-chia ssu-hsiang," *WW* 1975: 4, pp. 6–13.

30. Rather than "generals" the term normally expected would be "ministers," for the six great ministerial families were contending for power. However, as Wu Shu-p'ing points out (ibid, p. 6) in the Spring and Autumn period the great officials also served as the chief military commanders, assuming the ruler did not personally lead the troops. Thus the king's question refers to them as military leaders engaged in a violent struggle for power.

31. The "great families" were essentially clan groups rather than self-contained nuclear families.

32. Understanding "*wan*" as referring to the length of the side of the field rather than a unit of area, as Wu Shu-p'ing suggests (ibid, p. 7). Consequently, the

second character should also refer to a measurement of length ("breadth") rather than the area of an acre ("the 160-pace-acre"), even though Wu does not concur and the term usually designates acreage. However, the sentence is problematic, and despite the various contortions expended upon it, there is a basic inconsistency if the first term refers to a measurement of length and the second to a pace-acre. One possible—if far-fetched—resolution would be to understand both of them as simply defining two sizes of pace-acre, with the smaller perhaps being assigned to couples, the larger to those with dependents. Robin D. S. Yates, who notes the passage suggests that land reforms similar to those attributed to Lord Shang in the mid-fourth century were already occurring considerably earlier, thus understands *mou* in its traditional usage. (See "New Light on Ancient Chinese Military Texts," pp. 217–18.) Chan Li-po thinks the width of the field should be understood as two paces, with the acre then being 160 square paces ("Lüeh-t'an Lin-i Han-mu chu-chien *Sun-tzu ping-fa, WW* 1974: 12, p. 14).

33. Supplying the missing character "administration" from the parallel sentence below.

34. Supplementing the first part of the paragraph from the parallel passages above and below. The numbers clearly fall in sequence, giving 90 and 180.

35. While the tax on produce was remitted, there were obviously other exactions, including a military tax and required military and labor services to be rendered. (For a discussion, see Wu Shu-p'ing, "Ts'ung Lin-i Han-mu chu-chien *Wu-wen* k'an Sun Wu te Fa-chia ssu-hsiang," *WW* 1975: 4, p. 10.)

Selected Bibliography[*]

* Readers with expertise in Chinese and Japanese may also wish to consult the classified bibliograpy appended to our translation of *The Seven Military Classics of Ancient China*.

Abbreviations Used in the Bibliography

AA	*Acta Asiatica*
AM	*Asia Major*
BIHP	*Bulletin of the Institute of History and Philology*
BMFEA	*Bulletin of the Museum of Far Eastern Antiquities*
BSOAS	*Bulletin of the School of Oriental and African Studies*
CC	*Chinese Culture*
EC	*Early China*
GSR	*Grammata Serica Recensa (Bernhard Karlgrean, BMFEA 29 [1957])*
HJAS	*Harvard Journal of Asiatic Studies*
JAOS	*Journal of the American Oriental Society*
JAS	*Journal of Asian Studies*
JCP	*Journal of Chinese Philosophy*
JNCBRAS	*Journal of the North Central Branch, Royal Asiatic Society*
JRAS	*Journal of the Royal Asiatic Society*
KK	*K'ao-ku hsüeh-pao*
MS	*Monumenta Serica*
PEW	*Philosophy East and West*
TP	*T'oung Pao*
WW	*Wen-wu*

Because full bibliographic information for all works cited in the introductions and annotations is provided in the footnotes, only selected items from among them—together with additional, essential books and articles—are included herein. For the convenience of readers interested in pursuing focal topics, the entries are divided into several categories. With the great proliferation of academic books and articles in both Asia and the West, works of a tangential nature and a myriad of others that provide general contextual material cannot be included. Unfortunately, for every item listed several more are necessarily excluded, even though the bibliography must therefore be slightly less comprehensive. Preference has been given to items that are reasonably available to interested readers and to Chinese scholarship on fundamental historical issues.

Basic Texts

武經七書:

王雲五主編, 宋刊本武經七書, 商務印書館, 台北, 3 vol., 1971 (1935).

[宋刊武經七書], 中國兵書集成, 解放軍出版社, 遼沈書社, 北京, vol. 1, 2, 1987.

嚴一萍選輯, 百部叢書集成 (宋本子部), 藝文印書館, 台北, 1965.

武經七書直解 (劉寅):

景印明本武經七書直解, 史地敎育出版社, 台北, 2 vol., 1972.

武經七書直解, 中國兵書集成, 解放軍出版社, 遼沈書社, 北京, vol. 10, 11, 1990.

General Historical Works, Important Translations, and Specialized Monographs on the Period of the Seven Military Classics

Ames, Roger T., *The Art of Rulership*, University of Hawaii Press, Honolulu, 1983.

Baker, Hugh D. R., *Chinese Family and Kinship*, Columbia University Press, New York, 1979.

Balazs, Etienne, *Chinese Civilization and Bureaucracy*, Yale University Press, New Haven, 1964.

Beasley, W. G., and E. G. Pulleyblank, eds., *Historians of China and Japan*, Oxford University Press, London, 1961.

Bielenstein, Hans, *The Bureaucracy of Han Times*, Cambridge University Press, Cambridge, 1980.

———, *The Restoration of the Han Dynasty*, Elanders Boktryckeri Aktiebolag, Goteborg, 1953.

Bishop, John L., ed., *Studies in Governmental Institutions in Chinese History,* Harvard University Press, Cambridge, Mass., 1968.

Bodde, Derk, *China's First Unifier: A Study of the Ch'in Dynasty as Seen in the Life of Li Ssu,* Hong Kong University Press, Hong Kong, 1967 (1938).

———, *Essays on Chinese Civilization,* (Charles Le Blanc and Dorothy Borei, eds.), Princeton University Press, Princeton, 1981.

Chang, K. C., *Art, Myth, and Ritual: The Path to Political Authority in Ancient China,* Harvard University Press, Cambridge, Mass., 1983.

———, ed., *Studies of Shang Archaeology,* Yale University Press, New Haven, 1986.

Chang, Kwang-chih, ed., *Food in Chinese Culture,* Yale University Press, New Haven, 1977.

———, *Shang Civilization,* Yale University Press, New Haven, 1980.

———, *The Archaeology of Ancient China,* Yale University Press, New Haven, 1977 (3d ed).

Cheng Te'k'un, *Archaeology in China,* 3 vols.: *Chou China,* 1963; *Prehistoric China,* 1966; *Shang China,* 1960. W. Heffer & Sons, Cambridge.

———, *New Light on Prehistoric China,* W. Heffer & Sons, Cambridge, 1966.

———, *Studies in Chinese Archaeology,* Chinese University Press, 1982.

Ch'ü T'ung-tsu, *Han Social Structure,* University of Washington Press, Seattle, 1967.

———, *Law and Society in Traditional China,* Mouton and Company, The Hague, 1961; rev. ed., 1965.

Cotterall, Arthur, *The First Emperor of China,* Penguin, London, 1981.

Creel, Herrlee G., *The Origins of Statecraft in China:* vol. 1, *The Western Chou Empire,* University of Chicago Press, Chicago, 1970.

———, *Shen Pu-hai: A Chinese Political Philosopher of the Fourth Century* B.C., University of Chicago Press, Chicago, 1974.

Crump, J.I., Jr., *Chan-kuo Ts'e,* Oxford University Press, Oxford, 1970.

Dawson, Raymond, ed., *The Legacy of China,* Oxford University Press, Oxford, 1964.

de Crespigny, Rafe, *Official Titles of the Former Han Dynasty,* Australian National University Press, Canberra, 1967.

Dubs, Homer H., *The History of the Former Han Dynasty,* 3 vols., Waverly Press, Baltimore, 1938–55.

Duyvendak, J.J.L., *The Book of Lord Shang,* Arthur Probsthain, London, 1928.

Eberhard, Wolfram, *Conquerors and Rulers: Social Forces in Medieval China,* E. J. Brill, Leiden, 1970.

Fairbank, John K., ed., *Chinese Thought and Institutions,* University of Chicago Press, Chicago, 1957.

———, ed., *The Chinese World Order: Traditional China's Foreign Relations,* Harvard University Press, Cambridge, Mass., 1968.

Falkenhausen, Lothar Von, *Shang Civilization, Early China,* supplement 1, Berkeley, 1986.

Feng Han-yi, *The Chinese Kinship System,* Harvard University Press, Cambridge, Mass., 1967 (reprint of 1948 edition; originally published in *HJAS* 2 [1937]: 141–275).

Fong, Wen, ed., *The Great Bronze Age of China: An Exhibition from the People's Republic of China*, Knopf, New York, 1980.

Fung Yu-lan, *A History of Chinese Philosophy*, translated by Derk Bodde, 2 vols., Princeton University Press, Princeton, 1952 (1931) and 1953 (1934).

Gardner, Charles S., *Chinese Traditional Historiography*, Harvard University Press, Cambridge, Mass., 1938.

Graham, A. C., *Later Mohist Logic, Ethics, and Science*, Chinese University Press, Hong Kong, 1978.

Grousset, René, *The Empire of the Steppes: A History of Central Asia*, translated by Naomi Walford, Rutgers University Press, New Brunswick, N.J., 1970 (1939).

Herrmann, Albert, *An Historical Atlas of China*, edited by Norton Ginsburg, Aldine Publishing Co., Chicago, 1935; rev. ed., 1966.

Ho, Ping-ti, *The Cradle of the East*, Chinese University Press, Hong Kong, 1975.

Hook, Brian, ed., *The Cambridge Encyclopedia of China*, Cambridge University Press, Cambridge, 1982.

Hsu, Cho-yun, *Ancient China in Transition: An Analysis of Social Mobility*, Stanford University Press, Stanford, 1965.

———, *Han Agriculture*, University of Washington Press, Seattle, 1980.

Hsu, Cho-yun, and Katheryn M. Linduff, *Western Chou Civilization*, Yale University Press, New Haven, 1988.

Hsü Shihlien, *The Political Philosophy of Confucianism*, Curzon Press, London, 1932.

Hucker, Charles O., *A Dictionary of Official Titles in Imperial China*, Stanford University Press, Stanford, 1985.

Hulsewe, A.F.P., *Remnants of Han Law*, vol. 1, E. J. Brill, Leiden, 1955.

Jagchid, Sechin, and Van Jay Symons, *Peace, War, and Trade Along the Great Wall: Nomadic-Chinese Interaction Through Two Millennia*, Indiana University Press, Bloomington, 1989.

Kao, George, *The Translation of Things Past*, Chinese University of Hong Kong, Hong Kong, 1982.

Keightley, David N., *Sources of Shang History: The Oracle-bone Inscriptions of Bronze Age China*, University of California Press, Berkeley, 1978.

———, ed., *The Origins of Chinese Civilization*, University of California Press, Berkeley, 1983.

Lattimore, Owen, *Inner Asian Frontiers of China*, Beacon Press, Boston, 1960 (1940).

Lau, D. C., *The Analects*, Penguin Books, London, 1979.

———, *Mencius*, 2 vols., Chinese University Press, Hong Kong, 1984.

———, *Tao Te Ching*, Chinese University Press, Hong Kong, 1982.

Le Blanc, Charles, *Huai Nan Tzu*, Hong Kong University Press, Hong Kong, 1985.

Legg, Stuart, *The Barbarians of Asia*, Dorset Press, New York, 1990 (1970).

Leslie, Donald D., Colin Mackerras, and Gungwu Wang, *Essays on the Sources for Chinese History*, Australian National University Press, Canberra, 1973.

Li Chi, *Anyang*, University of Washington Press, Seattle, 1977.

———, *The Beginnings of Chinese Civilization*, University of Washington Press, Seattle, 1968 (1957).

Li Guohao, Zhang Mengwen, and Cao Tianqin, eds., *Explorations in the History of Science and Technology in China,* Shanghai Chinese Classics Publishing House, Shanghai, 1982.

Li Xueqin, *Eastern Zhou and Qin Civilizations,* translated by K. C. Chang, Yale University Press, New Haven, 1985.

Liao, W. K., *The Complete Works of Han Fei-tzu,* 2 vols., Arthur Probsthain, London, 1959.

Liu, James, *The Chinese Knight-errant,* University of Chicago Press, Chicago, 1967.

Lowe, Michael, *Crisis and Conflict in Han China,* George Allen and Unwin, London, 1974.

———, *Records of Han Administration,* 2 vols., Cambridge University Press, Cambridge, 1967.

Nakayama, Shigeru, and Nathan Sivin, eds., *Chinese Science: Explorations of an Ancient Tradition,* MIT Press, Cambridge, Mass., 1973.

Needham, Joseph, *Clerks and Craftsmen in China and the West,* Cambridge University Press, Cambridge, 1970.

———, *The Development of Iron and Steel Technology in China,* Newcomers Society, London, 1958.

———, *The Grand Titration,* George Allen and Unwin, London, 1969.

———, et al., *Science and Civilisation in China,* Cambridge University Press, Cambridge, 1962 (fourteen physical volumes to date, including vol. 5, part 7: *Military Technology).*

Nivison, David S. and Arthur F. Wright, eds., *Confucianism in Action,* Stanford University Press, Stanford, 1959.

Pirazzoli-t'Serstevens, Michéle, *The Han Dynasty,* translated by Janet Seligman, Rizzoli International Publications, New York, 1982.

Pye, Lucian W., *Asian Power and Politics: The Cultural Dimensions of Authority,* Harvard University Press, Cambridge, Mass., 1985.

Reischauer, Edwin O., *Ennin's Travels in T'ang China,* Ronald Press, New York, 1955.

Reischauer, Edwin O., and John K. Fairbank, *East Asia: The Great Tradition,* vol. 1, Houghton Mifflin Co., Boston, 1958.

Rickett, W. Allyn, *Guanzi,* vol. 1, Princeton University Press, Princeton, 1985.

Roy, David T., and Tsien Tsuen-hsuin, eds., *Ancient China: Studies in Early Civilization,* Chinese University Press, Hong Kong, 1978.

Sailey, Jay, *The Master Who Embraces Simplicity,* Chinese Materials Center, San Francisco, 1978.

Schram, Stuart R., ed., *Foundations and Limits of State Power in China,* Chinese University Press, Hong Kong, 1987.

———, ed., *The Scope of State Power in China,* Chinese University Press, Hong Kong, 1985.

Science Press, *Atlas of Primitive Man in China,* Science Press, Peking, 1980.

Swann, Nancy Lee, *Food and Money in Ancient China,* Princeton University Press, Princeton, 1950.

Tregear, T.R., *A Geography of China,* Aldine, Chicago, 1965.

Tsien Tsuen-hsuin, *Written on Bamboo and Silk: The Beginnings of Chinese Books and Inscriptions,* University of Chicago Press, Chicago, 1962.

Tung Tso-pin, *Chronological Tables of Chinese History,* Hong Kong University Press, Hong Kong, 1960.

Twitchett, Denis, and John K. Fairbank, eds., *The Cambridge History of China,* Cambridge University Press, London. vol. 1: *The Ch'in and Han Empires,* 221 B.C.–A.D. 220, 1986; vol. 3, part 1: *Sui and T'ang China, 589–906,* 1979.

Waley, Arthur, *The Analects of Confucius,* George Allen and Unwin, London, 1938.

——, *The Way and Its Power,* Grove Press, New York, 1958.

Wang Gungwu, *The Structure of Power in North China During the Five Dynasties,* Stanford University Press, Stanford, 1967 (1963).

Wang Zhongshu, *Han Civilization,* translated by K. C. Chang, Yale University Press, New Haven, 1982.

Watson, Burton, *Basic Writings of Mo Tzu, Hsün Tzu, and Han Fei Tzu,* Columbia University Press, New York, 1967.

——, *The Complete Works of Chuang-tzu,* Columbia University Press, New York, 1968.

——, *Courtier and Commoner in Ancient China,* Columbia University Press, New York, 1974.

——, *Early Chinese Literature,* Columbia University Press, New York, 1962.

——, *Records of the Grand Historian of China,* 2 vols., Columbia University Press, New York, 1961.

——, *Ssu-ma Ch'ien: Grand Historian of China,* Columbia University Press, New York, 1958.

——, *The Tso chuan,* Columbia University Press, New York, 1989.

Wheatley, Paul, *The Pivot of the Four Quarters,* Edinburgh University Press, Edinburgh, 1971.

Wing-tsit, Chan, *The Way of Lao-tzu,* Bobbs-Merrill, New York, 1963.

Wright, Arthur F., ed., *The Confucian Persuasion,* Stanford University Press, Stanford, 1960.

Wright, Arthur F., *The Sui Dynasty,* Alfred A. Knopf, New York, 1978.

Wright, Arthur F., and Denis Twitchett, eds., *Perspectives of the T'ang,* Yale University Press, New Haven, 1973.

Yang Lien-sheng, *Excursions in Sinology,* Harvard University Press, Cambridge, Mass., 1969.

——, *Studies in Chinese Institutional History,* Harvard University Press, Cambridge, Mass., 1969.

Yü Ying-shih, *Trade and Expansion in Han China: A Study in the Structure of Sinobarbarian Economic Relations,* University of California Press, Berkeley, 1967.

Western-Language Articles
on Ancient and Medieval History

Articles of particular relevance, excluding those found in collected
works listed under books or those that pertain generally
to intellectual or scientific history

Allan, Sarah, "Drought, Human Sacrifice and the Mandate of Heaven in a Lost Text from the *Shang Shu*," *BSOAS* 47 (1984): 523–39.

An Zhimin, "The Neolithic Archaeology of China: A Brief Survey of the Last Thirty Years," Translated by K. C. Chang, *EC* 5 (1979–80): 35–45.

Barnard, Noel, "Chou China: A Review of the Third Volume of Cheng Te'k'un's *Archaeology in China*," *MS* 24 (1965): 307–459.

———, "Chou Hung-hsiang, *Shang-Yin ti-wang pen-chi*" (review of), *MS* 19 (1960): 486–515.

———, "A Preliminary Study of the Ch'u Silk Manuscript," *MS* 17 (1958): 1–11.

Blakely, Barry, "In Search of Danyang I: Historical Geography and Archaeological Sites," *EC* 13 (1988): 116–52.

Broman, Sven, "Studies on the Chou Li," *BMFEA* 33 (1961): 1–88.

Bunker, Emma C., "The Steppe Connection," *EC* 9–10 (1983–85): 70–76.

Chang Ch'i-yün, "The Period of the Ch'un-ch'iu: A General Survey," *CC* 27, no. 2 (1986): 1–29.

Chen Ch'i-yün, "Han Dynasty China: Economy, Society, and State Power," *TP* (1984): 127–48.

Cheng Chung-ying, "Legalism Versus Confucianism: A Philosophical Appraisal," *JCP* 8 (1981): 271–302.

Cheng Te-k'ung, "The Origin and Development of Shang Culture," *AM* NS 6, no. 1 (1957); 80–98.

Cheung, Frederick Hok-Ming, "Conquerors and Consolidators in Anglo-Norman England and T'ang China: A Comparative Study," *Asian Culture* 13, no. 1 (1985): 63–85.

Chou Fa-kao, "Chronology of the Western Chou Dynasty," *Hsiang-kang Chung-wen Ta-hsüeh Chung-kuo Wen-hua Yen-chiu-so hsüeh-pao* 4, no. 1 (1971): 173–205.

Chun, Allen J., "Conceptions of Kinship and Kingship in Classical Chou China," *TP* 76 (1990): 16–48.

Cikoski, John S., "Toward Canons of Philological Method for Analyzing Classical Chinese Texts," *EC* 3 (1977): 18–30.

De Crespigny, Rafe, "Politics and Philosophy Under the Government of Emperor Huan 159–168," *TP* 66, nos. 1–3 (1980): 41–83.

Egan, Ronald C., "Narratives in *Tso Chuan*," *HJAS* 37, no. 2 (1977): 323–52.

Fields, Lanny B., "The Legalists and the Fall of Ch'in: Humanism and Tyranny," *Journal of Asian History* 17 (1983): 1–39.

Fu Pei-jung, "On Religious Ideas of the Pre-Chou China," *CC* 26, no. 3 (September 1985): 23–39.

Graham, A. C., "A Neglected Pre-Han Philosophical Text: *Ho-Kuan-Tzu*," *BSOAS* 52, no. 3 (1989): 497–532.

Haloun, Gustav, "Legalist Fragments," *AM* 2, no. 1 (1951–52): 85–120.

Harper, Donald, and Jeffrey Riegel, "Mawangdui Tomb Three: Documents" (Abstract), *EC* 2 (1976): 68–72.

Henricks, Robert G., "Examining the Ma-wang-tui Silk Texts of the Lao-tzu," *TP* 65, no. 4–5 (1979): 166–99.

———, "On the Chapter Divisions in the *Lao-tzu*," *BSOAS*, 45, no. 3 (1982): 501–24.

———, "The Philosophy of *Lao-tzu* Based on the Ma-wang-tui Texts: Some Preliminary Observations," *SSCR* Bulletin 9 (Fall 1981): 59–78.

Henry, Eric, "The Motif of Recognition in Early China," *HJAS* 47, no. 1 (1987): 5–30.

Hsü Cho-yün, "Some Working Notes on the Western Chou Government," *BIHP* 36 (1966): 513–24.

Hu Pingsheng, "Some Notes on the Organization of the Han Dynasty Bamboo 'Annals' Found at Fuyang," *EC* 14 (1989): 1–24.

Huber, Louisa G., "The Bo Capital and Questions Concerning Xia and Early Shang," *EC* 13 (1988): 46–77.

———, "A Commentary on the Recent Finds of Neolithic Painted Pottery from Ta-ti-wan, Kansu," *EC* 9–10 (1983–85): 1–19.

Hulsewe, A.F.P., "The Ch'in Documents Discovered in Hupei in 1975," *TP* 64, nos. 4–5 (1978): 175–217.

———, "Watching the Vapours: An Ancient Chinese Technique of Prognostication," *Nachrichten* 125 (1979): 40–49.

———, "The Wide Scope of Tao, 'Theft,' in Ch'in-Han Law," *EC* 13 (1988): 166–200.

Jacobson, Esther, "Beyond the Frontier: A Reconsideration of Cultural Interchange Between China and the Early Nomads," *EC* 13 (1988): 201–40.

Jan Yün-hua, "Tao, Principle, and Law: The Three Key Concepts in the Yellow Emperor Taoism," *JCP* 7 (1980): 205–28.

———, "*Tao Yüan* or *Tao: The Origin*," *JCP* 7 (1980): 195–204.

Kamiya Masakazu, "The Staffing Structure of Commandery Offices and County Offices and the Relationship Between Commanderies and Counties in the Han Dynasty," *AA* 58 (1990): 59–88.

Karlgren, Bernhard, "The Book of Documents," *BMFEA* 22 (1950): 1–81.

———, "The Early History of the Chou Li and Tso Chuan Texts," *BMFEA* 3 (1931): 1–59.

———, "Glosses on the Book of Documents, I," *BMFEA* 20 (1948): 39–315.

———, "Glosses on the Book of Documents, II," *BMFEA* 21 (1949): 63–206.

———, "Legends and Cults in Ancient China," *BMFEA* 18 (1946): 199–356.

———, "Some Sacrifices in Chou China," *BMFEA* 40 (1968): 1–31.

Keightley, David N., "The *Bamboo Annals* and the Shang-Chou Chronology," *HJAS* 38, no. 2 (1978): 423–38.

———, "Reports from the Shang: A Corroboration and Some Speculation," *EC* 9–10 (1983–84); 20–54.

———, "The Shang State as Seen in the Oracle-bone Inscriptions," *EC* 5 (1979–80): 25–34.

Lau, D. C., "The Treatment of Opposites in *Lao Tzu*," *BSOAS* 21 (1958): 344–60.

Li Zehou, "Confucian Cosmology in the Han Dynasty," *Social Sciences in China* 7 (1986): 81–116.

Loewe, Michael, "Han Administrative Documents: Recent Finds from the Northwest," *TP* 72 (1986): 291–314.

———, "The Han View of Comets," *BMFEA* 52 (1980): 2–31.

MacCormack, Geoffrey, "The *Lü Hsing*: Problems of Legal Interpretation," *MS* 37 (1986 87). 35–47.

McLeod, Katrina C.D., and Robin D.S. Yates, "Forms of Ch'in Law: An Annotated Translation of the *Fen-chen shih*," *HJAS* 41, no. 1 (1981): 111–63.

Negata Hidemasa, "A Diplomatic Study of the Chü-yen Han Wooden Strips," *AA* 58 (1990): 38–57.

Nivison, David S., "1040 as the Date of the Chou Conquest," *EC* 8 (1982–83): 76–78.

Pang Pu, "Origins of the Yin-Yang and Five Elements Concepts," *Social Sciences in China* 6, no. 1 (1985): 91–131.

Pankenier, David W., "Astronomical Dates in Shang and Western Zhou," *EC* 7 (1981–82): 2–37.

———, "*Mozi* and the Dates of Xia, Shang, and Zhou: A Research Note," *EC* 9–10 (1983–85): 175–83.

Rawson, Jessica, "Late Western Zhou: A Break in the Shang Bronze Tradition," *EC* 11–12 (1985–87): 285–95.

Riegel, Jeffrey, "A Summary of Some Recent *Wenwu* and *Kaogu* Articles on Mawangdui Tombs Two and Three," *EC* 1 (1975): 10–14.

Rosement, Henry, Jr., "State and Society in the *Hsün Tzu*: A Philosophical Commentary," *MS* 29 (1970–71): 38–78.

Rubin, V. A., "Tzu-Ch'an and the City-state of Ancient China," *TP* 52 (1965): 8–34.

Shaughnessy, Edward L., "The 'Current' *Bamboo Annals* and the "Date of the Zhou Conquest of Shang," *EC* 11–12 (1985–87): 33–60.

———, "The Date of the 'Duo You *Ding* and Its Significance," *EC* 9–10 (1983–85): 55–69.

———, "Historical Geography and the Extent of the Earliest Chinese Kingdoms," *AM* Third Series 2, no. 2 (1989): 1–22.

———, "'New' Evidence on the Zhou Conquest," *EC* 6 (1980–81): 57–79.

———, "On the Authenticity of the *Bamboo Annals*," *HJAS* 46:1 (June 1986), pp. 149–180.

———, "Recent Approaches to Oracle-Bone Periodization: A Review," *EC* 8 (1982–83): 1–13.

Silbergeld, Jerome, "Mawangdui, Excavated Materials, and Transmitted Texts: A Cautionary Note," *EC* 8 (1982–83): 79–92.

Thorp, Robert L., "The Growth of Early Shang Civilization," *HJAS* 45 (1985): 5–75.

Turner, Karen, "The Theory of Law in the *Ching-fa*," *EC* 14 (1989): 55–76.

Wallacker, Benjamin E., "Chang Fei's Preface to the Chin Code of Law," *TP* 72 (1986): 229–68.

Wang Gung-wu, "The Chiu Wu-tai shih and History-writing During the Five Dynasties," *AM* NS 6, no. 1 (1957): 1–22.

Wang Ningsheng, "Yangshao Burial Customs and Social Organization: A Comment on the Theory of Yangshao Matrilineal Society and Its Methodology," translation by David N. Keightley, *EC* 11–12 (1985–87): 6–32.

Watson, Walter, "Principles for Dealing with Disorder," *JCP* 8 (1981): 349–70.

Wu Hung, "From Temple to Tomb: Ancient Chinese Art and Religion in Transition," *EC* 13 (1988): 78–115.

Yamada Katsuyoshi, "Offices and Officials of Works, Markets and Lands in the Ch'in Dynasty," *AA* 58 (1990): 1–23.

Yates, Robin D. S., "Social Status in the Ch'in: Evidence from the Yün-meng Legal Documents. Part One: Commoners," *HJAS* 47,no. 1 (1987): 197–237.

Yu Weichao, "The Origins of the Cultures of the Eastern Zhou," translated by Terry Kleeman, *EC* 9–19 (183–85): 307–14.

Zhang Jinfan, "Administration and Administrative Law in Ancient China," *Social Sciences in China 7, no.* 3 (1986): 169–96.

Western-Language Articles on Weapons, Technology, and the Evolution of Mobility

Chariots and Horses

Bishop, C. W., "The Horses of T'ang T'ai-Tsung: Of the Antecedents of the Chinese Horse," *Museum Journal* (University of Pennsylvania) 9 (1911): 244–73.

Ferguson, John C., "The Six Horses of T'ang T'ai-Tsung," *JNCBRAS*, 67 (1936): 1–6.

Fernald, Helen E., "The Horses of T'ang T'ai-Tsung and the Steele of Yu," *American Oriental Society Journal* 55 (1935): 420–28.

Goodrich, Chauncey S., "Riding Astride and the Saddle in Ancient China," *HJAS* 44, no. 2 (1984), pp. 279–306.

Piggott, Stuart, "Chariots in the Caucasus and in China," *Antiquity* 48 (1974): 16–24.

Shaughnessy, Edward L., "Historical Perspectives on the Introduction of the Chariot into China," *HJAS* 48, no. 1 (1988): 189–237.

Yetts, W. Perceval, "The Horse: A Factor in Early Chinese History," *Eurasia Septentionalis Antiqua* 9 (1934): 231–55.

Weapons, Armor, and Related Technology

An Zhimin, "Some Problems Concerning China's Early Copper and Bronze Artifacts," translated by Julia K. Murray, *EC* 8 (1982–83): 53–75.

Barnard, Noel, "Did the Swords Exist" (Rejoinder), *EC* 4 (1978–79): 60–65.

Beveridge, H., "Oriental Crossbows," *Asian Review* Series 3, *The Imperial and Asiatic Quarterly Review* 32 (1911): 344–48.

Dien, Albert E., "A Study of Early Chinese Armor," *Artibus Asiae* 43 (1981–82): 5–66.

———, "Warring States Armor and Pit Three at Qin Shihuangdi's Tomb" (Research Note), *EC* 5 (1979–80): 46–47.

Gardner, Charles W., "Weapon of Power," *Military History* 12 (1989): 16–74.
Gordon, D. H., "Swords, Rapiers, and Horse-riders," *Antiquity* 27 (1953): 67–78.
Huslewe, A.F.P., "Again the Crossbow Trigger Mechanism," *TP* 64, no. 4–5 (1978): 254.
Karlgren, Bernhard, "Some Weapons and Tools of the Yin Dynasty," *BMFEA* 17 (1945): 101–44.
Keightley, David N., "Where Have All the Swords Gone? Reflections on the Unification of China," *EC* 2 (1976): 31–34.
LaPlante, John D., "Ancient Chinese Ritual Vessels: Some Observations on Technology and Style," *EC* 13 (1988): 247–73.
Loehr, Max, "The Earliest Chinese Swords and the Akinakes," *Oriental Art* 1 (1948): 132–42.
McEwen, E., R. Miller, and C. Bergman, "Early Bow Design and Construction," *Scientific American* 1991: 6 76–82.
Rogers, Spencer L., "The Aboriginal Bow and Arrow of North America and Eastern Asia," *American Anthropologist* NS 42 (1940): 255–69.
Sun Shuyun and Han Rubin, "A Preliminary Study of Early Chinese Copper and Bronze Artifacts," translated by Julia K. Murray, *EC* 9–10 (1983–85): 261–89.
Trousdale, William, "Where All the Swords Have Gone," *EC* 3 (1977): 65–66.
Wilbur, C. Martin, "The History of the Crossbow, Illustrated from Specimens in the United States National Museum," *Smithsonian Institution Annual Report* (1936): 427–38.

Western-Language Monographs and Articles
on Chinese Military History, Texts, and Topics

Allan, Sarah, "The Identities of Taigong Wang in Zhou and Han Literature," *MS* 30 (1972–73): 57–99.
Balmforth, Edmund E., "A Chinese Military Strategist of the Warring States: Sun Pin," Ph.D.diss. Department of History, Rutgers University, 1979.
Chang Ch'un-shu, "Military Aspects of Han Wu-ti's Northern and Northwestern Campaigns," *HJAS* 26 (1966): 148–73.
Duyvendak, J.J.L., "An Illustrated Battle-account in the *History of the Former Han Dynasty*, *TP* 34 (1939): 244–64.
Fan Yuzhou, "Military Campaign Inscriptions from YH 127," *BSOAS* 52, no. 3 (1989): 533–48.
Goodrich, Chauncey S., "Ssu-ma Ch'ien's Biography of Wu Ch'i," *MS* 35 (1981–83): 197–233.
Johnson, David, "The Wu Tzu-hsü *Pien-wen* and Its Sources," part I, *HJAS* 40, no. 1 (June 1980): 93–156; part II, *HJAS* 40, no. 2 (December 1980): 465–505.
Kierman, Frank A., Jr., and John K. Fairbank, eds., *Chinese Ways in Warfare*, Harvard University Press, Cambridge, Mass., 1974.
Lau, D. C., "Some Notes on the *Sun-tzu*," *BSOAS* 28 (1965): 317–35.
Marsh, Susan H., "Frank A. Kierman, Jr., and John K. Fairbank (eds.), *Chinese Ways in Warfare*" (review of), *JCP* 3 (1975), pp. 97–104.

Rand, Christopher C., "Chinese Military Thought and Philosophical Taoism," *MS* 34 (1979–80): 171–218.

———, "Li Ch'üan and Chinese Military Thought," *HJAS* 39, no. 1 (June 1979): 107–37.

———, "The Role of Military Thought in Early Chinese Intellectual History," Ph.D. diss., Department of History and East Asian Languages, Harvard University, 1977.

Vervoorn, Aat, "Taoism, Legalism, and the Quest for Order in Warring States China," *JCP* 8, no. 3 (September 1981): 303–24.

Wallacker, Benjamin E., "Two Concepts in Early Chinese Military Thought," *Language* 42, no. 2 (1966): 295–99.

Yates, Robin D. S., "The City Under Siege: Technology and Organization as Seen in the Reconstructed Text of the Military Chapters of Mo-tzu," Ph.D. diss., Harvard University, 1980.

———, "The Mohists on Warfare: Technology, Techniques, and Justification," *Journal of the American Academy of Religion* Thematic Studies Supplement 47, no. 3 (1980): 549–603.

———, "New Light on Ancient Chinese Military Texts: Notes on Their Nature and Evolution, and the Development of Military Specialization in Warring States China," *TP* 74 (1988): 211–48.

———, "Siege Engines and Late Zhou Military Technology," in *Explorations in the History of Science and Technology in China* (Li Guohao et al, eds.), Shanghai Chinese Classics Publishing House, Shanghai, 1982, pp. 409–51.

Glossary

A

action 動
administration 制, 治, 政
  civil 文制, 文治
  military 軍制, 軍政, 軍治
advance 進
advance force 前鋒
advantage 利
afraid 恐
agents (spies) 間
  double 反間
  expendable 死間
  internal 內間
  living 生間
  local 鄉間
All under Heaven 天下
alliances 交
altars (of state) (國) 社
ambush 伏
ancestral temple 廟
archers 弓者
armor 甲
army 軍, 師
  of the Center 中軍
  of the Left 左軍
  of the Right 右軍
  Six (Armies) 六師
  Three (Armies) 三軍
Army's Strategic Power 軍勢
artifice 譎
ascension and decline 盛衰, 興衰
assemble 合
  and divide 分合
attack 攻
  incendiary 火攻

orthodox 正攻
sudden 突攻, 襲
unorthodox 奇攻
augury 卜
auspicious 吉
authority (*ch'üan*) 權
awesomeness 威
ax
  fu 斧
  yüeh 鉞

B

balance of power and
  plans 權謀
bamboo slips 竹簡
barbarian 狄, 蠻, 番, 夷, 胡
  dress 胡服
barricade 塞
battalion 旅, 廣
battle 戰
battle array 戰陣, 陣
bells 鈴
beneficence 惠
benevolence 仁
besiege 圍
border 境, 垠
bows and arrows 弓矢
brigade 師
brigand 賊

C

calculate 算, 數
capture 擒
cavalry 騎, 騎兵

certitude 信
Chang Liang 張良
Chang-sun Wu-chi 長孫無忌
change 變
  and transformation 變化
Chao (state of) 趙
Chao Yeh 趙嘩
chaos 亂
character 性
  evaluating 知人, 考人
  flaws 隙, 過
chariot 車
  assault 衝車
  attack 攻車
  battle 戰車
  light 輕車
Ch'eng-p'u 城濮
Chi (clan) 姬
ch'i (pneuma, breath) 氣
Ch'i (state of) 齊
  Duke Huan of Ch'i 齊桓公
Ch'i Wei Wang 齊威王
Chi-fu 雞父
Chiang (clan) 姜
chieh (constraint, measure) 節
chien-tu 簡牘
Chin (state of) 晉
Chin Wen-kung 晉文公
Ch'in (state of) 秦
Ch'in Shih Huang-ti 秦始皇帝
Chou 周
  duke of 周公
  dynasty 周朝
  Eastern 東周
  Western 西周
Chou li (*Rites of Chou*) 周禮
Ch'u (state of) 楚
Chuan Chu 專諸

ch'üan 權
  authority 權
  tactical balance of power 權
Ch'un ch'iu 春秋
Chung Kuo (Central States) 中國
circuitous 迂
circular (formation) 圓 (陣)
city 城
civil 文
  and martial 文武
civil (cultural) offensive 文伐
civil virtue 文德
civilian affairs 文事
clamorous 譁
clarity (clearness) 明
clique 派, 朋
combat 戰
command 命, 號
commandant 尉
common people 平民, 老百姓
company 卒, 閭
compel others 致人
concentration of force 集力
configuration and designation 形名
configuration of power 勢
confront 當, 向
Confucius 孔子
confuse 惑
confusion 亂, 惑, 擾亂
conquer 勝, 克, 剋
constant 常
constraints 節
contrary virtue 逆德
counterattack 反攻, 逆擊
courage 勇
court 朝

crack troops 銳兵
credibility 信
criminal 罪者
crossbow 弩

D

danger 危
death 死
deceive 詭, 詐
decline 衰
defeat 敗
defense 守
defiles 阻
deflated in spirit 失氣
deploy 陣
deployment 陣
depths of Earth 九地之下
desert 逃
designation 名
desire 欲
destroy 破
dilatory 慢, 失時
disadvantage 害, 不利
disaster 災, 殃
discipline 兵制, 兵治
disharmony 不和
disordered 擾, 不治
dispirited 失氣, 挫氣, 傷氣
disposition and strategic
  power 形勢
disposition of force 形
disposition of power 勢
ditches 溝, 洫, 瀆
divine (divination) 卜筮
doubt 疑, 狐疑
drums 鼓

E

Earth 地
elite force 銳士
embankment 隄防
emotionally attached 親附
emotions 情
employing men 用人
employing the military 用兵
empty 空
encampment 營
encircle(d) 圍
enemy 敵
entice 利之, 動之以利, 誘
error 過, 失
estimate 計
estimation 計
evaluate 考, 策, 察, 測
  enemy 察敵情, 料敵
  men 考人, 察才
evil 凶, 惡
evil implement 凶器
excess (flaw) 過
execute 誅
exterior 表
external 外

F

failure 失, 敗
Fan K'uai 樊噲
Fan Li 范蠡
fatal 死
fathom (the enemy) 相, 測, 占
  (敵)
fear 畏
Fei Wu-chi 費無忌

feigned retreats 佯北
feudal lords 諸侯
few 少
fields 野, 田
fines 罰
fire 火
five 五
    affairs 五事
    colors 五色, 五彩
    flavors 五味
    grains 五穀
    notes 五音
    phases 五行
    weapons 五兵
flag 旗
flanks 偏, 旁
flee (run off) 走
flourish and decline 勝衰
foodstuffs 食
foot soldiers 步兵
force
    heavy 重兵
    light 輕兵
ford (rivers) 渡 (水), 濟 (水)
forest 林
formation 陣
    assault 衝陣
formless 無形
forms of etiquette (*li*) 禮
fortification 城, 壘, 保, 堡
foundation 本
four 四
    limbs 四肢
    quarters 四方
    Seasons 四季
Four Changes 四變
frightened 驚懼

front 前
frontal assault force 戰鋒隊
Fu-ch'ai 夫差
Fu-kai 夫概
full 實
funeral mounds 墳墓

G

gate 門
general 將帥
    commanding 主將
    enlightened 明將
    ignorant 闇將
    subordinate 副將, 裨將
ghost 鬼
glory 榮
gong 金
gorge 谿
grain 粟
granary 倉
guest 客

H

halberd 戈
Han (people) 漢
Han dynasty 漢朝
Han Fei-tzu 韓非子
Han-shih wai-chuan 韓詩外傳
handles of state 國柄
hard 剛
    and strong 強
harm 害
harmony 和
hasty 疾, 急

Heaven 天
Heaven's
  Fissure 天隙
  Furnace 天竈
  Huang 天潢
  Jail 天牢
  Net 天羅
  Pit 天陷
  Well 天井
heavy force 重兵
hegemon 霸
heights 高
heights of Heaven 九天之上
Heir Apparent 太子
helmet 盔, 胄
hero 雄, 傑
high official 大夫
hillock 丘
Ho-lü 闔廬
honor 貴
horse 馬
host 主
Hsia dynasty 夏朝
hsing (form) 形
Huai River 淮水
Huang Shih-kung 黃石公
human effort (affairs) 人事
human emotions 人情
hundred 百
  illnesses 百病
  surnames 百姓

I

I Yin 伊尹
implements 器

impositions 斂
incendiary attack 火攻
infantry 步兵, 徒
  heavy 重兵
  light 輕兵
insignia 表, 號, 符
instructions 教, 練
intelligence (military) 敵情
interior 裏
internal 內
invader 寇, 客

J

jails 囹圄

K

King Chou 紂王
King Hui 惠王
King Liao (of Wu) 吳僚王
King P'ing (of Ch'u) 楚平王
King Wen 文王
King Wu 武王
know yourself 知己
Kou-chien 句踐
Ku-su 姑蘇
Kuan Chung 管仲
Kuan-tzu 管子
kuang 廣

L

labor service 役

law 法
li (rites, forms of etiquette) 禮
Li Ching 李靖
light force 輕兵 (軍)
likes 好
limbs and joints 肢節
Lin-i 臨沂
local guide 鄉導
long weapons 長兵
Lord Shang 商君
lost state 亡國
love the people 愛民
Lü-shih ch'un-ch'iu 呂氏春秋

M

majesty 威
mandate 命
many 多
marsh 澤
marshy depression 圯澤
martial (the) 武
masses 衆
Master of Fate 司命
material resources 資, 財
measure 量
Mencius 孟子
merit 功
method 法
military
    administration 軍制
    campaign 軍旅, 行師, 出軍
    discipline 軍治
    power 軍勢
Military Pronouncements 軍讖
misfortune 患, 禍
moat 溝, 池, 塹

mobilize the army 起軍, 興兵,
    舉兵, 起師
mountains 山
movement and rest 動止, 動靜
Mu-yeh 牧野
music 樂
mutual
    change 相變
    conquest 相剋
    production 相生
    protection 相保
    responsibility 相任

N

name and action 形, 形名
Nang Wa 囊瓦
narrow pass 隘塞
nonaction 無爲
not being knowable 不可知
nurturing the people 養人, 養民

O

oath 誓
observation post 斥侯, 長關
observe (the enemy) 觀, 伺 (敵)
occupy 佔, 居, 處
offense 攻
officers 士, 吏
officials 吏, 官
old army 老兵
omen 兆
opportunity 機
oppose 當, 拒
order 令

ordinance 律
orthodox (*cheng*) 正

P

pardon 赦, 舍
pennant 旌
people 人, 民
perverse 邪
plains 原
plan 計, 策
platoon 隊, 倆 (兩) 屬
pleasure 樂
Po P'i 伯嚭
Po-chü 柏舉
power 勢
pray 祈禱
precipitous 險
preservation 全
press (the enemy) 逼, 壓, 薄, 迫
pretend 僞
probe (the enemy) 刺 (敵),
  角之
probing force 跳盪 (隊)
profit 利
prohibitions 禁
prolonged 久
protracted fighting 戰久
provisions 糧
punish 罰
punishment 罰
punitive expedition 討
pursue 追

Q

Questions and Replies 問對

R

raiding force 寇
rain 雨
ramparts 壘
rank 爵
ravine 險
rear 後
rectify 正
regiment 旅, 師
regimental commander 帥
regulations 律, 制
repel 禦
repress 挫
resentment 怨
responsibility 任
rested 佚
retreat 退, 北
rewards 賞
  and punishments 賞罰
righteous 義
rites (see *li*) 禮
river 川, 水
rows and files 行列
ruler 主
  enlightened 明主
  obtuse (ignorant) 無知之主
rules 法
rumor 讒讒

S

Sage 聖人
salary 祿
sated 飽
scouts (遠) 斥
seasonal occupations 時事, 季事

vital point 機
vulnerable point 空點, 弱點,
　　虛點 (地)

W

wage war 作戰
wall 牆, 城
war 戰
ward off 拒
warfare 兵, 戰
　explosive 突戰
　forest 林戰
　mountain 山戰
Warring States 戰國
warrior 士, 武
　armored 甲士
water 水
weak 弱
weapons 兵器
Wei (state of) 魏
Wei Liao-tzu 尉繚子
well 井
Wen Chung 文種

wetlands 沮, 澤, 沛
withdraw 却
Worthy 賢人
Wu (state of) 吳
Wu Ch'i 吳起
Wu Shang 伍尚
Wu She 伍奢
Wu-tzu 吳子
Wu Yüeh ch'un-ch'iu 吳越春秋

Y

yang 陽
Yangtze River 揚子江
Yao (Emperor) 堯
Yellow Emperor 黃帝
Yellow Pond 黃池
Yellow River 黃河, 河
Yen (state of) 燕
yin 陰
yin and yang 陰陽
Ying 郢
Yü 羽
Yüeh (state of) 越

Index

Extremely common terms, such as "army," "tactics," and "strategy" are noted only where of particular significance, they appear as specific terms in the translation, or are discussed in the introductory material. Similarly, references to Sun-tzu are noted only for the introductory material and not the translation where he is assumed to be the speaker throughout. Historical individuals, unless extremely prominent, are also omitted.

Art of War 43, 61–62, 79, 82, 92,
  108–09, 114–18, 120–21, 123,
  127–30, 133–34, 136, 138,
  140–45, 147–48, 150–51,
  156–61, 237, 244
Assault 56, 64, 66, 90, 113, 123,
  147–48, 160, 177, 203, 244–45
Attached (emotionally) 210
Attack 40, 46, 56, 59, 80, 90, 92–95,
  99–105, 109–10, 114–18, 121,
  123, 129, 132, 135–39, 141, 145,
  147–49, 152–54, 168, 177, 191,
  198, 204, 208, 213–15, 219–20,
  227–28, 232, 238–39, 241,
  244–45
Authority—See *Ch'üan*
Awesomeness 89, 153, 224
Axes 35–36, 42, 45, 50, 52, 81

B

Bamboo strips (slips) 61, 156, 237
Barbarian(s) 31–32, 37–39, 40–42,
  50, 52, 56, 67–71, 76, 85–88
Battalion 73–75, 111, 129, 177
Battle 34–36, 38, 52, 54, 58–60, 68,
  85, 88, 90–93, 95, 102–03,
  111–12, 115–17, 120–21,
  128–30, 136, 141–43, 145, 148,
  153, 158–60, 173, 177, 184,
  187–88, 191, 198, 203, 207–09,
  213, 219–20, 224, 228, 237–39
Benevolence 32, 38, 98, 133, 167,
  232
Birds 40, 208–09
Boats 45, 89, 100, 113–14, 221
Border 55, 83, 155, 222–23, 231,
  238–40, 243
Bows 35, 42, 99, 244
Bribes 41, 44, 104–06, 108, 112, 121,
  125
Brigade 36, 75, 102
Bronze 34–35, 52, 69–73, 87

C

Calculation 129–31, 133, 184
Campaigns (military) 33–34, 37,
  41–42, 47–48, 52, 54, 58, 85, 88,
  92, 94, 107–09, 111–13, 116,
  119, 121, 125, 128, 134, 143, 152,
  154, 157, 159–60, 173, 231
  prolonged 173–74, 177
Capture 55, 95
Cavalry 36–37, 52, 56, 63, 67–72,
  150, 239, 241–42
Chang Liang 61
Change(s) 136, 148, 154, 160, 187,
  198–99, 201, 203, 227, 237,
  244–6
  and transformation 111, 140, 193
Chaos 46, 95, 187–88, 209, 214–15
Character, exploiting 121, 204
Chariots 35–37, 50, 52, 63–71,
  73–75, 86, 88–89, 91, 93, 103,
  112–13, 119, 147, 158–59,
  173–74, 208–09, 221, 239–42
Ch'i (pneuma, morale) 93, 107–08,
  112–14, 116, 118, 142, 198, 220,
  243–44
Ch'i (state of) 43, 46, 50–52, 57–60,
  82–83, 90, 103–06, 121, 125,
  154, 157, 161
Chi-fu (battle of) 93–95
Chin (state of) 52, 56–58, 76, 83,
  86–89, 99, 103, 112, 116, 122,
  154, 156, 246–48
Ch'in (state of) 33, 52, 54, 57–61,
  68, 72, 87–88, 97–98, 101, 103,
  119, 144
Chou
  dynasty 34–35, 44–46, 54–45, 57,
    62, 64–65, 69–72, 74, 76, 82,
    85–86, 88–89, 102, 106, 108,
    116, 137, 140, 233
  state of 37–38, 40–42, 44–46,
    48–51, 53, 86, 107, 109
Chou li 74–75
Ch'u (state of) 54, 75–76, 80,
  82–103, 107–21, 131, 138, 141,
  152–54

Doubt 111, 178, 208, 221, 239–40
Drums 81–82, 123, 198, 237,
  240–43
Dust 208, 240, 241

E

Ears 198, 222, 240
Earth 130–31, 135, 140–41, 167,
  214–15
  depths of 132, 183
Earthworks 207
Emotions 131, 222
Employing men 58, 168, 188, 198,
  210, 215
Employing the military 82, 92, 136,
  147–48, 154, 173, 177, 184,
  198–99, 203–04, 219–22, 228,
  245–46
Encampment 60, 93, 123, 139, 197,
  203, 208, 242, 245
Enemy 41–42, 48, 65–66, 80, 85,
  93–95, 107–08, 111, 114–15,
  117–19, 121, 123, 129–32,
  135–36, 138–43, 146–49,
  153–54, 174, 177, 179, 183–84,
  187–88, 191, 197, 207–10,
  213–15, 220, 222–24, 231–32,
  238–43, 245–46
Entice (the enemy) 60, 134, 138,
  168, 188, 191, 197, 199, 203, 209,
  213, 232, 238–41, 243, 246
Equipment 146, 173, 177, 197
Errors 183
Escape 114, 117–18
Estimation 130, 136, 141, 165,
  167–69, 184, 192–93, 215, 245
Evaluating the enemy 33, 93,
  130–31, 137, 141, 167, 207–10,
  214
Exhaustion 91, 108, 110, 117, 119,
  125, 131, 134, 173–74, 197, 199,
  209, 231, 238
Eyes 198, 222, 240

F

Fame 114, 133, 183, 215
Fan Li 83, 121–22, 125, 152
Fear 45, 115, 118, 130–31, 188, 198,
  209, 239, 243
Feudal lords 40, 45, 47, 49–51, 53,
  55, 57, 74, 76, 82–83, 98,
  105–06, 119, 173, 178, 197, 203,
  219–20, 223
Few, the 93
  See also Many and Few
Fields 56, 238, 247
Fire 60, 111, 154, 198, 225, 227, 242
Five
  colors 148, 187
  flavors 148, 187
  grains 34, 45, 86
  notes 148, 187
  phases 187, 193
  unit of 111
Flags 174, 198–99, 209, 240
Flanks 68, 122–23, 139–40, 192,
  207–08, 240, 242–43
Flee 60, 94–95, 102, 115, 244
Forces 52, 55, 60, 65, 90, 93–95, 98,
  101–02, 111, 113, 115, 118,
  122–23, 138–40, 146, 149–50,
  167–68, 184, 192, 207, 209,
  241–43
Ford (rivers) 65, 117, 207–08, 221
Forests 56, 86, 95, 111, 113, 119,
  142, 197–98, 208, 219, 223
Form—See *hsing*
Formations 81, 95, 136, 148–49,
  227, 238
Formless 134–36, 137–38, 191–93,
  220
Fortifications 55, 59, 90, 110, 122,
  129, 159, 238–39
Four seasons 193
Front 123, 192, 207, 220, 239, 243,
  244–46
Fu-ch'ai 83, 103–06, 108, 120–23,
  125, 154
Fu-kai 102–03, 115–16, 118–19
Funeral mounds 102

O

Occupation 55, 85, 95, 121, 213, 219, 246
Offense 56, 129–32, 175, 177, 183
Officers 55, 73–74, 76, 80, 88, 94, 111–12, 114–15, 130, 137, 160, 167, 177–78, 209, 214, 221–22 238–39, 241–44
Officials 33, 39–41, 48, 55, 76, 95, 101, 108, 120
Omens 45, 94, 143, 221
Onrush 187–88
Opportunity 59, 90, 184
Orders 80–81, 130, 167, 198, 210, 221, 224, 244–45
Orthodox (*cheng*) 69, 131, 135, 147–50, 187

P

Passes 113, 219, 224, 238, 240, 246
Peace 209
Pennants 174, 198, 209, 243
People, the 40, 108, 174, 204, 210, 221–22, 231, 238, 248
   welfare of 32, 38, 42, 91–92, 107–08, 121, 128, 154
Peoples 119
Plains 66, 68, 87, 207
Plans 44, 80, 104, 129, 143, 177, 193, 197, 203, 210, 220, 223, 243–44
Platoon 74–76, 146
Pleasure 39, 91–92, 108, 125
Plunder 111, 174, 198, 220, 238–39, 241, 246
Po P'i 80, 83, 101, 104–06, 108, 113, 152–54
Po-chü (battle of) 102, 112–16
Power 49–50, 53–57, 65, 97, 108, 122, 125, 134
   See also *Shih*
Preparations 52–53, 90, 111, 120, 128, 135, 192, 203, 208, 213, 221, 227, 240–41, 243–44, 246

Prisoners 35, 55
Probe the enemy 134, 193, 242
Profession of arms 31–32, 52, 54, 76, 132–33, 159
Profits 46, 168, 174, 188, 191, 197–98, 203, 213, 224, 232, 246
Prosperity 31, 42–43, 53, 58, 131
Provisions 119, 173, 197, 213, 220, 223, 227, 238, 241, 243, 246
Punishment 32, 36, 39, 46, 81–82, 105–06, 133, 156, 209–10, 214, 232
Pursuit 94, 116–17, 239

Q

Questions and Replies 61–62, 147

R

Rain 45, 208
Ramparts 191, 241, 243
Rank 52
Ravines 56–57, 66, 118, 141–42, 208, 214, 219, 223, 238–40, 243, 246
Rear 114, 123, 140, 192, 207, 220, 239, 243–48
Rested, the 59, 94, 131, 142, 168, 191, 199, 240
Retreat 93, 117, 130, 178, 191, 198–99, 208, 215, 239–40
   feigned 117, 122, 140, 199, 240
Revolution 38, 45–48
Rewards 35, 43, 50, 52, 100, 108, 154, 160, 174, 198, 209, 224, 231–32, 241
   and punishments 130, 143, 167
Righteous 38, 40, 232
Rites—See *Li*
Ritual—See *Li*
Rivers and streams 66, 86–87, 89–90, 93, 111, 113–14, 117–18, 122–23, 142, 207–08, 221, 242

Roads 142, 203, 219–20, 223, 231, 238–40, 242–44
Rulers 32, 34, 39, 50, 54–57, 90, 92–93, 99, 107–08, 112, 115–16, 130, 132, 134, 153, 159, 167, 178–79, 197, 202, 214–15, 228, 231–32, 244–45, 247
Rumors 143

S

Sages 44, 46, 232
Sated 119, 131, 191, 199, 220
Seasons 32, 83, 86, 167, 187, 193, 227
Secrecy 42–43, 123, 135, 137, 139, 192–93, 220, 232
Security 167, 174, 228
Seize (the enemy) 210, 220, 227, 242, 245
Segmenting—See Dividing
Selecting men 52, 188
Seven Military Classics 31, 42, 61, 73, 75–76, 79, 111, 136, 143
Shame 99, 204
Shang dynasty 33–39, 41, 44–46, 48–49, 53–55, 63–65, 67–69, 72–73, 75, 91, 105, 233
Shang shu (Book of Documents) 38, 47
Shields 35, 55, 69–71, 81, 154, 174, 177
Shih (officers, warriors) 49, 80, 82
Shih (strategic configuration of power) 34–37, 53–60, 68, 90, 122, 125, 139–40, 143–49, 168, 185, 187–88, 213–14, 238, 241, 245
Shih chi 39–40, 43, 47, 65–66, 79–80, 82–83, 97, 107, 152, 154–57, 159
Shuaijan (snake) 221
Sickness 103, 105, 207
Siege (besiege) 56, 64, 94, 114, 117, 159–60, 177, 199
Silence 123
Six Armies 49, 76, 86

Six Secret Teachings 38, 42, 60–62, 67–68, 74, 82, 134, 140, 147, 237
Slaves 33, 35, 51
Soft, the 149, 222
Soldiers 54, 74, 94–95, 112, 114, 174, 221, 227, 239, 241
Spears 35, 52, 57, 71–72
Speed 33, 56, 65–68, 92, 111, 134, 159–60, 173, 191, 198, 220
Spies 135–37, 193, 208, 229, 231, 232–33
Spirit (morale)—See *Ch'i*
Spirits 40, 46, 231
Spring and Autumn Annals (Ch'un ch'iu) 47
Spring and Autumn period 35, 50–53, 55, 64–67, 69, 71, 74–76, 85–87, 112, 116, 128, 151, 158–60
Squad 36, 73–76, 111, 129, 177
Ssu-ma (Master of Horse) 98
Ssu-ma Fa 61–62, 66, 158
Standoff 54, 231
State 33–35, 40, 46, 50–53, 56, 59, 75, 86–87, 89–92, 94, 100, 107–08, 111, 119, 122, 125, 128–29, 131–32, 147, 152–53, 167, 173, 177–78, 215, 222–24, 228, 231
Stimulating troops—See Motivating Men
Stopping (halting) 111, 192, 219
Straight, the 197–98
Stratagems 45, 90, 92, 209, 243
Strategic advantage—See Advantage
Strategic configuration of power—See *Shih*
Strategic points 55, 246
Strategists 42, 47
Strategy 31, 38, 43, 49, 57, 59, 62, 79–80, 92, 97, 105, 110–11, 119, 127–29, 131, 134, 137–39, 143, 149, 151, 158, 160, 173, 177, 183, 193, 197–99, 219–20, 222, 224, 244
Strength 52, 57, 60, 88, 93–94, 108, 122, 130–31, 146–47, 173–74,

Transformation 222
See also Change and
Transformation
Trees 142, 207–08
Troops 98, 102–04, 107, 113,
117–18, 121–23, 131–32,
134–35, 137, 145, 147, 158–60,
167, 173, 177, 198–99, 209–10,
214–15, 220, 222, 238–42, 244
disordered 131, 168, 178, 187, 220
well-ordered 131, 142, 199, 220
See also Forces; Warriors; Soldiers
Tso chuan 67, 74, 79, 89, 107, 110,
113–14, 116, 140, 151–52, 159

U

Unconquerable 131–32, 183, 204
Undefended 191–92
Unexpected 65, 127, 134, 149, 168,
191, 220, 222, 238, 240
Unity 92, 112, 114, 168, 178, 198,
220, 222–24, 242–43
Unorthodox *(ch'i)* 45, 68–69, 122,
127, 131, 134, 147–50, 159, 160,
187, 239, 244–45
Unprepared 134, 168, 213
Upright(ness) 133, 147, 222

V

Vacuity 59, 113, 134, 138, 189, 191,
220, 238, 242
Vacuous 140, 187, 193
Valleys 34, 56, 207, 215, 244–45
Vanguard 214
Victory 37, 42, 59, 65, 92, 95, 102,
107–08, 115–16, 121–22, 129,
132, 134–35, 139–41, 148,
153–54, 167–69, 173–74,
177–79, 184, 187, 192–93, 198,
207, 213–15, 224, 228, 231, 240
Village 76
Virtue 32, 38, 40–42, 65, 107, 147

W

Walls 55, 109, 112, 177, 238–39
War 31, 52, 61
Warfare 31–36, 51, 54–58, 63, 82,
91, 99, 104, 115, 128–30, 131,
136, 138, 141, 143, 145, 148, 153,
155, 158–60, 167–68, 173–74,
177, 183–84, 187, 214–15, 247
Warring States 31, 33, 36, 43, 53–55,
57, 64, 67–69, 71–72, 75–76,
116, 159, 161
Warriors 35–36, 65, 71–72, 88, 92,
123, 241, 243, 247
Water 45, 117, 140, 145, 187, 193,
207, 209, 227, 245
Weak, the 93, 133
Weakness 94, 115, 131, 188, 214, 242
Weapons 33–37, 49, 52, 56, 63,
65–66, 69–73, 81, 87, 129, 149,
160, 173, 177, 209
Wei (state of) 54, 57–60
Wei Liao-tzu 57
Wei Liao-tzu 61–62, 147
Wetlands 119, 142, 197, 207–08,
219, 223
Wind 45, 111, 198, 221, 227
Wisdom 47, 133, 167, 183, 232
Withdraw 60, 81, 110, 178, 213, 239
Women 32, 44, 80–81, 97–98, 100,
156
Worthies 44, 98, 107
Wu (state of) 66, 71, 79–80, 82–95,
101–04, 106, 108–28, 131, 134,
138, 141, 152–54, 157–58, 160,
221
Wu Ch'i 43, 55, 57–58, 62, 67, 71,
84, 93, 155
Wu-tzu 43, 61–62, 67, 71, 84, 93,
237
Wu Tzu-hsü 80, 82–85, 87, 89,
95–110, 113, 115, 120, 152–54,
157, 161
Wu Yüeh ch'un-ch'iu 79–80, 152,
155, 157, 159

Y

Yang 43, 207, 213
Yang-tze River 87–88, 100, 106, 113, 148, 187
Yellow Emperor 64, 207